MOHAMMED

AND

THE RISE OF ISLAM

MOHAMMED

AND

THE RISE OF ISLAM

D. S. MARGOLIOUTH

GYAN

Published by

Gyan Publishing House
5, Ansari Road
Daryaganj, New Delhi-110002
Phone: 011-47034999, 9811692060
E-mail: books@gyanbooks.com

Distribution Network
gyanbooks.com
India, USA, Canada, UK, Australia

ISBN: 978-93-6920-867-8 (PB)

First Published, 1905

2nd Impression 2025

Printed at: Gyan Press, Delhi.

MOHAMMED AND THE RISE OF ISLAM
Author: D. S. MARGOLIOUTH

THE ASCENSION OF MOHAMMED.

From D'Ohsson's *Tableau Général de l'Empire Othoman.*

MOHAMMED

AND

THE RISE OF ISLAM

BY

D. S. MARGOLIOUTH

PREFACE

THE biographers of the Prophet Mohammed* form a long series which it is impossible to end, but in which it would be honourable to find a place. The most famous of them is probably Sir Walter Raleigh,† while the palm for eloquence and historical insight may well be awarded to Gibbon.‡

During the time when Gibbon wrote, and for long after, historians mainly relied for their knowledge of the life of Mohammed on the Biography of Abu'l-Fidā, who died in the year 722 A.H., 1322 A.D., of whose work Gagnier produced an indifferent edition.§ The scholars of the nineteenth century were naturally not satisfied with so late an authority; and they succeeded in bringing to light all the earliest documents preserved by the Mohammedans. The merit

* Of the *sources* of the biography of the Prophet a valuable account is given by E. Sachau, *Ibn Sa'd III.*, i., Preface.

† *The Life and Death of Mahomet*, London, 1637. (If genuine.)

‡ Among eloquent accounts of Mohammed, that in Mr. Reade's *Martyrdom of Man*, 14th ed., 260 foll., deserves mention. That by Wellhausen in the introduction to *Das Arabische Reich und sein Sturz* is masterly in the extreme.

§ Oxford, 1723. Abu'l-Fidā is referred to as the chief authority perhaps for the last time by T. Wright, *Christianity in Arabia.*

of discovering and utilising these ancient works is shared by G. Weil, Caussin de Perceval, F. Wüstenfeld, A. Sprenger, and Sir William Muir; and the Lives of Mohammed by the last two of these writers * are likely to be regarded as classical so long as there are students of Oriental history in Europe; notwithstanding the fact that Muir's Life is written with a confessedly Christian bias, and that Sprenger's is defaced by some slipshod scholarship and untrustworthy archæology.†

Since these works were composed, knowledge of Mohammed and his time has been increased by the publication of many Arabic texts, and the labours of European scholars on Mohammedan antiquities.‡ The works of I. Goldziher, J. Wellhausen, and Th. Nöldeke have elucidated much that was obscure, and facilitated the understanding of Arabian history both before and after the Prophet. And from the following Arabic works, most of which have been published since Sprenger and Muir wrote, many fresh details of interest and even of importance occasionally have been furnished.

1. The *Musnad*, or collection of traditions of Ahmad Ibn Hanbal, who died in 241 A.H., (855 A.D.: Cairo,

* Muir's, London, 1857–1861; Sprenger's (2d ed.), Berlin, 1869.

† Wellhausen's judgment of it (*Wakidi*, pp. 24–26) is absolutely fair and sound.

‡ The most important Lives of Mohammed which have appeared in Europe are those by L. Krehl (Leipzig, 1884), H. Grimme (Münster, 1892–1895), F. Buhl (Copenhagen, 1903). The new editions of Grimme's work and of Wollaston's *Half-hours with Mohammed*, and the magnificent work of Prince Caetani were published too late for the present writer to utilise.

1890, in six volumes, fol.). In this work the sayings of the Prophet recorded by different individuals are given in separate collections for each individual. The same tradition is sometimes given ten, twenty, or even a hundred times. Much of the matter is scarcely to be found elsewhere, and is likely to be genuine. The account of this work given by Goldziher, *Z. D. M. G.*, l. 463–599, is of course excellent.

2. The gigantic *Commentary on the Koran* by the historian Tabari, who died 310 A.H., (922 A.D.: Cairo, 1902–1904, in thirty volumes, fol.). This commentary is for the historian of far greater value than the popular commentaries of Zamakhshari and Baidawi, who lived many centuries later, and were influenced by later controversies.

3. The *Isabah*, or Dictionary of Persons who knew Mohammed, by Ibn Hajar (Calcutta, 1853–1894, four volumes). In spite of the late date of the author of this great dictionary, his work is historically valuable, owing to the fact that it embodies matter taken from sources which are no longer accessible. Ibn Hajar was possessed of an extraordinary library.

4. The works of early Arabic writers, especially the polygraph 'Amr, son of Bahr, called Al-Jahiz, who died in 255 A.H. (868 A.D.). Of his works there are now accessible three edited by the late Van Vloten, and the treatise on rhetoric published in Cairo. Though not dealing directly with Mohammed, they contain many an allusion which it is possible to utilise.

The present writer has gone through, in addition to these (so far as they were accessible to him), the authorities utilised already by his predecessors, of which the chief are enumerated in the Bibliography. One of these, the *Class Book of Ibn Sa'd* (*ob.* 230 A.H., 845 A.D.) is in course of publication.

Since the authors of books in this series have the number of their pages limited, it has been found necessary to abbreviate, and this has been done by omitting three kinds of matter:

1. Translations of the Koran (except in the rarest cases).

2. All anecdotes that are obviously or most probably fabulous.

3. Such incidents as are of little consequence either in themselves or for the development of the narrative.

Some principles for estimating the credibility of traditions are given by Muir in his Introduction, and by Goldziher in his *Muhammadanische Studien*. A few important observations bearing on this subject are also made by Nöldeke, *Z. D. M. G.*, lii., 16, foll. The number of motives leading to the fabrication of traditions was so great that the historian is in constant danger of employing as veracious records what were deliberate fictions. I can only hope that I have not displayed greater credulity than my predecessors. In condemning traditions as unhistorical I have ordinarily considered the obelus of Goldziher, Nöldeke, or Wellhausen as sufficient.

The standpoint from which this book is written is suggested by the title of the series. I regard Mohammed as a great man, who solved a political problem of appalling difficulty,—the construction of a state and an empire out of the Arab tribes. I have endeavoured, in recounting the mode in which he accomplished this, to do justice to his intellectual ability and to observe towards him the respectful attitude which his greatness deserves; but otherwise this book does not aim at being either an apology or an indictment. Indeed neither sort of work is now required. The charming and eloquent treatise of Syed Ameer Ali * is probably the best achievement in the way of an apology for Mohammed that is ever likely to be composed in a European language, whereas indictments are very numerous—some dignified and moderate, as is the work of Sir William Muir; others fanatical and virulent.† These works are ordinarily designed to show the superiority or inferiority of Mohammed's religion to some other system; an endeavour from which it is hoped that this book will be found to be absolutely free.

There are two forms of literature to which I should especially wish to acknowledge obligations. One of these consists of works in which we have authentic biographies of persons who have convinced many of their fellows that they were in receipt of divine communications; in particular I may mention the history of modern Spiritualism, by F. Podmore,‡ and the study on the founder of Mormonism, by I. W. Riley.§ For the employment of "revelations"

* *The Spirit of Islam*, London, 1896, Calcutta, 1902.

† Bottom is probably touched by the *New but True Life of the Carpenter, including a New Life of Mohammed*, by Amos: Bristol, 1903.

‡ *Modern Spiritualism*, London, Macmillan, 1902.

§ *A Psychological Study of Joseph Smith, Jr.*, London, Heinemann, 1903.

as a political instrument, and for the difficulties which attend the career of Prophet-statesman, the life of Joseph Smith (the founder of Mormonism) furnishes illustrations of the most instructive character; only the biographer of Mohammed must envy the wealth and authenticity of the material at Dr. Riley's disposal, without which the formulæ of modern psychology could not have been applied to the interpretation of Smith's career so successfully as Dr. Riley has applied them.

A second class of works are those in which savage life is described at first hand: and among these the *Autobiography of James P. Beckwourth* deserves special notice. There are chapters in that work where by substituting *camel* for *horse* we might find a reproduction of Bedouin manners and institutions; and the question of Beckwourth's veracity does not affect the general truth of his descriptions.

Finally, I have to thank various persons from whom I have derived assistance. I am indebted for many suggestions and improvements to the Editor of the Series, to J. P. Margoliouth, and to the Rev. W. J. Foxell, who have read and re-read the proofs; to Mr. A. E. Cowley, Fellow of Magdalen College, for advice in the selection of coins; to Dr. J. Ritchie, Fellow of New College, and Mr. R. B. Townshend for guidance with regard to medical and anthropological works; and to Mr. G. Zaidan, editor of the Cairene journal *Hilal*, for leave to reproduce certain plates that have appeared in his magazine, and also for the names of certain Arabic works with which I was not previously acquainted. Mr. Zaidan is well known in Arabic-speaking countries as a historian, novelist, and journalist; and I hope that ere long I may have the pleasure of introducing some of his works to English readers.

In the second edition certain errors have been corrected, to which the author's attention was called by Pére Lammens, S.J., of Beyrut, and Prof. I. Goldziher.

CONTENTS

ILLUSTRATIONS

TRANSLITERATION

In this matter the example of Nöldeke and Wellhausen in their popular writings has been followed. The mode of transliteration is similar to that in use at Cairo for ordinary purposes. The Arabic letters are represented by those English letters or combinations of letters which come nearest to the Arabic sounds: one who is acquainted with the original language will without difficulty be able to identify the words and names; whereas, to the reader who is ignorant of Arabic, further differentiation by means of diacritic points (*e.g.*, ṣ, ṭ, ḳ) is of no value. A few proper names that are familiar have been left in their popular forms.

CHRONOLOGY

COMPARATIVE tables of months and days as between the Mohammedan and Christian eras are to be found in Wüstenfeld, *Vergleichungstabellen der Muhammedanischen und Christlichen Zeitrechnung*, 2d ed., Leipzig, 1903; copied in *Trésor de Chronologie*, Paris, 1889. Others are in Dubbaneh's *Universal Calendar*, Cairo, 1896, and (in Arabic) the *Tawfikiyyāt* of Mukhtar Basha, Cairo, 1311. For the first nine years of Islam these tables are somewhat misleading, since they assume that the pre-Islamic Calendar was purely lunar, whereas it is certain that it was not. Moreover the occasional notices of the weather during the Prophet's expeditions, etc. (collected by Wellhausen, *W*. p. 17, *sq*., *Reste*, pp. 94–101), disagree seriously with Wüstenfeld's synchronisms; in some cases by antedating the events by two and a half months tolerable correspondence is obtained. It is not however possible to make out enough of the pre-Islamic Calendar to substitute a detailed scheme for Wüstenfeld's; and it has been pointed out by Winckler (*Altorientalische Forschungen*, ii., 324–350) that the Calendar of Medinah may well have been different from that of Meccah, the same month-names having quite different values at the two cities. His investigations into the origin of the Arabic Calendar, which have been amplified by D. Nielsen, *Die Altarabische Mondreligion*, Strassburg, 1904, are of no practical importance for fixing the dates of events during the early years of the Hijrah. The date of the Flight itself (8 Rabi' I., Sept. 20, 622) is fixed by the tradition that the Prophet arrived at Kuba on the Jewish Day of Atonement. Another date, that of the burial of the Prophet's son Ibrahim, is fixed by the solar eclipse, 7–9 A.M., Jan. 27, 632; but the synchronism, 28 Shawwal, A. H. 10, is not in agreement with the Arabic records, which put the event in some other month. The traditions bearing on this subject are discussed by Rhodokanakis, *W. Z. K. M.*, xiv., 78; another synchronism suggested *ibid.* from the lunar eclipse of Nov. 19–20, 625, identified with 13 Jumada II. A. H. 4, is useless, since the month and year in the Arabic tradition are uncertain. To a further synchronism, connected with the Prophet's birth, discussed by Mahmoud Efendi, *Sur le Calendrier Arabe avant l' Islamisme*, an allusion is sufficient.

GEOGRAPHY

THE political conditions of Arabia will have altered very considerably before any scientific exploration and surveying of the country are possible. The maps which have been added to this volume are intended as an unpretentious aid to those who would follow the campaigns of the Prophet and the gradual extension of his sphere of influence. For both, the author has availed himself of Sprenger's classical works on Arabian geography—*Die Post- und Reiserouten des Orients*, Leipzig, 1864, and *Die alte Geographie Arabiens*, Bern, 1875. For the map of Central Arabia, use has further been made of Wüstenfeld's *Das Gebiet von Medina*, Göttingen, 1873, and also of the measurements given by Al-Bekri in his *Geographical Dictionary*, ed. Wüstenfeld, 1876; valuable information about the modern nomenclature of this part of Arabia is to be found in the monographs *Die geographische Lage Mekkas*, by J. J. Hess, Freiburg (Schweiz), 1900, and *Der Hedjaz und die Strasse von Mekka nach Medina*, by B. Moritz, Berlin, 1890. The map of the location of Tribes is based on the monograph of Blau, *Z.D.M.G.*, xxiii., *Arabien im sechsten Jahrhundert*, whose results have been modified in part from Hamdani's *Geography of the*

Arabian Peninsula, ed. Müller, 1891, and in part from the authorities already mentioned. The results of exploration in Arabia down to the year 1875 are well summarised by A. Zehme in the work called *Arabien und die Araber seit 100 Jahren*, Halle, 1875; while D. Hogarth's *Penetration of Arabia*, London, 1904, summarises more recent enterprise. The plan of Meccah which is reproduced, is that of Burckhardt, as modified by Wüstenfeld in the fourth volume of his *Chroniken der Stadt Mekka*, Leipzig, 1861; its correctness is attested by the greatest modern authority on Meccah, Snouck Hurgronje, who adopts it with very trifling alterations in his article in the *Verhandlungen der geographischen Gesellschaft zu Berlin*, xiv., 138, foll., 1887, as well as in his classical work on Meccah.

BIBLIOGRAPHY*

1. Lives of Mohammed and Histories of the early days of Islam:

Ibn Ishak (quoted in the notes as Ishak), ob. about 150 A.H., 767 A.D.: his work (so far as is at present known) exists in two abridgments only: that by Ibn Hisham, ob. 218 A.H., 833 A.D., which has been published by Wüstenfeld, Göttingen, 1860, and later by Zubair Pasha; and that by Tabari, ob. 310 A.H., 922 A.D., embodied in his *Chronicle*, published at Leyden, 1882–1885.

Wakidi, ob. 207 A.H., 823 A.D., author of a treatise on Mohammed's Campaigns, of which an imperfect edition was issued by von Kremer, Calcutta, 1856; an abridged translation of a far more perfect copy was made by Wellhausen and published with the title *Muhammed in Medina*, Berlin, 1882. To this last reference is made as Wakidi (W.).

Ibn Sa'd, Secretary of Wakidi, ob. 230 A.H., 845 A.D.; author of an encyclopædic work on the Prophet, his followers, etc., of which three volumes have thus far been published at Berlin under the superintendence of E. Sachau.

Ya'kubi, ob. about 292 A.H., 905 A.D., author of a history in two parts, Pre-Islamic and Islamic, published by Houtsma, Leyden, 1883.

Ibn al-Athir, ob. 630 A.H., 1233 A.D., author of a Universal History, published at Leyden and in Egypt.

Diyarbekri, ob. 982 A.H., 1574 A.D., author of a Life of the Prophet, followed by a sketch of Islamic history, called *Ta'rikh al-Khamis*, published at Cairo, 1302 A.H.

* Works mentioned in the Preface are not repeated here.

Halabi, ob. 1044 A.H., 1634 A.D., author of a Life of the Prophet, called *Insan al-'uyun*, published at Cairo, 1292 A.H.

2. Books of Tradition (*i.e.* collections of sayings attributed to the Prophet, and traced back to him through a series of trustworthy witnesses):

Musnad of Ibn Hanbal. See Preface.

Collection by Bokhari, ob. 256 A.H., 870 A.D.: the unfinished edition by Krehl, Leyden, 1864–1868, is quoted as Bokhari (K.); for the parts wanting in this edition that of Cairo, 1312, has been used; Bokhari (Kast.) refers to the sixth edition of the Commentary of Kastalani, Cairo, 1306 A.H.

Collection by Muslim, ob. 261 A.H., 875 A.D., published at Cairo, 1290 A.H.

Collection by Tirmidhi, ob. 279 A.H., 892 A.D., published at Cairo, 1292, in two volumes, and Lucknow, 1301, in one volume.

Collection by Nasa'i, ob. 303 A.H., 916 A.D., published at Cairo, 1314 A.H.

These collections are enumerated in order of importance. The remaining authentic collections, by Malik Ibn Anas, ob. 179 A.H., 795 A.D., Ibn Majah, ob. 273 A.H., 887 A.D., and Abu Dawud, ob. 275 A.H., 889 A.D., have not been cited.

3. Commentaries on the Koran:

Tab. or Tabari (Comm.) refers to the Commentary on the Koran by the historian whose date has been given above, recently published at Cairo. Other commentaries occasionally cited are those by Zamakhshari, ob. 538 A.H., 1144 A.D.; Baidawi, ob. 691 A.H., 1292 A.D.

Of modern works on the Koran, Preserved Smith, *The Bible and Islam*, New York, 1897, is occasionally cited; the author has further profited by the treatises of H. Hirschfeld, though he has had no occasion to cite them. The remaining Arabic works occasionally cited in the notes will be familiar to scholars.

4. History of Meccah and Medinah:

History of Meccah by Azraki, ob. about 245 A.H., 859 A.D.,

edited by Wüstenfeld, Leipzig, 1858. The editor has appended in two volumes extracts from other and later historians of Meccah, and in a third volume a German epitome of the whole.

History of Medinah by Samhudi, ob. 911 A.H., 1505 A.D., published at Cairo, 1285 A.H.: epitomised by Wüstenfeld in his *Geschichte der Stadt Medina*, Göttingen, 1873.

Modern works on Meccah and Medinah.

Burckhardt's *Travels*, quoted from the French translation, Paris, 1835.

Burton's *Pilgrimage to Al-Medinah and Meccah*, Memorial edition, London, 1893.

A. H. Keane, *Six Months in the Hejaz*, London, 1887.

Soubhy, *Pêlerinage à la Mecque et à Médine*, Cairo, 1894.

Muhammad Basha Sadik, *The Pilgrim's Guide* (Arabic), Cairo, 1313 A.H., 1895 A.D.

Gervais-Courtellemont, *Mon Voyage à la Mecque*, Paris, 1897.

Sabri Pasha, *Mirror of the Two Sanctuaries* (Turkish), Constantinople, 1886.

5. Works of I. Goldziher:

M.S., abbreviation for *Muhammadanische Studien*, Halle, 1889, 1890.

Abhandlungen zur arabischen Litteratur, Leyden, 1896, 1899.

6. Of Th. Nöldeke:

Geschichte des Korans, Gôttingen, 1860.

Das Leben Muhammeds, Hannover, 1863.

Geschichte der Perser und Araber zur Zeit der Sasaniden, Leyden, 1879.

Die Ghassanischen Fürsten aus dem Hause Gafna's, Berlin, 1887.

Sketches of Eastern History, trans. by Black, London, 1896.

7. Of J. Wellhausen:

Muhammed in Medina, see above; the introduction and notes are cited as Wellhausen (W.) or (Wakidi).

Reste arabischen Heidenthums, Berlin, 1897.

Skizzen und Vorarbeiten, viertes Heft, Berlin, 1889.

Die Ehe bei den Arabern, Göttingen, 1893.
Das arabische Reich und sein Sturz, Berlin, 1902.

Numerous articles by these writers in the Z. D. M. G. (*Zeitschrift der deutschen morgenländischen Gesellschaft*) and W. Z. K. M. (*Wiener Zeitschrift für die Kunde des Morgenlandes*) are also cited; J. R. A. S. stands for *Journal of the Royal Asiatic Society*.

MOHAMMED

MOHAMMED

CHAPTER I

THE BIRTHPLACE OF THE HERO

AT some time in the year 594 of our era, a caravan bearing the merchandise of a wealthy woman at Meccah was safely conducted to Bostra and safely brought back with profits proportionate to the risk of the undertaking. Of the qualities necessary for the conduct of such an expedition many differ little from those required by a successful general: ability to enforce discipline, skill in evading enemies and courage in meeting them, the power to discriminate false news from true, and to penetrate into other men's designs. And when the mart has been safely reached, and the leader of the caravan or agent has to sell the goods entrusted to him so as to obtain the best return, another set of qualities are called into play; of which fidelity to his employer is the chief, but patience and shrewdness are also indispensable. The leader of the expedition to Bostra, Mohammed, the orphan son of Abdallah, then a man of twenty-five, had displayed the necessary qualities, and given satisfaction to his employer, the widow Khadijah, who was perhaps some years his senior. As a reward for his services the widow bestowed on him her hand, thereby securing for herself and for her spouse a place in history.

Over the country which they made famous there lies a veil which even at the beginning of this twentieth century is only lifted at the fringe.* The explorer still enters the interior at the risk of his life. Official chronicles of the vicissitudes of its governments are rarely kept; their historians are visitors, to whom curiosity or some other motive gives courage to enter the forbidden land. Religious fanaticism was introduced by Islam, as an addition to the dangers of the country; otherwise the Arabia of the twentieth century is similar to the Arabia of the sixth.

Of the Arabs before Islam, an account is said to have been given † by one of their princes in answer to the Persian king, who declared every other race superior to them. What nation, he asked, could be put before the Arabs, for strength or beauty or piety, courage, munificence, wisdom, pride, or fidelity? Alone among the neighbours of the Persians, the Arabs had maintained their independence. Their fortresses were the backs of their horses, their beds the ground, their roof the sky; when other people entrenched themselves with stone and brick, the Arab's defence was his sword and his hardihood.

* See *D. Hogarth*, *Penetration of Arabia*, 1904.

† To be found in many "Adab" books, *e. g.*, *Ikd Farid*, *Alif-Bā*.

Other nations knew nothing of their pedigrees, but the Arab knew his genealogy up to the father of mankind, whence no man could ever obtain admission into a tribe which was not his own. So liberal was he that he would slaughter the camel which was his sole wealth to give a meal to the stranger who came to him at night. No other nation had poetry so elaborate or a language so expressive as theirs. Theirs were the noblest horses, the chastest women, the finest raiment; their mountains teemed with gold and silver and gems. For their camels no distance was too far, no desert too wild to traverse. So faithful were they to the ordinances of their religion that if a man met his father's murderer unarmed in one of the sacred months he would not harm him. A sign or a look from one of them constituted an engagement which was absolutely inviolable. If he guaranteed protection, and his clients came to harm, he would not rest till either the tribe of the injurer were exterminated or his own perished in the quest of vengeance. If other nations obeyed a central government and a single ruler, the Arabs required no such institution, each of them being fit to be a king, and well able to protect himself; and unwilling to undergo the humiliation of paying tribute or bearing rebuke.

This description, like many an encomium, requires considerable modification before it will tally with the truth. After the spread of Islam men began to care for their pedigrees, and genealogy came to be a recognised subject of study. But before Islam, genealogies were never committed to writing and only in exceptional cases were they remembered. The population of Central Arabia had the vaguest notion of the way in which they had come there. The introduction of the Old Testament was a boon to the archæologists, when such arose, because in it they found the beginnings of genealogies, to which, by calculation of time and arbitrary insertions, they could attach the pedigrees with which they were acquainted. Only in the rarest cases are those pedigrees likely to be historical for more than a couple of generations before the commencement of Islam: the theory of the genealogists which derives all tribes from eponymous heroes, and so makes all Kurashites descendants of Kuraish and all Kilabites descendants of Kilab, breaks down over a variety of facts which modern research has rightly appraised, and of which ancient archæology was not wholly ignorant: totemism, the institution of polyandry, the separation of the ideas connected with parentage and procreation, all of which are attested for the nomad Arabs. The genealogical unity of the tribe was a fancy often superimposed on what in origin was a local unity,* or union of emigrants under a single leader,† or some other fortuitous combination.‡ Genuine family ties, if any were preserved, were thus mixed by the genealogists with products of the fancy, till the fragments of real history were absorbed beyond recognition in the artificial tables. A man was known to belong to a clan,

* *Goldziher*, *M. S.*, i., 64.

† *Nöldeke*, *Z. D. M. G.*, xl., 159.

‡ *Sprenger*, *Alte Geographie Arabiens*, 290.

and that clan was likely to be considered a branch of a tribe. But the steps which connected the individual with the founder of the clan, and those whereby the clan was deduced from the tribe, represented theory, rarely a genuine tradition; and instances are not wanting of both persons and clans being artificially grafted on tribes with which they had no physical connection.

Greater accuracy may be attributed to the statement about the piety of the Arabs, so far as it concerns the observation of the sacred months; for Greek writers attest the same. For three autumn months * and one spring month a truce of God was observed by many tribes, who therein laid down their arms and shed no blood. This institution, in the fixed form which it had assumed by the commencement of Islam, must have been the result of many stages of development, and was itself fruitful in effects. It cannot be severed from the desire to visit a sanctuary and celebrate a feast, and indeed the two seasons correspond with those of the birth of domestic animals and the harvesting of fruit. The month before and the month after that in which the more important visit was paid may have been included in the time for the benefit of distant visitors, who thereby were enabled to arrive and return in safety. For those who had no great distance to traverse the truce provided a period in which they could recover from the ravages of constant warfare, and by secure communication

* Nonnosus and Procopius: "two months after the summer solstice, and one in mid spring."

interchange ideas as well as produce. In the neighbourhood of the sanctuaries fairs arose, at some time or other so organised that the period of waiting was divided between them. Thus then the tribes that visited the shrine preserved or evolved the idea of a common nationality: while some of the ceremonies kept up the memory of original distinctions. The fair of 'Ukaz * in particular served a purpose similar to that for which the great games of Greece were utilised. Matters which were thought to concern the whole Arabian family could be communicated there, and opportunities were given for the gratification of other than warlike ambitions. Regarded as the home of the Arabian family, 'Ukaz was a place where women could be wooed.†

Meccah, the Prophet Mohammed's home, where dwelt a trading society, was within easy distance of several of these fairs. The community which had settled there had abandoned the nomad life, though it maintained the memory of it ‡; and early writers § preserve the tradition of a time when Meccah was inhabited in only two seasons of the year, the winter being spent in Jeddah on the coast, and the summer at the neighbouring oasis of Ta'if. Though theological speculation made the Moslems assign to their religious capital a fabulous

---

* A brilliant description of it in *Wellhausen*, *Reste*, 88–91. He holds that the localities of the fairs must originally have been sanctuaries.

† *Wellhausen*, *Ehe*, 442.

‡ *Jahiz*, *Mahasin*, 226.

§ *Jahiz*, *Opuscula*, 62.

TOMB OF EVE AT JEDDAH.

antiquity, more sober tradition placed the building of the first house at Meccah only a few generations before Mohammed's time; this act being ascribed to a member of the tribe Sahm, whose name was variously given as Su'aid son of Sahm * and Sa'd son of 'Amr. † The former would be separated by three generations from the Prophet, while the latter would be still nearer his age. ‡ This first house is not described, but was probably a primitive form of dwelling. Although a poet speaks of the people of the Tihamah as building houses with clay and mortar, it is probable that construction of this sort was carried on at Meccah on a small scale. The second Caliph § found fault with brick building; as indeed the Prophet had done before him ‖; the best houses were probably rude erections of roughly hewn stone. The remaining dwellings were probably enclosures, containing variations between huts and tents.¶

The community which had settled in the valley of Meccah, or Beccah, a ravine about a mile and a half long and a third of a mile broad stretching from north-east to south-west, somewhere about the middle of Arabia, at a distance of seventy miles from the western coast, cannot, when they selected this spot, have hoped to live by its produce; for that the soil

* *Chronicles of Meccah*, iii., 15.

† *Isabah*, ii., 915.

‡ *Wüstenfeld*, *Genealogische Tabellen*.

§ *Jahiz*, *Bayan*, ii., 25.

‖ *Musnad*, iii., 220.

¶ From *Azraki* it would appear that the Prophet's house had no roof.

is incapable of producing anything is attested by all who know it, from the author of the Koran to the present day. Their presence there is to be accounted for by their sanctuary, called the Ka'bah, not indeed the only Ka'bah, or cube-shaped God's house, in Arabia, yet one that attracted many visitors. It stood in some relation to the Black Stone, let into the north-west corner, kissed by devotees; and since both Greek and Arabic writers attest that the Arabs worshipped stones, many have thought this to be the real god of the Meccans, the Ka'bah itself being an ideal enlargement of it. On the other hand, the Ka'bah in Mohammed's time certainly contained the image of one god as well as representations of others. There was yet another theory that the Ka'bah contained a tomb, whence it may in origin have been a tent erected over a grave by a mourner, anxious to remain near the lost one *; and indeed that the stone Ka'bah replaced an original tent is attested by its being roofless, save for a cloth, till Mohammed's time.† Sanctity being a quality that spreads by contact, either the Black Stone or the Image or the Tomb originally gave sanctity to the Ka'bah which contained them; and the area of sanctity by Mohammed's time extended over some square miles. If we are justified in referring the statements of Greek writers concerning a great Arabic sanctuary to the Meccan Ka'bah, and in supposing those statements to be correct, the sanctity of this building was in the sixth century A.D.

* For this practice, see *Goldziher*, *M. S.*, i., 255.

† *Azraki*, 106.

recognised over a considerable portion of Arabia. Visits were paid to it both at fixed seasons of the year and at times dictated by the pilgrims' convenience. Persons who wished to curse their neighbours or enemies came even from a distance to the Ka'bah, where their imprecations were certain to be heard.* And a vast number of customs and ceremonies grew up round this building, many of which are not yet obsolete, and offer the anthropologist scope for conjecture, while the theologian can find in them some profound significance. The real import of most of them was probably forgotten before Mohammed's time.†

The Arabs suppose, and indeed are compelled by their system to suppose, that the Ka'bah was earlier than the Kuraish, the tribe which we find dominant at Meccah in the sixth century of our era. It is probable that this is correct. The possession of a temple to which pilgrimages are made is a valuable asset, since pilgrims can be made to pay for leave to visit the god; such a tax was levied by the Kuraish on foreign visitors,‡ and the right to collect it is likely to have been a matter for contention. Even without this material advantage the seizure of a temple is a natural proceeding, since thereby control of the god who inhabits it can be obtained. The name Kuraish tells us nothing of the history of the tribe thus called; either it is a totem-name (meaning swordfish), or one arbitrarily fabricated from three

---

* *Azraki*, 299.

† *Wellhausen*, *Reste*, 71.

‡ *Ibn Duraid*, 172.

successive letters of the alphabet *; and the Arab genealogists, who make Kuraish a person, forfeit thereby their claim to be regarded as serious authorities. Ali, the Prophet's cousin and son-in-law, declared that the Kuraish were Nabatæans from Kutha in Mesopotamia; which may only have meant that they were descended from Abraham; yet the story that the tribal god Hubal came from Hit on the Euphrates, and that Kutha, † the name of a familiar town on the Euphrates, was also a name for Meccah or part of it, lends some slight colour to the statement; which is somewhat strengthened by the commercial and political ability which the tribe displayed. ‡

It is doubtful whether any actual history is to be got out of the lengthy series of fables dignified with the title *Chronicles of Meccah*. A tribe called Jurhum, resident in historical times on the Yemen coast, claimed to have been supreme at Meccah for centuries.§ They were supposed to have been displaced and forbidden to enter the precinct ‖ by the Khuza'ah, a tribe actually resident in Meccah at the commencement of this period, and so closely connected with the Kuraish that the blood of the latter was not thought pure unless it had a Khuza'ite strain.¶ Their displacement is described in a myth of which the purpose appears to be to show that their

* *Chronicles of Meccah*, ii., 133.

† *Yakut;* see *Amedroz's Hilal*, Index.

‡ *Wellhausen*, *Reste*, 93.

§ *Ibn Duraid*, 253, gives a specimen of their dialect.

‖ *Wellhausen*, *Reste*, 91.

¶ *Jahiz*, *Bayan*, ii., 16.

conqueror was really one of themselves. Kusayy, a member of the tribe, whose mother, having married a man of another tribe, had taken him to Syria, returned and married the daughter of the governor of Meccah, at whose death Kusayy claimed the succession. His claim being disputed, he appealed to his relations by his mother's second marriage; after some skirmishing, an umpire being called in recognised the claims of Kusayy, who, however, made no attempt to banish the Khuza'ah from their homes. The meaning of this story is probably that the Khuza'ite settlement was earlier than the Kuraish settlement, and that the newcomers, though not an unwelcome accession, had, by showing greater activity and ability than the older settlers, secured the dominant place. During Mohammed's early life there were at times, however, open ruptures between the Khuza'ah and the Kuraish,* which led to a series of fights and the intervention of arbiters †; and in the history of Islam before Meccah was taken the Khuza'ah joined the side of Mohammed against the Kuraish. It would appear that the supremacy of the latter was not to the taste of the Khuza'ah, though they waited till fortune had declared itself before they finally made common cause with Mohammed. Of all the myths that seems to be nearest history which makes the head of the Kurashite settlement at Meccah one Hisham, son of Mughirah,‡ of the tribe Makhzum. Traditions which seem

---

* *Baihaki, Mahasin*, 495, 17.

† *Ibn Duraid*, 106.

‡ *Ibid.*, 94.

valuable state that *Hisham* and *Meccah* were at one time interchangeable terms; and that at Hisham's death the people were summoned to the funeral of their "lord."

The Kuraish formed a group of tribes, supposed, according to the ordinary theory of the ancients, to be descended from the father of the main tribe. The names of these clans will frequently meet us in the sequel, but the memory need not be burdened with them at this point. They dwelt side by side in groups of habitations at Meccah. The oldest guide-book to Meccah, composed in the third century of Islam, enumerates thirty-six such groups; the nobler clans living in the middle of the valley while the less noble dwelt on the hillside. Many of the clans had attached to them allies, corresponding with the Greek *metics*, persons who for some reason—ordinarily blood-guiltiness, but often poverty—had left their original homes and come to live at Meccah under foreign protection; and certain manufactures were probably in such metics' hands.* Some of the metics, however, were of wealth and even station, though a metic could not protect a native.† Similar to them in status were the clients, persons who had come to Meccah as slaves and been manumitted, though by the fiction of adoption such persons, as well as other clients, could become actual members of their owner's clans. ‡ Finally, the slaves made up the rest of the population. Intermarriage between the clans

* Cf. *Jacob*, *Beduinenleben*, 150.

† *Tabari*, i., 1203.

‡ *Nallino*, *Nuova Antologia*, 1893.

was common; but for the purpose of the blood-feud they, with their respective clients, were distinct, though the conflicting theories of male and female kinship appear at times to have produced complications.

For the economical basis of the community we have some data though little in the way of statistics. The possession of a popular sanctuary ensured a certain revenue from strangers; taking the form partly of a visitors' tax, partly of fees paid to the worker of the oracle (said to be 100 dirhems and a camel for each consultation), and partly of remuneration for entertainment and garments furnished to visitors; for by a lucrative rule the pilgrims might not use food or clothes brought by themselves.* Secondly, the sanctity which attached to the neighbourhood of the temple rendered it a suitable place for the pursuit of the arts of peace. Hence our authorities enumerate a number of trades that were practised at Meccah: such as those of carpenter, smith, sword-maker, wine-merchant, oil-merchant, leather-merchant, tailor, weaver, arrow-maker, stationer, money-lender. On the goods which were imported from the Byzantine Empire, partly for use in those industries, the Meccans levied a tax of ten per cent.† If a Bedouin wished to purchase an idol for his tent he would come to Meccah to procure it.‡ But in the third place the sacred character which attached to "God's neighbours"

* *Jahiz, Mahasin*, 165.

† *Azraki*, 107.

‡ *Ibid.*, 78; *Wakidi* (*W.*), 350.

gave them a great advantage for the prosecution of the carrying trade. By wearing certain badges merchants could in many places secure themselves from attack.* Much will be heard in the sequel of these caravans and the sums which they earned. The profits of the export trade greatly exceeded the revenue provided by the other sources, and upon it the constantly increasing community depended for their bread—which was made of corn brought from Yemamah in the north-east. He who wished to have Meccah at his mercy had but to stop their caravans. But before this plan occurred to their illustrious Exile, the carrying trade had furnished Meccah with considerable wealth; and gold that had been dug out of mines in the country of the Sulaim was sometimes brought to Meccah,† where it could be profitably employed. Ayeshah, the Prophet's girl-wife, perhaps inclined to exaggerate, estimated her father's property in the "Days of Ignorance" at a million dirhems—about £40,000.‡ Perhaps 40,000 dirhems was a truer estimate.§ Four hundred dinars, or about £150, is given as the price of a dwelling at Meccah before it was taken by Mohammed. Fifty dinars, or about £20, is said to have been given by a Meccan for an antique robe ‖; 300 dirhems, or about £12, for an excellent war-horse.¶ If the accounts of

---

* *Jahiz*, *Opuscula*; *Azraki*, 155. This badge was of bark; according to *Wellhausen*, *Wakidi*, 400, a humiliating badge of subjection.

† *Wakidi* (*W.*), 290.

‡ *Alif-Bā*, i., 319. The text has "ounces."

§ *Ibn Sa'd*, iii., 122.

‖ *Musnad*, iii., 403.

¶ *Wakidi* (*W.*), 42.

SHERIF'S HOUSE AT MECCAH.

traditions, or on the numbers and fighting power of the clans. The Banu 'Amir Ibn Luway could not protect a stranger against the Banu Ka'b *; the Banu 'Adi Ibn Ka'b were regarded as inferior to the Banu 'Abd Manaf. † "People whose traditions could not point to distinguished ancestors were liable to be despised, and the contempt which they experienced condemned them to humiliating occupations which degraded them still more." ‡ Intermarriage with an inferior clan was regarded as disgraceful. § Of these social distinctions something will be heard in the sequel, where it will appear that they provided one of the factors which helped the cause of Islam.

That a community which had attained this degree of pacific development could dispense with a similarly developed political and judicial organisation seems remarkable; yet there would appear to have been little beyond the rudiments of either. ‖ Within the clans and tribes there was patriarchal organisation of a kind. Thus it appears that the sole will of Abu Talib prevented the Hashimite clan from giving Mohammed up. Those persons who disagreed appear, however, to have been able to dissociate themselves from their brethren. Contributions were said at times to be levied on the clans for the covering of the Ka'bah ¶ and the entertainment of pilgrims, and

* *Tabari*, i., 1203.

† *Azraki*, 448

‡ *Goldziher*, *M. S.*, i., 40.

§ *Wellhausen*, *Ehe*, 439.

‖ Compare Wellhausen's lecture *Ein Gemeinwesen ohne Obrigkeit*, Göttingen, 1900.

¶ *Azraki*, 176.

this, if true, also implies some sort of municipal organisation. The same is implied for the state by the traditions that visitors paid taxes, and that imports paid customs; for a budget requires a variety of officials. The principle on which the chief of the clan was appointed is unknown. Ordinarily some wealth went with the office—for our authorities note as exceptional the case in which a poor man was chief *; oratorical ability, personal courage, and personal dignity were essentials.† The chief, however, was not necessarily or indeed ordinarily leader of the tribe in war. Our authorities actually provide us with a list of offices of state held at Meccah, and we cannot doubt that the sanctuary and its ceremonies led to the existence of certain officials: thus there was a sacristan who kept the key of the Ka'bah, and a priest who worked the oracle of the god (Hubal) whose image was inside; and the entertaining of the pilgrims is said to have been the perquisite of certain persons. None of these functions appear to have acquired political significance. In time of war, as in many communities, the fighters subjected themselves (in some degree) to a leader; but in time of peace there was little government. Some matters indeed were settled at a council, or comitia, in which heads of tribes, other free citizens, and even strangers,‡ it would appear, might be heard; yet the theory of deciding by a majority of votes was certainly unknown.

---

* *Wakidi* (*W.*), 51. 'Utbah, son of Rabi'ah.

† *Nallino*, *Nuova Antologia*, 1893, Oct., p. 618.

‡ *Tabari*, i., 1230.

Where conflicting claims arose within the community, they might be settled (perhaps) by an appeal to the oracle of the god Hubal, whose minister decided by the drawing of arrows; or the opinion of a sorceress might be asked. These sibyls indeed play a rather important part in the early history of Arabia: combining the professions of lawyer, physician, and priest, they yet enjoyed little respect. Or the claim could be submitted to some man whose celebrity for justness or keenness gave him the unofficial position of judge: some of these persons are even said "to have judged the judgment of Islam in the days of Ignorance."* They were not, however, necessarily resident in Meccah; and when there was a quarrel between two men in that city, they might even go as far as Yemen to get it settled.† All such modes of obtaining justice were not only costly and haphazard, but, as they were unofficial, there was no certainty of the award being executed; and if it consisted in death or mutilation, the culprit's tribe might interfere to prevent its being carried out.‡ Probably then monetary penalties were more commonly prescribed, and indeed we hear of an ancestor of the Prophet paying away a house in atonement for a blow §; the chief business of the arbiter would be then to assess a claim for damages. We have no authority for asserting that there was in consequence much unpunished injury committed

* *Ibn Duraid*, 234.

† *Aghani*, viii., 51.

‡ *Ibn Duraid:* case of Abu Lahab.

§ *Azraki*, 452.

at Meccah; and a league of which we hear—called the league of the Fudul, meaning perhaps a number of persons named Fadl—instituted during Mohammed's youth, for the purpose of preventing injuries, was chiefly directed against those inflicted on strangers visiting Meccah. From the history of Mohammed we should infer that the fear of civil strife and its consequences led to an extraordinary amount of mutual forbearance.

Between Hubal, the god whose image was inside the Ka'bah, and Allah ("the God"), of whom much will be heard, there was perhaps some connection; yet the identification of the two *suggested** by Wellhausen is not yet more than an hypothesis. It seems possible that Allah, really a male deity, of which Al-Lāt was the female,† identified by Mohammed with the object of monotheistic adoration, was the tribal god of the Kuraish; and indeed in lines which may possibly be pre-Islamic the Kuraish are called Allah's family.‡ At the ceremonies of Muzdalifah the Kuraish and their co-religionists used to say, "We are the family of Allah"§; and by this name they were known in Arabia.‖ Something of this sort is also assumed in the polemic of the Koran.¶ According to ancient custom the Kuraish, when they became supreme, gave their deity a place beside the deities of the older tribes, such as Al-'Uzza, Al-Lāt, Manāt,

* And hesitatingly approved by *Nöldeke*, *Z. D. M. G.*, xli., 715.

† *Wakidi* (*W.*), 362.

‡ *Ibn Duraid*, 94; *Z. D. M. G.*, xviii., 226.

§ *Tirmidhi*, i., 167.

‖ *Azraki*, 98, 155.

¶ Chapter v., *ultra*.

and others; a process described in the Koran by the commercial term "associating" or "taking into partnership," which probably had no underlying theological speculation. That association did not lead to a distinction of functions between different gods and goddesses,* which was only found in Arabia by those who had been schooled in the theology of Egypt or Greece. In Arabia each tribe had its god or patron, from whom it expected everything, and where tribes were confederate the relation between the gods was a friendly one, whence a man might call different sons after different gods; as indeed was done by Mohammed's grandfather. It is possible, in some cases probable, that these gods or some of them had been in earlier stages of Arabic development impersonations of some moral or physical quality, or belonged to a system of astronomical theology †; but such associations had long since vanished, just as the ordinary worshippers of Zeus or Jupiter were unaware that his name meant the sky. The number of the gods who had a place near the Ka'bah would seem to have been very large and some of these were also identified with trees or stones in the neighbourhood, which pious persons visited, bringing offerings. Of the same and perhaps of others there were also household representations, which received homage in domestic rites. Their number is to be accounted

---

* "Auf keinen Fall dürfte man es versuchen die arabischen Götter durch eine förmliche Mythologie zu verknüpfen." *Nöldeke, Z. D. M. G.*, xli., 714.

† An Egyptian writer has recently endeavoured to take them all to Egypt.

for in part by the practice of exogamy or obtaining wives outside the husband's tribe, whose gods would often accompany them; in part by the trading of the Meccans, who had opportunities of learning of the existence and power of foreign deities.

Paganism is called by the Koran the period of Ignorance—a phrase in the opinion of some borrowed from the New Testament*; in the Koran it is thus explained: the Meccans had, we are assured, no previous revelation; no Prophet, no books, no guidance.† The only reason which they could assign for the rites they practised was that their fathers had done the same.

It seems likely that this account is near the truth. We should miss much in the origin of Islam if we failed to keep before our minds its claim to be a *first instruction* to the people whom it addressed. Against any previous code, therefore, the Koran does not argue, just as it does not lean upon any such background. It is true the Moslems suppose that the Arabs had been originally bound by the code of Abraham and Ishmael, and that to certain Arab races other prophets had been sent. But this was only assumed in order to prove fetish worship and the practices of the pagans to be innovations; and the Arabs could even name the miscreant who was responsible for their introduction.

The Koran makes indeed an exception when it denies that the Arabs had any previous guide. It is

---

* *Wellhausen*, *Reste*, 71. Wrongly according to *Goldziher*, *M. S.*, i., 225, who renders it "Barbarianism."

† *Surah* xxxiv., 43, xxxvi., 5.

recorded* that some of those who enquired about Islam declared that they had before been in possession of the Book of Lukman, and the Koran once reproduces a certain number of maxims addressed by Lukman to his son. Many more such maxims are quoted by Moslem writers, but unfortunately we have rarely any good reason for believing them to be handed down from very early time. The Koran clearly supposes Lukman to have been a monotheist, and the sayings ascribed to him are ordinarily in the style of the Biblical Proverbs—containing a mixture of religious, moral, and worldly counsels. Some of his precepts may have been employed in instructing the Arab youth; and he was ordinarily supposed to have been an Arab, though some legends† make him out to have been a black. But of any reverend and beloved name being made responsible for pagan practice we do not hear. Against the Prophet Mohammed the general practice of a series of generations was quoted, but not apparently any authoritative code.

Where these practices are described—and many of them had been forgotten by the time when the Moslems came to study them with some sort of sympathy—they continually admit of easy illustration from, if not of identification with, the practices of other pagan races. To the religious institutions (such as prayer, vows, sacrifices) which the Arabs shared with the nations of classical antiquity we

---

* *Tabari*, i., 1207.

† *Jahiz, Opuscula*, 58.

need do no more than allude. That there should be many rites of a superstitious nature connected with the camel is natural, considering the importance which attached to that animal in the life of the Arab. Of the practice of Tabu, so richly illustrated in Mr. Manning's *Old New Zealand*, the customs of Central Arabia contain many examples. Of ancestor worship,* sacrifices to the dead,† human sacrifices,‡ and even cannibalism traces have been preserved. Cases occur in the biography of the Prophet of women biting the liver or drinking out of the skull of a fallen foe. Rich illustration is also provided of the sanctuary or domain controlled by a god whose force permeates it somewhat after the fashion of an electric current; a doctrine so lucidly explained in Frazer's *Golden Bough*. A mythology of a naive sort was taught by nurses to children, a few details of which crop up from time to time. The soul was thought at death to take the form of a bird.§ The sun was supposed at eventide to sink into a well.

Although the practices of paganism were exceedingly numerous and complicated, it does not appear that there was any systematic knowledge of them; old men could state, so far as their memory served them, what had been the invariable custom, but it is unlikely that any one had been taught to observe or to make collections of cases; and it is only

---

* *Goldziher*, *M.S.*, i., 230.

† *Ibid.*, 239.

‡ *Wellhausen*, *Reste*, 115.

§ In *Globus*, 1901, 358, etc., parallels to this superstition are collected.

where this is done that any system can come into being. We must not therefore make the mistake of supposing that there were definite notions and fixed rules, where at best there may have been a vague tendency towards uniformity.

It has been asserted by some authors that the insufficiency of paganism as a satisfaction of the religious need was felt at Meccah, and that the whole of the Arabs were ready for something better. If this be interpreted as meaning that paganism was becoming unfashionable, it is correct; devout believers in Al-Lāt and Al-'Uzza were thought by those who had been in the great world to be behind the times. Practices which savoured of savagery were already condemned by the common sense of influential men; and those who, having travelled, learned that paganism was despised and ridiculed in the Roman Empire and in Persia, often thought it proper to despise and ridicule it themselves. But that the fetishism of the Arabs was otherwise insufficient for their religious needs is an assertion which does not admit of proof. A god is an imaginary being who can do good or harm; and everything goes to show that the Arabs who had not seen the great world were firmly convinced that their gods or goddesses could do both. Hence the images of the gods provided sanctuary for persons whose lives were forfeit, and this sanctuary was respected by all save the enlightened.* Of the *real* philanthropists and reformers among them, men who squandered their substance in saving the lives of

***Ibn Duraid*, 235.

girls doomed to death* or in releasing prisoners,† or who kept their word at any cost, some were faithful adherents of the cults of Al-'Uzza and Al-Lāt. Occupied with the reform of their own lives and the righting of actual wrongs, these persons made no noise, and being earnest, did not suppose that the setting up of one cult for another would make men virtuous; and Mohammed himself had occasion to draw a contrast between the conduct of his pagan and that of his believing son-in-law, greatly to the disadvantage of the latter. So far as the religious sentiment required gratification, there is no evidence to show that paganism failed to gratify it. We gather from the inscriptions of the pagan Arabs that a wealth of affection and gratitude was bestowed upon their gods and patrons. Few indeed were prepared to die for their deities, when told to reject them or be executed. But then with sound though rare logic they inferred from their reduction to this strait that their gods were impotent and had been vainly worshipped.

A great scholar, indeed, from whom it is unsafe to differ, finds a difference between the central and the southern Arabians, and supposes the latter to have been earnest worshippers, while the former were indifferent. The ground for this assertion appears to lie in the absence of religious inscriptions from Central Arabia; but there is no saying when

---

* This act is also ascribed to the monotheist, Zaid, son of 'Amr. *Ibn Sa'd*, iii., 277.

† *Ibn Duraid*, 193: Sa'd, son of Mushammit, vowed that he would never see a prisoner but he would release him.

this gap in our knowledge may be filled up, and little can be inferred on such matters from negative evidence. The fact, moreover, that several of the chief objects of worship were goddesses suggests that the Arabs of Central Arabia were not wanting in piety, since the cult of goddesses all over the world appears to be conducted with special fervour, and calls into play sentiments which a male cult is not capable of exciting. Doubtless too the identification of these objects varied very much with the mental capacity of different worshippers; to some they may have been stars, or fetishes, or sentiments, but to the greater number they were women, not indeed often to be seen, but neither quite invisible nor far off, who were more powerful certainly than the women of the tribe, but resembling them in character and disposition.

With regard to morals, there is no doubt that the Arabs possessed the notions of right and wrong, but the denotation assigned to these notions was ordinarily very different from what we expect in civilised countries. Mr. Beckwourth tells us how when he lived with the Blackfeet, he one day struck down his wife for disobeying him; her supposed death, however, occasioned no resentment on the part of her father, who gave her husband his second daughter as a substitute the selfsame evening; and when the husband discovered that the former wife had been merely stunned, not killed, the situation was in no way complicated thereby. How many violations of European morality he committed thus within twenty-four hours it would not be easy to count. In a civilised state he would have been arrested for murder, and imprisoned for bigamy; tabooed on half a dozen grounds and ousted from decent society. Among the Blackfeet his conduct was normal and praiseworthy, nor was his father-in-law's conduct—to us heartless and indecent in the extreme—improper. Similarly with the people of the Ignorance a moral stigma attached to certain states and certain acts; but not always to those states and acts which the experience of ages of civilisation has shown to be deleterious to the community, and which members of organised states taboo. To the taking of human life it is clear that no moral guilt was thought to attach; and between accidental homicide and intentional murder the Arabs seem to have been quite unable to distinguish; when some men, building up a lion pit, accidentally pushed,* or pulled,† each other in and were killed by the lion, their relatives could with the greatest difficulty be prevented from avenging the deaths; and of the right to blood-money there was no question. On the other hand not to avenge a murder was disgraceful. The taking of blood-money by the relatives was thought degrading, but not because it implied heartlessness or sordidness: rather because it suggested weakness and fear. Only when the steady accumulation of wealth began to be found attractive, and peace was seen to be a necessary condition of this, did the presence in the tribe of a swashbuckler prove inconvenient. Such a person

* *Musnad*, i., 77.

† *Ibid.*, i, 128

therefore was apt to be publicly discarded. But if he remained in the tribe, murders committed by him were likely to involve the tribe in war, since the blood-feud demanded the death of any of the murderer's tribesmen, and to hand over a murderer to the vengeance of the heirs of the murdered man was thought in the highest degree dishonourable.

In another matter which civilisation has hedged in with a variety of rules and ordinances, Central Arabia exhibits the simultaneous existence of many stages of development. The institution of marriage in our sense had certainly existed for untold centuries; of polyandry in its various forms only faint traces survived; even in a rather backward community like that of Medinah, a girl in order to be marriageable required a dowry—in our sense of the word *; and there is evidence that concubinage was in some tribes considered improper.† The question whether the wife should enter the husband's tribe or the husband enter the wife's was settled by the circumstances of the case; in normal cases the former took place. Still the social condition described by Beckwourth appears to have existed in certain of the Arab tribes. Those men who did most for the community married many women; but it would rather appear that the dissolution of a marriage was the right of the woman, not of the man. It does not appear that dishonour everywhere attached to unchastity in women, though ideas on this subject varied very much in different tribes. In some the

* *Ibn Sa'd II.*, ii., 78.

† *Z. D. M. G.*, xlvi., 2; *Wellhausen, Ehe*, 440.

birth of a daughter was the occasion for special felicitation,* containing an allusion to the dowry or purchase-money she would bring her parents; on the other hand the Koran asserts that the birth of a daughter was regarded as a misfortune, and that the practice of burying girls alive was common, and such occurrences are attested for the period with which Mohammed's early life coincided.† That practice cannot be altogether dissociated from fears concerning female frailty, and even in the most civilised period of the Caliphate we find the death of a daughter in childhood regarded as a subject for congratulation, the father being thereby saved from a possible source of danger to his honour. "Were it not," says the author of a letter of condolence on such an occasion, "for my knowledge of your late daughter's rare virtues, I should be more inclined to congratulate you than to condole with you, since the hiding of one's weak points is an advantage, and the burial of a daughter is a desirable thing." ‡ With an allusion to the same notion, poets praising women speak of them as having been buried before death in the secrecy of the harem, or at death being transferred from one harem to another. A still older theory, however, is that the father is in any case disgraced by giving his flesh and blood into another man's power. ‖ Where infanticide was not practised, fear of dishonour (or perhaps a religious scruple) led to

* *Hariri, Sch.*, 334.
† *Musnad*, i., 398. For this subject, see *Wellhausen, Ehe*, 458.
‡ *Letters of Khwarizmi (Const.)*, 20.
‖ *Wellhausen, Ehe*, 433.

child marriage, seven or eight being the normal age at which girls became wives. *

The general freedom of pagan days, and the varieties of the practice of different tribes, permitted of much abnormal development. Sensuality and unchastity were normal; but in some tribes the erotic sentiment took a sublime and romantic form, and many a legend tells of the ennobling of the passion into fastidious chivalry and refinement. Deprived by custom of the right of inheriting,† women not unfrequently accumulated and disposed of wealth; as poetesses they could fan the embers of feuds into flame, and as prophetesses direct the movements of their tribes. Following the men into the battle-field, they could encourage the fighters by savage music, or could themselves (like Beckwourth's "Pine Leaf") deal wounds and death; or, more often, strip and mutilate the slain. The institutions (if that term may be used) of paganism were not unfavourable to the prominence of those women who had the requisite gifts of courage or insight. And the ensuing narrative will show examples of women acting with originality and resolution, when there was room for the display of those qualities.

Of respect for property and loyalty and honour, pagan Arabia shows no exalted standard. The institution of private property would appear to have existed, and indeed to have been fairly developed at Meccah, in spite of its apparent contradiction to the doctrine of the blood-feud. Thus the Meccan heads

* *Alif-Bā*, i., 394.

† *Perron, Femmes Arabes avant et depuis l'Islamisme*, 1858.

of houses are represented as forming a joint-stock company for the purpose of foreign trade, the profits on each occasion being divided proportionately among the investors, and by them expended or hoarded, or invested in fresh speculations. Sales of various sorts between individuals are recorded for the period before the taking of Meccah. Probably, therefore, this community was somewhat further advanced in commercial civilisation than the Crows or Blackfeet of Beckwourth's time.

The course of the following narrative will show that Mohammed's mission at Meccah was a failure, and that it was only at Medinah, which had been suffering for years from the curse of civil war, that he readily found a hearing, and that having turned Medinah into an armed camp, he was able partly by force and partly by bribes to subjugate Meccah, whence he proceeded quickly to subdue the rest of Arabia. The conquest of Arabia speedily led to that of the surrounding nations. From this we may draw with regard to Meccah certain inferences which correspond very well with the historical tradition. It had clearly acquired at the time when Mohammed arose a position of importance in Arabia, since its example was so speedily followed, and indeed many an Arabian state seems to have waited to submit to the Prophet till Meccah had submitted. That importance was not due to military strength, but either to the respect felt for the deities of the Meccan temple, or to the intellectual and political superiority of its inhabitants; an early writer perhaps with justice attributes it to the miraculous repulse of the Abyssinian invasion, which impressed the Arabs with the idea that the Meccans were the favoured of heaven *; Wellhausen on the other hand ascribes it mainly to the ability of the Kuraish, "who understood better than others how to draw water out of their own well, and make their neighbours' water flow in their channels." †

Meccah then was in a sufficiently healthy condition to be able to throw off without serious trouble such a civil disease as is represented by a secret society, aiming at reconstruction of the social fabric. But outside Meccah there was much instability, and much opportunity for the intervention of a strong will. The title of king was maintained by a few heads of tribes, ‡ and certain other historic appellations were not yet extinct among the populations of the south and centre of the peninsula; but these chieftains resembled the feudal barons, whose authority reached but a little way beyond the fortresses whence they could conduct their raids, and was of no avail for the protection of life or property.

These neighbours of the Meccans still lived the nomad life—a life in which the raiding of camels was the only manly occupation, and in which the blood-feud was the most important of existing institutions. That Bedouin institution was still retained by the Meccans, though they had abandoned the nomad state; blood shed by another tribe demanded vengeance, and therefore some trivial cause was likely

* *Azraki*, 98.

† *Reste*, 93.

‡ Kindah; also in Hajar, and Oman.

at any moment to involve the state in war, or cause the constituent groups to be arrayed against each other. War meant such an upsetting of arrangements that we find the Meccan magnates dominated by the desire for peace.

The wealth which some of the community had acquired made them sufficiently important to be honoured with appeals from various disputants: in such cases we find it the policy of the arbiters to do anything rather than make a pronouncement which is at all likely to produce a broil. A legend which may have a basis of truth makes Abu Sufyan, of whom much will be heard, appointed arbiter by persons who were disputing over the claims of their respective clans. To favour either would have probably involved both the favoured party and the arbiter in a dispute*: Abu Sufyan therefore refused to say more than that they were like the "Knees of a camel" and declined to state which was the right knee. The other Kurashite leaders were no less cautious; and resorted to great sacrifices to stifle disputes at their commencement.

For the north and east two Christian or partly Christian outposts were formed by the Ghassanide kingdom which held the Gulf of Akabah and was dependent on Byzantium, and the kingdom of Hirah which held the approaches to Mesopotamia and was dependent on Persia.

In both cases civilised powers employed Arabs to keep Arabs in order†: the purpose of these Arab

---

* *Agh.*, xv., 54.

† *Rothstein*, *Lakhmiden*, 127.

kingdoms being to form bulwarks against the raiding Bedouins. But the dynasty of Hirah was abolished about 602 A.D. by the Persian suzerain—for a variety of reasons: and a few years after at Dhu Kār the Bedouins had an earnest of their future conquest of the empire of the Khosroes.

It appears that some goods had been entrusted to a certain Arab tribe by Nu 'man, son of Mundhir, King of Hirah, shortly before his deposition, and that the new viceroy had demanded that these, consisting chiefly in weapons and armour, together with hostages, should be given up. A chieftain of the Banu 'Ijl, Hanzalah, son of Tha 'labah, was brought to the front by this demand, which was backed with the terrible force of the Persian empire. He resolved to resist it: the arms instead of being handed over to the Persians were distributed among men capable of bearing them; and plans were devised by which the organisation of the Persians and their skill as bowmen should be rendered unavailing. The Persian forces were lured into a place where there was no water, and the soldiers were speedily incapacitated by thirst; an ambush was prepared whence a body of Bedouins could emerge at a critical moment in the fray; and finally the Arab allies of the Persians were induced to leave the field when the battle had begun, and drag the rest of the army into rout. The battle of Dhu Kar, so called from the spring near which it was fought, exposed the *Sawad* or fertile land watered by the Euphrates to the incursions of the Bakr Ibn Wa 'il and other Arab raiders: but it also shook the belief in the power of

Persia, which had long been an article of faith in Arabia.

In Golan, in Palæstina Secunda, reigned the Ghassanidæ of the house of Jafnah, whose rule at one time embraced the land of Hermon to the Gulf of Akabah; and who indeed were responsible for all nomads "permanently or temporarily settled in Palæstina II., Arabia, Phœnicia ad Libanum, probably also Palæstina III., and perhaps even in the provinces of N. Syria."* About 583 the dynasty had for a time been suspended, owing to disputes with the Byzantine suzerains, who, however, appear to have restored it again, till it was overthrown in 613 or 614 by the Persian invaders, after which it is uncertain whether it was restored.

In other South and North Arabian states the religion of the world-power had penetrated, and certain tribes were wholly or partly Christian.† But it was seed sown on stony ground, whose product had no power of resistance when the heat came: it perished without leaving a trace, when Islam appeared. A strange fact: these Christian Arabs had bishops and priests and churches, and even heresies of their own; yet we cannot to this day make out from our authorities whether the Christian Scriptures were ever rendered into the vernacular of those converts, or whether only the priests had religious books, and these in a language which they must go abroad to learn. The

* *Nöldeke, Die Ghassanischen Fürsten aus dem Hause Gafna's*, Berlin. 1887, from whom the statements in the paragraph are taken.

† There were churches in the Farsan islands, *Sprenger*, *Alte Geographie Arabiens*, 254.

last is most likely to have been the case, and to have been one of the causes of the unresisting collapse of Arabian Christianity. Even before Mohammed's time it had given way in South Arabia to Judaism, some Sabæan king having been won over by the Jews of Yathrib, and for once men of the Jewish persuasion had possessed the courage to fight and even to die. A conquering state, governed by the law of Moses! That Jewish state was indeed of short duration. Like other religious communities which preach toleration when oppressed, they became persecutors when they had acquired sovereignty: and for once * an inquisition arose in which Jews piled fagots and lit fires, and Christians were burned. Those pyres gleam out as a ray of light in the darkness of Arabian history before Islam: the Syriac letter in which the story of the Najran martyrs is told is like a fragment of a pre-Islamic Chronicle.† The persecution was an act of folly, no less than of cruelty; the Jews had indeed much to avenge, but to remain unavenged had been safer. The news spread that the Church was in danger: from Christian Abyssinia a force was sent to aid the persecuted followers of the Gospel: defeated by some accident the Jewish king died a hero's death. But the Abyssinians had not conquered for the Najranites, but for themselves. Kings of their own were set up in South Arabia, who oppressed the Arabs, and set

* A. D. 523. *Fell* in *Z. D. M. G.*, xxxv., 74. *Nöldeke, Sasaniden*, 186, n.

† *Mordtmann, Z. D. M. G.* xxxv., 700, regards it as spurious: *Nöldeke* and the majority as genuine.

COIN, WITH ABYSSINIAN KING APHIDAS ON OBVERSE, AND ON REVERSE THE LAST JEWISH KING OF YEMEN, DHU NUWAS OR DIMEAN.

From Rüppell, *Reise in Abessinien*, t. viii., pl. vi.; vol. ii., pp. 344 and 429.

themselves to spread Christianity with the sword. The year in which the Prophet was ordinarily supposed to have been born,* long known as the year of the Elephant, the South Arabian ruler, provoked indeed by insults offered to his own sanctuary, is said to have sent an army to destroy the sanctuary at Meccah; but the legend says he failed, some disaster attacking his force similar to that which befell Sennacherib of old: for occasionally the gods defend their temples. After his return to San 'a, still the capital of Yemen, Arab discontent found a leader in Saif, son of Dhu Yazan; who importuned the Persian court till at last help was given against the Abyssinian usurpers; whom he drove out, substituting vassalage to Persia for the other. The films of Judaism and Christianity torn off the face of South Arabia, paganism it seems was restored: not indeed at Najran, where Christianity remained, as in an island; but the rulers were pagans, and in league with the worst enemy of the Cross. Meanwhile the matters about which the sects were at variance were evoking interest in minds that had been alien from them.

The introduction of both the Christian and Jewish religions was attended at times perhaps with the spread of certain virtues. Fidelity was regarded as the result of both Judaism and Christianity: the King of Hirah was supposed to have turned Christian because of a brilliant specimen of fidelity shown to him by a member of the Christian tribe of Tay.†

* *Nöldeke*, *Sasaniden*, 205, gives reasons for placing the expedition much earlier.

† *Jahiz*, *Mahasin*, 75.

In the main the effects on the life and character of the people were vanishingly small. A member of this tribe, 'Adi, son of Hatim, was taunted by Mohammed with appropriating a fourth of the spoil contrary to the principles of his religion and in accordance with the practices of paganism. Ali declared that the Christianity of the Taghlibites was confined to the drinking of wine.* The King of Hirah, though a Christian, had more than one wife †; as also had the Ghassanide Al-Mundhir.‡ A long story is told of the Christian Haudhah, son of 'Ali, a member of the tribe Hanifah. He undertook to escort the Persian King's caravan safely to the Persian frontier: but it was attacked and raided by the Banu Sa'd. Haudhah redeemed the prisoners out of his own purse, naturally with a view to a reward from the Persian King, who richly fulfilled his hopes. At the Persian King's request he presently decoyed the Banu Sa'd, under pretext of selling them corn in a year of famine, into a building, where they were killed one by one as they entered. We are not surprised to find him regarding conversion to Islam as merely a matter for bargaining.

We should require thus to know more of the inner life of these Christianised tribes before we could be certain whether their conversion did much else than take away the restraints which pagan superstitions had placed upon them. Thus it appears that, whereas pagan Arabia respected the

* *Fell*, p. 49.

† *Nöldeke*, *Sas.*, 329.

‡ *Id.*, *Ghass.*, 29, n. 1.

four sacred months, it was unsafe during those months to traverse the land of the Christian tribes without safe conduct.* A Tai'ite Christian, who at baptism had received the well-known name of Sergius, and was converted to Islam in Mohammed's lifetime, explained to his new friends some remarkable expedients which he had invented for camel raiding: he used to store water in ostrich eggs and bury the latter at points in the desert known only to himself; hence he could drive the camels to regions whither no one cared to follow him.† His whole tribe were regarded as expert thieves.‡ Of one of these Christians § we possess a considerable volume of poems: they were composed certainly in the days of the second Islamic dynasty, but the spirit they breathe is that of the Arabs before Islam. The poet taunts his enemies with preferring goods and chattels to vengeance; with accepting blood-money where men of honour would have been satisfied only with blood. If he ever heard of a future life, it affected his calculations no more than the thought of the Elysian Fields affected Horace; when once the earth should close over him, no more pleasure, he was convinced, was to be had. He had a keen idea of the glories of his tribe: which consist of old victories, in which they had slain, if not thousands and ten thousands, yet respectable numbers of the foe. His Muse is readily roused by the thought of wine, the quality of which he thoroughly

* Cf. *Muslim*, ii., 254.

† *Ishak*, 985.

‡ *Tirmidhi*, 481 (ii., 158.)

§ *Al-Akhtal.*

understood. It has even been conjectured that the fragments of pre-Islamic poetry which have been preserved emanated to a great extent from professing Christians, and these are as a rule characterised by the Pagan spirit. Traces of the higher morality which we are accustomed to associate with Christianity are not easily found in this literature.

The life then of these Christianised Arabs seems in many respects to have resembled that of their pagan brethren. With some of the old vices they retained the old virtues, among which personal prowess was chief; but a certain class of the population kept out of the fighting and lived in quiet—the monks and nuns. These probably did not abound in Arabia—for the love of and pride in offspring which is so characteristic of that country would have a tendency to render monastic institutions unpopular, even before they were branded by Mohammed as a wicked innovation: but there were monks and nuns,* and probably the introduction of this form of life was the most important alteration produced by the conversion of the Arab tribes to Christianity. It would seem likely that the application of the modern Arabic alphabet to the Arabic language originated with these men†: and that the diffusion of that alphabet over the Arabian peninsula was due to their intercommunication. As some of these persons assuredly spent their ample leisure in some form of study, the notion that the true religion was a learned religion spread about.

---

*Cf. *Goldziher*, *Z. D. M. G.*, xlvi., 44.

† *Rothstein*, *Lakhmiden*, 27, places it with the Christians of Hirah.

The earlier portions of the Koran give evidence of the extreme respect with which "Knowledge of the Book" was regarded by the Arab who was without it. The very vagueness of the notion contributed to the wonder which it inspired. The Jews and Christians were literate, and pagans illiterate.* Early in his career Mohammed assumed that the evidence of one of the people of the Book could settle any historical question beyond the possibility of contradiction. Of the veracity of the Book he, at no time, held any doubt whatever. Novelists sometimes depict the awe which book-learning evokes in those who are absolutely without it; and this, which for a time was Mohammed's attitude, was, if not normal, at any rate common among the pagans of Arabia who had come into contact with Jews and Christians.

Some of the Meccans even before Mohammed had, it is generally supposed, the curiosity to pry into this awful mystery of the Book.† Interest therein may have been aroused by the Abyssinian captives or deserters left behind after the unsuccessful invasion in the year of the Elephant ‡; perhaps they account for the presence at Meccah of some Abyssinians who became prominent at the commencement of Islam. We hear besides of certain Ghassanide Christians who were settled at Meccah under the protection of the Banu Zuhrah,§ the Prophet's uncles on the mother's side.

---

* Ali, not over accurate in his statements, declared that when Mohammed rose, not an Arab could read a book.—*Nahj al-balaghah*, 51.

† For a list see *Sir C. Lyall, J. R. A. S.*, 1903.

‡ *Azraki*, 97.

§ *Ibid.*, 466.

Further, the wine-taverns led to a circulation of Christian and Jewish ideas among heathen topers.* One of the Meccan inquirers, Warakah, son of Naufal, cousin of Khadijah, is likely to have had much to do with the beginnings of Islam. He is credited with having translated a Gospel, or part of one, into Arabic; it was probably the Gospel of the Nativity, and was afterwards useful to the Prophet. The legend credits Kais, son of Nushbah, of the tribe Sulaym, which dwelt near Meccah, with some Book-knowledge; he is thought to have put questions thence to Mohammed—out of books unknown to us—which the latter answered correctly.† Whether the study of the Book was regarded by the Meccans as equivalent to the adoption of the Christian religion we know not; but most likely it was. The days are not so far off when Europeans took an analogous view, and any acquaintance with heretical books was thought to imply free-thinking. Moslem tradition records very little about these "precursors" of Mohammed, as they are called, which can be trusted. Most of them lived at a time when not to be against Mohammed was to be with him.

Even outside this small circle (supposing it to be historical) the influence of Judaism and perhaps Christianity had spread. The assertion that the Ka'bah contained a picture of the Madonna may of course be rejected as an error; but old names for Friday and Sunday‡ must have been derived from

---

* *Rothstein*, *Lakhmiden*, 26.

† *Isabah*, iii., 522.

‡ See *Fischer* in *Z. D. M. G.*, l., 224.

Jews or Christians, and there is reason for supposing that some ceremonies belonging to these sects were imitated at Meccah. Since in pagan Rome it was not unfashionable to respect the Jewish holy days, it is not surprising that at Meccah enlightenment should have taken the form of aping the ways of the enlightened communities. Some of the Meccans are credited with having practised a form of flagellation "after the fashion of Christian priests"; baring themselves they twisted their garments into scourges and lashed each other.* Abstention from wine—as a form of religious asceticism—is said to have been practised by several of the pagan Kuraish. Christian preachers were occasionally heard at the national fairs, and a proverb appears to perpetuate the name of one who, on such occasions, exhibited a previously unattainable degree of eloquence. Kuss, whose name appears to be a mispronunciation of the Syrian *Kasha*, "priest," said to be Bishop of Najran, delivered such an address at the market of 'Ukaz in the hearing of the Prophet †; and the address, as the Arabs preserve it, bears a marked likeness to early passages of the Koran, and may have contributed something to that book.‡ It is not suggested by our authorities that the persons who either adopted Christianity or showed inclination towards it suffered much inconvenience at Meccah. Even therefore if

---

* *Musnad*, iv., 191.

† *Bayan*, i., 119.

‡ A long story is told about Kuss in *Baihaki*, *Mahasin*, 351-5, where Kuss figures as a fortune-teller; it is probably pure invention. Further myths about him in *Al-Dhakha'ir*, 254.

the Abyssinian invasion caused some recrudescence of paganism at the beginning of Mohammed's life, the effect of it had disappeared by the time he was a young man.

Speculation is perhaps fruitless when directed to the probable course of history under circumstances differing from those that actually occurred. Had Meccah continued to increase in wealth and power under her sagacious leaders, it is not probable that her people would have remained satisfied with a religious system that was thought barbarous in the countries whence she would have been compelled to obtain science and learning. Yet the fact that the old religion was the source of her material prosperity would have rendered the substitution for it of either Christianity or Judaism impracticable. The ideal solution of the problem was clearly that discovered in time by Mohammed, of superseding both the enlightened religions; retaining the old source of wealth, but in a system which, so far from being backward, was in advance of the cult of the Roman Empire. So tortuous, however, was the process by which this solution was discovered and enforced that the symmetry of the edifice was lost—as perhaps ordinarily occurs when a stone rejected by the builder becomes the headstone of the corner.

CHAPTER II

EARLY LIFE OF MOHAMMED

MOHAMMED was the child of Meccan parents whose names are given as Abdallah (Servant of Allah) and Aminah (The Safe or Secure). The latter belonged to the Banu Zuhrah, the former was the son of Abd al-Muttalib, of the clan named Banu Hashim. It is certain that the future Prophet's father died before his son was born; it is said, when visiting Yathrib, afterwards better known as Medinah. Nor did his mother long survive him, and her grave was by some* said to be at Abwa, a place midway between the two cities, where, some fifty years after, her bones lay in some danger of being exhumed. Their son inherited from them a strong constitution capable of enduring fatigue, privation, and excess. On the other hand the notion current among Christian writers † that he was subject to epilepsy finds curious confirmation in the notices recorded of his experiences during the process of revelation—the importance of which is not

* *Azraki*, 481. Perhaps an etymological myth, the word seeming to mean "two parents."

† *Nöldeke*, *Gesch. d. Korans*, 18.

lessened by the probability that the symptoms were often artificially reproduced. That process was attended by a fit of unconsciousness; accompanied (or preceded) at times by the sound of bells in the ears * or the belief that some one was present †; by a sense of fright, such as to make the patient burst out into perspiration ‡; by the turning of the head to one side §; by foaming at the mouth ‖; by the reddening or whitening of the face; by a sense of headache.¶ Still we read of only two cases in his later life in which the fits were not subject to his own control, once when he fainted at the intense excitement of the battle of Badr, and once when he had himself bled after fasting.** And some of the signs of severe epilepsy—biting of the tongue, dropping what is in the hand,†† and gradual degeneration of the brain power—were wanting.

He was received into his father's family, and is said to have spent the first eight years of his life in the charge of Abd al-Muttalib. The condition of a fatherless lad was not altogether desirable; and late in life Mohammed was taunted by his uncle Hamzah (when drunk) with being one of his father's slaves.‡‡

---

* *Gowers*, *Epilepsy*, p. 70.

† *Ibid.*, 69.

‡ *Ibid.*, 80.

§ *Tabari*, *Comm.*, xxviii., 4. According to *Gowers*, to the side on which the convulsion is more severe.

‖ *Gowers*, 169.

¶ *Alif-Bā*, ii., 29.

** *Musnad*, i., 148.

†† *Gowers*, 130.

‡‡ *Bokhari* (*K.*), ii., 270.

Mohammed being a posthumous child, little in the way of romance gathered about his father; with his grandfather on the other hand the fancy of pious Moslems was industrious. Perhaps one or two actual facts can be made out about him. It seems clear that Mohammed came of a humble family; this crops up in many places. The Kuraish in the Koran wonder why a Prophet should be sent them who was not of noble birth. When their Prophet became all-powerful, they compared him to a palm springing out of a dung-hill.* On the day of his triumphal entry into Meccah he told the people that an end had now come to the pagan aristocracy by blood.† He himself rejected the title, "Master and son of our master," offered him by some devotee.‡ On the ground of these anecdotes we reject as fabulous all those in which Abd al-Muttalib figures as a leading man at Meccah.§

In the treasury of Ma'mun, whose reign began in 812 A.D., a document was preserved in which a Himyarite of San'a acknowledged to owing Abd al-Muttalib one thousand silver dirhems of the standard of Hudaydeh; "witness thereunto, Allah and the two angels"; the writing was Abd al-Muttalib's, and like a woman's hand.‖ "The two angels" stand, we suppose, for "the two 'Uzzas," *i. e.*, the goddesses Al-Lāt and Al-'Uzza, whose names may

* *Musnad*, iv., 166.

† *Ishak*, 821.

‡ *Musnad*, iii., 241.

§ Cf. *Nöldeke, Sas.*, 291.

‖ *Fihrist*, p. 5.

have figured in the original document.* The document may have been spurious; yet it is difficult to see why a forgery should have taken this form. If it was genuine, we should infer that Abd al-Muttalib was possessed of some capital, and occasionally lent it out; with which the anecdote that makes his son Abbas lend money to the people of Ta'if agrees. In order to harmonise the fact of his wealth with the fact of his being in a humble station we have to suppose that the profession in which his money was made was not an honourable one. Now a tradition which cannot easily be set aside† gives him the functions of providing the pilgrims with water and also with food. The water of the well Zemzem (which a later legend made him dig) being brackish, he used to render it potable by mixing it with camel's milk, honey, or raisins—the last procured from Ta'if, where his son Abbas afterwards possessed a vineyard.‡ That he put himself to this trouble and expense without remuneration is not credible; hence it would seem that the offices of "waterer and entertainer" which later writers represent as posts of honour at Meccah resolve themselves into a trade, and one that was not honourable; since the Prophet afterwards forbade the sale of water, and lavish hospitality is characteristic of the Arab noble. The other profession (of money-lender) was also of little esteem in the eyes of the

* Cf. *W. R. Smith*, *Kinship and Marriage*, 60.

† Thus *Wakidi* (*W.*) makes Hamzah refer to it on the battle-field of Uhud.

‡ *Azraki*, 70.

THE WELL ZEMZEM.
From *Ali Bey's Travels.*

Arabs, and many a poet boasts of his skill in eluding the creditors' claims.* The name Abd al-Muttalib, "slave of al-Muttalib," of which a fanciful explanation is given by our historians, is probably to be interpreted as meaning that its owner was at one time actually a slave, though afterwards manumitted and enrolled in the Hashim clan.†

The names of his ten sons and six daughters are probably historical, and indeed four of the former and two of the latter play parts of importance in the sequel. All ten sons, it is said, were of massive build and dark colour.‡ From the names of some of them we learn that Abd al-Muttalib was piously disposed towards the deities Allah, Manat, and Al-'Uzza. 'Abbas appears to have inherited the money-lending and watering businesses, and to have succeeded well in them. He also imported spices from Yemen which he sold at the time of the feast.§ Abu Talib dealt in cloth and perfume,‖ and succeeded less well. Another son, Hamzah, made his living by hunting. A fourth, Zubair, was engaged in the carrying trade, and this perhaps furnished the remainder with the means of livelihood. Abdallah, the Prophet's father, is supposed to have died while absent from Meccah on a business journey.

---

* *Nöldeke, Beiträge zur Kenntniss der Poesie der alten Araber*, 183–199.

† *Baihaki, Mahasin*, 393, makes him originate the custom of dyeing the hair black.

‡ *Jahiz, Opuscula*, 75, 5.

§ *Tabari*, 1162, 13.

‖ *Jahiz, Mahasin*, 165.

The name Mohammed (of which Ahmad and Mahmud were varieties) * was given the future Prophet; it was apparently not uncommon, and belonged to a distant connexion. † At a later time, when Mohammed's enemies wished to insult him, they called him the son of Abu Kabshah. Great uncertainty prevails as to the identity of this person; some holding that he was an ancestor of the Prophet ‡ or ancient Kurashite, § who had endeavoured to change the national religion, substituting the worship of Sirius for that of stones; whence Mohammed, when he began his religious innovations, was regarded as his moral descendant. A fragment of interesting history may be imbedded in this tale. Mohammed, it is said, occasionally spoke of his foster-father, and many assumed that Abu Kabshah was the man. With this statement there is connected a legend that Mohammed was nursed by some woman other than his mother: and this woman's husband would, according to Arabian ideas, bear a relation to Mohammed not much inferior to that of father. At a late period in his career a captive woman claimed to be his foster-sister, and proved her claim to the Prophet's satisfaction by showing where he had once bitten her in

* The discussion of these names by *Rösch, Z. D. M. G.*, xlvi., 432–440, leads to no results.

† It is worth noticing that the name of the Elephant brought by Abrahat against the Ka'bah was Mahmud (*Azraki*, 96) Was the Prophet thence supposed to have been born in the year called after it?

‡ *Baidawi* on *Surah* liii., 50.

§ *Zamakhshari*, *Ibid.*

ARAFAT.

the back. The foster-sister, however, refused an offer to remain in the neighbourhood of her distinguished relation, whence we are perhaps to infer that she was an impostor; while from the proof which she adduced of her identity, it would appear that Mohammed acknowledged having been a passionate child. The family to whose charge he was committed are all of them shadowy figures; their tribe is said to have been the Banu Sa'd, a branch of the Hawazin, who encamped at no great distance from Meccah.* The identification of Abu Kabshah with the father of the family seems very clearly to rest on a combination which may be sound, but which is by no means certain. The patronymic† Abu Kabshah would appear to have been fairly common, and calling Mohammed Abu Kabshah's son conveyed some sting; but what the nature of the insult was we cannot define with certainty. Another woman to whom the honour of having nursed Mohammed is ascribed was Thuwaibah, slave of his uncle Abu Lahab.

It is said that Abd al-Muttalib died when his grandson was eight years of age, leaving him to the care of his uncle Abu Talib. Abu Talib probably employed him in looking after the sheep and camels which he kept at 'Uranah, near Mt. Arafat,‡ just as his son Ja'far was employed in looking after sheep at Badr.§ When Mohammed had attained to power and

* According to *Al-Bekri*, at Hudaibiah, afterwards the scene of some famous negotiations.

† "Father of so-and-so," not "son of so-and-so."

‡ *Azraki*, 71.

§ *Wakidi* (*W.*), 73.

eminence he still used to tar his own camel,* and to divert himself by branding the camels and sheep † that were brought in as alms, in which business he displayed some technical skill ‡; and used to amaze his followers by his familiarity with the details of Bedouin life. In such societies as that of Meccah the difference between the occupations of the grand and the humble is at all times small, most of all in the time of youth. Mohammed probably did much the same as was done by his cousins and those of his uncles who were near his age. There are some games which Bedouin children play; certain weapons of which they learn the use in early life. A legend § shows us the youthful Prophet playing at "white bone." A bone of "dazzling whiteness" is thrown to a distance at night; and the boy who finds it becomes leader. In another tradition ‖ Mohammed confesses that twice when he was feeding his flock, he had left the care of the beasts to one of his companions, in order that he might take part in the revelries of the town; on both occasions, if we are to believe him, sleep fell on him miraculously before he could so disgrace himself.

Mayeux would have it that the Bedouins still attach vast importance to the study of eloquence, of fluent and correct delivery; and Mohammed may have had some early practice in this accomplish-

---

* *Musnad*, iii., 175.
† *Ibid.*, iii, 254.
‡ *Isabah*, i., 525.
§ *Alif-Bā*, i., 322.
‖ *Chronicles of Meccah*, ii., 7.

ment, in which he afterwards excelled. The Arabs who speculate on the subject observe that the Arab eloquence is invariably improvisation *; the elaborate preparation of a discourse which gives value to European oratory is unknown to them.

Further, the love of horses which characterised Mohammed at a later time † is likely to have been imbibed in early youth. Many traditions record his admiration for the Arab steed, and some of them are likely to be authentic; even when Prophet and sovereign of Medinah he is said to have encouraged and taken part in horse-racing.‡ Not a few of the Meccans possessed horses, as appears from the history of his campaigns; yet their employment seems to have been confined to war; for travelling they used the camel. The horse, however, is a favourite subject for poetic descriptions, and pride in the horse is characteristic of the Arab race. Dogs were detested by the Prophet, and he was near giving orders to extinguish the species.

If for the forty years of Mohammed's life which elapsed before his "mission," we omit what is evidently or most probably fabulous, it is surprising how little remains to be narrated. There appears, however, to be no ground for disputing the statement that he acted as helper, supplying arrows to his uncle Zubair, at a series of battles which took place when he was in his teens. Those battles belonged to what is known as the second Fijar war, waged

* *Jahiz, Bayan.*

† *Musnad*, v., 27; *Wakidi* (*W.*), 402.

‡ *Musnad*, iii., 160; *Wakidi* (*W.*), 184.

between the Kuraish with their allies, the Kinanah, and the collection of tribes called Kais. The quarrel arose like most of these quarrels, from the chief constituents of Arab life, the blood-feud and the relation of patron and client. The King of Hirah desired the protection of a central Arabian chieftain for the goods which he was sending to the 'Ukaz market. This was offered by a man named Al-Barrad, who had been ejected from tribe after tribe owing to his bad character, but whom the Kurashite Harb, father of Mohammed's antagonist Abu Sufyan, had undertaken to protect. The King perhaps wisely preferred the guaranty of a chieftain, of the Kaisite tribe Hawazin, named 'Urwah, whom Al-Barrad, out of pique, waylaid and slew. But then he remembered the troublesome fact that with the Hawazin his own life would not count as the equivalent of their kinsman's; they would want not an outcast like himself, but some eminent member of the tribe that had foolishly taken him in.* It was suggested to Abdallah Ibn Jud'an, an eminent Meccan, with whom the tribes that came to the fair of 'Ukaz deposited their arms, that he might seize those of the Hawazin, and so render them harmless; but he refused to take this unfair advantage, and instead restored to all the tribes their arms and bade the Kuraish return to Meccah; on the way thither they were attacked by the Hawazin, who, after an uneventful battle, arranged to continue the fight the same time in the following year. For four years successively the war, or rather the game, was renewed, with varying

* *Kamil*, ii., 239; *Procksh, Blutrache.*

success; at the fourth battle the Kuraish were victorious, but a Kurashite woman who had married a man of Kais was permitted to grant their lives to any Kaisites who took refuge in her tent, which she had enlarged on purpose; in the fifth year the Kaisites got the better, and after that the warfare dwindled down to occasional murders, when members of the rival tribes met. Finally the parties decided to count the slain and pay blood-money for the surplus. The series of mock battles was dated by the Arab archæologists from the fact that Mohammed took no part in the first, but witnessed the remainder. It was naturally inferred that he was prevented by youth from being present at the first fight, and his own practice at a later time was to allow no recruits younger than fifteen. If this reasoning be correct, the period covered by the war would be 584–588 A.D. He himself dated one of the fights as fought in his twentieth year.

It is not recorded (except indeed in a legend which scarcely professes to be historical) that Mohammed distinguished himself in any way during these wars; but when he came to rule a state himself we find that two of the lessons which they suggest to the modern reader had impressed themselves deeply upon his mind. One was the necessity of settling affairs of blood by some expedient less wasteful and more satisfactory than that which was illustrated by the war of the Fijar; and a second was that war should be regarded not as a game which might be played for an indefinite period, but as a mode of obtaining decisive results. His enemies arranged, when they were successful, to continue the battle next year, but not he. Nor do we find him imitating the conduct of the chivalrous Abdallah, son of Jud'an, who furnished a vindictive foe with weapons to be used against his friends.

The story of this war is of interest, since of those who figured in it, many were fathers of men who became prominent in the Prophet's time, and some continued their activity into that period. Abdallah, son of Jud'an, probably loomed in the eyes of the youthful Prophet as a mighty figure. The legend makes him fabulously wealthy, as having discovered a mass of jewels hidden in a hill, with the aid whereof he became chief of his tribe, and indeed the leading man in Meccah, profuse in gifts and lavish in hospitality*; late in life Mohammed could recall banquets given by the great man, at which verses in his praise were recited.† Harb, son of Umayyah, who commanded on one of the days,‡ was the father of the Meccan who opposed to Mohammed the most dogged resistance. Al-Zubair, the Prophet's uncle, who was at times in command, appears on few occasions in history; he is, however, said to have been a poet, and to have practised hospitality on a liberal scale to poets of other tribes; and on one occasion to have taken his nephew with him on a journey into Yemen. A story (which we have no means of checking) makes him venture to dispute the patronage of Harb, father of Abu Sufyan,

---

* *Goldziher*, *Z. D. M. G.*, xlvi., 7.

† *Isabah*, ii., 706.

‡ *Kamil* of *Mubarrad*, i., 187.

when his own father, Abd al-Muttalib, was prepared to respect it.*

There is no doubt that Mohammed often accompanied the Meccan caravans to their various destinations. The leading men of Meccah were constantly engaged in the conduct of these caravans, in which, as has been seen, many military qualities could be displayed. Their caravans regularly visited Syria and Yemen, but occasionally Egypt, Abyssinia, and Persia provided them with markets: the last of these countries not being in regular commercial relations with them.† The Christian kingdom of Hirah was also said to be visited by Meccan merchants; and one of the lovers of Hind, daughter of 'Utbah, of whom more will be heard, is said to have been a courtier of the King of Hirah, whose assistance he could demand for matrimonial projects.‡ In a tradition the Prophet speaks of the white palaces of Hirah, seen by him (professedly) from Medinah. The Koran shows him acquainted with travelling by sea as well as by land; he there describes the motions of ships and the results of storms with a realism which savours of experience. He knows too of a sweet sea as well as of a salt sea; the former he calls Euphrates; the two, he supposed, were kept from combining by a dam. His language about Egypt seems also to imply that he had been there§; and there is reason for supposing

**Jahiz, Mahasin*, 154. † *Isabah*, iii., 379.

‡ *Aghani*, viii., 50. Probably an anachronism is involved.

§ *Nöldeke, Sketches*, c. ii., shows that Mohammed was unaware that no rain falls in Egypt; perhaps, however, the error is due to momentary forgetfulness.

him to have seen the Dead Sea. The rock-tombs of Al-Hijr had deeply impressed his imagination before he passed by them at the head of an army. He had visited Bahrain in the Persian Gulf, and late in life could well remember the names of many villages there, as well as the local names of several varieties of dates *; just as his attention had been struck by a breed of tailless sheep in Yemen. †

That Mohammed on these journeys made acquaintances who afterwards proved serviceable seems likely, and indeed we know the names of some of his foreign or provincial friends, though ordinarily only the names. Khalid, son of Hawari, is given as the name of an Abyssinian acquaintance; the dialect of the father's name makes it likely that this statement is correct. Iyad, son of Himar, of the tribe Mujashi, is given as another.‡

To none of these journeys can we assign any date, except that to which reference has already been made, when he himself conducted an expedition to Bostra. On all of them he would appear to have picked up information. Sometimes this was gained from visits to places, as to smelting works; for such a visit may well be inferred from his curious comparison of the torrent, which carries away scum and bears fertilising water, to the molten metal, of which the slag is carried away, whereas the substance of which utensils are made remains. But most of his information was doubtless gathered from conver-

* *Musnad*, iv., 206.
† *Ibid.*, iv., 297.
‡ *Ibn Duraid*, 147.

BEDOUIN ARABS STORY-TELLING.

Drawn by Alfred Fredericks.

sations (*e. g.*, at wine-shops) or from listening to story-tellers. To any well-guarded caravan in Eastern countries some strangers are sure to attach themselves, who are anxious to enjoy the security and who in return will make themselves useful or agreeable. Among such would doubtless be Jewish dealers who traded in clothes* and other goods. From intercourse with these persons the Prophet is likely to have derived many an anecdote, and also many an outlandish expression. Some of these would figure in his conversation †; and his sacred book afterwards contained a number of phrases which even his intimate associates at Meccah did not understand.‡

What is known as education he clearly had not received. It is certain that he was not as a child taught to read or write, though these arts were known to many Meccans, as will appear from the sequel; their use in commerce was so great, as Mohammed himself afterwards emphasised, that his failing to learn them was probably due to the neglect into which an orphan ordinarily falls. For the other Arab fine art, poetry, he had absolutely no ear: hence we may infer that the form of education which consisted in learning by heart the tribal lays § was also denied him. Yet even here his power of picking up information did not altogether fail. The Tradition could name verses which had specially attracted

* *Goldziher*, *Z. D. M. G.*, xlvi., 185.

† *Kamil*, i., 27.

‡ *Comm.* on *Surah* xvi., 47.

§ *Jahiz*, *Bayan*, i., 107.

the Prophet's fancy.* The language of the Koran was thought by experts to bear a striking likeness to that of the early poetry: and though for us it is difficult to pass an opinion on this point, seeing that the early poetry is largely fabrication modelled on the Koran, we may accept the opinion of the Arabs. Of those lays which were recited on solemn or festive occasions some verses then stuck in his memory and provided the form of future revelations. Notwithstanding this fact he had a sincere aversion for poetry,† and an equally strong one for the only other known form of literary composition‡—rhymed prose. Perhaps he thus avenged himself for the want of education which had rendered him unable to handle either.

From intercourse with Arabian Jews and Christians he derived a sort of biblical phraseology, § such as is to be found in the works not only of Eastern Jews and Christians, but even in the modern languages of Europe. Of phrases like "tasting death," "to bring from darkness to light," "to pervert the straight way of God," "the trumpet shall be blown," "to roll up the heavens as a scroll is rolled up," "they have weights in their ears," "the new heavens and the new earth," "the first and second death," "that which eye hath not seen nor ear heard nor hath

* *Jahiz, Mahasin*, 186; *Musnad*, vi., 31.

† *Goldziher, M. S.*, i., 53., regards this as a *theological* aversion, the poets being the chief exponents of pagan ideas. *Surah* xxxvi., 69.

‡ *Musnad*, iv., 245; *Jahiz, Bayan*, i., 112.

§ *Preserved Smith* suggests that many of these phrases may have been merely Semitic.

entered into the heart of man," "a camel entering a needle's eye," "as far as the East is from the West, so far hath he removed our sins from us" *—a biblical scholar would have easily been able to tell the source: Mohammed probably heard them in the conversation of his pious friends and automatically adopted them. To the last he appears to have adhered to the habit of picking up information and then utilising it: he heard casually from his girl-wife Ayeshah that a Jewess had talked to her about the torment of the grave; after this he introduced a prayer to be delivered therefrom into his ordinary devotion. Having heard a Mary mentioned in the story of Moses and another in the story of Jesus, it did not occur to him to distinguish between them. Late in his career he casually heard from a visitor to Najran that they were separated by some thousands of years; he did not reject this information, but found a means of reconciling it with his former statement.† When at times some Jew or Christian testified publicly that Mohammed had correctly reproduced the information which he had picked up, it occasioned him the keenest pleasure.‡

Of the superstitions of the Arabs, which differ slightly, if at all, from those of other races, he would seem to have imbibed a fair share. To omens, especially those connected with names, he attached great importance. When a man was wanted to milk

* *Musnad*, vi., 57.

† *Muslim*, ii., 168. There is a controversy on this subject; see *Ed. Sayous*, *Jésus-Christ d'après Mahomet*, Paris, 1880, p. 36.

‡ *Muslim*, ii. 380.

a camel, he disqualified one applicant after another, till one offered whose name meant "long life."* Whenever the name of a new adherent contained anything ill-omened, it was his custom to alter it; if a convert was named Rough, he called him Smooth. At the most important crisis in his career, the preparation for the battle of Badr, and at other times,† he was guided in his strategy by the names of the places on the different routes. Just as Bedouin tribes were guided in their migrations by the instincts of their camels, so Mohammed, at times, left the determination of his policy to the conduct of the beast which he happened to be riding. He was a firm believer in the evil eye, and the possibility of averting it by means of charms; nor does he ever seem to have doubted the efficacy of incantations. As such he at one time recommended the Lord's Prayer—or as much as he knew of it‡; when portions of his Koran had become classical he approved of their being used for this purpose; and even claimed part of the fee when a serpent's bite was healed by the aid of one of the verses.§ Belief in the *Jinn*, mysterious beings who haunted the desert, was authorised by him, whether he shared it himself or not. From some superstitions he emancipated himself in time. It is recorded that when his followers wished to attribute

* *Isabah*, i., 655.

† *Wakidi* (*W.*), 266.

‡ *Musnad*, vi., 21. It was similarly used by Christians: *J. M Robertson*, *A Short History of Christianity*, 125.

§ *Musnad*, ii., 183.

an eclipse of the sun to the death of his son Ibrahim, he assured them that eclipses were not connected with the fortunes of any persons, however important. Still he continued to regard eclipses as events of a serious nature, for which a special form of prayer was desirable.

Experience as a caravan-boy taught him the art of scouting; the power of inferring from minute signs and indications much about the whereabouts, the numbers, and the equipments of the enemy, perhaps not more than many of the caravan-leaders knew, yet sufficient to stand him in good stead when he became a captain of banditti. At times secret ways of procuring information stood at his command, the nature of which we can scarcely divine. But nature, rather than experience, had endowed him with one gift more to be envied than any other: knowledge of mankind. His instinctive judgment of men and people was rarely, we might say never, wrong.

The personal appearance of the Prophet in middle life was recorded by many persons. According to the ordinary tradition he was "of middle height, bluish coloured, with hair that was neither straight nor curly: with a large head, large eyes, heavy eyelashes, a reddish tint in his eyes, thick-bearded, broad-shouldered, with thick hands and feet"*; another description adds "with a large mouth, with eyes horizontally long, and with little flesh on the heels"†; according to one account his hands were

* *Musnad*, i., 89; *Bokhari* (*K*.), ii., 392.

† *Muslim*, ii., 217.

abnormally soft, which the palmists tell us signifies "a natural tendency towards the miraculous." His style of dress seems to have varied at different times: his favourite costume being a striped dress of Yemen make,* though sometimes he wore a Syrian *jubbah* with narrow sleeves,† or a cloak (*mirt*) of twisted black hair,‡ or a red gown (*hullah*).§ On the day of the taking of Meccah he wore a black turban.‖

What is recorded of his tastes and habits exhibits ordinarily a high degree of refinement and delicacy. He abhorred anything that produced an evil odour: garlic and onions were described by him as evil vegetables,¶ and his loathing of anything that tainted the breath was used as a lever by members of his harem. When sovereign he found fault with those whose hair was untidy, or whose clothes were dirty,** being himself particular as to his appearance. He disliked yellow teeth,†† and almost made the use of the toothpick a religious ordinance.

We know, from the Koran,‡‡ that Mohammed was a young man of promise, and, indeed, should expect that the astounding talents which he afterwards displayed would give evidence of themselves in youth.

---

* *Hibrah. Muslim*, ii., 154.

† *Musnad*, i., 29.

‡ *Ibid.*, vi., 162.

§ *Bokhari* (*K.*), ii., 392.

‖ *Musnad*, iii., 363.

¶ *Ibid.*, iv., 19.

** *Ibid.*, iii., 356.

†† *Ibid.*, iii., 442.

‡‡ *Surah* xi., 65.

And of his ambition we have evidence in the comfort which his notoriety afforded him at a time when few things were going well with his project: "Have we not expanded thy breast and exalted thy name?" is the form which the divine consolation takes, when the Prophet is in trouble. Expansion of the breast, the organisation of life about a new centre, as Professor Starbuck expresses it, and celebrity, were then things for which he yearned; but his early promise led to none of those fiascos in which the efforts of persons who are anxious to distinguish themselves are apt to result.

And how could Mohammed distinguish himself? Like Beckwourth, doubtless, who, in every fight, killed the rival chieftain, or at every assault was the first to scale the wall; so the battles of Fijar (and others perhaps of which there is no record) gave Mohammed the chance of proving himself the first man of the Kuraish. At these battles his future antagonists, Abu Sufyan and his brother, had won the title "The Lions." * Men, too, who played a rôle similar to that of David were not wanting in Arabia. The poet-king Imru'ulkais, being driven from home by his father, had collected a number of outcasts round him with whom he raided his neighbours. The sequel shows that Mohammed was not born for that sort of distinction. Care for his life and safety was invariably his first consideration; in the presence of danger, indeed, he kept his head, and even fought, if necessary, bravely. But he lacked the courage of the man who, when a champion is called for, hurries

* *Ibn Duraid*, 103.

to be first. The four Fijar battles therefore brought him no laurels.

The lads who were prepared to pass their lives in camel-driving, or similar occupations, doubtless took to themselves wives at seventeen or eighteen, and so settled into a slough of poverty, whence they could not, save by marvellous luck, emerge. Mohammed, though not without his share of that passion of which the Talmud rightly says nine parts have been given to the Arabs, and only one to the rest of the world, waited to marry till he could better himself thereby. He had indeed made an offer for the hand of his cousin, Umm Hani, Abu Talib's daughter, a girl of whom he doubtless saw much in his childhood and youth. For the character of the relations between the sexes at this time an analogy should be drawn rather from Bedouin life than from the town life introduced by the founder of Islam; and in the Bedouin life these marriages between cousins, which are normal, are often preceded and determined by attachment.* Mohammed's proposal was rejected by his uncle, who preferred another and probably richer cousin. This early rebuff may have had something to do with the future career of the Prophet, on whom the ills of poverty had thus been painfully impressed. Long after, Umm Hani, relieved of her husband, desired Mohammed to renew the offer, but he refused. When he was twenty-five years of age, Khadijah, the wealthy woman whose

* *Mayeux*, iii., 143. The well-informed novelist in the Egyptian magazine *Ra'is*, ii., 93, makes it a rule of the Bedouins that love must not precede marriage.

caravan he had safely conducted, offered him her hand. Arab ladies have to this day no *gêne* in such matters, and in pagan times women were doubtless freer than after Islam had introduced the veil; some of the privileges dating from the old days of matriarchate remaining.* She was some years older than Mohammed, but assuredly not forty, as Mohammed's biographers assert; though the legend makes some of the Bedouin ladies keep their good looks till eighty or even one hundred,† and the Kurashite women were regarded as an exception to the law which renders childbearing impossible after sixty.‡ Her nephew Hakim, son of Hizam, was one of the Meccan magnates. At a later period he figures as a trader, and, indeed, a speculator in corn.§ He professed to have liberated forty slaves in Pagan times.‖ If it be true that he gave four hundred dirhems¶ for the slave Zaid, son of Harithah, and then presented him to his aunt, he must, indeed, have had means—accumulated, it is said, by rigid economy.** Khadijah's cousin Warakah is said to have blessed the union in the homely language of the Bedouins, calling Mohammed a camel "whose nose would not be

* *Robertson Smith*, in his *Kinship and Marriage*, has an excursus on Khadijah's marriage, but brings no fresh light.

† *Jahiz, Mahasin*, 205.

‡ *Id., Opuscula*, 78, 5.

§ *Musnad*, iii., 403.

‖ *Ibid.*, iii., 434.

¶ *Ibn Sa'd*, iii., 27.

** *Baihaki, Mahasin*, 315. He was one of those who ran away from Badr. *Ibn Duraid*, 103.

struck."* The future Prophet left his uncle's camels to become master of a house—or part of one, for Khadijah lived in the house of her above-mentioned nephew, in the Hizamiyah street, with a covered walk and a garden, where there was a door leading to the house of 'Awwam, who had married an aunt of the Prophet. †

That great step in a career had been taken whereby a man, freed from the absorbing care of his daily bread, like a balloon loosed from its moorings, begins to ascend. Henceforth he either led no camels, or led his own. But indeed he appears to have been set up in business in Meccah, having for his partner Kais, son of Al-Sa'ib, whose fidelity he afterwards commended highly. The tradition appears not to know with what goods he supplied his fellow-citizens, though it has preserved this detail in the case of his immediate associates. In the one shopping scene of which we have a record for this period the Prophet is buyer, not seller. Suwaid, son of Kais, said: "Makhramah, the Abdite, and I brought a bale of clothes from Haji to Meccah; the Prophet bargained with us for a pair of breeches; there were in the shop some persons who were weighing with pieces of clay, and the Prophet told them to give us good measure." ‡ Since breeches could scarcely be sold by weight, perhaps the Prophet gave them some grain or fruit in return. Mohammed and

---

* *Mubarrad, Kamil*, i., 93. Another tradition ascribes the words to Abu Sufyan, when Mohammed married his daughter. *Letters of Hamadhani*, p. 216.

† *Azraki*, 463.

‡ *Musnad*, iv., 352.

his partner offered their goods for sale in the dwelling of the latter,* and the traces of this calling are found all over his Sacred Book. A dissertation has been written on the commercial language of the Koran, showing that the tradesman Prophet could not keep free of metaphors taken from his business. "God," he repeatedly says, " is good at accounts. The Believers are doing a good business, the unbelievers a losing trade. Those who buy error for guidance make a bad bargain." The shake of the hand which closes a bargain became with him and his followers the form by which homage was done to a sovereign. Even when he was sovereign at Medinah he did not disdain to buy goods wholesale and make a profit by selling them retail †; while occasionally he consented to act as auctioneer.‡

Children were born to the couple, four daughters and one son or more; whence Mohammed could call himself honourably Abu'l-Kasim, father of Kasim, after the style of the Arabs; whether they held like the Indians that a sonless man goes straight to hell, or whether without a son a man had no full franchise. But the son or sons died in infancy,§ and the girls were weaklings, of whom the most long-lived did not see her fortieth year; whence some who understand medicine have drawn their inferences about their father. The names of some of the children show that their

* *Azraki*, 471.

† *Musnad*, i., 255.

‡ *Ibid.*, iii., 111. Hence he is supposed to have invented auctions. *Baihaki*, *Mahasin*, 393, 3.

§ One of these was born in Islam, according to our authorities, after his mother was fifty-two. *Ibn Sa'd*, iii., 2.

parents when they named them were idolators. Nor is there anything to indicate that Mohammed was at this time of a monotheistic or religious turn of mind. He with Khadijah performed some domestic rite in honour of one of the goddesses each night before retiring.* At the wedding of his cousin, Abu Lahab's daughter, he is represented as clamouring for sport †; and indeed even when Prophet he had a taste for the performances of singing girls.‡ He confessed to having at one time sacrificed a grey sheep to Al-'Uzza §—and probably did so more than once, since after his mission he used to slaughter sheep for sacrifice with his own hands.‖ A story which may be true shows us Mohammed with his stepson inviting the Meccan monotheist Zaid, son of 'Amr, to eat with them—of meat offered to idols: the old man refused; thereby inspiring Mohammed with a dislike for such food.¶

Of Khadijah's children—and Mohammed appears to have had both stepsons and stepdaughters—not much is recorded. Mohammed was at all times of an affectionate disposition, and even demonstratively so; he expressed disgust at a man who having ten children declared that he had never kissed one of them **: and he remained demonstratively affectionate to the end towards the slave Zaid, whom he

* *Musnad*, iv., 222.
† *Ibid.*, iv., 67.
‡ *Ibid.*, iii., 391.
§ *Wellhausen*, *Reste*, 34.
‖ *Musnad*, iii., 99.
¶ *Ibid.*, i., 189.
** *Tirmidhi*, 321 (i., 348).

adopted as a son. In his prayers he would at times hold a child in his arms when he stood up, putting it down when he prostrated himself.* At Medinah † he would let a little girl take his hand and lead him where she chose. Affectionate treatment of step-children is attested for a later period of his life.‡ He is not likely to have failed in his duty towards Khadijah's children: and indeed one of these is said to have lost his life in endeavouring to save Mohammed from the fury of the populace when he first preached the unity of God. Of another a story is told in which he offers friendly counsel to his step-father.

As Mohammed's daughters grew up, they were given in marriage: Umm Kulthum to her cousin on the father's side, son of Abu Lahab, presently Mohammed's bitter enemy; Zainab to her cousin on the mother's side, Abu'l-'Asi. All this was normal and in order. Abu'l-'Asi was a brave man and true,§ accustomed to spend his evenings in Mohammed's house.‖ This marriage was one of affection, which Islam could not change. Zainab in after times repeatedly made use of her privileges as the Prophet's daughter to save the life of her unbelieving husband; and his faithfulness to her won him warm encomiums from her father.

For the rest we imagine Mohammed during these

---

* *Nasa'i*, i., 132.

† *Musnad*, iii., 174.

‡ *Ibid.*, vi., 101.

§ *Ibid.*, iv., 326.

‖ *Isabah*, iv., 223.

fifteen years to have been a respected and undistinguished tradesman. The little that we glean of his sayings during the period is commonplace. One 'Arfajah, son of Al-As'ad, had lost his nose in a pre-Islamic battle, and had one of silver fitted to his face; as this became foul, Mohammed recommended him to try one of gold.*

In the case of many of the Heroes of the Nations it is possible to point to the occasion which first led them to play their heroic part; a crisis called and they responded. In Mohammed's case it is impossible to indicate any such event. For many years he was, as we have seen, a respectable citizen, an undistinguished tradesman; at the age of forty we find him the nucleus of a secret society, aiming at reconstruction of the entire social fabric. At the age of forty, it is asserted, a Meccan citizen had access to the Council Chamber; and there may be some truth in this statement, though only a vague interpretation can be given it, since there were no registers at Meccah, and when the Prophet died, it was uncertain whether he was sixty-three or sixty-five. Supposing him to have been harbouring his scheme of reform for years, he may have waited first till he could gauge the possibilities of the Council Chamber for launching it. If the Council Chamber resembled any other debating body, the Prophet would have had little chance of succeeding there; for he was not a ready debater, and when he became a religious controversialist, he received divine orders to avoid public disputation. Still it was in Mo-

* *Musnad*, v., 23, etc.

hammed's character to try easy and normal methods before he attempted abnormal and difficult ones, and there may be some connection between the facts of the fortieth year being the time for the acquisition of the franchise and the period of Mohammed's life at which his mission commenced. And since it was his custom only to launch his schemes when they were mature, the part which he was to play may have been present to his mind for many years, suggested by conversations with Jews, Christians, and Parsees; shown to him to be imperatively called for by the difficulties and injustices which arose from the need of it.

The Jews, the Christians, the Magians, the Sabæans, had all one thing which the Arabs had not: a legislator, who had acted as divine commissioner. None of the members of these sects hesitated a moment when asked what code he followed, or from whom it emanated. Moses, Jesus, Zoroaster, St. John the Baptist, they would severally and immediately reply. But whom did the worshippers of Hubal, Al-Lāt, and Al-'Uzza follow? No one at all. Foreigners indeed told them that they had Abraham for their father, but only foreigners knew anything about him; to the Meccans he was not even a name. Those who tried to discover either an Abrahamic community or an Abrahamic code traversed the world in vain. Yet each nation ought to have a leader.* Here then was an opportunity for a Prophet.

In what form the conviction comes to a man of

* *Surah* xiii., 8.

the existence of a need which he can or should supply is rarely recorded, perhaps not often remembered. Of the evils of the tribal system and the blood-feud Mohammed had ample experience; and visits to countries where the whole population was subject to the law of God may well have convinced him that the Arabs were backward, and that the revelation of a divine code was an indispensable preliminary of progress. Such a code was associated with the God of the Jews and the Christians, but not with the Meccan Allah, Al-Lāt, and Al-'Uzza, though it is likely that these deities approved and disapproved of various acts. But the name of the God of the Jews and Christians was identical with that of the god of the Kuraish. The inference that there was room for a messenger of Allah lay in the premises which the phenomena provided; Mohammed's greatness is to be found in the two facts of his drawing the inference, and of his ability to render that knowledge effective.

The execution of this resolve closes this period of forty years or more; his soaring spirit had found the outlet upwards through which it proceeded to make its way. It is more often the seeker who finds than one who is not searching. When Starbuck wished to collect cases of conversion, he had to go to sects in which it was normal, and where men and women might expect to be converted. And the conversions which he studied were found by him to resemble cases in which persons feel after an idea with unrest and perplexity until the result is finally presented to clear consciousness ready made.

"The unaccomplished volition is doubtless an indication that new nerve-connections are budding, that a new channel of mental activity is being opened, and in time the act of centring force (trying) in the given direction may through increased circulation and heightened nutrition of that point itself directly contribute to the formation of those nerve-connections through which the high potential energy which corresponds to the new insight expends itself."

Into this psychological explanation we cannot in the present case follow him; but the evidence which he has produced of conversion meaning the starting of a fresh career, the bringing of the converted individual into fresh connection with his fellows, is very much to the purpose. To the enlarging of the breast and the exalting of the name the Koran adds the forgiveness of sin. Normal cases of conversion bring out only the last sensation, the forgiveness of sin; the enlarging of the breast and exalting of the name are found in cases where the converted person has abnormal talents.

The idea of reproducing the rôle of Moses, Jesus, or Zoroaster must not be judged from the modern standpoint, whence those characters are either wholly unhistorical, or owe that which is enviable in their history to myth and legend. To Mohammed the first two (of the third he may not have heard) were men, highly favoured by God, it is true, but still flesh and blood, "eating food."

To carry out in practice the part of a mythical hero was, as he afterwards found, exceedingly difficult; but that his predecessors were mythical never entered into his mind. The idea that a Prophet was expected in Arabia, that either Jews or Christians foretold the arrival of one, may be dismissed as a *vaticinium post eventum;* so, too, when Islam had conquered Persia, it was discovered that portents occurred in Persia when Mohammed was born. The Meccans, as we see them in the Fijar wars, or at the building of their Ka'bah, appear by no means desolate at the want of a Prophet. They enjoyed their life exceedingly; even when the battle of Badr was looming, they went to the fight in high spirits, spending lavishly; wine and music were at their feasts. And the best proof that they enjoyed life is to be found in the good nature with which they fought. They gladly displayed their courage, but bore no ill-will against the foe.

That Mohammed in the course of his conversations with Jews and Christians had become convinced of the general truth of their systems is fairly clear; or rather it had not occurred to him to doubt it. He shared the general attitude of the people of Meccah towards their learned neighbours. But these conversations had further forced upon his attention the divisions that existed, not only between Jews and Christians—who each denied that the other had any standing ground—but also between the Christian sects, which anathematised each other. It is curious that the founder of the Mormons similarly received an early impulse from his observation of the differences between the rival sects.* Which were in the right, Jews or Christians, and if the latter, which

* *The Mormons*, London, 1851.

of the sects? Clearly a new Prophet was needed to settle this point, and Mohammed, at Medinah, claimed that it was his mission to put them right where they disagreed. The notions, however, which he acquired of both Jewish and Christian doctrine were, as has been seen, those of a superficial, though shrewd, observer. If he thought the Christians worshipped a goddess and two gods, that was the practical as opposed to the theoretical character of all but Nestorian Christianity in the East.* Nor could he fail to observe that the Christians were more lax in the matter of food than the Jews. With each community he sympathised in one point or another; to have joined either of the communities and to have become a missionary for either would have been a serious mistake, and utterly unsuited to Mohammed's plans. Christianity could not be dissociated from subjection to the suzerainty of Byzantium; and Mohammed was far too great a patriot to contemplate the introduction of a foreign yoke. A convert to an old established religion, he could not have pretended to such knowledge of it as older members possessed; and even appointed head of a new congregation, he would have been compelled to affiliate it to some existing branch. It is certain that a fundamental dogma of his system was the personal one that he was God's Prophet; agreement on other points presently became useless, if that were not conceded.

Hence it would appear that Mohammed regarded these systems chiefly as systems founded respectively

* *J. M. Robertson, A Short History of Christianity*, 1902, p. 184.

by Moses and Jesus—a point of view from which they are not ordinarily regarded, since men think rather in each case of the code than of the authority for it. Whoso honours not himself shall not be honoured, Zuhair sings: the ambitious Christian or Jew hopes to be a bishop, perhaps, or a rabbi, but regards the founders of the systems as beyond all possibility of competition. But thoughts are not impracticable because they are bold, and this Arab conceived the idea which a proselyte's notion of Judaism or Christianity would have rendered beyond his reach. To the proselyte both figures would have seemed simply inaccessible, placed on pinnacles beyond climbing. To the cool-headed student of human nature they were men, and what they had done he could do.

It is likely, we might say certain, that Mohammed's notion of a Prophet underwent some growth in the course of his career; we can even trace the steps by which the mission was extended from Meccah to the world; and before Mohammed reached Medinah he may not have been quite familiar with the Hebrew word for prophet. But there were certain notions connected with the office which were in his mind from first to last. A messenger of God was quite certain to be successful. The messengers, he was to learn, were harassed by opposition and unbelief, but they succeeded in time. The notion that Jesus was crucified was repugnant to his system, he was convinced that the truth was with the Julianists who held that the traitor Judas had been crucified: the true Prophet was naturally and certainly victorious. Of the whole

THE BLACK STONE.
From *Ali Bey's Travels.*

number, from Abraham to Mohammed, this held good.

Belief therefore in himself was the dogma which he taught himself first, and afterwards taught others. Of strong convictions on other subjects we cannot be so sure; and in any case, of the charge of fanaticism, brought against him by several writers, he can easily be cleared. Reasons of policy and reasons of humanity were sufficient to make him modify or at times even abandon each one of the doctrines and practices on which he set the greatest store. To these voices the ears of fanatics are closed, but his were invariably open. Of exaggeration, whether in religious exercises or in liberality, he always had a horror: beneath the mask of the enthusiast there was the soundest and sanest common-sense. Though he railed against idolatry, he clearly had not that physical repugnance to it which men have often had: otherwise the Kissing of the Black Stone would not have been a ceremony for which he yearned when deprived of it, and which he permanently retained. His physical repugnance seems to have been not to fetishes but to representations, which, according to some anecdotes that are recorded, he found worrying and distracting. His identification of the god Allah with the God of the Jews and Christians was in a manner accidental; it is precisely parallel to St. Paul's endeavour to make the "Unknown God" paramount at Athens to the exclusion of all the other deities. But the Jewish and Christian records narrated how their Allah had despatched messengers, and such a messenger he might be. The message was in many cases subordinate to the dignity of the office, just as we think of a king's ambassador as a high official, rather than as the bearer of a definite message. For the contents of the message he had to go back to Jewish and Christian Scriptures, until the course of events provided him with plenty to say.

Why and how the idea of playing that part should have come into the mind of this particular Arab, or in the case of this particular Arab have found a man with the patience and resolution and ingenuity to make it a success—about that we cannot even hazard a conjecture. As Carlyle says, from the time of Tubal Cain there had been iron and boiling water; but through all these millennia no one invented the steam-engine. Either men wanted the ingenuity to see the possibilities of things, or they wanted the patience to make their discoveries fruitful. The daughter of Abu Jahl, one of Mohammed's chief opponents, declared that her father might have been Prophet had he chosen, but was unwilling to create sedition.* Prophets indeed had arisen in Arabia before Mohammed: in Yemen among the Himyarites one Samaifa had imitated the exploit of old Zamolxis: had hidden himself for a time and then re-appeared, when one hundred thousand men prostrated themselves before their risen lord.† Legends containing probably some germ of truth recorded how shortly before Mohammed one Khalid, son of Sinan, had been sent to preach to the

Azraki, 192; *Wakidi* (*W.*), 343.

†*Isabah*, i., 1003.

tribe of 'Abs, and one Hanzalah, son of Safwan, to some other of the inhabitants of Arabia. In Yemamah, too, one Maslamah had given a sign that he was sent from God: through the narrow neck of a bottle he introduced an egg unbroken to the bowl.* Since Yemamah supplied Meccah with corn, the tradition that makes Mohammed a pupil of Maslamah has certainly some foundation. But Mohammed had far more to teach Maslamah than to learn from him. Maslamah's aspirations scarcely rose above those of a conjurer; his pupil, far less able to mystify, saw how a Prophet could become the head of a state.

When the plan had become an assured success, others were inclined to try it for their own benefit. To Mohammed their claims did not seem to merit a moment's consideration, he treated them as the people of Meccah had at first treated him. The wish that all the Lord's people were prophets, probably never felt by any who uttered it, was not even expressed by him. If men failed to agree with his second dogma, his own apostleship, he devised ingenious reasons for showing that they disagreed with him concerning the first dogma, the Unity of God. Hence we are justified in supposing that the second was the dogma to which he attached the greater importance. And if a Prophet was not a subject charged with painful duties, but a sovereign privileged with extraordinary rights, the unity of

* That Maslamah had taken the title Rahman before Mohammed left Meccah is attested by *Wakidi* (*W.*), 58; see also *J. R. A. S.*, 1903.

God's Prophet was no less certain than the unity of God. The sayings that are recorded of the Prophet show that he never compromised that high dignity by any of the humility, genuine or affected, which meets us in the speeches of those who preached a doctrine without political ambitions. In dicta which are ascribed to him he declared himself to be the best in character and the most perfect in beauty among mankind. His was the most noble pedigree,* consisting entirely of well-born men and chaste women. He was the most eloquent of all who had pronounced the characteristic Arabic letter *dād*. In the Koran he repeatedly points out what a privilege his presence is, and how he is a proof or embodiment of God's mercy to the world. If ever he spoke of himself in a less exalted strain, it was when some reverse, the blame for which he refused to accept, compelled him to tell his followers that they had expected too much. Hence we are driven to the assumption that however many motives may have led to the adoption of the rôle of Prophet, the desire for personal distinction, which the Koran puts into the mouth of Noah's adversaries,† —or let us rather say for a place in the community whence he could enforce his ideas on the rest,—was one of them; and we shall more easily be able to appreciate and admire the skill with which he piloted his way, if we keep clearly in our minds the destination for which he was steering.

**Musnad*, iv., 107, 166.

† *Surah* xxiii., 24.

CHAPTER III

ISLAM AS A SECRET SOCIETY

IN his thirty-ninth year Mohammed became acquainted or became intimate with Abu Bakr, son of Abu Kuhafah, a cloth merchant, Mohammed's junior by two years. He possessed some business ability, whereby he had acquired a considerable fortune, and, his father being blind, was the head of the household. He was a man of a kindly and complaisant disposition, of charming manners and ready wit, though of an occasionally obscene tongue, and his company was much sought after. Since the Meccan tribes, like other Arabs, habitually gathered in circles at evening time, and some ladies * held salons in the courts of their houses, there was at Meccah every opportunity of conversing. Abu Bakr was a hero worshipper, if ever there was one; he possessed a quality common in women, but sometimes present in men, *i.e.*, readiness to follow the fortunes of some one else with complete and blind devotion, never questioning nor looking back; to have believed much was with him a reason for

* *Azraki*, 467.

believing more. Mohammed, a shrewd judge of men, perceived this quality and used it.

A year after their intimacy had begun, Mohammed's call came, and the proselytising was then done not by Mohammed, but by Abu Bakr. Whether Mohammed had sounded any one before, to find out the possibility of winning disciples, is not known; what is certain is that in this person Mohammed discovered a man capable of believing that one of his fellow-citizens had a message from God, which it was incumbent on him to receive and promote. It is so much easier to invite men to recognise the claims of another than of oneself that in the later history of Islam we find those Mahdis most successful who could keep hidden while some follower proclaimed their advent. But these were ordinarily cases of collusion, where each party anticipated some definite advantage from such an arrangement: in Abu Bakr's case the notion of acknowledged collusion cannot be admitted. Mohammed used to assert that if he were to make any man his confidant (*khalil*) he would make Abu Bakr, but that he had not made a confidant of any one. Abu Bakr, though an invaluable assistant, was not an accomplice. He never forgot the distance between his master and himself.

When a man professes to produce messages from another world, he has to make both their form and their manner correspond in some way with supernatural origin. The problem before the medium is to produce a message without appearing to furnish it himself; and Mohammed had to solve that problem no less than a modern medium. When revelations came to him in public he seems instinctively * (or, perhaps, after the example of the Kahins) to have adopted a process common to the prophets of all ages ; just as to the Sibyl :

> "talia fanti
> Ante fores subito non voltus, non color unus,
> Non comptæ mansere comæ; sed pectus anhelum,
> Et rabie fera corda tument: majorque videri
> Nec mortale sonans, adflata est numine quando
> Jam propiore dei,"

so Mohammed would fall into a violent state of agitation, his face would turn livid, † and he would cover himself with a blanket, from which he would afterwards emerge perspiring copiously, ‡ with a message ready. At some period or other the articulate message seems to have been preceded by an inarticulate one, letters of the alphabet forming no words—curiously resembling the initial movements of a planchette. § We have already seen reason for believing that Mohammed at some time had epileptic fits; whence the phenomena accompanying such a fit may

---

* One of the chief authorities for traditions of the Prophet used at times to introduce his recollections of the Prophet's utterances with a similar performance. *Tabari*, *Comm.*, xii., 9.

† *Tabari*, *Comm.*, xxviii., 4.

‡ *Bouveret*, *Les sueurs Morbides* (Paris, 1880), says : "Adamkiewicz has shown that perspiration can be provoked by artificial or voluntary incitation of the muscles and their nerves."

§ *Nöldeke's* ingenious explanation of the mystic letters as signatures of MSS. is abandoned by him in his *Sketches* for a theory resembling the above.

have suggested a form which could afterwards be artificially reproduced. The process described, at times accompanied by snoring and reddening of the face,* presently came to be recognised as the normal form of inspiration, and could be produced without the slightest preparation; the Prophet would receive a divine communication in immediate answer to a question addressed him while he was eating; and would, after delivering it in this fashion, proceed to finish the morsel which he held in his hand when he was interrupted †; or a revelation would come in answer to a question addressed him as he stood in the pulpit. ‡ In revelations which appear to be very early Mohammed is addressed as "the man in the blanket," or "the man who is wrapped up." Whatever may have been the occasion for this process, the Prophet appears to have retained it from first to last.

The other questions which the medium must solve concern the matter of the revelation. Once the head of a state Mohammed had plenty to say; but at the commencement of his career, the matter was not provided by the circumstances. Mediums who are similarly placed as a rule hit on the same plan. They put into God's mouth sayings which are generally acknowledged to be His—*i. e.*, verses of the Old or New Testament. These being recognised as God's Word, no one is compromised by their iteration. When Mohammed, forced by circum-

---

* *Musnad*, iv., 222. *Bouveret*, p. 47: "*La peau peut rougir simultanément*," when perspiration is the result of a violent emotion.

† *Musnad*, vi., 56.

‡ *Ibid.*, iii., 21.

stances to produce revelations in increasing quantities, followed this safe method, he could declare that it was a miracle by which he was made acquainted with the contents of books which he had never read. When his style as a preacher had justly won him the applause of large audiences, he could change his ground somewhat and declare that the miracle lay in his unrivalled eloquence.

This however is to anticipate. The earliest scraps of revelation, which were communicated to Abu Bakr, appear to have been imitations of the utterances of revivalist preachers, whom Mohammed had heard on his travels. There is (as we have seen) a tradition that he had heard sermons from "the most eloquent of the Arabs," Kuss, son of Sa'idah, who bade men remember the transitoriness of life, and infer the existence of the Creator from the phenomena of the world. The subjects on which these preachers dwelt were doubtless the Day of Judgment, the pains of hell fire, and the necessity of worshipping Allah rather than the idols; these being the ordinary themes of Christian revivalists. Experience, moreover, shows that warnings of the approaching end of the world readily find a hearing.* Those who describe the first discourses of the Prophet speak of them as warning the Meccans of the divine punishment: the speaker comparing himself to one who gives the alarm when the enemy is raiding.† As we shall presently see, this doctrine is not really to be dissociated from that of resurrec-

* *History of the Mormons*, London, 1851.

† "I am the naked alarm-giver," *Alif-Bā*, i., 133.

tion; and the distinctive features of Mohammed's teaching, as opposed to the ideas of paganism, were from first to last the doctrine of a future life, and of the unity of God. Arabian oratory seems to have been in some sort of rhyme, and this Mohammed imitated though he little understood its nature.

Against the supposition that Mohammed deliberately mystified his contemporaries, objection has been taken both in ancient and modern times from the uprightness of his character, which is even said to have earned him the name of "the Trusty." Hence the story that he trained a pigeon to peck grains from his ear has called forth bitter indignation from Carlyle and others. And indeed the Moslem tradition does not record any occasions on which he received revelations from pigeons. Still, many scenes are recorded in which he appears to have studied theatrical effect of a scarcely less naïve kind. In an empty room he professed to be unable to find sitting-place,—all the seats being occupied by angels. He turned his face away modestly from a corpse, out of regard for two Houris who had come from heaven to tend their husband. There is even reason for supposing that he, at times, let confederates act the part of Gabriel, or let his followers identify some interlocutor of his with that angel.* The revelations which he produced find a close parallel in those of modern mediums, which can be studied in the history of Spiritualism by Mr. F. Podmore, whose researches cast great doubt on the proposition

* *Ibn Sa'd II.*, ii., 52. One Harithah Ibn Al-Nu'man declared he had seen Gabriel twice.

that an honourable man would not mystify his fellows; and also make it appear that the conviction produced by the performances of a medium is often not shaken by the clearest exposure. Of one of the mediums whose career he describes, this author observes that he possessed the friendship and perfect trust of his sitters, was aided by the religious emotions inspired by his trance utterances, and could appeal to an unstained character and a life of honourable activity. The possession of these advantages greatly helped this medium in producing belief in his sincerity; but the historian of Spiritualism, though uncertain how to account for all the phenomena, and acknowledging the difficulties which attend his explanation, is inclined to attribute all that is wonderful in the medium's performances to trickery. What is clear is that Mohammed possessed the same advantages as Podmore enumerates, and thereby won adherents; that nevertheless the process of revelation was so suspicious that one of the scribes employed to take down the effusions became convinced that it was imposture and discarded Islam in consequence.* But to those who are studying merely the political effectiveness of supernatural revelations the sincerity of the medium is a question of little consequence.

We regard then Mohammed's assumption of the rôle of medium as due to the receptivity of Abu Bakr.† It was in the Prophet's character to bide

---

* *Musnad*, iii., 121, etc.

† *Nöldeke, Z. D. M. G.*, lii., 16–21, makes the order of converts Khadijah, Zaid, Ali, some slaves, Sa'd, son of Abu Wakkas, and Abu Bakr, with other Kurashites.

his time—to wait, before taking any step, till the favourable moment had arrived. But such a new rôle cannot be taken up quite suddenly—there must be some period of transition between the old life and the new. Most mediums have for such transition a period of solitude. Thus Joseph Smith, founder of the Mormon sect, wandered into a wood, and there, under the guidance of angels, unearthed the Book of Mormon. The Seer of Poughkeepsie, in March, 1844, "wandered into the country under the guidance of his inward monitor, and fell into a spontaneous trance, during which Galen and Swedenborg appeared to him in a churchyard, and instructed him concerning his message to mankind." His work, *The Principles of Nature*, afterwards delivered by him in trance, if not quite so successful as the Koran, nevertheless went through thirty-four editions in thirty years, and is still * quoted by some as a divine revelation. Now that Mohammed's prophetic career began with a period of solitude seems attested, though there is some inconsistency between our authorities as to the details. For one month of the year—and it would appear the month of Ramadan, afterwards stereotyped as the Fasting Month of Islam—the Meccans practised a rite called *tahannuth*, of which the exact meaning is indeed unknown, but which apparently was some sort of asceticism. During this month it was Mohammed's custom to retire to a cave in Mt. Hira, some three miles from Meccah in the direction of Ta'if. He would appear to have taken his family with him:

* *Contemporary Rev.*, Oct., 1903.

yet probably their daily worship of Al-Lāt or Al-'Uzza * would not be carried on at such a time. Moreover, a month devoted to ascetic observance was one specially suited for aspirations towards a more spiritual form of religion than the ordinary paganism. At some time then in this month, when he had descended by himself to the midst of the valley, occurred the theophany (or its equivalent) which led to Mohammed's starting as a divine messenger.

The idea of Joseph Smith was to communicate to the world the contents of certain hidden tablets only accessible to himself, and in a language which he only could translate "by the grace of God." Mohammed's was very similar; he was empowered (or, according to one account, forced) to read matter contained in a well-guarded tablet—he having previously been unable to read or write. To the miracle whereby he was enabled to read without having learned—which may have been suggested by narratives current about other prophets—he alludes,† but he does not insist on it. His idea of being permitted only occasionally to get access to the guarded tablet was a better one than Smith's, because it enabled him to legislate as occasion demanded. In the traditions which bear on this subject the communication is done by Gabriel, the angel who in the New Testament conveys messages; but in the theophany recorded in the Koran, it appears to be God Himself who descended, and at a

* *Musnad*, iv., 222.

† *Surah* xxix., 47.

distance of rather less than two bowshots * addressed the Prophet, and on a second occasion was seen by him "at the lotus of the extreme end, where is the garden of lodging." The substitution afterwards of Gabriel is probably due to the development of the Prophet's theology.

More than a shadowy outline of this commencement of revelation will never be known. The earliest account makes the Prophet so much alarmed by his experience, and so afraid of becoming a *Kahin* or a poet, that he all but commits suicide; Khadijah, finding him, comforts him with the assurance that he is going to be the national *nabī* (Prophet)—a word which she can scarcely have known; and consults her learned relative Warakah, son of Naufal, who is equally encouraging. His words are given as, "Kaddosh, Kaddosh, this is the Greater Nomos." The first two words are Hebrew, and mean "Holy, Holy!" The last is Greek for "Law." The curious and hybrid nature of the expressions makes it possible that there may be some truth in this story; but that the exclamation did not suit the occasion on which it is supposed to have been uttered is implied by the commentators, who make the "Law" mean King's messenger, and apply it to Gabriel. Another account made Khadijah consult not Warakah, but a Christian slave, who recognised the name Gabriel. Warakah figures no further in the narrative,† and it would be rash to assert that the interview between

* The original is obscure.

† In *Usd al-ghabah*, i., 207, he is said to have witnessed the torture of one of Mohammed's followers.

him and Khadijah was historical; it was known that a relative of Khadijah was enlightened, and the legend could scarcely do less than make him acknowledge her husband's mission. Nor do we assign any historical value to the tradition that Mohammed dreamed he saw Warakah after his death in white raiment, signifying a place in Paradise.* But that Khadijah may have been prepared by her cousin's speculations and studies for a revolt from the Meccan religion is not improbable. In Khadijah's case moreover we might expect *a priori* that maternal grief over her dead sons would enter into the process of conversion, and this is confirmed by a story told in the memoirs of Ali.† If idolators went to hell, she asked her husband, were her parents in hell? Mohammed replied that they were, and, seeing that she looked pained, assured her that if she could see them with their true nature revealed, she would detest them too. Next she asked were their dead children in hell also? To this question the Prophet in reply produced a revelation: "And whoso believe and are followed by their seed in faith, unto them shall we attach their seed.‡ A brilliant answer; since thereby the bereaved mother was assured that the eternal happiness of her dead sons was made conditional on her believing; the chance being thus given her not only of recovering them, but of giving them access to the Garden of Delight. No wonder that Khadijah devoted herself

---

* *Musnad*, vi., 68.

† *Ibid.*, i., 135.

‡ *Surah* lii., 21.

heart and soul to the mission, and received a promise of a very special place in Paradise.*

It is clear that some of the ordinances of Islam must have commenced from the moment that the revelations were communicated to Abu Bakr and Khadijah. For it is by no means sufficient to warn people of the terrors of the Day of Judgment; some answer must be given to the question, What shall I do to be saved? And that answer, in order that it may satisfy, must involve certain injunctions. There appear to have been commands to wash the clothes, and to avoid the idols. The first of these was an easy symbolical act—with many races the clothes are all but identical with the wearer.† The second was difficult in a community where people saw much of each other; from stories which shall be mentioned we gather that worship of idols was a familiar feature of every-day life. Abandonment of idolatry could not easily be concealed from the household; hence the secret of the Prophet's mission had to be revealed almost at the first to the two lads who were about Khadijah's house, Zaid, son of Harithah, the adopted son, and Ali, the Prophet's cousin, son of Abu Talib, for whom Mohammed had undertaken to provide, owing to his uncle finding difficulty in maintaining his numerous family.‡ The latter was about ten years of age; the former was ten years the Prophet's junior §—according to

* *Musnad*, iv., 356.

† *Wellhausen*, *Reste*, 196.

‡ *Nöldeke*, *Z. D. M. G.*, lii., 19, regards this as a fiction.

§ *Ibn Sa'd*, iii., 30.

the most likely account—but, as we shall have occasion to see, entirely subject to the Prophet's authority.

It is stated that the revelations ceased for a time after they had begun—a phenomenon which may be compared with the fact made out by Starbuck in the cases of conversion which he studied: complete relapses, he shows, are few, but periods of inactivity and indifference numerous. Khadijah is credited with having consoled the Prophet during the temporary suspense of the divine visitations; which perhaps we may interpret as meaning that the strong-minded woman who kept him faithful during the years in which his master-passion must have been strongest compelled him to adhere to the line which he had taken. But indeed he was compelled to continue by Abu Bakr, who immediately started proselytising. Doubtless at the Prophet's desire the mission was conducted with profound secrecy. Abu Bakr communicated nothing save to persons in whom he had confidence; and on whom he was able to obtain some leverage. But neither he nor the Prophet were impatient, and they were satisfied if the first year of Abu Bakr's propaganda produced three converts.* There is strong reason for thinking that he was helped from the first by an Abyssinian slave, Bilal, of whose antecedents we should gladly know more; for Omar declared that Bilal was a third part of Islam †; and, lest we should mistake the meaning of the phrase, a later follower used to call himself

* *Isabah*, ii., 162.

† *Jahiz*, *Opuscula*, 58.

the quarter of Islam,* because, when he visited Mohammed at 'Ukaz, he found him followed as yet by one freeman, Abu Bakr, and one slave, Bilal. The tradition clearly does not know for certain whose slave he was. In want of better information we are inclined to attribute to him some of the Abyssinian elements in the Prophet's productions.† He was after a time purchased and manumitted by Abu Bakr.

How Abu Bakr proceeded is not recorded in many cases. There is, however, one anecdote which is likely to be true and characteristic. Othman, son of 'Affan, six years the Prophet's junior, was a cloth merchant, having for partner a cousin of Mohammed‡; he also did some business as a money-lender, advancing sums for enterprises of which he was to enjoy half the profits,§ and in money matters showed remarkable acuteness.‖ His sister was a milliner, married to a barber,¶ and he himself was unusually handsome, fond of personal adornment, and dignified; Mohammed even did not venture to appear in déshabille before him,** or allow slave-girls to beat drums in his presence.†† He was no fighting man, as his subsequent history proved, for he shirked one battle-field, ran away from

* *Musnad*, iv., 385.

† Enumerated by *Wellhausen*, *Reste*, 232.

‡ *Isabah*, i., 1036.

§ *Ibn Sa'd*, iii., 111.

‖ *Wakidi* (*W.*), 231.

¶ *Isabah*, i., 714.

** *Muslim*, ii., 234.

†† *Musnad*, iv., 353.

another, and was killed, priest-like, ostentatiously reading the Koran. He loved Mohammed's fair daughter, Rukayyah, and learned to his chagrin that she had been betrothed to another. Hearing the sad news he came to pour his grief into Abu Bakr's friendly ears. Abu Bakr in reply asked him whether he did not think the Meccan gods stocks and stones?—a question of doubtful appropriateness, it might seem, unless their services had been called in by the lover; but a conversation followed, whence Othman inferred that if he chose to declare the Meccan gods worthy of contempt and acknowledge that Mohammed had a mission to suppress them, Mohammed's daughter might still be his. Mohammed presently passed by, Abu Bakr whispered something into his ear and the affair was arranged. Othman became a believer and Rukayyah became his wife.

In this case the process of conversion is laid bare, and offers no further difficulty to the reader. In each of the other cases the shrewd missionary must have seen his opening, though we do not often know what it was. Abu Bakr probably was aware that women are more amenable to conversion than men, resident foreigners than natives,* slaves than freemen, persons in distress than persons in prosperity and affluence. When Islam was found out, the humble character of many of Mohammed's followers was a stumbling-block to the Meccan aristocrats, who requested him to send away this scum before they would argue with him. Indeed the

* *Wellhausen, Reste*, 221.

Koran acknowledges so distinctly that the followers of the Prophet were the lowest of the people* that grave doubt attaches to early traditions which conflict with this statement. The phraseology employed, "the worst of us—at first sight," is curiously lucid. And later on, when the aristocrats had been forced into Islam, they were wont to reproach their new brethren with their earlier condition.† For many a man the honour of being Abu Bakr's first convert was afterwards claimed; and the length of time in which the mission remained a secret rendered their claims difficult to assess. When men were asked what first led them to Mohammed they were apt to give fantastic answers; perhaps they had forgotten the real motive or preferred to conceal it. Khalid, son of Sa'id, the fourth or fifth convert, dreamed that his father was pushing him into a lake of fire, whence another man saved him. He asked Abu Bakr to interpret‡; Abu Bakr took him to Mohammed, then in retreat at Ajyad, near Safa; in whom the dreamer recognised his Saviour, and was converted. Do men really dream thus? Flammarion and Myers would answer that they do. Abdallah, son of Mas'ud, a client and serf, declared that when feeding the herds of 'Ukbah, son of Mu'ait (afterwards a prominent opponent of Mohammed) in the country, he had been solicited for a bowl of milk by Mohammed and Abu Bakr, who were walking together away from

* *Surah* xi., 27.

† *Wahidi*, 118.

‡ Abu Bakr regularly figures as dream interpreter. *Wellhausen* (*W.*), 14.

men; and Abdallah was converted by perceiving the goat's udder swell and contract at the Prophet's pleasure.* Othman, son of Maz'un,† a man of ascetic turn of mind, came one day to sit with the Prophet; the Prophet gazed up into heaven, presently looked at a certain spot, went thither, came back, and again gazed up into heaven. Asked the meaning of this performance, he replied that he had been visited by a messenger of God, who told him to preach justice, kindness, chastity, etc.; and Othman believed. Several declared that dissatisfaction with pagan beliefs was what had led them to the Prophet; and if there was a trace of this feeling in a man, Abu Bakr would not let it escape him. Such a convert may have been Sa'id, son of Zaid Ibn 'Amr; his father had rejected polytheism and idolatry before Mohammed's mission was started, without, however, adopting Judaism or Christianity. Sa'id's conversion was early, but he is not reckoned among Abu Bakr's proselytes. Such a convert may also have been 'Abd al-Ka'bah (servant of the Ka'bah), son of 'Auf, re-named 'Abd al-Rahmān; for the Ka'bah was not yet dissociated from paganism.‡ This man was a merchant, partner of a certain Rabāh, called by his new friends the trustworthy; he had a rare talent for making money, with which he was free-handed. Years after, when he§ with the other Refugees arrived at Yathrib destitute, he asked for

---

* *Musnad*, i., 462.

† *Ibid*, i., 318.

‡ His original name is doubtful; others give it as servant of 'Amr.

§ *Alif-Bā*, i., 437

no further provision than to be shown the market; once there he could get on, though he had no capital.* He is said to have been a total abstainer before conversion; to have disapproved of fighting in the cause of Islam, yet when the practice had once begun, to have been inferior to none in courage. Such a man might not seem to be promising material for Abu Bakr; but he was some eight years Abu Bakr's junior, and may have been subject to his influence. Or in his case, too, a lady may have been involved. There was at Meccah a certain Mikdad, who had fled from his own tribe for a murder, and been received by the Kindah; among them, too, he shed blood, and fled to Meccah, where he was adopted by a man named Al-Aswad, of the tribe of Mohammed's mother. 'Abd al-Ka'bah advised him (in conversation) to marry, yet refused him his daughter, with scorn; but he found consolation from Mohammed, who gave him the daughter of his uncle, Zubair, already dead, on the same conditions (we suspect) as those to which Othman had been compelled to assent. The further steps which led to the winning over of 'Abd al-Ka'bah are unknown. With Mikdad there was won another convert, 'Utbah, son of Ghazwan, also a client, and probably poor.

Three men who figure among the earliest converts are Al-Zubair, son of 'Awwam; Sa'd, son of Abu Wakkas, and Talhah, son of 'Ubaidallah. The first of these, according to different traditions was eight, ten, or seventeen at this time; he was a cousin of

* *Isabah.*

the Prophet, son of a corn-chandler, in training to be a butcher, and is said to have experienced rough treatment at home. If his conversion be rightly placed at this time, perhaps he was a playmate of Ali, initiated in the mysteries that he might not reveal them; for, as we have seen, their houses were connected.

Talhah was certainly grown up, and professed to have been directed to Mohammed by a monk whom he met when travelling on business to Syria. If any value attaches to this statement, it probably means that he had heard the Arabian paganism ridiculed by followers of the fashionable creed, and though their jibes were without effect on most minds, some were impressed thereby. Later in life he won celebrity by his freehandedness with money.*

Sa'd claimed to have been for a whole week the third Moslem, in which case he was actually Abu Bakr's first convert. He was by trade an arrow-maker, and was thought to have shed the first blood in the new cause. He was aged seventeen at the time of his conversion.

Every convert when brought to Mohammed exhibited some repugnance, except Abu Bakr. This was afterwards acknowledged by the Prophet: but he did not state what it was that the newcomers disliked. Nor have we any record of the procedure at these solemn scenes: at most we hear that the Prophet taught the proselytes to pray. At a later time, however, admission to see the Prophet meant

* *Ghurar al-Khasa'is*, 245.

that the proselyte was prepared to swear allegiance, and bound himself to abstain from certain immoral acts; for the commission of which he was to undergo punishment in this life, if he meant to escape punishment hereafter*; and besides at a still later period (in the case of men) to fight all nations till they adopted the new religion. We can scarcely doubt that from the first the proselytes undertook some serious obligation, such as those who are admitted to other secret societies undertake; those obligations are not ordinarily some definite performances in the present but readiness to act when called upon in the future. It would appear that from the first the Prophet instituted brotherhoods between pairs of believers, whose new relationship was to supersede the claims of blood just as the Christianity of the tribes who formed the '*Ibad* or Christians of Hirah had provided a bond different from that of the tribe. The repugnance observed by the Prophet probably lay in the anxiety which even the young feel in committing themselves to something for life, especially when that something is an unknown quantity, a course of which the issue is obscure.

Of the evolution of the Mohammedan ceremony called *salāt*, the name of which was borrowed from either the Jewish or the Christian name for prayer, we possess little detailed knowledge. In the form afterwards stereotyped the Jewish practice of standing erect, the Christian of prostration,‡ and a third

---

* *Tabari*, i., 1213.

† *Rothstein*, *Lakhmiden*, 25.

‡ *Von Kremer*, *Streifzüge*, 15.

POSTURES OF PRAYER.

of inclination (the back horizontal with the hands on the knees) were combined; and certain formulæ were prescribed. "We used at first," said a convert, "not knowing what to say when we prayed, to salute God, Gabriel, and Michael; the Prophet presently taught us another formula instead."* A prayer corresponding to the *Pater Noster* was composed probably at a later time: it contains polemical references to some sect or sects not specified.† As will be seen, the *salāt* was afterwards employed as a sort of military drill: at the first it was ascetic in character, the devotee "tying a cord to his chest."‡ That the division of the day into periods for the purpose of performing *salāt* five times was an innovation of the late Meccan period is asserted by the tradition; and the details of the purity legislation appear to have been still later. Yet the theory that God should be approached only by persons in a state of purity was known in South Arabia before Mohammed's time, whence it is probable that his earliest converts were instructed therein; and indeed the washing of the garments which marked conversion belongs to the same range of ideas.

The *salāt* was during this early period performed in strict privacy, and doubtless meetings of believers were fixed with great caution. Whatever part the

* *Musnad*, i., 423.

† "Lead us in the straight path, the path of those unto whom Thou hast been gracious, not those with whom Thou hast been angry [the Jews?], nor those who go astray [the Christians?]" This is Tirmidhi's explanation.

‡ *Tabari*, *Comm.*, xvi., 90. Probably the other end of the cord was attached to the roof; *Histoire du Bas-empire*, xiii., 312.

converts had previously taken in the Meccan worship they doubtless continued to take. Whether the sanctity of the Ka'bah was maintained at this time by the Prophet we do not know: more probably it was rejected. And if the question of a direction to be taken in prayer was considered at this time, we can scarcely doubt that the Temple of Jerusalem was the point to which he turned. The connection of the Abraham-myth with the Ka'bah appears to have been the result of later speculation, and to have been fully developed only when a political need for it arose.

A fair amount of the Koran must have been in existence when Abu Bakr started his mission; at least he must have been able to assure the proselytes that his Prophet was in receipt of divine communications, such as he could allege in proof of his personal acquaintance with the real God; and it is probable that with the gradual increase in the numbers of the believers, the Koran transformed itself from the "*mediumistic*" communications with which it began to the powerful sermons with which its second period is occupied. For a very small audience the processes undergone by the medium are exceedingly effective. The necessity of excluding strangers keeps those present in a state of alarm; the approach of the "superior condition" shown by the medium collapsing, requiring to be wrapped up, and then revealing himself in a violent state of perspiration, is highly sensational; the marvellous processes which the spectators have witnessed make them attach extraordinary value to the utterances which the medium produces, as the result of his trance. If any unbelievers are present the medium (in many cases) cannot act: and the words of the biographers imply that in the case of these early converts they signified their belief before they were brought into Mohammed's presence.

As the Prophet more and more identified himself with his part he endeavoured to live up to it. It is said that he habitually wore a veil,* and this practice may have begun at the time of these mysterious séances, of which it served to enhance the solemnity. In course of time he acquired a benign and pastoral manner; when he shook hands he would not withdraw his hand first; when he looked at a man he would wait for the other to turn away his face.† Scrupulous care was bestowed by him on his person: every night he painted his eyes, and his body was at all times fragrant with perfumes.‡ His hair was suffered to grow long till it reached his shoulders; and when it began to display signs of grey, § these were concealed with dyes.‖ He possessed the art of speaking a word in season to the neophytes—saying something which gratified the special inclinations of each, or which manifested acquaintance with his antecedents. How many of the stories which illustrate the latter talent are true it is hard to say; but there is little doubt that he was acquainted with the devices known to modern

* *Jahiz, Bayan*, ii., 79, 84.

† *Tirmidhi*, 410 (ii., 80).

‡ *Alif-Bā*, ii., 29.

§ *Musnad*, iv., 188.

‖ *Ibid.*, iv., 163. This is disputed.

mediums by which private information can either be obtained, or the appearance of possessing it displayed. Moreover, in the early period none were admitted to see the Prophet in character of whom the missionary was not sure, and who had not been prepared to venerate.

The needs of his profession do not appear to have made him actually a student—yet there is no question that as the Koran grew in bulk, its knowledge of biblical stories became somewhat more accurate: and though this greater degree of accuracy may have at times been due to the Prophet's memory, it is more likely that he took such opportunities as offered of acquiring more information. The following story gives us an idea of his method. Jabr, a client of the Banu 'Abd al-Dar, was a Jew* who worked as a smith in Meccah. He and Yasar (also a Jew) used to sit together at their trade and in the course of their work read out their sacred book; the Prophet used to pass by and listen. Presently Jabr was converted by hearing the Prophet read the Surah of Joseph.† It has been suggested that some of the Christian matter in the Koran may have been learned from an early follower named Suhaib, who was a Greek from Mosul.‡ The tradition names more than one person who was thought by the Meccans to be the Prophet's mentor, and the Koran even refutes this charge by stating that the person to whom they allude had a foreign tongue, and could

* Or a Christian; the Moslems are careless about distinguishing.

† *Isabah*, i., 452; *Wakidi* (*W.*), 349.

‡ *Loth* in *Z. D. M. G.*, xxxv., 621.

not therefore be the author of an Arabic Koran. Perhaps that reply is unconvincing; but the impression which the Koran leaves is that of information picked up casually rather than acquired by any sort of methodical study.* In a Surah delivered at Medinah in which the story of Saul should be told, Saul's name is mutilated to *Talut*, clearly a jingle with Galut, the nearest that the Prophet could get to Goliath: the name of Samuel is forgotten, he is confused with Gideon, and the story of Gideon is told wrongly. This phenomenon almost disposes of the theory of a mentor, for no mentor could be so ignorant of the Bible. Moreover the sources of the Koran are very numerous—Abyssinian and Syriac, as well as Hebrew and Greek.† So far then as the biblical tales of the Koran were not reproductions of matter heard by Mohammed on his early travels, they are likely to have been all picked up by listening when services or Bible readings were going on. The Jinn were thought by him to listen at the heavenly councils in the same way, and in consequence to pick up intelligence which was only partially correct. That danger there was no way of averting, except engaging a teacher, which would have involved still greater risks.

Publicity was expressly discouraged by him. A Syrian ('Amr, son of 'Abasah) who claimed at a later time to have been the fourth Moslem, asserted

* *Nöldeke*, *Sketches*, c. ii.

† The best evidence for this is the form assumed by the proper names. *Sye*, *Die Eigennamen im Koran*, 1903, does scant justice to this theme.

that having himself abandoned the worship of idols,* he had come to Mohammed, who, he heard, was in possession of the truth; he found Mohammed bent on maintaining the secrecy of his mission: he offered to join Mohammed openly, but was forbidden to do so, since he would serve the cause better by returning to his country and—we may presume—playing the part of Abu Bakr. Some early revelations are said to have been delivered in a cave, a natural form of hiding-place†; and in the anecdotes that have already been told Mohammed is found in seclusion; when Abu Dharr, afterwards a famous ascetic, came from a distance to learn about the Prophet's views (according to one account), the latter was hiding in the mountains.‡ But one fact that emerges from the obscurity which is spread over the early days of the mission is that Mohammed, after some conversions had been made, went into "the house of Al-Arkam, on Mount Safa." This Al-Arkam was a member of the tribe Makhzum, and must have been about seventeen when the mission started: some made him out to be the seventh, others the tenth convert. His house on Safa appears to have served as a meeting-house, where the Prophet could receive neophytes or hold séances without fear of being disturbed. So we are told of two converts, both Greek slaves, Suhaib, son of Sinan, and 'Ammar, son of Yasir, accidentally meeting at the door of Al-Arkam's house, entering to make their profession of faith, and

* *Musnad*, iv., 111.

† *Muslim*, ii., 194.

‡ *Isabah*, iii., 1173.

then at eventide skulking away.* Many years lapsed before Mohammed was able to reward his faithful entertainer by presenting him with a dwelling at Medinah. Even if secrecy had not been desirable, the intense curiosity of Orientals would have seriously interfered with séances held in a thickly populated town. But that curiosity would not induce them to go a short journey outside it, hence Mohammed could hold his meetings in peace. Since at the first conversion did not interfere with a man's business, it is likely that these meetings were at irregular intervals.

We should gladly be able to make use of the tables drawn up by Professor Starbuck in analysing the next set of conversions; but the ages recorded are absolutely irregular, and the phenomena can be brought under no rule. The persons who went to the house of Arkam were of all sorts of ages, the oldest ten years the Prophet's senior, some in middle life, forty-six or thirty-four, several quite young. Several were slaves or freedmen—persons for whom a new system which holds out prospects of equality had an easily intelligible attraction. And indeed their condition speedily bettered itself —for the manumission of believers was soon declared to be a pious duty.† Some belonged to the metic class, who were without relations in Meccah. Hatib, son of Abu Balta'ah, probably a Christian from Hirah, who will meet us once or twice in the sequel, is a specimen. Most of them are however to us mere names.

* *Ibn Sa'd*, iii., 162.

† So Abu Bakr bought and manumitted 'Amir Ibn Fuhairah.

In a few cases families were converted wholesale, three sons of Jahsh, three sons of Al-Harith (Hatib, Hattab, and Ma'mar), four sons of Al-Bukair, three sons of Maz'un, are enumerated among the accessions of this period; and in several cases the conversion of one brother was succeeded by that of another; so Ali's older brother Ja'far joined the movement, in which he was destined to play a part of some importance, though less distinguished than that of the Prophet's son-in-law. The privilege of re-naming followers was one of which other prophets had availed themselves, and this Mohammed claimed wherever a proselyte was called after an idol, or otherwise had an ill-omened appellation. Special titles of honour were also conferred, but probably at a later time: Abu Bakr was called the Faithful Friend, Zubair, the Apostle, Abu Ubaidah, son of Jarrah, the Faithful, Omar, the Saviour. These were like the decorations conferred by the sovereign in modern times on persons who have either done some public service, or are intrusted with some important charge.

The precursors of Mohammed do not enter on the scene at this period, and it is not probable that they were in the secret, supposing more than one of them to have been alive at the time. "Those that are whole need not a physician," and the proud possessors of monotheistic book-learning were at no time promising material for proselytism. Moreover these persons (it would appear) had not kept their opinions secret.

That conversion could be concealed for any

length of time is rather surprising, for, even if the positive part of the new system could be performed in secrecy, the negative part would speedily give evidence of itself. The worship of the gods was a feature of every-day life. Visits to their abodes for a number of days, accompanied by sacrifices of sheep and camels, were not uncommon.* Mohammed's partner (or his son) described some of the household rites: "My parents used to churn the milk till it was done, when they would pour some of it into a vessel, and tell me to take it to the gods. Then a dog might come and drink the milk or eat the butter, and afterwards pollute the vessel." This rite was no more and no less ridiculous than any other in which an imaginary person is treated as a human being; but it can be made out to be ridiculous: and the persons whose eyes had been focussed to the point whence the sacrifice of milk to Al-Lāt appeared ridiculous would feel the greatest repugnance when called upon to take part in it: the young and thoughtless would burn to play the part of Abraham who broke his father's idols. And indeed Ali asserted that Abraham's act had been imitated by the Prophet himself. The two went secretly to the Ka'bah to destroy an idol that was on the roof. First Mohammed tried to mount on Ali's shoulders: but Ali was not yet strong enough, and therefore Mohammed had to support his cousin; who wrenched the idol from its place, and caused it to crash in pieces on the ground.† Probably this story

* *Azraki*, 81.

† *Musnad*, i., 84, etc.

represents rather what they ought to have done than what they actually did. Still we see the need for proselytising only persons in whose self-control confidence could be felt. At a later period Mohammed is recorded to have recommended a certain procedure to persons who, in order to save their lives, had to go through some of the ceremonies of idolatry: to appear to men to worship while in secret venting some expressions of contempt upon the idol. Those who found the idols unable to resent this behaviour would be only confirmed in their contempt for them. Meanwhile the worship which was to be substituted for the old rites was carried on in strict privacy.

To what extent the secret society was conscious of its potentialities we know not. The advantage of the darkness for the first few years of its growth was great. That darkness saved it from being crushed at the outset. Ridicule and contempt could be more easily endured when some hundred persons were involved, than if the Prophet had been compelled to endure them by himself. It saved him, too, from the character of the eccentric sage (such as Warakah and the others had borne), investing him from his first public appearance with that of the leader of a party: it gave the Prophet time to secure over a reasonable number of persons that influence which he could exercise to such an extraordinary degree. It prepared him for ruling men on a great scale. Gathered in the house of Al-Arkam there were specimens of most of the classes with whom his further career brought him in contact: there were examples of the religious enthusiast and gloomy fanatic—Othman, son of Maz'un, seems to have been of this type; some of the weak-minded and superstitious; many of the persons who find in religion the possibility of a career. The skill of both Abu Bakr and the Prophet was displayed in retaining their hold on this slowly growing company. In the case of the poor it was done by subsidies; presently, when Islam was penalised, the Prophet found he had whole families on his hands; but we need not doubt that from the first the wealth which he controlled proved useful. Unlike the Christian missionaries who had to be supported by their converts, he could claim that he sought no reward, and to the end refused either to enjoy the Alms himself, or to allow any members of his family to enjoy them. The most successful of the mediums played this card. Home with its aid won his way into the society of princes.

Like most of those who have known mankind thoroughly, Mohammed held, and at times all but openly avowed, the doctrine that every man has his price, and indeed a price to be estimated in camels.

But where "temporal relief" was not required, the promise of the Garden worked wonders. The glowing descriptions thereof contained in the Koran are still a powerful instrument in the hands of Moslem missionaries. The history of Islam is a record of sacrifices gladly made in order to obtain those gaudily painted delights. Its character is not unlike that of some savage Paradises: "there are prettier women in the Land of the Great Spirit than any of your squaws, and game in much greater abundance," said a Crow to Beckwourth,* urging him to fight. Its name was taken from Jews or Christians, its description in part from Ta'if, where the wealthy Meccans had gardens, but various touches were added as occasion required.

So soon as Islam became strong, the ordinary rule of the secret society was avowed: whereby whoso joins it once joins it for ever, his life being forfeit if he quits. This rule, which to the present day renders the conversion of a Mohammedan all but an impossibility, is so intimately connected with the nature of secret societies that we should place the beginnings of it very early; and a suspicion at least of its existence was probably what kept many a proselyte faithful under persecution. Yet the religion which is embraced for sordid motives is often retained for honourable reasons; and early observers found that among the most sincere believers in Islam were persons who had been lured into it by bribes.†

Moreover, to some persons secrecy has an attraction, and some gratification is afforded by leading a double life. Secret societies still exist, meeting where no one suspects their object, sometimes probably for mummeries, sometimes to discuss schemes of far-reaching import. One writer of ability suspects that at Mohammed's early meetings some socialistic scheme was discussed, some better division of wealth between rich and poor.‡ For this

---

* *Autobiography*, 161.

† *Muslim*, ii., 212; *Musnad*, iii., 175.

‡ So, too, preachers describe Mohammed as sent that he might obtain justice for the poor from the rich. *Hariri*, p. 328.

there is little evidence. That the harsh things said at these meetings about the worship of idols included condemnation of the representatives of the official worship at Meccah is exceedingly probable; and the notion that a Prophet ought to be an autocrat probably was developed very early. But if one of the secret society asked another why he belonged to it, he would probably have replied: in order to gain Paradise and escape the Fire.* Men were initiated into the mysteries of Eleusis for some similar reason. Examples are not wanting of converts whose faith received some sudden shock, or who (as unbelievers might say) suddenly woke up to the unreality of the whole system.

New sects require some freemasonry by which members may know each other, and perhaps the greeting "Peace upon you" was introduced at this early period, though a visitor to Medinah fifteen years after the commencement of the mission declared that it was new.† This greeting was doubtless usual among Jews and Christians; but it seems to have deeply affected Mohammed, who constantly refers to it in the Koran. God pronounces it over the Prophets, the angels taught it to Abraham, with it the beatified dead are greeted in Paradise, where indeed it is the whole conversation. By adopting this salutation, Mohammed practically identified his system with that of Jews and

---

* Cf. *Tabari*, i., 1218, 10.

† *Isabah*, iii., 70; but *Wellhausen* (*W.*, 75) renders this differently. In *Muslim*, ii., 255, Abu Dharr claims to have invented it. See also *Goldziher*, *Z. D. M. G.*, xlvi., 22.

Christians. If this greeting was not at first permitted in public, perhaps the Moslems could recognise each other by some slight peculiarity in their attire; thus the Moslems let the end of the turban hang down the back, whereas the pagans tucked it in.* So at a later time members of the chief sects of Islam could be distinguished by their mode of disposing their turbans.†

Finally a name had to be given to the new sect, and either accident or choice led to its being called the sect of the Muslims (Moslems) or Hanifs. Were these originally names by which the followers of *Maslamah* the prophet of the Banu *Hanifah* had been known? Or had some other sect, monotheistic and professedly following Abraham, whose descendants according to the Bible some of the Arabs were, been thus designated? We cannot say; no Arab seems to have known anything about the Hanifs, except that Abraham was one, and *perhaps* one or two of the precursors of Mohammed; and since in Hebrew the word means "hypocrite" and in Syriac "heathen," pious followers of Mohammed did not care to study its etymology. The other name, Muslim, meant naturally "traitor," and when the new sect came to be lampooned, it provided the satirists with a witticism; Mohammed showed some want of humour in adopting it, but displayed great ingenuity in giving it an honourable meaning: whereas it or-

* *Hariri*, *Schol.*, 346.

† *Hamadhani*, *Makamas*, 199. So now Kaisites and Yemenites (*Goldziher*, *M. S.*, i., 84). There is also incidental evidence that Mohammed at the first wore his hair in the Jewish style, and in such particulars he was likely to be followed by the disciples.

dinarily signified one who handed over his friends to their enemies, it was glorified into meaning one who handed over his person to God; and though, like Christian, it may conceivably have been first invented by enemies of the sect whom it designated, divine authority was presently adduced for the statement that Abraham coined the name. Like the Jews, these new Abrahamites called their pagan brethren the Gentiles, using an Abyssinian word. The pagans appear to have ordinarily called the new sect, when it had ceased to be secret, Sabian, * a word properly meaning Baptist, and belonging to a community still perpetuated as the Soubbas, whose home is in the marshes of the Euphrates.† The application of the name to Mohammed's followers may have been due to mere ignorance, as the Arabians of our day called Doughty a Jew, because he was a Christian; or it may have been due to the prominence given by Mohammed to the ceremony of washing.

* The passages are collected by *Wellhausen*, *Reste*, 236, 237.

† *Siouffi*, *Les Soubbas*.

CHAPTER IV

PUBLICITY

WHO first professed the new religion before the world is not certain: a tradition* ascribes the act to a certain Khabbab, son of the Stammerer, a slave who worked at sword-making and a starveling.† To avow Islam meant to renounce publicly the national worship, to ridicule, and, if possible, break down idols, and unabashedly to use the new salutation and celebrate the newfangled rites. For it must be remembered that Islam was in its nature polemical. Its Allah was not satisfied with worship, unless similar honour was paid to no other name; and his worship also was intolerant of idols, and of all rites not instituted or approved by himself. This then was the meaning of the meetings in the house of Al-Arkam, and doubtless of the knowing glances which the members of the new sect had been observed to interchange. Mohammed and Abu Bakr were planning an attack on the national religion, that cult which every Meccan

* *Isabah;* in *Musnad*, i., 404, seven persons are named in this contest, but not Khabbab.

† *Tirmidhi*, i., 181.

proudly remembered had within their memory been defended by a miracle from the Abyssinian invaders and in their myths had often thus triumphed before. The gods they worshipped were, Mohammed and Abu Bakr asserted, no gods. For their worship these innovators would substitute that of the Jews whose power in South Arabia had recently been overthrown, and of the Christians with whose defeat the national spirit of Arabia had just awakened.

Mr. Grote in his treatment of the affair of the Hermocopidæ taught men to judge one age by another. Persons who are tolerant of opinions which differ from their own become indignant when their own beliefs are ruthlessly assailed. When the assertions of Mohammed were first heard by those who had not been sounded and prepared for them, it was natural that they should appear ridiculous, and wicked, and suicidal. Ridiculous, because the gods were thoroughly familiar figures. "Their partners,"* Al-'Uzza and Al-Lāt, did not exist? Why, many a man could state the occasions on which they had done him personally a service, many a child owed its existence to their intervention, and recorded the fact by its name. To many they had appeared in dreams; to some doubtless in waking hours; soliciting and bestowing favours. And if the men's attachment to their deities was weak at times, that of the women who needed their help more was strong.

But what weighed with the men who could think calmly† was the fact that Meccah lived mainly by

* *Surah* vi., 137.

† *Wellhausen*, *Reste*, 220.

its being a religious centre, and by the pagan institution of the four months of peace. That valuable institution the Christians were known not to observe; and since Mohammed's followers prayed toward another sanctuary and no longer kissed the Black Stone,* it could be inferred that he wanted to destroy the Ka'bah; and indeed till a late period in his career there were Moslems who wished for its destruction.† An early revelation seems intended to reassure the Meccans on this point; and Mohammed, whose practical sense never deserted him, was careful to find a place for the Ka'bah in his system.

Some of our authorities introduce the first public preaching of Islam with a theatrical scene. Mohammed goes to the precincts of the Ka'bah and calls on the assembled throng to utter the formula, "There is no God but Allah"; the blasphemous words cause him to be mobbed; news of his danger spreads to his family, and one of Khadijah's children, Al-Harith, son of Abu Halah, rushing to defend his stepfather, perished, the first martyr of Islam.‡ But indeed the transference of the Islamic doctrine from secrecy to publicity must have taken place by some definite act of delivery—if the phrase may be employed. When one member of the community after another was found to be tainted with heresy, and each referred to Mohammed as his guide, Mohammed was, we suppose, confronted by some of those in authority, and challenged to declare his

---

* *Ibn Sa'd*, iii., 88, 10.

† *Wellhausen*, *Reste*, 69, n. 1.

‡ *Isabah*, i., 60.

views. And he confessed and denied not. On later occasions when compelled to risk much on an effort, he spared no pains in preparation, and his first public address to the people of Meccah was doubtless elaborately prepared. Whether the assembly broke up in mirth or in tumult, the Rubicon was now crossed. The husband of Khadijah claimed to supersede all existing authority, and to be the accredited representative of the God of the tribe. And there were in Meccah something like a hundred persons who recognised his claims. But the announcement came as a surprise to those who were not in the secret; and Abu Sufyan, then in Yemen, receiving a letter to the effect that one of his relations claimed to be God's Apostle, had to ask which of his relations it was.*

The view prevalent at Meccah concerning Mohammed appears to have been that he was mad—under the influence of a Jinn, one of the beings who were supposed to speak through poets and sorcerers. That this charge stung Mohammed to the quick may be inferred from the virulence with which he rejects it, and the invective with which he attacks the "bastard" who had uttered it.† He charges the author of the outrage with being unable to write and with being over head and ears in debt, and threatens to brand him on his "proboscis."

Against the humbler followers‡ of the new

---

* *Aghani*, ii., 96.

† *Surah* lxviii., 10–16.

‡ Such as Khabbab, Suhaib Ibn Sinan, 'Amir Ibn Fuhairah, 'Ammār and his family. (*Ibn Sa'd.*)

doctrine violence was speedily put in motion; to increase, as time went on, to burning with hot irons, or exposure face upwards to the midday sun; till some found refuge in the houses of their more powerful brethren, or were ransomed by the more wealthy; or (with Mohammed's approval) denied with their lips,* while believing in their heart. Five only are said to have actually returned to paganism in consequence.† Even strangers visiting Meccah who inquired after the Prophet were subjected to violence.‡ Against those who were wealthy and powerful violence could not at first be tried; the very young could indeed be rebuked and punished by their fathers, but the grown men were safe for a time owing to that institution of paganism which made the ties of clan and family more powerful than any moral law; which made a man's kin necessarily accomplices in his misdeeds. In some cases parents tried to reclaim their sons by appealing to their affections: the mother of Sa'd, son of Abu Wakkas, vowed that she would take no food until he recanted; but he recanted not, and food was forced down her throat.§ Abu Talib, who for some reason appears to have been the head of his clan, undertook to protect Mohammed from the fury of the orthodox, not without their approval. Probably he had been in the secret for some time. He is said to have surprised

---

* *Ibn Sa'd*, iii., 178,

† *Ya'kubi*, ii., 28.

‡ *Muslim*, ii., 254.

§ *Ibid.*, ii., 24.

his son Ali with Mohammed prostrating themselves in the valley of Nakhlah, and when the nature of the performance was explained to him, to have declared that he had no objection to it, but did not like the idea of raising his séant above his head, a jest the thought of which caused Ali to laugh years afterwards.* This story is likely to be true, and characteristic of Abu Talib, apparently a good-natured man, not inclined to take things seriously, yet rigidly attached to old-fashioned ideas of duty.† But other members of the family opposed Mohammed vehemently, notably his uncle, Abu Lahab, and his cousin, Abu Sufyan, son of Al-Harith.‡

For a time then the war between Mohammed and the Meccans was to be one of words,—a long time, no less than eight, or, according to most, ten years, so tenacious was the Meccan community of the cult of the *clan*, so timid of the consequences which arise from the shedding of kindred blood. If the head of Mohammed's clan had let him be outlawed, then Meccah might have been rid of him, but Abu Talib could not be persuaded to do this, and his veto blocked the way. Perhaps Abu Talib and his numerous family could not afford to abandon their wealthy relative; and, indeed, had Mohammed not had some power over his uncle, it is unlikely that the latter would have submitted to the inconvenience which his nephew's mission brought on him.

* *Musnad*, i., 99.

† Abu Talib was supposed to be a poet, but most of the verses attributed to him were suspect in very early days. Some few are regarded by modern scholars as genuine. *Z.D.M.G.*, xviii., 223.

‡ *Wakidi* (*W.*), 328.

The clear-headed man who played the part of Prophet could have at any time secured his own safety by taking refuge in a Christian country, but his aim was to be not a subject but a sovereign, and so he made no such mistake. Truly the hand with which he started contained some good cards: Khadijah's devotion and her fortune; Abu Talib's affection and his influence; Abu Bakr's blind trust and his persuasiveness. When the first two cards were withdrawn by fortune, better ones were substituted, and so Mohammed won the game.

Three separate deputations from the Meccans to Abu Talib are reported (or invented) by the biographer: the leading men of Meccah are sent to the Sheykh to request him to abandon his nephew: on one occasion they offer to provide him with a substitute—'Umarah, son of Al-Walid,—as good a man as any in Meccah, if it is only a question of not losing a member from the family. This 'Umarah appears to have been an Adonis, who turned women's heads: he went on an expedition to Abyssinia once with 'Amr, son of Al-'Asi, and would have killed his companion to seize his wife; and presently seduced one of the Abyssinian's queens, and was punished, not with death, but with what, to an Arab, was as bad. He was, besides, a hard drinker. Perhaps Abu Talib was not satisfied that he would gain peace by the exchange; whatever his reason, he held out bravely and induced the rest of his clan to join him in protecting their kinsman.

Mohammed is to be admired for having profited to the utmost from the sanctity of the clan, while himself yielding nothing in consequence. At a later period sons suffered their fathers to be killed in the cause of Islam without the faintest scruple: but even at an early period of the mission the converts began to treat their pagan relatives with gross disrespect. Mohammed is said to have been struck with the rudeness of the neophytes towards their unconverted fathers,—a phenomenon which had its origin in the sentiment illustrated by Lecky, which sometimes renders religion incompatible with the domestic affections.

The history then of the first years of Mohammed's preaching at Meccah is not without events, but it is, in the main, the history of a debate, and a debate in which the speeches of the counsel of one side only are preserved. The Meccan Surahs of the Koran are rarely to be dated with precision: many are reports or notes of the same course of lectures repeated over and over again by the lecturer. Hence, the order in which question after question was posed by the adversary is not known.

Of the procedure by which a reform in religion spreads, history gives so many examples that from one or other we can picture to ourselves what happened at Meccah as the adherents of Mohammed increased. The reformers invariably become aggressive and endeavour to interfere with the worship which they regard as improper. We need not doubt that followers of Mohammed pursued this course with the rites to which they were taught to object at Meccah. The Koran praises the conduct of Abraham who knocked down the idols in his father's shop and ascribed the act ironically to the largest idol. The early converts at Medinah are known to have acted in the style of Abraham, and it is probable that the Meccan converts had set the example. Violent scenes were certain to be the result of such actions.

The old pagan religion was certainly not wanting in rules on the subject of food—though the concepts "clean and unclean" may have been strange to it. It is expressly stated that some foods were permitted to men only, and others probably were only lawful for women; and of other regulations we occasionally hear details.* Mohammed's conversations with Jews and Christians had taught him to assign a far higher importance to that subject than the pagans are likely to have assigned it. All his life he had a hankering after the Jewish regulations on this subject; only as the Jewish system forbade the use of camel's flesh, he could not well adopt it: he preferred therefore that of the Christians who followed the regulation of the Council of Jerusalem described in Acts xv. Blood, meats offered to idols, strangled beasts, and swine † were to be forbidden, but other meat lawful. Probably at a later period carnivorous beasts, birds of prey, and the domestic ass were declared unlawful. ‡ This apparently easy regulation would suffice to render it impossible for a Moslem to join in the meals of most of his countrymen §; for

* *Nöldeke*, *Sasaniden*, 203; *Wellhausen*, *Reste*, 125, n. 1, 168.

† Bentley conjectured χοιρείας for πορνείας.

‡ *Musnad*, i., 302.

§ A Moslem prisoner at Meccah at a later time implored his guards not to give him meat offered to idols. *Isabah*, iii., 963.

doubtless the slaughter of an animal was in the majority of cases a religious act *; and Mohammed made "eating of our slaughtering" a test of Islam.† One convert used to speak with regret of his enjoyment of blood in the time of paganism.‡ Unwillingness to eat the food of others ordinarily in such cases implies loathing and disgust for it. Hence we can conjecture with ease the indignation with which this idea of purity was viewed by those whose conduct was impugned by it.

The debates with which the earlier years were filled were conducted in a variety of ways. Occasionally the Prophet himself condescended to enter the arena, and confront his antagonist: he was indeed a powerful preacher, and "when he talked of the Day of Judgment his cheeks blazed, and his voice rose, and his manner was fiery" §; apparently, however, he was not a ready debater, and was worsted when he tried this plan. Moreover his temper in debate was not easily controlled, and he was apt to give violent and insulting answers to questioners.‖ He therefore received divine instructions not to take part in open debate, and if addressed and questioned by unbelievers, to evade the question and retire.¶ More often then the controversy was conducted as it is in this country in election times, when different speakers address different meetings.

* *Wellhausen* (*W.*), 160.

† *Isabah*, iii., 943.

‡ *Ibid.*, iii., 670.

§ *Musnad*, iii., 371.

‖ *Tabari, Comm.* xxiii., 19.

¶ *Surah* vi., 67.

The points are recorded and reported by members of the audience to the antagonists; who then proceed, if they deem it worth while, in some manner to reply. It is also certain that the Koran at an early period circulated in writing, though we do not know in what form. A revelation could then be published in answer to an objection, sometimes with the formula "it will be said by" * prefixed.

Some of the scenes which the tradition describes in connection with the debates may be historical. By the time when the Prophet's revelations had attracted curiosity, any public appearance on his part betokened the occurrence of something new. He is found in the Precincts by Abu Jahl who asks scornfully for the latest. The Prophet replies that he has been carried to Jerusalem and back during the night. Abu Jahl does not contradict, wishing to know what effect the statement will have on the Prophet's followers. He summons the clans to an assembly: the Prophet repeats the assertion. Persons present who had visited Jerusalem request him to describe it. He complies, but gets involved in difficulties. The tradition adds that thereupon a divine model of the city was placed before him to enable him to describe it accurately.† It also adds that the story of the nightly journey made some of Mohammed's followers fall away‡: Abu Jahl had hoped it might shake the faith of Abu Bakr; but Abu Bakr retorted that he had already

* *Surah* vi., 149.

† *Musnad*, i., 309.

‡ *Tabari*, *Comm.*, xv., *init.*

MOSQUE OF OMAR, JERUSALEM.

From Archer and Kingsford's *Story of the Crusades.*

believed greater improbabilities on Mohammed's authority.

It has been asserted that the Meccans obtained the aid of Jews to assist them in their refutation of the Prophet. This would appear to be an anachronism; after the Flight, when the Prophet began to quarrel with the Jews of Medinah, there is no doubt that some of the latter went to Meccah and delighted the Meccans with ridicule of the Prophet's ignorance; but during the first years of the Meccan mission, there is strong reason for believing that so far as the Jews interfered it was on the side of Mohammed. The Jews were appealed to by the latter as a final authority *; he positively asserts that they (as opposed to "the Gentiles") believe in him: indeed, when in doubt concerning his own mission, he is invited to appeal to them to make sure. † So long as his campaign against idolatry and in favour of "Allah" showed no sign of interfering with their interests, there was no reason why he should not find them friendly and ready to support him. Since there was great danger of all Arabia becoming Christian, they may even have deemed it sagacious to encourage a non-Christian teacher. But there were also persons "to whom Knowledge had been given aforetime" who prostrated themselves when the Koran was read: which implies that the Prophet had also Christian supporters at Meccah. ‡ One authority informs us that the Kuraish

* *Surah* xiii., 43; xxviii., 52; xxix., 46.

† *Ibid* x., 94.

‡ *Ibid* xvii., 108, 9.

had Parsee prompters*; and this is not wholly improbable.

The objections recorded and ostensibly answered in the Koran appear to have been directed against every part and feature of the new system; against Mohammed personally, against his notion of prophecy, against his style, his statements, his doctrines. It is impossible to suggest any chronological order for them.

From the first he had followed the example of the New Testament prophets in threatening that a terrible day was at hand. The stories which are repeated so often in the Koran are mainly intended as warnings. Prophets whose names he had partly from Jews, partly from Christians, partly from pagans, had before this time done the same. They had come to announce a terrible judgment, only to be averted by obeying them and following their law. Those who disobeyed them were shortly overtaken by the judgment, and perished: while the prophet and his followers escaped.

Into this scheme the histories of the Old Testament are worked. Moses, *e. g.*, was sent to Pharaoh, a King of Egypt, who had for colleagues or ministers Haman and Corah. Pharaoh had divided his people into castes, one of which oppressed the other. Moses comes claiming to be the messenger of the Lord of the world. Pharaoh desires him to prove his claim by a sign, which he does. Pharaoh refuses to believe, and in consequence is drowned with his host, whereas the oppressed caste who followed Moses

* *Tabari*, *Comm.*, viii., 12.

inherit the country. This is the framework of the story of Moses as Mohammed first grasped it. Further conversation led him to find out rather more of the history of Moses, which he worked up into his peculiar style, and repeatedly told; at Medinah he even learned a great deal about the history of the children of Israel. But when he had to deal with pagans only, the tale as told above was what he required.

The story in certain cases makes the Prophet's message condemnation of some definite vice. The purpose of the mission of Lot to Sodom naturally suggests itself; a prophet named Shu'aib * is sent to Midyan to warn against deceitful weights and measures; the prophet Hud warns the people of 'Ad against pride, etc. Most frequently the exhortation would seem to have been against polytheism. Mohammed identifies himself in thought with each of these prophets in turn, and in their persons he overcomes the objections of his opponents. He, therefore, in warning the Meccans of the troubles that would befall them could point to all these examples.

It is probably an error to distinguish this punishment very clearly from the Day of Judgment and the future world. To John Bunyan the two were certainly not distinct; the consumption of the earth by heavenly flame and the resurrection to shame and everlasting contempt were sides of the same event; the concepts fade into one another, like the doctrines of Virgil's inferno. At a later period

* Halévy's suggestion that this is a misreading of the Syriac form of Jobab seems adequate.

Mohammed styles the banishment of his enemies, the Nadirites, "the beginning of the resurrection" —a first instalment of the final Judgment.* It is probable that Mohammed wished the Meccans to think that unless they obeyed him they would be swallowed up by the earth, or be crushed by the falling of the sky. And there were at Meccah men who, though true to the rites of paganism, took a philosophical view of the order of events, and justly ridiculed any threat of temporal punishment for disobeying a Prophet. Of the order of events they knew less than the twentieth century knows; but that the moral conduct of mankind had nothing to do with it they were well aware. Hence they scornfully told him to bring down the sky as soon as he pleased, or at any rate required a date for the exhibition. Finding that no amount of threats caused nature to vary her course, the Prophet ingeniously declared that his presence in Meccah prevented the calamity; or that the experience of Allah with other cities which had failed to be convinced by miracles was what prevented him from sending one by Mohammed.†

For indeed a criticism to which the stories of Moses, etc., gave rise was that Mohammed provided no miracle. Moses at the start had been armed with a whole stock of miracles; and though not every prophet appears to have been thus furnished, there was no question of it in the leading cases of Moses and " 'Isa," who made live sparrows out of clay, and

* *Surah* lix., 2.

† *Ibid.* xvii., 61.

Æ. EARLY MOSLEM COIN.
(Bodleian Library.) *Cf.* Lane-Poole, *Or. Coins of the British Museum*, i., p. 174, 4.

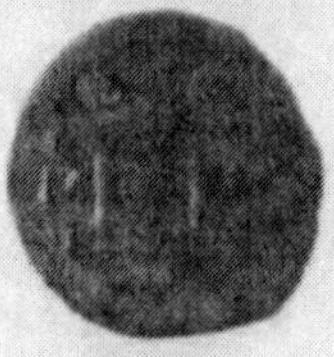

AR. COIN OF KHOSROES II., WITH MOSLEM FORMULA ADDED.
(Bodleian Library.)

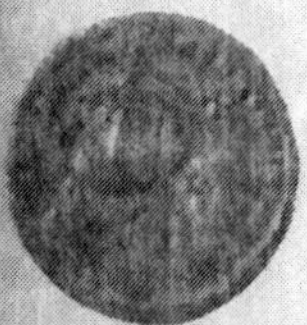

AV. COIN OF HERACLIUS I. AND HERACLIUS CONSTANTINE.
(Bodleian Library.) *Cf.* Sabatier, *Monnaies Byzantines*, pl. xxix., 18.

AR. COIN OF KHOSROES II.
(Bodleian Library.) *Cf.* Longpérier, *Dynastie Sassanide*, pl. xi., 4.

Æ. MOSLEM IMITATION OF COIN OF HERACLIUS, STRUCK AT EMESA.
(Bodleian Library.) *Cf.* Lane-Poole, *Or. Coins of the British Museum*, ix., p. 6.

performed various miracles of healing. It is worth noticing, in order to transfer ourselves into a region of thought so different from that of modern times, that none of the miraculous stories in the Bible or out of it appears to have been received by Mohammed with the semblance of a doubt: hence he repeated those tales in perfectly good faith; thereby laying himself open to this serious objection to his own mission. The miracle which would have pleased the Meccans best would have been some decided improvement in the physical condition of Meccah, especially the production of a perennial river *; but the appearance of an angel, or even supernatural sustenance provided to the Prophet, would have satisfied them: or, like the relations of Dives, they would have wished to see the founder of the tribe—Kusayy, son of Kilab,—rise from the dead and testify to Mohammed's veracity. Or they would have gladly seen Mount Safa turned into gold.† Only on one occasion does he appear to have been induced to venture on a prophecy—the famous declaration that though the Greeks had been defeated by the Persians "in the nearest part of the earth," they would yet again be victorious. The interest of the prophecy for us is that it gives us a date for a Meccan Surah of the Koran; according to the tradition the Meccans at this time favoured the Persians and the Moslems the Greeks; and the prophecy was occasioned by the gratification of the Meccans at the victory of Chosroes over the nearer East in 616. Abu Bakr

* *Ishak*, 185.

† *Musnad*, i., 242.

seems to have made the mistake of betting that it would be fulfilled within five years,* and to have lost in consequence. The guess was not an unnatural one to hazard: and the ambiguity of the Arabic script rendered it as safe as the Delphic communication of Crœsus.†

Many years had to elapse before he could triumphantly meet the demand for a miracle: the battle of Badr, when three hundred Moslems defeated twice the number of Unbelievers, was alleged as a miracle at last. Before that he had to make shift with the Koran. If he had no miraculous power he could reply that he had miraculous knowledge. He had previously been unable to read or write and now he could do both. He had not been present at the scenes of ancient history which he described, and lo and behold, he knew them. If the genuineness of his narrations were disputed, the people who knew—*i. e.*, the Jews and Christians—would attest them. Finally when the Prophet had become perfect in his own peculiar style he could boast that no one without divine aid could compose so well. Let all mankind, with the aid of the Jinn, try to produce ten Suṙahs, or even one, and they would fail.‡

The criticisms on these assertions were numerous and powerful. The reading and writing miracle was

* *Musnad*, i., 276.

† Compare *Riley's* remarks on Joseph Smith's prophecy of the American Civil War, *l. c.*, p. 184.

‡ Similarly Joseph Smith, rebuking one of his associates: "William E. McLellin, the wisest man, in his own estimation, endeavoured to write a commandment like unto one of the least of the Lord's, but failed." *Riley*, p. 322.

probably not urged, because the Prophet was never an adept at either; but to the miraculous character of both the matter and the style of the Koran exception was repeatedly taken. If the Prophet told stories to be found in the Christian and Jewish books, his opponents declared that there were people who taught him and they even undertook to name his mentor. It is not in our power to say with precision whether this charge was just or not: the facts that have been stated in the last chapter are rather against the theory of a mentor. But whether there was a mentor or not, probably the stories were not altogether new to the Meccans, who in the course of business or pleasure had come into contact with Jews and Christians and had heard allusions to the subjects. Hence these Acts of the Prophets were termed "Stories of the Ancients," or perhaps "Old Wives' Fables," which it required no divine interposition to reproduce. One man, Al-Nadir Ibn Harith, accepted the challenge to produce anything as good, and either versified or put into rhyme the tales of the Persian kings which Firdausi some four centuries later rendered immortal—or perhaps those of the kings of Hirah. These "surahs" he read out at séances similar to those in which the Prophet published the Koran. The effect of this criticism must have been very damaging; for when the Prophet at the battle of Badr got the man into his power, he executed him at once, while he allowed the other prisoners to be ransomed.

A further objection to the Koran was that it was revealed in portions or parcels, as occasion required; if really copied from "a well-guarded tablet," why could it not have been produced in a final edition once for all? The reason given by the Prophet was his own personal comfort or convenience*; and similarly we find that Joseph Smith, having published his *Book of Mormon* as a volume, was compelled to supplement it from time to time with occasional revelations. The theory of the "well-guarded tablet" appears to have been more useful to later generations of theologians than to the Prophet himself. It was as a living well of revelation that he won the reverence of his followers: not as one who had access to an otherwise inaccessible book.

Doubtless as the debate between Mohammed and the Meccans continued, the critical powers of the latter were greatly sharpened, and their attention was called to a variety of matters on which they had not previously speculated. The Meccans were constantly taunted with having no sacred book or authority which they could cite for their practice, whereas Mohammed could quote his revelation for the Moslem precepts.† Inquiries were made into the character of other sacred books, which, it was discovered, were mainly in dead and sacred languages: some notions were obtained as to the qualifications and character of persons who were supposed to deliver supernatural messages, and inquiries were suggested concerning the lives of persons whose names were known among the Jews and Christians. Ibn Ishak has a story to the effect that the Meccans

* *Surah* xvii., 107.

† See especially *Surah* vi., 145, 6.

sent two envoys to Medinah to get the opinion of the Jews there, who suggested three questions which Mohammed was to answer if he were to show himself a true Prophet. According to the biographer, Mohammed undertook to answer the questions in a day, and was unable to do so until a fortnight had elapsed, a fact which confirms the theory of the mentor very strongly, which is scarcely weakened by the advice given in the Surah to the Prophet to consult no one.* Since, however, the questions concerned the Seven Sleepers and Alexander the Great, we may be sure that they were not suggested by Jews.

The Koran bears traces of criticisms which his answers to these questions occasioned. Mohammed clearly made a mistake in the number of the Sleepers; in a later edition of the Surah, while adhering to the number which he had originally given, he acknowledged that there were various opinions on the subject, but declared that God must know best. Another statement which had to be corrected was that what is worshipped will be punished as well as the worshipper—a doctrine learned from a Rabbinical Midrash. An ingenious Meccan argued that Jesus would be among the lost in that case. A fresh revelation came to give the necessary exception.†

One who knew mankind less profoundly than Mohammed would probably have been induced by fear of this sort of criticism to have recourse to study to prevent the recurrence of such errors. But Moham-

* *Surah* xviii., 22.

† *Ishak*, 237.

med knew that accuracy and scholarship were of no use for such an enterprise as his. The persons who were prepared to believe in the Revelation were not likely to be affected by the clearest refutation of the errors of the Koran. The danger to be feared from reliance on any living authority was far greater than that which could arise from the most demonstrable misstatements concerning ancient history. Unhesitating assertion and assurance would win respect from Abu Bakr and the like, and be supported by them against all the learning of the "People of the Book," if that could be produced on the other side. There was, however, at this period some difficulty in obtaining it; for, as we have seen, the "People of the Book" were on Mohammed's side.

On the doctrines as opposed to the history of the Koran many criticisms are recorded, such as free-thinking persons would naturally make. The doctrine of the future life could not be dissociated by Mohammed from that of the resurrection of the body, against which there are some very obvious objections. The pagans had believed in some sort of "survival of human personality," but the notion of the reconstruction of the decayed body seemed to them in the highest degree absurd, and Mohammed's promise of heavenly spouses occasioned mirth.* Mohammed was asked to prove his point by bringing them their deceased ancestors. His only reply was the sophism that the resurrection of the body was not more wonderful than its original formation—a process which he is never weary of describing. This, of course, may

* *Wakidi* (*W.*), 131.

be so, but the pagans probably thought that this argument left the matter precisely where it was.

We must, however, acknowledge his wisdom in adhering to this doctrine. His most effective sermons were, as we have seen, descriptions of torture and enjoyment, both of which require and imply the possession of bodily organs. He did not hesitate therefore to assert that the body would be restored for the purpose of enjoying and suffering; and even provided for the danger that suffering might consume the body, by the declaration that it would be renewed repeatedly in order to suffer continuously. These descriptions were not indeed without careless statements which gave rise to ribald criticisms; of which, if no other explanation was forthcoming, he could say that the purpose had been to test the faith of believers, * to see, as we might put it, how much they would be prepared to accept. Or, if the imprudence committed had been too considerable, the verse could be withdrawn. To do this, withdraw a revelation and substitute another for it, was, he asserted, well within the power of God. Doubtless it was, but so obviously within the power of man that it is to us astonishing how so compromising a procedure can have been permitted to be introduced into the system by friends and foes.

Of the mode in which the doctrine of the future life produced conversions we have some anecdotes which may well be true. 'Amr Ibn Al-'Asi† professed to have been converted by the arguments of one who

---

* Joseph Smith used the same plea at times.

† *Isabah.*

asked him whether the Meccans were or were not *better than* the Byzantines and Persians. He replied naturally that the Meccans were better. The next question was whether the Meccans were *better off than* those other nations. He had to reply that they were worse off. Being therefore surpassed in this world, if their superiority were to display itself, it must be in another world. But who knew about such another world save Mohammed? This argument sank in his mind; but he waited to join Mohammed till Fortune had definitely declared herself on the Prophet's side. His former allies noticed his growing coolness, and finally he abandoned them.

Another controversy which occasioned Mohammed some difficulty was that old one of free-will and determinism. The description in the Koran of the omnipotence of God led to the belief that men's acts were God's acts, whence the worship of idols might be regarded as willed by God, and the idolators freed from blame. Mohammed was fortunately too little of a philosopher to perceive the rigidity of this consequence, and the Koran answers this objection as it answers others. Owing however to his repeated declarations on the subject of appointed terms, and events designed by God, the opinion that he was a fatalist has gained ground; traditions were invented in which he positively asserted that human action was all arranged beforehand without the possibility of innovation,* and indeed many of the phenomena of Islam are explained on this supposition. The fact is that his mind was not of a sort to

* *Musnad*, iv., 67, etc.

which contradictory propositions occasion any difficulty. When discontented subjects urged that if their friends had stayed at home instead of going to war they would not have been killed, he could assert with the conviction of common-sense that those who were destined to die on a certain day would have died on that day in any case; but with equal common-sense he could warn men of the consequences which would follow according to the course which they took. The Islamic controversy on this subject belongs to a later age—one in which the works of Aristotle had begun to influence the thinkers of Baghdad.

Thus then the years of the Meccan controversy rolled on; in which the parties increased in vehemence and antagonism, and in which the successful polemics of the Meccans on the new religion were met by ridicule and refutation of the religious notions current among the pagans. As has been said, the Meccan side is known only from the statements of the adversary, whose acquaintance with the Meccan religion may not have been deep. If his statements were to be trusted, we should fancy the Meccans to have been very near monotheism. We should infer that Allah was the national God, to whom they appealed in any trouble, whereas in times of comfort and quiet they slid back into polytheism. We should suppose that they recognised Allah as the Creator of heaven and earth, and assigned the other deities quite subordinate functions. "How many deities do you worship?" Mohammed is supposed to have asked a Khuza'ite (Hasin, son of

'Ubaid),* sent to reason with him by the Kurashites. "Seven on earth and one in heaven," was the reply, and further conversation elicited the confession that in all serious trouble the God of heaven (Allah) only was invoked. And doubtless to other followers Mohammed's innovation appeared to lie in the merging of all minor cults in that of the heaven God. At a later time the chief of the tribe Muzainah, who broke the idol Nahum, declared in his verse that he henceforth worshipped the God of heaven.† A Thakafite convert (from Ta'if, twin city to Meccah) asked Mohammed whether he should keep a vow made before conversion; since questioning elicited the fact that the vow had been made to Allah, not to an idol, Mohammed declared that it should be kept.‡

The above assumptions are frequently required for the reasoning of the Koran and are unhesitatingly made. The Meccans are taunted with worshipping additional deities who, being feminine, are called Allah's daughters, and who are identified by them with the Christian angels. These beings, though theoretically inferior to Allah, are said to receive a larger share in the offerings. Naturally we cannot implicitly trust a case as stated by the adversary; and it is even permissible to suppose that the Meccan worship of Allah consisted of no more than a belief in the power of the God worshipped by Jews and Christians; but the statements that the Meccan

---

* *Isabah*, i., 692.

† *Ibid.*, i., 874.

‡ *Ibid.*, iii., 581; *Musnad*, iii., 419.

deities were daughters of Allah and worshipped as intercessors may have been ventured in the course of the argument with Mohammed, when perhaps for the first time the Meccan reasoners began to reflect on the nature of their religion.* Yet difficulties assail us at every turn. The theory that Allah had daughters is refuted by the statement that a daughter is regarded as a misfortune, so that if Allah had children at all, he would certainly have had sons instead; implying that this theory of the children of Allah did not apply to the *male* deities, which however the Meccans as well as other Arab tribes are known to have worshipped. We fancy that this argument about daughters brought on Mohammed some well-deserved taunts about having only daughters himself; and indeed a Surah is revealed endeavouring to console him and clear him of the charge of being *abtar* or sonless.

From some texts† and traditions we should gather that the Meccan objection was not to the glorification of *Allah*, but to the identification of their familiar deity with him whom the Jews called *Rahmān* (the Merciful), a title applied to pagan deities also. But the reason of this objection lies beyond our reach.

In estimating the arguments of the Koran with the Meccans we must constantly remember that Mohammed is playing the part of a Hebrew Prophet, recalling his countrymen to the sole worship of the national God, whose rites have been abandoned for

* So *Wellhausen*, *Reste*, 208.

† So *Surah* xvii., 110.

other and idolatrous cults. That part he may indeed have sincerely believed himself to be playing; and in the scene as he represents it, he probably assigned corresponding rôles to his antagonists. But if the paganism of Meccah really came so near monotheism as the Koran represents it, it is clear that with a little good-will and candour the differences of detail might have been made up.

Those qualities, however, were not present. As the controversy progressed, there arose among the Meccans a personal dislike of Mohammed which to us does not seem unintelligible. Although the later myths represent him as a member of a noble family, the Koran confesses that this was not so: if the Meccans were to be reformed, they would have preferred being reformed by a man of rank either of Meccah or of Ta'if. Political and religious headship could not be separated: and they were not prepared to see Mohammed at the head of the state.

Hence the debate went on, not to be settled till more powerful weapons than words had been brought to bear upon it. Though Mohammed's life was spared, he had, apparently, to put up with much rudeness, and occasionally even with personal violence. As he prostrated himself in his newly invented ceremony of prayers, some one threw some camel's refuse over his back, and probably similar insults were not uncommon. The persons on whom the Prophet invoked curses were four,—Abu Jahl, 'Utbah, son of Rabi'ah, Shaibah, son of Rabi'ah, Umayyah, son of Khalef. Legends were afterwards invented showing how all who either injured the

Prophet or mocked at the Koran were divinely punished. During the vicissitudes of this period, its successes and failures, conquests and rebuffs, the Koran served as the Prophet's faithful confidant —like Lucilius, thither he would recur whether he were doing well or badly. In it he records—or lets Allah record for him—the sayings and doings of his enemies, his own chagrin and despondency, and the reflections wherewith he is consoled. Were its verses only dated, we should know his state of mind from day to day, in the years which witnessed the struggling of Islam into the light. But even during these years Apollo was not always drawing his bow. Much of the Koran is not polemical, but homiletic or narrative. Whatever fragments of the Old or New Testament, of the Lives of the Saints, of the Sayings of the Jewish Fathers, or of ordinary folklore happened to be in the Prophet's memory were regarded by him as suitable matter for the Koran. He does not often venture to quote his sources by name; in exceptional cases he mentions that some sentiment or other is "written by Us" in the Psalms of David or the Law of Moses: and in quite early passages the Rolls of Abraham and Moses are cited. The name of the Law appears to have been learned by him in the course of controversy; and there is some probability that the "Sayings of the Fathers" called by the Jews *Perakim* lie hidden in the name of a sacred book which he calls *Furkan.*

At times his homilies are somewhat like those to be heard from modern pulpits, in which a preacher tells a biblical story, adding some detail from his fancy and amplifying or explaining on the way. The story which is told at greatest length and with most continuity is that of Joseph—that famous biblical romance which Eastern Christians never tired of versifying or re-telling in a variety of ways. Once or twice, too, he recollects enough of the Bible to be able to tell the history of Moses and Aaron with an approach to accuracy. A story of Moses and a prophet whom the Moslems identify with Elijah seems to be a conflation of a number of anecdotes about different persons. Of several heroes he knows the story but is unable to give names: this is notably the case with Dhu'l-Karnain, who is doubtless Alexander the Great. But of the greater number of biblical and other heroes his knowledge is clearly meagre in the extreme. He knows of Solomon's acquaintance with the Jinn and with the Queen of Sheba—this story, as being connected with Arabia, was doubtless familiar even to some of the Meccans; his knowledge of it, however, comes from Jewish story-tellers, not from the Bible. We should have expected him to know of Solomon's judgment,* being a narrative of a style which would have suited him; evidently he had not heard of it, but had heard of David and Nathan, though he has very seriously misstated the episode. Of Penelope's web he had also heard, but the Arabs, who find a native Penelope, had not.

Ingenuity has been well spent in discovering the sources of the Koran, and the amount that is of un-

* Knowledge of it is ascribed to him in the Tradition.

certain origin is not large. Probably the author should not be denied to possess some felicity of expression, some exuberance of fancy, and even some poetical sublimity. If, to us, the repetitions in the Koran seem intolerable, it must be remembered that the men who have impressed the world most are those who have always been saying the same about the same things. Napoleon said there is only one rhetorical figure of serious importance and that is repetition.* Just as the hearers of Socrates were prepared to be told or questioned about the tailor and the shoemaker, so the hearers of Mohammed could not hear too often the tales of 'Ad and Thamud, or the legends of Abraham and Lot.

In some cases the Surahs appear to be merely the product of an exuberant and poetical fancy, to which it can only be regretted that theological value should have ever been assigned. Such a Surah is the narrative of the Jinn listening to his preaching and being converted; they profess horror at the blasphemies of the idolators; they acknowledge that the shooting stars are now driving them away from the heavenly councils where they used to listen. This Surah is a pleasing effusion, to be compared with Horace's account of his vision of Pan, whose followers, the spirits of the woods, are not very unlike the Jinn, who were spirits of the desert. Such, too, was the lost Surah in which the Prophet described his nocturnal visit to Jerusalem, which, as we have seen, gave offence, and was withdrawn.

**Lebon*, *Crowds*, p. 126.

But, besides the recitation of the Koran, to which direct descent from heaven was ascribed, there were utterances of the Prophet called "The Wisdom," which were only made infallible at a later time through logical necessity. These were nearer the modern sermon in that their delivery was neither accompanied nor preceded by the signs of possession; and they appear to have consisted of aphorisms on a variety of subjects, of which conduct was perhaps the chief. The writing down of this table-talk was forbidden by the Prophet, and of the great mass of the matter which is ascribed to him we cannot be sure that as much as a tenth was actually said by him. At times, however, the reports of this table-talk circulated and gave rise to criticisms no more sparing than those which the Koran called forth. Occasionally, too, the Koran makes allusions to the Prophet's sayings, when their author had special reason to be gratified with them. Large numbers of the dicta ascribed to him are aphorisms, pithy sayings either about himself or others, such as that the three things about which he cared were scent, women, and prayer; or formulæ in which he summarised the theological view which for the moment dominated his mind, as that a man's heart is between two of God's fingers, to be turned whither God will, or that every new-born child is attacked by Satan, and cries in consequence. "When a man dies three follow him, but only one stays with him: he is followed by his family, his property, and his works; his works abide, and the rest return." *

* *Bokhari*, iv., 81.

"Three things gladden the eye of the gazer: green fields, running water, and fair faces." *

Of any moralising or demoralising effect which Mohammed's teaching had upon his followers, we cannot speak with precision. When he was at the head of a robber community it is probable that the demoralising influence began to be felt; it was then that men who had never broken an oath learnt that they might evade their obligations,† and that men to whom the blood of the clansmen had been as their own began to shed it with impunity in the cause of God; and that lying and treachery in the cause of Islam received divine approval, hesitation to perjure oneself in that cause being reprehended as a weakness. ‡ It was then, too, that Moslems became distinguished by the obscenity of their language. § It was then, too, that the coveting of goods and wives (possessed by Unbelievers) was avowed without discouragement from the Prophet. Yet it was then, too, that the theory of mutual obligations between the members of the Moslem brotherhood became clearly evolved, and the morality which is necessary for the existence of the state was most earnestly enforced. At Meccah, however, it is not likely that these developments showed themselves. On the other hand, there is no evidence that the Moslems were either in personal or altruistic morality better than the pagans, though persons who had

---

* *Schol. Hariri*, 492.

† *Bokhari*, iv., 90; *Musnad*, iv., 256.

‡ *Musnad*, iv., 79.

§ *Ishak*, 433, 744; *Ibn Sa'd*, iii., 116, 13.

been successful traders before conversion found their new life incompatible with business.* Liquor was not yet forbidden, and even in Medinah we find Mohammed's uncle savage from drink, while an ordinance that Believers were not to pray when in a state of intoxication, for fear they should maul their prayers, implies that intoxication was no uncommon state for Believers to be found in.† The suppression of gambling was also a measure of the Medinah period; but since the gambling practised at Meccah was probably a religious ceremony, it is likely that the adoption of monotheism prevented the Believers from taking part in it. Of improvements in sexual morality it is difficult to speak with precision; it is probable that prostitution was already forbidden by the Prophet, though there is reason for supposing that it was regarded at Meccah somewhat as it has been regarded at most great capitals: as an offence against decorum, but not as involving any serious stigma on the man. It was recorded in after times for the benefit of posterity, that "the Apostle" Zubair, son of 'Awwam, gave his wife so sound a beating that he broke her arm‡; and our authorities frequently entertain us with specimens of conjugal bickerings among the converts.§ There can be no doubt, however, that the liability to persecution under which the Moslems suffered led to a more stringent morality on their part than they

* Abu'l-Darda, *Isabah*, iii., 89.

† Cf. *Musnad*, iii., 447.

‡ *Jahiz, Mahasin*, 235.

§ So *Ibn Sa'd II.*, ii., 86.

had previously practised; for it is only so that persecuted communities can survive; and the need for mutual support certainly led to some degree of altruism.

Further, Islam had the effect rightly emphasised by Wellhausen, of making men earnest. The experience of even our own day shows that revivalistic preaching can be highly effective in this way; those whom experience of earthly misery does not affect are often made earnest by being threatened with eternal fire and eternal contempt. Some of the converts certainly wished to be ascetics, and were only prevented by the express admonitions of Mohammed, who resolved to have no monkery in Islam. Of one it is recorded that, alarmed by Mohammed's declaration that the Day of Judgment was at hand, he went and sold his five hundred sheep, probably spending the proceeds in the path of God. *

* *Isabah*, ii., 128.

CHAPTER V

HISTORY OF THE MECCAN PERIOD.

THE fact that Mohammed kept his mission secret as long as possible shows that he was aware that it was fraught with danger. What steps were thought legitimate at Meccah in the case of one who had abandoned the gods of his country we know not; it is, however, certain that the gods suffer by the neglect of their dues, and as they have representatives on earth, some men suffer thereby also. And since the favour of the gods is thought to be necessary for the well-being of the state, many persons who have no other commercial interest in the matter are anxious to suppress heresy for fear of offending their masters. From whatever motives, then, there were many persons in Meccah from whom Mohammed anticipated opposition. By the time that he was compelled to face it, he was fairly well entrenched.

With perhaps the exception of Abu Sufyan, the Meccan magnates are obscure figures. When they died unconverted tradition is silent about them; when they lived to embrace Islam it wilfully perverts their biographies. Abu Sufyan probably was not a prominent opponent till after the battle of Badr, when he headed the Meccans against Mohammed till the taking of the city; proving himself throughout the period not altogether incompetent or wanting in energy, but intellectually no match for the Prophet. A tradition * makes him one of a party of free-thinkers, who had learned atheism from the "Christians of the Harrah": and to his scepticism he added loose morality.† The callousness to insults and injuries which formed so remarkable a trait in his son Mu'awiyah appears to have characterised him also, since we find him employing as lieutenant Khalid, son of Al-Walid, whose brother had killed a man protected by Abu Sufyan, thereby causing the death of many Kurashites.‡ Of Mohammed's opponents before the Flight the most prominent appear to have been Abu Jahl, or Abu 'l-Hakam, son of Hisham, of the tribe Makhzum; and the Prophet's uncle Abu Lahab Abd al-'Uzza.§ The former enjoyed a great reputation for sagacity; at thirty years of age he had been admitted to the Council Chamber, whereas other Meccans had to wait till their fortieth year.‖ The latter, like Abu Sufyan, is said to have been a loose liver, involved among others in the theft of the golden gazelles placed in the Ka'bah, which he and his companions melted down to distribute among

---

* *Lata'if al-Ma'arif*, 64.

† *Ibid.*, 63.

‡ *Ibn Duraid*, 295.

§ The name means "father of flame," and was given him, it is said, owing to his red complexion.

‖ *Ibn Duraid*, 97.

their singing women; an act for which he would have lost his hand, had not the Khuza'ah, to whom his mother belonged, interceded.* He professed great devotion to the goddess Al-'Uzza,† as a speculation, however, on the chance of her having an existence; ready to console himself, in the other event, with the fact that her arch-enemy, Mohammed, was his nephew. These two persons appear, at times at least, to have used violence, and the same is asserted of Abdallah, son of Umayyah, the Prophet's cousin; whereas the others who are named seem to have done more to suppress rioting and brawls than to have deliberately brought them on. The hands of all alike were tied by fear of bloodshed; but in the case of humble converts they were ready to come very near that limit. The persons whose accession to Islam was most welcomed were men of physical strength, and much actual fighting must have taken place at Meccah before the Flight; else the readiness with which the Moslems after the Flight could produce from their number tried champions would be inexplicable. A tried champion must have been tried somewhere: and no external fights are recorded or are even the subject of an allusion for this period. The Prophet himself is said on one occasion after reciting Surah xxxvi. to have flung dust on the heads of his opponents.‡ And the wise principle of hitting back when hit appears to have characterised the new religion from its start, and to

---

* *Ibn Duraid*, 76.

† *Azraki*, 81.

‡ *Wakidi* (*W.*), 51.

have been the cause of its speedy success. We learn incidentally * that the Prophetic office did not prevent Mohammed from continuing to work at his business; but those of his followers who were in dependent situations certainly lost them. Those who like Khalid, son of Sa 'id, were driven from their homes by indignant parents had to be fed at the Prophet's table. The growth of the new religion tended to spread discord between families and so keep the city in a state of turmoil and confusion. Those who for any reason felt aggrieved with their condition could gratify their ill-will by joining Mohammed; and some probably did this in momentary pique. Desperadoes of whom the whole city was ashamed seem to have been received into the fold of Islam; they could then on the strength of their faith claim to be better than their neighbours.

A measure which seems to us both natural and harmless was taken by the Meccans; the Moslems were kept out of the Precincts of the Ka'bah. When they came there their devotions were rudely interrupted.

From personal violence the Prophet himself was ordinarily secured by the protection of his relations, especially when his uncle, the mighty hunter Hamzah, joined Islam—we know not why: one tradition says, because of his indignation at the insults inflicted on Mohammed by Abu Jahl; another that he demanded (like Philip) to be shown the Angel Gabriel, and with this request Mohammed complied; the Angel, whose feet were of emerald, appearing

* *Ishak*, 189.

mounted on a clothes-horse in the Ka'bah.* If this story be true, we should couple with it another, presently to meet us, where Hamzah figures disgracefully intoxicated.† Hamzah's sword was destined to do good service later on.

After a time the situation became intolerable. The resources of the Believers who were independent were insufficient to support the strain of their starving brethren, nor was the life of the latter endurable, amid ceaseless vexations and persecutions. A few, as we learn from the Koran, fell away, though the Prophet assured them that their sufferings were slight compared with those which monotheists in former times had to endure. The idea which so readily occurs, and which has so often proved the salvation of persecuted communities suggested itself. God's earth was wide, so why should not those who were injured in their native country flee to another? Thus a few generations ago the Mormons, vexed and persecuted, fled to a new land and started a now thriving colony. That the Moslems did not do this may be attributed to their being essentially artisans and traders, accustomed to the handling, not to the production, of raw materials. Moreover, the permanent abandonment of Meccah seems never to have entered the Prophet's mind, though the mode in which the Meccan sanctuary was worked into his system was probably the product of slow develop-

---

* *Ibn Sa'd*, iii., 6.

† Still it may have been a case of "hypnotic hallucination,"—the mode whereby *Riley* explains the evidence of the three witnesses who saw Joseph Smith's gold plates. *Loc. cit.*, p. 212.

VIEW OF MASSOVA.
From a lithograph.

ment. Still a temporary refuge was clearly desirable and Mohammed had not to look far to find it. In that country which had sent effective aid to the persecuted Arabian Christians and which had manifested detestation of the Meccan idolatry, Mohammed resolved to find a refuge for his followers, perhaps looking forward to seeing them return at the head of an Abyssinian army.* Among those with whom he had associated there had certainly been Abyssinians, and indeed he had himself most likely visited the country, so as to know something of its conditions.

The Meccans were in commercial relations with the state of Axum, whose port Massoua is separated by an easy journey from the Arabian coast. The beginnings of Christianity in that country are lost in obscurity, and its chronicles up to the Portuguese invasion are all fabulous. But Greek authors attest the Arabian legend which makes the Negus in the sixth century send an army to the relief of the persecuted Christians in South Arabia; and every Meccan child knew that an Abyssinian force had been sent to destroy the Ka'bah and had been miraculously repelled. Thither (in the fifth year of the mission, it is said)† the Moslems began to slink away, probably in small groups, though the number of refugees reached in time eighty-three families. At the head of the list one tradition places the weakly Othman, son of 'Affan, with his wife Rukayyah, Mohammed's daughter, whereas another

* This suggestion is made by Sir William Muir.

† *Wakidi* in *Dhakha'ir wa A'lak*, 204.

makes the first refugee a certain Hatib, son of 'Amr, who occupies otherwise no prominent place in the history. The remainder of the list seems to include nearly all the persons who were enumerated among the converts. Ja'far, Abu Talib's son, was one of the emigrants. Abu Bakr started for Abyssinia, but was recalled by the promise of protection of a certain Ibn Dughunnah. Abu Bakr, however, performed his orisons with so much ostentation, and thereby attracted so much attention that his patron had publicly to withdraw his protection. In some cases the Meccans endeavoured to prevent the flight of their persecuted brethren: this is recorded of Salamah, brother of Abu Jahl.

Little is known of the condition of the refugees in Abyssinia. The bulk of our information is derived from the narative of Umm Salamah, wife of Abdallah Ibn Abd al-Asad, who afterwards became wife of the Prophet. Some of the matter contained in this narrative is certainly afterthought; but the employment of some Ethiopic words in the speeches of the King of Abyssinia which she records, seems evidence of authenticity. How these people lived in Abyssinia is not known, nor do we even know whether they and the Abyssinians were mutually intelligible.* Their life there was not of a sort which can have been very enjoyable, since they all manifested great anxiety to return, with the exception of such as became Christians. One of the refugees (Asma, daughter of Unais) described it as miserable to the last

* Interpreters are required between Abyssinians and Arabs, *Nöldeke, Sass.*, 220.

degree.* Perhaps they found some menial employments, enabling them to earn a livelihood. No great interest was at first manifested in them by the King, who was probably not averse to the reception of immigrant aliens.

According to Umm Salamah, however, the Meccans were not disposed to lose so considerable a number of their fellow-citizens. At a later time we find them unreasonably tenacious of citizens who by abandoning their religion had ceased to be of any use to themselves; they preferred keeping them in chains at home to letting them go free. The reason for this is in part to be found in the institution called *munāfarah*,† a sort of contest in which men endeavoured to prove their families to be the biggest; ridiculed in the Koran, where some one is said to swell the list by counting gravestones. Hence a voluntary exile was said to bid defiance to his friends.‡ A deputation consisting of Abdallah (then called Bujair), son of Abu Rabi'ah, and father of a celebrated poet, and 'Amr, son of Al-'Asi, afterwards famous, was sent to induce the King to extradite them. 'Amr, son of Al-'Asi, was well known at the Abyssinian court, where he had revealed to the King the unfaithfulness of one of his queens,§ and so avenged his own wrong while he avenged the King's. They were told to take presents to the nobles and approach the King through

* *Muslim*, ii., 265.

† *Goldziher*, *M. S.*, i., 56.

‡ *Ibn Duraid*, 223.

§ *Agh*, viii., 53.

them. The way having been duly paved, the envoys submitted their desire that their misguided brethren might be handed over to them; returned, we must suppose, with an Abyssinian escort to the Arabian coast. The King wished to know first what the new religion was. An assembly was called at which Ja'far, being summoned to reply, read out *the earlier part** of Surah xix., a discourse specially prepared by Mohammed for this occasion. Its description of the experiences of the Virgin Mary moved the Negus to tears; and he resolved never to abandon these followers of Christ. The disappointed envoys endeavoured to show the King that Mohammed's views of the nature of Christ were unorthodox, but the King, to their vexation, declared the Koranic doctrine on that matter to be the solely true one.

How much of this narrative is true is not known. From a later anecdote Ja'far appears incidentally to have had some experience of the Negus's court.† It is in any case a fact that the Negus favoured the cause of Mohammed against the Kuraish, and remained Mohammed's faithful friend to his death; when success had crowned Mohammed's arms he restored his followers to him, and went to the expense of finding the dowry of one of his numerous brides, Ethiopian Christianity, unlike most other branches, tolerating polygamy. Without an Abyssinian account of the affair we cannot make out certainly the King's motives or the actual course of Mohammed's policy.

---

* *Wakidi*, *Dhakha'ir*, 205.

† *Wakidi* (*W.*), 302.

OBELISKS AT AXUM.
From an engraving.

The XIXth Surah is (like many others) a summary of the Prophet's teaching, only in it the story of the Nativity occupies the chief place; we fancy Warakah's translation of the Gospel must have come in useful at this period. The indignant denial which it contains of the divine sonship of Jesus is without question an addition inserted at a later time; Mohammed avoided that thorny matter till it became politic for him to quarrel with Christians. The part which is likely to have been read before the King is an innocent reproduction of statements current in Christian books, with some touches from the Prophet's fancy; the story that Christ spoke in the cradle is likely to have been known in Abyssinia, and, even if heard for the first time, would have given no offence. We cannot well believe that Ja'far translated this Surah, which derives so much of its beauty from the rhyme, into another language; hence we fancy the Abyssinian audience must have been able to guess at the meaning of a tale in a dialect so closely allied to their own.

When Moslems began to persecute Christians, they were doubtless taunted with the memory of this timely help, whereby the early community had been saved from destruction. Fictions were then excogitated showing how the Negus had been, not a Christian, but a follower of Islam. On the analogy of similar scenes we should suppose that the envoys of Mohammed urged the Negus to take an active part in suppressing paganism, reminding him of the Abyssinian rule in South Arabia, a fact which gave him some sort of title to the country; and that the idea of regaining this ancient possession was what led him to favour the Meccan insurgents.

An important event, the conversion of Omar, is placed about the time of the first secession.* This man was some ten years the Prophet's junior, a famous horseman and of herculean strength; like Hamzah he was addicted to wine; in his youth he had suffered from extreme poverty†; like the rest of the Meccans he was engaged in trade, and had a Bedouin's cunning.‡ He tried in his trading expeditions to evade the tax on gold exacted by the Ghassanides, by making a camel swallow the money, and afterwards slaughtering the camel and recovering the coins. The Ghassanide official let himself be cheated once this way, but a second time he was able to detect the camel that had been tampered with, and outwitted Omar. Omar's camel had to disgorge the money, and its master to satisfy himself with threats of vengeance. Like St. Paul, to whom he has been compared, he persecuted the religion of which he afterwards became a champion. Mohammed, with his unfailing skill in judging men, eagerly desired to have this man among his supporters; and though our authorities are silent concerning the steps which he took to obtain this end, the facts that Omar was converted after his sister, and that the sister was married to the son of a monotheist, supply materials for reconstruction of the process. A story

* Dhu'l-Hijjah of the year 6 of the Mission. *Ibn Sa'd*, iii., 193.

† *Baihaki*, *Mahasin*, 301.

‡ *Isabah*, ii., 21. Verses by him are occasionally quoted. *Ibn Duraid*, 225.

was circulated that the husband's father had died searching for that faith which Mohammed was authorised to preach.¶ Of Omar's conversion a variety of accounts are given, several agreeing in that they ascribe it to the charm of the Koran. The most popular make him embrace Islam at the house of his sister Fatimah (or Ramlah), wife of Sa'id, son of Zaid, both of them secret proselytes. Khabbab, son of Al-Aratt, was reading a Surah (No. xx.) at their house, when they were surprised by the entry of Omar. The scripture-reader fled precipitately, leaving the roll with Fatimah, who tried in vain to hide it; Omar demanding it, and being refused, wounded his sister with his sword. The sight of the blood made him penitent; he begged humbly to see the roll, which was granted him, if he washed before touching it. He read a portion of the Surah and asked to be taken to Mohammed, to make his confession of faith. The scripture-reader, hearing this, emerged from his hiding-place, and escorted Omar to the Prophet. Hamzah, who was hiding with the Prophet, undertook to kill Omar if he meant mischief, but he came as a proselyte and was warmly welcomed. He proceeded at once to communicate the intelligence of his conversion to the amateur town-crier, and visited Abu Jahl, the inveterate enemy of Islam, who thanked him for the information by shutting the door in his face.

The Moslems could now come out of their places of concealment, and even pray openly in the precincts. Such was the fear which his strength inspired. "If Satan were to meet Omar," said

Mohammed, "he would get out of Omar's way."* Yet we have no record of any occasion on which Omar displayed remarkable courage, though many examples are at hand of his cruelty and bloodthirstiness; at the battle of Hunain he ran away,† and on another occasion owed his life to the good nature of an enemy.

Probably the above story is in the main true. Novelists sometimes employ similar motives; an impetuous but chivalrous man finds that he has rushed into an ungentlemanly act, and in his extreme desire to atone loses command of his will. The shock which Omar experienced at having wounded his sister made him anxious to do anything which would atone for it; the most obvious course being to express admiration for the Koran and become a Moslem, he hastens to adopt that; he is admitted into the society, and becomes its most fanatical member. Moreover, to this sister he appears to have been fondly attached; when, as children, they looked after their mother's camel in the desert, Omar used when it grew hot to throw his garment over his sister and tend the beast, exposed without any covering to the sunshine.‡ This explains the difficulty that Omar's conduct on other occasions displays no trace of chivalry. He was a wife-beater§; he went to the length of scourging some women for weeping over the death of one of Mohammed's daughters‖; and

* *Muslim*, ii., 234.

† *Wakidi* (*W*.), 361.

‡ *Baihaki*, *Mahasin*, 301.

§ *Musnad*, iii., 328.

‖ *Ibid.*, i., 237, etc. Cf. *Goldziher*, *M. S.*, i., 253.

at other times interfered with women's concerns in a manner which displays a nature of extreme coarseness. It must further be added in explanation of his conversion that he belonged to a humble clan, and had therefore something to gain by the equality which Islam promised. Years after, when Caliph, he took a delight in humiliating the aristocrat Abu Sufyan, thanking God that through Islam a member of his humble family could command one of the illustrious Abd Manaf.* Mohammed, who with the view of breaking the family and tribal ties instituted brotherhoods between pairs of his followers, coupled Omar with his principal adherent, Abu Bakr †; and in spite of the difference of their dispositions we hear of only one serious quarrel between them. ‡ Where they agreed the Prophet regularly took their advice. § The tradition regularly represents Omar as recommending violence where Abu Bakr is for gentle measures; Mohammed did not often take his advice in such cases, yet made him one of the innermost cabinet; the formula, "I, Abu Bakr, and Omar," was constantly on his lips. ‖ When the Prophet adopted his suggestions he ordinarily professed to have arrived at them independently. This process by no means weakened Omar's confidence, whose belief was only shaken when the Prophet allowed his rights as Messenger of Allah to be curtailed. When the

* *Azraki*, 448.
† *Ishak*, 934.
‡ *Musnad*, iv., 6.
§ *Ibid.*, iv., 227.
‖ *Muslim*, ii., 232.

Prophet, having declined to wear silk himself, on one occasion offered a silken robe to Omar, the latter burst into tears.*

If the Kuraish were indignant before these developments their fury now rose many degrees. The envoys whom they had despatched to Abyssinia returned with the news that their presents had been refused by the lord of Axum, who had trusted Mohammed's followers rather than them; *they* knew all about Mohammed and his antecedents, and their opinion had no effect with the Negus; the starveling Refugees had greater weight than they. The affront involved assuredly made the Meccan aristocrats feel sore. But what was more important, Abyssinian assistance must have reminded every Meccan of their invasion of Arabia, and the misconduct which led to the heroic efforts of Saif, son of Dhu Yazan, to eject them. The return of their presents to the Meccan envoys looked like a declaration of *war;* as such we find this act regarded in negotiations between the Wahhabis and Ibrahim Pasha, recorded by Palgrave.† What more likely than that the anticipation of Mohammed would be fulfilled, and an army be sent to abolish the Meccan rites, and with them the Meccan commerce? There is little reason for doubting that the founder of Islam, in sending his followers to Axum, designed some such dénouement. A few years afterwards he readily allied himself with another city—it is said—with the express object of fighting all the world in the cause of his religion.

* *Muslim*, ii., 153.

† *Travels*, ii., 51.

The reason why this fear was not realised is suggested by Umm Salamah. Shortly after the arrival of the Refugees the Negus was involved in a frontier war: with whom, she does not record; but the history of Abyssinia suggests many possibilities. The Refugees awaited with the extremest anxiety the result of the battle, which would be likely to influence their fate. It turned out (she says) favourably for the Negus; but is likely to have put the Meccan business out of his head.

The story of the conversion of Omar represents him as endeavouring to find Mohammed, armed with a sword for the purpose of freeing Meccah from the impostor. This trait is probably borrowed from the Omar of later days, who was accustomed to solve every knot with that weapon. The fear of a blood-feud between the Meccan families acted like an impassable barrier, keeping that expedient out of the Meccans' reach. The time was not ripe for their bracing themselves to contemplate such a thing, and even when it came their clumsiness and timidity rendered the attempt abortive. There was, however, a process, known to pagan Arabs no less than Christians, which they could attempt without violating their consciences. This was *excommunication*, depriving the culprit's family of the *jus connubii* and *jus commercii:* a purpose for which special confederacies were established. * Rolls would seem to have been in common use at this time in Meccah: a solemn league and covenant was made, written on a roll, and suspended in the Ka'bah, by which the heads

* *Goldziher*, *M. S.*, i., 65.

of the Meccan households pledged themselves to exclude the Banu Hashim and the Banu 'l-Muttalib from these rights, until, we may presume, Mohammed was declared outlawed, and handed up to vengeance. The scribe was himself a member of the Hashim clan; but it apparently was open to members of the clan to forswear their clanship, and so escape the ban. Abu Lahab, the Prophet's uncle, was one of those who took advantage of this option; and he is perhaps cursed in the Koran in consequence; Mohammed's cousin, Abu Sufyan, son of Al-Harith, was another.* The whole Hashimite clan, with these exceptions, congregated in Abu Talib's ravine, where they probably lived on Khadijah's resources. The ravine was capable of holding as many as four thousand persons and could be defended against attacks.† Like other prisoners, the Hashimites could obtain food, but at famine prices. The careless generosity of the Meccans and their vacillating wills did much to render the blockade ineffective. One Mut'im, son of 'Adi, rendered such services that Mohammed afterwards would have made him a present of all the prisoners of Badr. Hisham, son of 'Amr, who was remotely connected with the Hashimites, used to send beasts laden with provisions into the ravine.‡ There were other persons, some of whom, like Sahl, son of Wahb, afterwards professed to have been secret converts, to whom the "Scroll" was distasteful, and

* *Wakidi* (*W.*), 328.

† *Chronicles of Meccah*, ii., 31.

‡ *Ishak*, 247.

who endeavoured to get it cancelled. Meanwhile the Moslems then no more than at any other time believed in the doctrine of turning the other cheek. One of the Prophet's cousins, Tulaib, son of 'Umair, actually wounded Abu Lahab, and being captured by the Kuraish would have been dispatched, but that Abu Lahab, generous as usual, protected him.* Abu Jahl also is said to have been battered in an encounter with some of Mohammed's friends.†

The duration of the ban is given as two or three years. The number of persons who were affected by it is not exactly known, but it is certain that it must have been very considerable: a sufficient number to render a feud a serious matter. One of those affected was the Prophet's uncle Abbas, whose son Abdallah, born during the ban, became eminent among the fathers of the Mohammedan Church.

The period of the ban is artistically filled by the biographers with notices of Koranic controversies; but it is probable that the controversy belonged to an earlier period, and that the war of deeds was after rather than simultaneous with the war of words. The Abyssinian card was one of enormous value—not so valuable as that of Medinah afterwards proved to be, yet capable of being played with great effect. All the argumentation of the Koran, which indeed few in Meccah could understand,‡ was far outweighed by the testimonial of the great man. The Negus believed Mohammed was a

---

* *Isabah* after *Baladhuri*.

† *Tabari*, i., 1190.

‡ *Surah* xi., 93.

prophet; that fact could now be flaunted in advertisements, and the Meccans who probably saw in this testimonial merely a desire on the part of the Abyssinians to interfere with their affairs, found that Mohammed from being vexatious had become dangerous. He had, in fact, by the Negus's patronage of the cause become *a political power;* a person hated, indeed, but feared rather than despised. Meanwhile Mohammed's resources were being severely strained, and he probably had to bear many a reproach from the clansmen whom he had so seriously compromised; but developments from Abyssinia were worth awaiting, and the result of the Abyssinian campaign was probably watched for in Meccah with considerable anxiety.

What we know is that a compromise was presently arrived at: and the causes which led to the compromise may be thus divined. After the Abyssinians' campaign had proved successful, it was important for the Meccans to persuade their fugitives to come home, so that there might be no further fear of an Abyssinian invasion. On the other hand, the Prophet was probably aware that such an invasion would be a doubtful advantage to himself, since the Abyssinians would conquer, if at all, for themselves. Let Mohammed make some reasonable concession to Al-Lāt and Al-'Uzza, and Allah's Prophet would be recognised.

This was in effect what happened. The Prophet produced a revelation in which Al-Lāt, etc., were raised from the position of "names invented by your fathers for which Allah has given no authority" to that of "intercessors whose intercession might be hoped." The scene for its delivery seems to have been carefully prepared. The inhabitants of Meccah thronged the precincts; the Prophet appeared, delivered his discourse, and paid his high compliment to the goddesses whom he had previously treated so cavalierly. He prostrated himself at the end of the discourse, and the congregation prostrated themselves also. One whom the stiffness of old age prevented from joining in the ceremony took soil from the ground and applied it to his brow. The news flew fast that Allah and the goddesses had become friends—that the Kuraish had accepted Islam, or that Mohammed had fallen back into paganism. The ban on the Hashimites was withdrawn; the Abyssinian Refugees returned.

The compromise, which to us appears wise and statesmanly, was regarded as the most discreditable episode in the Prophet's career, and in the chief edition of his biography it is suppressed. In the edition which preserves it Mohammed is represented as returning to monotheism the same day.* The release of the Hashimites from the ban is disconnected from the compromise, and ascribed to the action of certain individuals whose tender hearts were afflicted with the thought of a Kurashite tribe perishing. They therefore resolved to induce the Kurashites to destroy the roll, which, it is then discovered, has already been destroyed by worms. The fact however of the Abyssinian Refugees returning in consequence of the compromise shows that it was an event of

* *Tabari*, i., 1195.

more than momentary importance. It would be utterly unlike Mohammed to make such a concession unless at least an equivalent was to be obtained. Such an equivalent would doubtless be the removal of the ban. The ascription of that step to the good nature of certain persons we regard therefore as due to the desire to bring the compromise into oblivion. How came the ban to be withdrawn? was a natural question. The most pious answer was that the worms ate up the document on which it had been inscribed—with due reverence for the name of God which was at the head of it. To those who thought this unlikely the good nature of certain Meccans furnished a likelier reply. Our authorities give us a combination of the two. Yet in ascribing to the pagans such tenderness of feeling they appear to be right.

What it was that spoiled the satisfactory syncretism which had restored concord is not known; most probably it was the fact that many of Mohammed's followers were earnest. Indeed the long persecution they had undergone had burned out the elements that were not genuine metal. The trials which they had faced had endeared the doctrine to which they were due; and those persons, accustomed to speak of Al-Lāt and Al-'Uzza with contempt and abhorrence, refused to turn round so sharply and admit their efficacy with God. It was not the only occasion on which Mohammed discovered that his followers were not all adventurers but some of them enthusiasts. Men to whom he held out the prospect of worldly goods replied at times that they did not need them *;

* *Musnad*, iv., 197.

converts who were told to profit from their conversion by embezzling goods entrusted to them by unbelievers declined to make theft their entry into the new condition*; men tried hard to get permission to become ascetics.† Mohammed, like others who raise spirits, could not always control them. The compromise threatened to mean a complete victory for one side. Nor indeed are the Meccans likely to have suppressed their delight at having extorted such a concession.

Some one, therefore, an Abyssinian Refugee, or perhaps Omar—whose faith at a later time was all but wrecked by a tergiversation of the Prophet's,—demanded that this concession should be withdrawn. We were not there, as Mohammed would say, when the discussion went on; yet we know that disputes rage no less fiercely because posterity forgets all about them. Strong as was the Prophet's will, there were times when he could be bent; and having resigned himself to approving the Meccan polytheism, he had now to resign himself to declaring that he had made a mistake. As we have seen, the retractation of errors committed in the Koran was a fairly familiar process. Allah was not proud. The compromising verses were erased from the Surah, and an apology substituted. In this he declares that whenever a prophet recites his oracles the devil is quite sure to interpolate. God, however, revises the proofs, and throws out the devil's interpolation. The fruit of the long negotiations was thus lost; the

---

* *Ishak*, 470.

† *Musnad*, i., 175, vi., 122.

Refugees for the most part returned to Abyssinia, few of them having even entered Meccah. Thirty-three who remained had to obtain patrons. The persons who had procured the compromise were more than ever embittered at Mohammed's slipperiness and bad faith.

The strategy of the Meccan leaders had, however, averted a serious danger. The fugitives had left Abyssinia, spreading the rumour of the conversion of their enemies, a rumour which doubtless had been magnified in their mouths, for exiles feed so much on hopes. Abyssinian aid was, they declared, no longer required to force their countrymen to respect the Chosen of God. These persons coming back after a month, and saying it was all a regrettable mistake, cut rather a sorry figure; nor dared they, we fancy, tell the story of the devil's interpolation. Hence the danger from Abyssinia had been averted.

The interval between the failure of the compromise and the next events of importance is filled in by the biographer with miraculous tales or such as are clearly inventions requisite for the interpretation of passages in the Koran. Hard as it is to injure a reputation, it is probable that Mohammed's concession and retractation had seriously injured his. The grand scene in the precincts would be remembered by the citizens of Meccah, and many a sarcasm be bestowed on the Prophet who could not distinguish the inspirations of Satan from those of God. Few proselytes are likely to have been won at Meccah from the time of the abrogation of the verses till the exodus.

The next events of consequence are the deaths in one year of Khadijah and Abu Talib: this is given as year 10 of the Mission, and it is stated that the events were after the blockade was over and the Hashimites had issued from their ravine. Probably the proximate cause of the death of both is to be found in the agitation due to the scenes of which we can only reproduce so faint an outline, and the privation and annoyance which the blockade had occasioned; or more probably in the prospect of a renewal of the same privations after they had stopped for a time. Mohammed is said to have tried hard to get the dying Abu Talib to pronounce the Islamic confession, but unsuccessfully; whereas he could assure Khadijah on her deathbed that she with three other famous ladies—the Virgin Mary, Potiphar's wife, and "Kulthum, Moses' sister"—would share his chamber in Paradise; and wishing her husband "Peace and Offspring," the ordinary nuptial greeting, she passed away.* Of Abu Talib the Prophet appears to have spoken with very moderate affection; his protection had doubtless been like the brake, which, while it saves the vehicle from destruction, retards its pace. Moreover, with Mohammed failure to recognise his Mission could not be atoned for by any services, however great. Abu Talib therefore was doomed to hell; the utmost that his nephew could procure for him was that whereas other evil-doers were in a lake of fire, he was to be in a puddle, without, however, much alleviation of the suffering involved. Ali, more fanatical than the

* *Isabah.*

Prophet, displayed some reluctance when ordered to bury his father who had died in unbelief.*

Of Khadijah, on the other hand, Mohammed is said to have spoken with affection and appreciation, and in later years used regularly to treat with favour women who had been recipients of Khadijah's bounty, declaring faithfulness to be part of faith.† He thereby roused the jealousy of one of her many substitutes. For indeed the widower consoled himself within a month by marrying Saudah, daughter of Zama'ah, whose brother strewed ashes on his head when he heard of her betrothal ‡; and ere long, by engaging himself to the infant daughter of Abu Bakr, Ayeshah, of whom more will be heard. A child of seven, she was sent by her father with a basket of dates to the Prophet, whose manner inspired her with alarm and aversion. § But this of course strengthened the Prophet's resolve, though she was already betrothed to the son of his patron Mut'im, who, however, was not anxious for alliance with a Moslem.

Mohammed's numerous marriages after Khadijah's death have been attributed by many European writers to gross passion, but they would seem to have been mainly dictated by motives of a less coarse kind. Several of his alliances were political in character, the Prophet being anxious to bind his chief followers more and more closely to himself.

---

* *Musnad*, i., 97.

† *Alif-Bā*, i., 141.

‡ *Musnad*, vi., 210.

§ *Mikhlat*, 156.

This was doubtless his object in marrying the daughters of Abu Bakr and Omar; while a political motive of a different sort is to be found in his alliances with the daughters of political opponents or fallen enemies. Victory over an enemy would seem to have been consummated only when the enemy's daughter was introduced into the conqueror's harem.* The remainder are to be explained by his extreme anxiety to have a son, and thereby escape a reproach to which he was keenly sensitive. "The owner of this castle was in great grief because he had no son; so he did not cease selecting bride after bride till at last there was prospect of success." This is mentioned by an Arabic writer † as a normal occurrence, and indeed the institution of marriage is among the Arabs based on the first two only of the reasons given in the Anglican marriage service. ‡ In Khadijah's lifetime, as has been seen, Mohammed could not follow the dictates of either of the motives that have been alleged. Viewed in the light of his subsequent conduct, his behaviour prior to her death illustrates in a striking way his extraordinary self-control and determination to wait for the favourable moment before putting any plan into execution. Women in the East, especially Meccan women, are more attached to their native homes than men, § and Khadijah's death probably rendered the Flight practicable. The death of Abu Talib rendered it a natural

* *Wellhausen, Ehe*, 435, n. 5. He gives a reason for this.

† *Hariri*, 430.

‡ *Ibid.*, 329.

§ *Wellhausen, Ehe*, 470.

solution of the Prophet's difficulties, and one which the legend made Abu Talib himself suggest to his nephew on his deathbed.* For to no other of his relations was he bound by ties similar to those which attached him to the uncle whose protection he had enjoyed so long, nor was there any of the unconverted left who was likely to interfere so actively in his behalf. The tradition would fain give Abbas a similar part; but there is grave reason to suspect that he first got it when his descendants had climbed Mohammed's throne.

After Abu Talib's death the Prophet is said to have suffered severe persecution, dust being thrown on his head.† He therefore left Meccah, with the view of obtaining a footing elsewhere; his first visit was to Ta'if, the city that was connected with Meccah by so many ties. He could not apparently have made a worse choice; the people of Ta'if were no less devoted to their goddesses than the Ephesians to Artemis; years after they made a tougher fight for their religion than any other Arab town. In the fact that he went no farther than Ta'if we have evidence of the caution and timidity which characterised his movements: one of the ruling family at Ta'if had a Kurashite wife; hence as a Kurashite Mohammed could claim the protection of the ruling family, which they appear to have granted till he began to explain his views, which were received by the sheikhs with contempt and withering rebuffs. Abashed by their tone—this story is too characteristic to be

* *Ibn Sa'd II.*, ii., 91.

† *Tabari*, i., 1196.

omitted—the Prophet begged them not to mention what his views were, so determined was he to keep out of danger's way. His request was not granted, and he was mobbed by the fanatical populace, his sufferings being witnessed by some of his Kurashite opponents, who, however, as usual, treated him with generosity. Long after a late convert remembered seeing him on a high place at Ta'if, leaning like a Kahin * on a staff or bow, and reciting a Surah (lxxxvi.) in which he argues the resurrection of the body from the nature of its origin, and assures the hearers with strange oaths that he is serious. The rôle of the Prophet assuredly resembled that of a madman ; but the convert professed to have committed the text to memory at the time, though it was not till long after that he acknowledged it to be the Word of God. † At the time he accepted the opinion of some Kurashites who told him that they knew the Prophet well, and would have followed him had he been genuine. ‡ One woman (Rakikah) is said to have given the Prophet water, and indeed to have been converted ; and since open conversion would have meant death to her, she was permitted to adopt a compromise similar to that of Naaman the Syrian ; she was to assert that her God was the Thakafite idol, but she was to turn her back to it when she prayed. §

To Meccah he durst not return without a promise

---

* *Isabah*, iii., 1127.

† *Ibid.*, i., 826.

‡ *Musnad*, iv., 335.

§ *Isabah*, ii., 212.

of protection, for whoever succeeded Abu Talib as chief of the Hashimites was not disposed to grant it; it was at last with difficulty procured from Mut'im, son of 'Adi, whose name has occurred before. Nothing further of importance occurred during this trip save an interview with a Christian slave whom he moved to rapturous admiration by knowing that Nineveh was the home of Jonah.

Truly the inhabitants of one town care little for the concerns of another. Ta'if is not two days' journey from Meccah, and, as appears from this story and other evidence, many Meccans had property there. Yet clearly Mohammed's prophetic mission, which had now continued for ten years, had not reached the ears of the people of Ta'if. We, knowing nothing of Meccah, save what Mohammed's biographers record, suppose the Meccans to have been exclusively occupied with him and his mission. But it is evident that they must have had other and more important concerns, else the neighbouring and sister city must have known something about their Prophet.

The Prophet then had at the first attempt less honour in another country than even in his own; but the first failure never made any difference when he had once conceived a plan. Since, however, missionary journeys were not free from danger, he resolved to take advantage of the immunity which the time of the festival provided. On those occasions the neighbouring tribes came *en masse* to the neighbourhood of Meccah, and set up their tents in groups, as indeed is probably done still. For twenty days from the commencement of Dhu'l-Ka'dah they had their fair at Ukaz, for ten at Majannah, and for eight at Dhu'l-Majaz. Nothing could be easier than to go the round of these encampments, as doubtless many a pedlar did, and recite passages of the Koran; offering Paradise to any tribe that was prepared to receive him.* And years after the Mission had become a success old men remembered seeing the Prophet at the fair of Dhu'l-Majaz delivering his message; he was clad in red, and at that time had a white complexion and copious black hair. Abu Jahl was near, throwing clods at the preacher and warning those present not to abandon their gods.† When the feast itself came near, and the two sects of the Arabs separated, Mohammed used to surprise the youthful Meccans by standing with the sect which was not his own.‡ One tribe, indeed, the Banu 'Amr Ibn Sa'sa'ah, appear to have thought his proposition worth considering, though the conditions which they demanded were not accepted. To the rest the Prophet seemed either a blasphemer or a buffoon; and Abu Lahab is said to have followed him closely, to warn the Arabs to attach no importance to his proposals. On the other hand Abu Bakr is represented as utilising his genealogical knowledge to win the Prophet credit.

Since favours are usually granted with conditions attached to them, we are entitled to infer from the Prophet's conduct after the death of Abu Talib that

---

* *Musnad*, iii., 339.

† *Ibid.*, iv., 63.

‡ *Azraki*, 130.

he was only permitted to enjoy the protection of a Meccan family on condition that he confined his proselytising endeavours to strangers. Such conditions are not uncommonly imposed on Christian missionaries who work in Moslem countries, where they are permitted to convert Jews and Christians at their pleasure, provided they leave privileged citizens alone. Those who stipulated this probably had ceased to regard Mohammed as a source of danger, and felt confident that his preaching would have no other effect than that of making him ridiculous. Hence he was permitted to try what he could do with the visitors whom the feast attracted in numbers, and also with such casual guests as a variety of causes might bring to Meccah. Thus it came about that one Tufail, son of 'Amr, of the tribe Daus, came to Meccah and believed; his tribe had produced, if not a prophet, yet a man who had inferred the existence of a Creator, not knowing who He was; his disciple came to Meccah prepared to learn. He offered Mohammed a sure refuge in his fortress, but Mohammed was not satisfied with the proposal.* Thus, too, a man of the tribe Hamdan offered Mohammed refuge, but as he bethought him of getting the consent of his tribe and returning the next year to fetch the Prophet, he was too late.† Thus, too, it came about that Mohammed was on the lookout when envoys from Yathrib arrived, and another cause had meanwhile been conspiring to make the people of Yathrib ready to receive Mohammed.

* *Muslim*, i., 44; *Isabah*, ii., 578; *Musnad*, iii., 370.

† *Musnad*, iii., 390.

This would appear to have been the course of events during the Meccan period, of which precise dates were rarely remembered, while the falsification of parts of it was naturally attempted.

Throughout, the conduct of the Meccan leaders seems to have been that of respectable and good-natured men. They were not hard on Mohammed's eccentricity, supported as it was by Khadijah's wealth and social position, but naturally they were merciless to the humble individuals, who, having neither wealth nor station, or only a little of either, chose to think for themselves.

When Mohammed's successful diplomacy threatened to wreck the independence of their city, they adopted forcible measures, but even then were ready to make an honourable compromise. When this failed, and a succession of misfortunes reduced Mohammed to impotence, they took no advantage of his weakness, but suffered him to hold his own opinions, so long as he gave the citizens no further trouble. If, says an Arabic proverb, the end of a course were as clear as the beginning, no one would ever be found regretting. Neither they nor any one else could then foresee the possibilities of Islam.

In Mohammed's conduct we may see the influence of what Carlyle calls a fixed idea—determination to be recognised as the Prophet of Allah. A legend makes the Kurashite chiefs offer him anything he chooses, wealth beyond the dreams of avarice, sovereignty, or anything else, if he will only resign his claims to be a Prophet, but he refuses. To this legend we naturally attach no credence, but even in the case of the fixed ideas which Carlyle has rendered immortal—Boehmer's determination to sell his necklace, Rohan's determination to be reconciled to the Queen—their abandonment would have been attended with much personal inconvenience, and going back was little less awkward than going forward. After the part of divine ambassador had been acted for ten years with very considerable success it could not well be given up.

CHAPTER VI

THE MIGRATION. *

UNLIKE Meccah, Yathrib lies in a fruitful plain. "Walled habitations, green fields, running water, every blessing the Eastern mind can desire, are there." † And indeed the richness of the soil finds expression in the name Taibah, "the pleasing," which its Arab colonists were at one time inclined to substitute for the Egyptian *Athribis*, *Atrepe*, "Residence of Triphis." The name whereby it is now known, "the City," is an abbreviation for "the City of the Prophet." The Egyptian settlement was apparently not quite identical with the present site, but somewhat to the north, at the confluence of the streams which unite at Zaghabah to work their way to the sea.

The Arab chronicles take us back but a little way in elucidating the circumstances which led to the reception of Mohammed. That so favoured a region would be early colonised is certain, and indeed in pre-Christian days Yathrib figures as a prosperous

* In Arabic, *hijrah*, often wrongly written *Hegira*.

† *Keane*, p. 219.

commercial city*; but the native tradition knows little of earlier inhabitants than Jews.

Some of these professed to have settled there in the time of Moses; others to have joined their brethren after the taking of Jerusalem by the Romans.† Jewish settlers were certainly to be found in most of the oases that lie between Syria and Yemen. A considerable number of Jewish tribes at Yathrib (some twenty) are enumerated by the Arabs, though only three figure much in the life of Mohammed. The names of none of these tribes are Hebrew; most of them are Arabic, and similar to the names of Arab tribes; one or two being derived from totems, while one or two are Aramaic. Hence it is improbable that the blood of these Jews was mainly Jewish. Their goods were protected by seventy forts.‡

The Arabic history accounts for the facts that the Jews in Mohammed's time formed a minority of the people of Yathrib, and that many of them were clients of the Arabs instead of being supreme, by certain hypotheses. At the dispersion caused by the breaking of the dam at Marib,§ the Aus and Khazraj had wandered towards the Yathrib oasis, and had indeed been allowed land, but had no capital. As the Arabs increased, they incurred the envy and suspicion of the wealthy Jewish residents, who, imitating the treatment of their ancestors by Pharaoh,

* *Winckler*, *Altorientalische Forschungen*, ii., 339.

† *Aghani*, xix., 94.

‡ *Samhudi*, 80.

§ This event is still regarded by some as not wholly mythical.

proceeded to oppress the settlers: one Jewish chieftain (with the curious name Bedchamber)* even exacting the *jus primæ noctis.* By an expedient which rarely failed in anecdotes of this style, the brother of one of the brides, disguised in bridal attire, assassinated the tyrant; and presently † by two acts of gross perfidy the supremacy had been won for the incomers. A Ghassanide king, at the instance of a Khazrajite, Malik, son of 'Ajlan, had invited the chiefs of the Jews to a banquet and beheaded them, leaving Malik to achieve the work of subduing the Jews. Malik accomplishes this by a second banquet, which the remaining chiefs were credulous and infatuated enough to attend. After this double massacre the Jews were no longer able to make head against the newcomers, but sank into a condition of vassalage. When a Jew was attacked, instead of calling his brethren to help him, he besought the aid of an Arab patron. And, indeed, that the Banu Kainuka, who owned the market of Yathrib, were dependents of the Khazraj, appears from a tale which shall presently be told.

It cannot now be discovered whether the above story contains any germ of truth, or whether it is wholly the product of the fancy. It is certainly true that to many of the Yathrib tribes Jews were attached: but the victims of the treachery cannot well have been the tribes Nadir and Kuraizah, who play a part in the scenes to which we are coming;

* So *Samhudi* (Kaitun): but probably Fatyun (*Ibn Duraid,* 259) is better.

† *Samhudi,* 81.

for at the commencement of Islam, these were not in a condition of vassalage. It rather appears as if these tribes had kept aloof from the affairs of their pagan neighbours till shortly after the commencement of Islam. Yet the fact of these tribes having names with specifically Arabic consonants requires some explanation. Israelites in most countries take names by which they are assimilated to their neighbours; but the fact of their doing so implies that they feel themselves to be aliens, and would, at least to a certain extent, conceal this circumstance. Had these Israelites, coming from their home in Canaan, colonised a new country, they would surely have retained both their language and their national names. Now, it seems clear that these Jews of Medinah were no more retentive of the former than of the latter. They spoke Arabic—an idiom of their own, it would appear, but not more different from the language of their neighbours than is Yiddish from German.

Hence we cannot credit the Arabic tale, and yet the obvious hypothesis that these tribes were not of Jewish origin, but Judaised Arabs,* can only be accepted to a moderate extent.† The characteristics which they are found displaying are too national for us to suppose they had imbibed their Judaism from strangers. Perhaps, then, these tribes had migrated to Yathrib after the break-up of the Jewish state in South Arabia. Of the superiority

---

* *Ibn Duraid*, p. 259, seems to be in favour of this view. Ya'kubi asserts it positively.

† So *Nöldeke*.

of their culture to that of the Arabs there was no question. They were better equipped with instruments for agriculture, and understood many industries to which the Arabs were strangers. They were also adepts in magic and preferred the weapons of the black art to those of open warfare. At the time when this history opens they had some renown as warriors. Mohammed, a good judge of men, rated it, as we shall see, quite correctly.

There is no doubt that the Jewish communities had, by aid of their peaceful industry, acquired considerable wealth, and a poet of early Islam couples the palaces of the Banu Nadir with those of the Persian and Byzantine monarchs; deterioration of the race had, he thinks, led to the fall of all alike. They had certain public funds, with a treasurer to manage them. We hear incidentally of valuable plate possessed by members of the tribe. Some of their wealth was doubtless acquired by money-lending; on several occasions in the subsequent history Jews figure largely as money-lenders,* and when the Prophet died his cuirass was held by a Jew in pawn. This fact makes their abandonment to destruction by the people of Yathrib easier to understand.

The reputation for learning which, as we have seen, they enjoyed at Meccah, seems to have been deserved. They had one or more schools in which the Torah was taught: and it seems likely that members of their community were at the first employed by Mohammed as scribes, or at any rate as accountants; for few of the pagans at Yathrib could

* E. g., *Wakidi* (*W.*), 174.

as yet write Arabic.* They would seem to have written Arabic in their familiar Hebrew character, and among the fragments of antiquity which may some day be unearthed are letters or contracts in this language. Their command of the "clear Arabic tongue" was in some cases sufficient to enable their poets to compete on equal terms with those of the pagan Arab tribes, and more than one of their number counts among the classics of the Days of Ignorance. In their compositions they arrogate to themselves the virtues and the distinctions of the pagan chieftains or knights errant: and from a scene to which allusion shall presently be made we should gather that they seriously believed themselves to possess these qualities.

The tribes called Aus and Khazraj formed, however, the bulk of the population of Yathrib. From the tribe to the family there were (as elsewhere) a series of groups of smaller or greater numbers, which, however, did not admit of precise limitations. Separate groups dwelt in separate quarters surrounded by their own palm plantations. These quarters were groups of mud huts; some of the groups had meeting houses, but we do not hear of sanctuaries.† Some had towers or fortresses where at times of danger they could secure their families and property. In an ancient description of such a

* Ibn Sa'd mentions as writers Abu 'Abs Ibn Jabr, Ma'n Ibn 'Adi, Ubayy Ibn Ka'b, Sa'd Ibn Al-Rabi', Abdallah Ibn Rawahah, Bashir Ibn Sa'd, Abdallah Ibn Zaid, Aus Ibn Khawali, Al-Mundhir Ibn 'Amr, Usaid Ibn Al-Hudair, Sa'd Ibn 'Ubadah, Rafi' Ibn Malik.

† The breadth of one quarter is given as thirty cubits. *Ibn Sa'd, II.*, ii., 10.

tower it is said to have been built of black stone "with an eminence of white, with another on that which would be seen from a distance." They appear ordinarily to have been square in shape. They were required only in emergencies, since the rules of war forbade the conqueror to enter the quarters of the vanquished.

The pagan Yathribites seem to have lagged behind the Meccans in civilisation: a "perfect man" was in their nomenclature one who could write Arabic, swim, and shoot *; and few of them possessed all these accomplishments. Their occupation in time of peace lay mainly in the cultivation of the palm. Many of the necessaries of life were imported by Nabatæans, who had a market called after them in Yathrib; payment was probably in dates, which were as much the measure of value at Yathrib as was the camel at Meccah. Though we hear the names of one or two wealthy Yathribites, the bulk of them appear to have been poor. "In Yathrib in the Prophet's time there was only one wedding garment; ornaments had to be borrowed from the Jews." † This poverty was probably aggravated by the Jewish money-lending.

There appears to have been as at Meccah no recognised government at Yathrib, no regular mode of administering justice. A tribal group was, however, responsible for the actions of its members. Bloodshed was common, as the result of petty brawls, and caprices or conflicting interests often led on these

* *Ibn Sa'd II.*, ii., 91.

† *Wellhausen, Ehe*, 443.

occasions to cross-grouping: clans for various reasons taking the part of more remote relations against their nearer kin. Yet the petty wars seem to have been fought with strict observation of the rules of the game. Routed in the field the enemy was not pursued into his habitation. After many battles the affair was patched up by the payment of blood-money: the number of the slain was counted, and the family that had lost most men received compensation from the victor. Frequently doubtless disputes were settled without bloodshed by the appointment of arbitrators, * who however constantly found it difficult to get their dooms recognised by the party against whom they gave sentence.

Of the origin of the dissensions at Yathrib which led to the summoning of Mohammed a complicated account is given. It would appear that dispute was frequently caused by a chieftain according his protection to some stranger, whom a native wantonly would injure or kill. The patron's honour was injured by such an act, and his demand for vengeance would lead to an affray of serious dimensions. Yet the consequences of such acts were so well known that we fancy those who committed them had ordinarily some ulterior object—the acquisition of land or spoil, if they thought the patron whom they had injured would succumb in combat. A member of the Aus, Hatib, of the clan Mu'awiyah, had accorded his protection to a stranger, of the tribe Tha'labah of Dhubyan: while in the Jewish market-place, a

* *Ibn Duraid*, 266, mentions Al-Mundhir Ibn Haram as arbitrator between the Aus and Khazraj.

Khazrajite (Yazid, son of al-Harith) offered a Jew his robe if he would box the stranger's ears. The Jew accepted the offer, and gave the man a blow which rang throughout the market-place—for which assault he paid with his life, when Hatib, incensed at the treatment of his client, arrived on the scene.* The Khazrajite who had instigated the outrage rushed after Hatib, but failing to catch him, slew in his stead a member of his clan. Each of the tribes gladly rushed to arms, and there followed a series of encounters, in which the Aus met with serious reverses, and one of their clans, called Nabit, were expelled from their lands, and forced to leave Yathrib.

In the final explosion, known as the battle of Bu'ath, dated six years before the Flight,† the Jewish tribes Kuraizah and Nadir were involved. Till this time it would appear that they had been cultivating their lands in peace: and even if the story told above be true, they apparently had taken the loss of their men quietly, preferring a battle of curses and imprecations to the use of the sword or spear. The defeated Aus, catching like drowning men at a straw, negotiated with these tribes for assistance in their war, and the Khazraj, hearing of this, sent to warn the Jews against interference, and demanded forty lads as hostages. These were provided: but the real purpose of the Khazraj was to force the Jews into a quarrel with the view of obtaining their lands, and the game which they played was afterwards

* *Ibn Athir*, i., 247.

† *Ibn Sa'd II.*, ii., 135.

imitated by Mohammed with most signal success. The Khazraj demanded the lands of the Jews under threat of killing their hostages: and the Jews suffered the hostages to be killed. So the Jews were driven to help the Aus, and to take part in the war of which they had kept clear. They opened their doors to the fugitive Nabit. Fighting under foreign commanders, and by the side of brave men, the Jews have often proved themselves as good soldiers as other men ; and in the battle which resulted after long preparation, the Khazraj were defeated by the Aus with their Jewish allies. In following up the victory and exacting full vengeance the Jews were not restrained by the usages which the Arabs respected.

One of the Khazrajite chiefs played a part in this history of which he was destined to give many reproductions after the arrival of Mohammed. This was Abdallah, son of Ubayy, of the clan Balhubla. In the crime of murdering the hostages he would not participate ; he endeavoured to dissuade the others, and sent back the hostages that were deposited with him. From the battle, too, he kept aloof—out of conscientious scruples. Hence when the tide of fortune had turned against the Khazraj he was able to secure the deliverance of his own fortress. But to take full advantage of a victory was a proceeding which the Arabs had to learn from Mohammed. The battle of Bu'ath left the Aus victorious, but the enemy were not exterminated—only humiliated, with a heavy score against them which every member of the tribe was under a solemn obligation to pay in blood. The hostile tribes were still living side by side, and the life of no man was safe when he went outside his house. The day of Bu'ath, said Ayeshah, had been arranged by God for the benefit of the Moslems.*

During the civil war some of the antagonists, it is said, had appealed to distant Meccah, and had tried to ally themselves with the Kuraish, but without success. To the disappointed envoys Mohammed offered Islam as a substitute, but this was not accepted. Others visited the sacred places on pilgrimage at the usual times, when, as we have seen, it was the Prophet's custom to provide part of the spectacle. Two Yathribites, As'ad, son of Zurarah, already a monotheist in belief,† and Dhakwan, son of Abd Kais, on one of these occasions, were engaged in a contest concerning their claims to distinction, which they submitted to the highly respected Meccan, 'Utbah, son of Rabi'ah, who probably, after the fashion of his colleagues, refused to decide. While waiting for his decision they heard at Dhu'l-Majaz the Prophet's discourses, and became the first of the Helpers,‡ as the people of Yathrib who joined Islam were afterwards called. Another account§ makes Rafi', son of Malik, the first convert; he heard the Surah of Joseph, and took it with him to Medinah. Yet another‖ makes the first convert from Medinah Mu'adh, son of Al-Harith. Other

* *Samhudi*, 90.

† *Ibn Sa'd II.*, ii., 22.

‡ *Isabah* i., 988.

§ *Ibid.*, i., 102; *Ibn Duraid*, 272.

‖ *Isabah*, iii., 874.

accounts make the first converts a band of six, or seven, or eight.* It is likely that the persons whose attention was roused by the Prophet's words were chiefly members of the Khazraj, and it is stated that As'ad, son of Zurarah, the foremost of the Helpers, was a hater of the Jews.† The Khazrajites were fresh from a severe defeat which they had sustained from the united forces of the Aus and the Jews; and the native tradition represents them as having taken up with Mohammed in order to outwit the latter. The Jews had talked in moments of despair (as they talk still) of the Messiah who would one day appear and conquer the world for them. If this Prophet was the Messiah—and he claimed to be something of the sort—would it not be excellent policy to secure him before the Jews could claim him? So argued the Khazrajites. Hence they listened gladly to the Prophet's sermon.

The history which has come down to us is meagre and one-sided: we hear little of the triumph of the Aus or of the pride of the Jewish tribes in their victory over their oppressors. When men have had to endure failure and humiliation, a little success turns their heads. That the victory of Bu'ath was regarded by the Jews as a direct intervention by their God can scarcely be doubted; and since the gods of the Aus had failed to secure them victory, it prepared their enemies to recognise the transcendent power of the Israelitish God, whose emissary and agent Mohammed claimed—as we have seen, with

* *Ibn Sa'd II.*, ii., 55.

† *Wakidi* (*W.*), 414.

some Jewish support—to be. Perhaps Mohammed confirmed them in this view of the situation. What more natural than that Allah should help his worshippers? The Khazrajites returned home with much food for reflection.

Thus we can interpret the saying of the keen-witted Ayeshah. In the civil war at Yathrib the side that had long been defeated had won a signal victory by the aid of Allah, the God of the Jews. The Jews however care little to make proselytes, and took no advantage of the event for religious propaganda. But some of the defeated side learned of a man who could obtain for them the favour of Allah, and so were disposed to give a favourable hearing to Mohammed's preaching; and to the victors the name of Allah was associated with success, and they were not willing that the favour of his assistance should be transferred to those whom they had defeated. The expedient which had originally been intended for the continuance of the civil war resulted in uniting the parties. The Jews of Yathrib, impolitic and unforeseeing in the extreme, are likely to have attested the correctness of the first principles of Islam which reached them—the Unity of God, necessitating the destruction of idols, and the resurrection of the dead; the fact that prayer was to be directed towards their Temple clenched the matter. Moreover a century before they had made a convert of an Arab chieftain who had established a Jewish throne in South Arabia. Further, there are classical precedents of a prophet being called in to treat a state which was suffering from *stasis* (internal dissension); some new cult was the expedient whereby the disease was curable. Such precedents were not indeed known to the Yathribites, but history is homogeneous. Hence the soil of Yathrib was thoroughly prepared for Islam. In a healthy community like that of Meccah it gained no hold; but in one that was ailing from long years of civil strife it could spread apace.

At next year's feast the Khazrajites returned, their numbers increased to twelve, a few members of the rival faction accompanying them. These persons were inaugurated in the elements of Islam and put through a rough catechism: they were made to promise to abstain from infanticide, theft, adultery, and lying, and to obey Mohammed in lawful things. One of Mohammed's followers—a man resembling him in appearance, and on whose suavity and amiability he could rely,*—Mus'ab, son of 'Umair, was sent back with them to lead prayer, and teach them such portions of the Koran as had already become part of the ritual. This was Mohammed's first choice of a lieutenant. When they returned—for only one or two of them remained † at Meccah—their numbers, increased probably by clients and dependents, speedily grew to forty, and a place for prayer was extemporised in the Harrah of the Banu Bayadah, a clan of the Khazraj. ‡

By what means the converts spread their religion among the people of Yathrib we do not know. But

* *Ibn Sa'd*, *iii.*, 82.

† *Ibn Sa'd II.*, ii., 93, 128, 131.

‡ *Ishak*, 290.

the missionary whom Mohammed had sent was an earnest man. In early life he had been a fop, who rejoiced in fine raiment and dainty perfumes. He had concealed his conversion till the secret was betrayed to his parents by one who saw him pray. Then he openly espoused the cause, losing his all. He fled to Abyssinia, and returned with the others. Poverty and privation had changed his dainty complexion so that the Prophet wept to see it; rags scarcely sufficient to cover him were the substitute for his smart apparel. Presently a martyr's death awaited him. If other Moslems reaped some of their reward in this world the first Refugee reaped none. Fops and dandies were thought good material by Epictetus, who perhaps knew men well.

A valuable convert won by him almost as soon as he had arrived was Mohammed, son of Maslamah,* a namesake of the Prophet, in his thirty-first year; but the persons whose conversion decided the fortunes of Islam at Yathrib were two chieftains of the Aus, Usaid, son of Huraith, and Sa'd, son of Mu'adh. The conversion of both is told with the same formulæ; each approaches the missionary with threats, is persuaded to listen and is charmed by the Siren's song. The rights of clients and of kindred furnish some of the machinery here as so often. As'ad, son of Zurarah, is the Khazrajite in whose protection the missionary is dwelling at Yathrib. The Ausite chief, Sa'd, son of Mu'adh, is his cousin: hence the protection of the missionary falls partly on Sa'd, who is induced to hear him on the pretext that

**Ibn Sa'd II.*, ii., 19.

his cousin is likely to suffer injury for his opinions. But if the idea of the first converts was, as the historian says, to heal the ulcer which was ruining Yathrib by introducing a religion which would unify the combatants, Mus'ab's audience had been well prepared for his sermons. In the case of these men we might well look for analogies in the lists of conversions which some recent writers have collected. Earnestness and asceticism, joined to refinement, effect wonders. A roseate picture could be drawn of the Prophet, somewhat like those which devout Mohammedans so often paint. Perhaps the Jewish hopes of a Messiah were recalled to these allies of the Kuraizah and Nadir, and their chieftains urged to seize, while it was still there, the chance of securing him for themselves. It was to Allah, the God who had won the battle of Bu'ath, that the missionary summoned them; and his representative was to be not one of the Jews, but a distant connexion of one of the Yathribite tribes. A later age than ours may know something definite about the physical or psychological conditions which determine the propogation of idea-germs; to us the process is absolutely mysterious. Whatever the arguments employed, Mus'ab succeeded. Sa'd, son of Mu'adh, became so enthusiastic about his new faith that he not only brought Mus'ab and As'ad into his lodge,* but vowed to hold converse with none of his clan, the Banu Abd al-Ashhal, till they were converted; and this energetic measure led to the conversion of the whole clan.† In the sequel he maintains the character

**Ibn Sa'd II.*, ii., 2. † *Isabah.*

of the fanatical convert. And when these chieftains had been won to the new movement, Islam became fashionable at Yathrib. Soon there was only one clan (the Ausallah) left in Yathrib of which no member was a Moslem. Yet some years elapsed before the blood-feud between the Aus and the Khazraj was forgotten, and desultory murders continued for a time.*

What the Jews of Yathrib thought of the new movement we know not; when the Prophet's régime began to fall heavily on them there were not wanting persons among them who professed to have foretold it all; but it is probable that they favoured any movement which was likely to result in quiet and security. It was not Mohammed's custom to break with people till he was quite sure of the upper hand, and till he left Meccah he probably was on good terms with the Jews there, from whom favourable reports might spread to their brethren at the northern oasis. The tradition makes a Jew the first to recognise the Prophet on his arrival, which would imply that accurate accounts of him had circulated between the Israelites of the two cities.

Of the other magnates of Yathrib the only figure of interest is Abdallah, son of Ubayy, who has already appeared on the scene. This "arch-Hypocrite" was a man who commanded respect by his talents and virtues—both of them of a sort which is of little use to a statesman, especially in times of trouble and confusion. He disliked bloodshed; he abhorred treachery. His mental powers placed him

* *Isabah*, iii., 1179.

above all the theological disputants; he cared little for these things. When he tried to interfere in politics he failed through want of practice, of readiness, and of dexterity.

Once Islam had begun to spread in Yathrib the younger converts burned to give some exhibition of their zeal. Idols were attached to dogs and sunk in wells, and that which was too much honoured beforehand was now eagerly trampled in the dust; in their enthusiasm for the new God the fiery proselytes indulged in a fit of iconoclasm—breaking the heads of idols, instead of those of the rival tribesmen. Fetishes have a bad time when their devotees can be got to wake up; and the people of Yathrib were now wide awake—on this subject.* Of the Prophet's own reflections and deliberations during this period we have no record. He was of course kept constantly informed of what was going on in Yathrib, and regularly sent instructions to his agent.† As the reports of that agent's success reached him he began to frame the scheme of conduct to be pursued when the invitation to Yathrib should arrive. To this able agent's communications it may be attributed that the Prophet was well acquainted with the affairs of Yathrib before he got there.

The next scene is what the Moslems call the second (or the third) Akabah. The number of converts who visit Meccah at the next feast‡ is swollen

---

**Isabah*, i., 452.

†*Ibn Sa'd*, iii., 84.

‡Or in the month Rejeb. *Musnad*, iii., 390.

to seventy; the party is headed by As'ad, son of Zurarah, followed by his daughter.* For the Moslems of Yathrib had been taking counsel together (probably at Mus'ab's suggestion) saying, "How long shall we leave the Prophet of God to wander about the mountains in fear of his life?"† At dead of night they meet the Prophet at the appointed place, the ravine under the hill of Akabah. An invitation can now be given him to come over to Yathrib, and allegiance definitely sworn him. At the first Akabah the neophytes had promised very little: to keep about half the ten commandments. At the second, we are told, they promised something more: *to fight men of all colours in order to defend the faith.* For meanwhile, as the Moslems put it, the use of the sword had been divinely authorised. It seems however that this is projecting into the past the theory of a later time; for in the earliest expeditions of the Prophet the Helpers took no part, their contract binding them to defensive but not offensive operations. Still there must have been something in the attitude of the Prophet's followers or the nature of his utterances, since the prospect of the sovereignty of Yathrib had been opened out, which rendered it probable that he would embark on such an enterprise. As'ad, son of Zurarah, put before his hearers the momentous character of the undertaking to which they were binding themselves, but there were no faint-hearts among them.‡ The

* *Isabah*, iii., 1135.

† *Musnad*, iii., 322.

‡ *Ibid.*, 323.

Prophet even nominated officials—twelve, in imitation of the number of the Apostles—to preside over the new community.*

The meeting was secret, and only accomplices knew of it. But a secret cannot well be kept between seventy persons, and next morning Meccah knew that the Prophet whom they had rejected had secured an alliance and a retreat likely to be more valuable than Axum; for to Yathrib there was no sea to traverse, and, more important still, its people were to be not Mohammed's patrons, but his subjects. Remonstrances were directed to some Yathribites who were in Meccah, but they, not being in the secret, could only express surprise. An abortive attempt was made to retain as hostages some of those who had sworn, and Sa'd, son of Ubadah, received some rough treatment before he was allowed to escape. But the Meccan rulers were not men who could either foresee emergencies or know how to act when one arrived. Vaguely indeed they could perceive that their enemy had won to his side a city which lay on the main route of their caravans. Rather less vaguely they may have been aware that men only preach patience under injuries when they have no chance of avenging them, and that the scruples which had fettered their own action might be abrogated by a messenger from heaven.

The second Akabah was followed by an exodus

* Our authorities make Abbas secure that the Prophet shall enjoy the same protection at Yathrib as he was enjoying at Meccah. Since Mohammed was enjoying the protection of Mut'im, son of 'Adi, this is probably a fiction to glorify the Abbasides.

from Meccah. Some persons had even made their escape after the first Akabah, so soon as the prospect of refuge at Yathrib was opened out; Abdallah, son of Abd al-As'ad, was named as the first Refugee. * The Meccans tried to stop the flight of their fellow-citizens; some they pursued and even brought back by force or deceit, some, precluded from access to the new refuge, fell away and returned to paganism. Omar, Hisham, son of Al'Asi, and 'Ayyash made an arrangement to escape together; Omar and 'Ayyash got away, but Hisham was detained, and 'Ayyash was afterwards lured back. † Of one man, Nu'aim, son of Sallam, famous as a philanthropist, it is recorded that the Meccans, fearing to lose the advantage of his presence, persuaded him to stay, with the right of holding any religion he chose. But the same half-heartedness which led to the collapse of the Meccan resistance made most of their measures abortive. Of those who wished to escape the greater number succeeded. Some had relatives in Medinah on whom they could quarter themselves; as Sa'd, son of Abu Wakkas, a brother of whose had fled from Meccah through blood-guiltiness, and settled at Kuba. ‡ Lots were drawn by the converts at Yathrib for the honour of entertaining the other Refugees §; as a poet of the Helpers afterwards boasted, ‖ they shared their possessions with the newcomers, as in old times the

* Said to have arrived Muharram 10. *Ibn Sa'd*, iii., 171.

† *Ibn Sa'd*, 194.

‡ *Ibid.*, iii., 99.

§ *Bokhari* (*K.*), ii., 163.

‖ *Isabah*, iii., 1157.

camels were shared by the arrow-game. Sa'd, son of al-Rabi', offered Abd al-Rahman, son of 'Auf, the half of his property, including one of his wives.* So liberally were the Refugees treated that they began to fear their colleagues might get the whole of the heavenly reward.† A place of worship was started at Kuba—one hour's distance from Yathrib, in the direction of Meccah—and Salim, freedman of Abu Hudhaifah, owing to his acquaintance with the Koran, was made minister there.‡

The sagacious founder of Islam waited till the end, though Abu Bakr kept urging him to leave, and cried for joy when at last he resolved to do so.§ The faith of the people of Yathrib was to be tested before the Prophet committed himself to them. If they were to receive him, they must first receive his followers. If they welcomed in the name of Allah and his Prophet all those hungry mouths, the Prophet might leave his stronghold and enter into his palace. But even if the people of Yathrib should prove fickle, these Refugees would form a bodyguard of desperate men, of whose loyalty he could be absolutely sure. "When we return," said a Hypocrite at a later time, "the stronger of us shall eject the weaker." The stronger were those who had sacrificed every hope and every conviction to one.

The departure from Meccah was brought about by the action of Mohammed's enemies. The idea of a

---

* *Musnad*, iii., 190.

† *Ibid.*, 200.

‡ *Isabah*, ii., 110.

§ *Tabari*, i., 1238.

man having friends and adherents of a new sort alarmed them; the defence of the madman by his kindred had been entirely in accordance with their views of what was proper, and provoked no resentment. But when for protecting kindred there was substituted a guard of followers, belonging to a different city and different tribes, some of the most intelligent realised in a dim way to what consequences that might lead. Arabia would have remained pagan had there been a man in Meccah who could strike a blow; who would act, and be ready to accept the responsibility for acting. But many as were Mohammed's ill-wishers, there was not one of them who had this sort of courage; and, as has been seen, there was no magistracy by which he could be tried. The history tells how they met in their Senate-house, and bethought them of one plan after another; and the final issue was that Mohammed should be assassinated, every tribe in Meccah sending a representative to take part in the murder. Mohammed's tribe, too weak to demand blood-vengeance from all the other tribes, would have to accept blood-money, which would be easily paid, perhaps even readily received. Abu Bakr's son Abdallah possessed some talent for espionage, and managed to be present at their deliberations.* The resolute man with whom they were dealing was quickly apprized of this design, and had his measures ready for outwitting it. When the trembling conspirators reached his house, to execute their melodrama as he rose from sleep, he was not there. He had escaped from

* *Isabah*, ii., 619.

a window in the back of Abu Bakr's house, accompanied by Abu Bakr, who took with him five thousand dirhems—all that remained to him of his fortune.* The son-in-law, Ali, was sleeping in Mohammed's blanket, and would have served for a hostage. But the Kurashites were too chivalrous to take so mean an advantage of their foe. They satisfied themselves with offering a reward of one hundred camels for the heads of the Prophet and Abu Bakr, † and employing professional trackers to follow their trail. ‡

When convicts escape from prison, their plan is, it is said, § to hide in the neighbourhood for three days, before they seek another country. The hue and cry has then calmed down, and not every man they meet is a detective. Mohammed's plan was the same. Before leaving Meccah a refuge was secured, known ever since as the Cave. It is in the mountain called Thaur, in the region called Mafjar; to the south of Meccah. Few of the Meccans were cunning enough to search for him in the direction which was opposite to that in which Yathrib lay; or if they searched, they failed to find the hiding-place, though one Kurz, son of 'Alkamah, professed afterwards to have followed the Prophet's trail as far as the Cave.‖ A few trusty persons were admitted to the secret. One was 'Amir, son of Fuhayrah, freed-

* *Ibn Sa'd*, iii., 122.

† *Musnad*, iv., 176.

‡ *Muruj al-dhahab*, i., 233.

§ *Boisgobé, Trente années d'aventures.* Mohammed's followers did the same: *Wakidi* (W.), 171.

‖ *Isabah*, iii., 585.

man of Abu Bakr, and an early convert, whose conversion had won him his liberty: he served in Abu Bakr's household, and presently shared his employer's camel in the flight. He undertook the difficult task of providing the fugitives with food, visiting the Cave at evening for this purpose—so we read; but the convicts who stock their lurking places with provisions beforehand do more wisely, and Mohammed's forethought was not less than theirs. Another was a guide who knew the way from Meccah to Yathrib; which Keane says is 375 miles by the shortest road, but Burton puts at 248. This guide was a pagan called Abdallah, son of Arkat,* who kept the camels which had been procured for this journey, and brought them to the Cave at the appointed time. The Prophet afterwards recorded in the Koran how he and his companion had waited by themselves in the Cave, and how he had prophetically assured Abu Bakr of the assistance of God, and told him not to grieve.† Nor need we doubt that Mohammed, whose mental powers were at their best in times of extreme danger, comported himself with coolness and courage.

The distance then which the fugitives proposed to traverse was about equal to that between London and Newcastle, or perhaps London and Edinburgh. Those who have accomplished this journey once only do not make light of its difficulties and terrors. Part of it lies over bare rocks, through narrow ravines; part over a great glaring dirty plain.

* Different accounts were current of his origin and status.

† *Surah* ix., 40.

"Every yard into that dead barren waste with its constant flitting mirage phantoms, made you feel more dismal and insignificant than an hundred miles into the bright, sparkling, briny ocean : even the Red Sea itself, with a temperature of one hundred degrees in the shade, is nothing to the desert for downright misery and helplessness."

So writes Keane; Burckhardt compares part of the way to the Nubian desert. Burton speaks of the same as "a desert peopled only with sand: a place of death for what little there to die in it: Nature scalped, flayed, discovering all her skeleton to the gazer's eye." The Egyptian Soubhi, having to go from Meccah to Medinah, envies the European travellers in Switzerland or the South of France.

The hesitation of Mohammed to migrate to Yathrib may have been in part due to unwillingness to encounter those physical horrors, which, though less trying to an Arab than to a European, are not likely to have been underrated: and indeed he hated travelling,* and in the Koran couples exile with death.† The Prophet was, like many men, timid at the start, courageous when he had experience.

The road followed by the guide appears to have been not quite identical with any of the four mentioned by Burton. The first two days' journey brought them near Usfan, thirty-six miles from Meccah; this is at the extreme edge of the hills, and apparently retained its name as late as Burck-

* *Muslim*, ii., 107.

† *Baihaki*, *Mahasin*, 326.

ON THE ROAD TO MEDINAH.

hardt's time. Of the rest of the names that figure in the narrative of the Prophet's flight few would seem to be known to European travellers. The guide intentionally followed bye-paths, only occasionally crossing the ordinary route. The true form of some of the names was doubtful in the third century of Islam. The fabulous incidents with which some of the chronicles embellish the journey need not be repeated, but it is characteristic that when they reached 'Arj, and Mohammed was told that the land belonged to the tribe Aslam, whose name means "safest," the Prophet gladly accepted the omen. * His camel broke down here, and another was supplied him by a member of the tribe; according to one account, one of a family with whom a daughter of Abu Bakr was being nursed, which also supplied a guide acquainted with a short cut to Medinah † over the difficult mountain called Rakūbah, where the Prophet succeeded in pressing a couple of robbers into his service.‡ The Aslam were a branch of the Khuza'ah, and in conciliating them the Prophet had taken the first step towards the recovery of Meccah; for, as we have seen, the Khuza'ah remembered that they had been ousted from their privileges by the Kuraish. § It is not certain that the Meccan pursuers went far on the road to Medinah, and it is likely that the Kurashite leaders, guiltless of forethought, congratulated themselves on being rid of

* Perhaps, however, this story is an embellishment by the biographer. Similar tales are often told.

† *Isabah*, ii., 180.

‡ *Musnad*, iv., 74.

§ Cf. *Wellhausen*, *Wakidi*, 320, 374.

their vexatious countrymen without bloodshed. 'Akil, an unconverted son of Abu Talib, seized and sold the dwellings of Mohammed and the other Moslem members of his family *; and a similar raid was made on the houses and goods of the other Refugees. For a time the city was to enjoy complete rest.

On Monday the 8th of Rabi' I of the year 1 A.H., corresponding to September 20 of the year 622 A.D., the Prophet reached Kuba, now a great place for gardens and orchards. Here the guide left them and returned to inform Abu Bakr's family of his safe arrival.† He arrived there at midday and the neophytes could not tell which was the Prophet and which Abu Bakr, both being clothed in white garments sent them by Talhah, son of Ubaidallah ‡; presently, however, they saw the latter shading the former with his coat, and they had been taught thus much, that a Prophet comes to be served. Hospitality was offered by an aged convert, Kulthum, son of Hind, the name of whose slave "Success" seemed to the Prophet of good augury. § It was accepted, though for receptions the house of another convert was found to be more convenient. At Kuba they determined to remain till Ali joined them, which happened on the Thursday; with him was Suhaib, son of Sinan, ‖ who had been forced to hand over his savings to the Kuraish. Iconoclasm

* *Azraki*, 389.

† *Isabah*, ii., 696.

‡ *Ibn Sa'd* iii., 122.

§ *Isabah*, iii., 1138.

‖ *Ibn Sa'd* iii., 163.

appears to have been rife among the inhabitants and the Prophet is said to have started the building of a mosque—a matter about which there is, however, some doubt. There is evidence that the people of Kuba afterwards manifested some pique at the Prophet's failing to make their village his permanent residence. Since Yathrib was so close, it might have been expected that all the city would have come out to Kuba to bring their Prophet home in state; inhabitants of Eastern cities will ride out many hours' journey to welcome guests of moderate distinction. Since the people of Yathrib did not do this, it is probable that the cautious Prophet, who had escaped from Meccah with such skill, like Ulysses of old at first kept the fact of his arrival a secret known to the select few; and indeed Abu Bakr, who was known to the people on the road, when asked who his companion was, replied, "a guide to lead me." * The Prophet was not a man to accept roseate statements without some scepticism. From Kuba he communicated the fact of his arrival to As'ad Ibn Zurarah and other converts at Yathrib, but his time was doubtless well spent in finding out the truth about the welcome he was to receive.

On the Friday † the Prophet rode from Kuba towards Yathrib, and is said to have performed service in the Wadi Ra'unah, which forms the route between the two places. This appears to be an anachronism;

* *Musnad*, iii., 122.

† Anas, son of Malik, makes the Prophet stay fourteen days at Kuba. *Musnad*, iii., 212.

the adoption of Friday as a sacred day came later, at the suggestion of a Medinese, and after the relations with the Jews had become unfriendly; and, indeed, confirmation of this is found in the fact of his choosing the Friday for travelling. It is asserted that each tribe by which he passed desired the honour of his presence and requested him to take up his abode with them; that he refused all these offers, in order to excite no jealousy, and left it to his camel to choose a site; it chose that of the future mosque, the Prophet only accepting hospitality till his own house was built. Anas Ibn Malik asserted that five hundred of the Helpers came out to meet him,* and that an Abyssinian war dance was got up by way of welcome.† These stories may or may not be true. We know that he was at first unable to sleep at night owing to his alarm, and could only close his eyes when he found that some of his faithful adherents from Meccah were mounting guard.‡ The terrors of the attempted assassination and of the days and nights in the Cave were still on him. And he was aware also that one of his new adherents, Nufai', son of Al-Mu'alla, had been murdered before his arrival in consequence of the blood-feud.§

Till a residence had been built for him he had lodgings in the house of Khalid, son of Zaid, a Khazrajite who was among the earliest converts

---

* *Musnad*, iii., 222.

† *Ibid.*, 161.

‡ *Isabah*, ii., 163.

§ *Ibn Duraid*, 271.

from Yathrib, and who was on an intimate footing with Mus'ab, son of 'Umair, the missionary whom he had despatched to prepare the way. An early step taken by him was to create between some of his chief followers from Meccah with converts of Medinah a relationship which he called brotherhood, and which was to involve many of the rights which belonged to that name. He had tried the same method before, and so successfully broke down the superstition about kinship. The measure at Medinah appears to have been a temporary one only, and to have been abrogated after the battle of Badr.*

That the office of a Prophet involved all the duties of a King, and both religious and political headship, was doubtless understood by him. And we can imagine the delight with which a man thoroughly qualified for ruling found himself at last in a position in which his talents could be exercised. He did not, however, enter upon all his duties at once. For a time the old soothsayers continued to retain some of their clients, when disputants required their differences settled,† though presently resort to them was forbidden, under pain of forfeiting the merits of forty days' prayers‡; and their fees were declared illegal.§ The rudimentary organisation which had existed among the tribes before his arrival did not immediately disappear. Gradually, however, the

---

* *Ibn Sa'd II.*, ii., 121, etc.

† *Wahidi*, 121.

‡ *Musnad*, iv., 68.

§ *Ibid.*, 118.

principle that all authority emanated from Mohammed permeated the constitution of Medinah. He claimed the right to depose the heads of tribes and replace them by chiefs of his own choice.* Disputes between his followers were naturally brought to him to settle, and presently disputes between them and their neighbours.

He inherited the devotion and adulation which had hitherto been bestowed on the idols; and though he never permitted the word worship to be used of the ceremonies of which he was the object, he ere long became hedged in with a state which differed little from that which surrounded a god. Enthusiastic converts habitually struggled for the honour of washing in the water which the Prophet had used for his ablution, and then drinking it up. Ere long he took to bottling up the precious liquid and sending it, after the style of the relics of saints, to new adherents. When he employed the services of a barber, the Moslems crowded round, and even scrambled for the hair,† and nail-parings, which they preserved as charms and relics.‡ The ease of approach which had characterised the old Bedouin chiefs was soon prohibited, and a divine revelation forbade the Moslems to address the Prophet as they addressed each other. At one time he commanded his followers to make an offering to the poor before they addressed him, but this had to be rescinded.§

---

* *Ibn Duraid*, 274; *Wakidi* (*W.*), 249.

† *Musnad*, iii., 133.

‡ *Ibn Sa'd II.*, ii., 87.

§ *Surah* lviii., 13.

He made a rule to enter no house of Medinah with one exception save his own,* and perhaps broke it only when it was necessary for him to administer the last consolations to the dying; but after a time it became the custom to bring the dying or dead to him.† Yet from costly paraphernalia, such as pleased the childish taste of other monarchs, he abstained to the end; he rejected a proposal of Omar that he should purchase a silken robe in which to receive deputations; neither when his resources were slender nor when they were swollen were they ever wasted on jewels or mosaics or cloth of gold. They were employed in purchasing arms and men.

The Koran at Medinah entered on a new stage of its existence, serving as a medium for legislation, and so discharging the functions of an oracle, but also as an official chronicle in which current events were criticised from the Prophet's standpoint. ‡ To the end Mohammed appears never to have let even his most intimate associates into the secret of his revelations; though at times he gave notice in advance of the import of a future revelation, and affirmed that words of his had the same force as the words of God. A whole staff of scribes presently came to be employed in taking down his effusions; and one of them is said to have gone back to paganism by observing that the Prophet allowed him to write whatever

---

* *Bokhari* (*K.*), ii., 212. The contrary is asserted *Musnad*, iv., 393.

† *Musnad*, iii., 66.

‡ Sprenger's phrase, "Leading Articles," describes these Surahs so accurately that it has been adopted in the sequel.

he chose.* The faithful however did not reason thus. Omar records in perfectly good faith how when the Prophet went to say prayers over the dead Hypocrite Abdallah Ibn Ubayy, he remonstrated with the Prophet for paying such honours to his enemy; not without astonishment at his own boldness in thus criticising the conduct of the messenger of God. But shortly after the Prophet produced a revelation "Pray not thou over any of them who dies at any time, neither stand thou upon his grave." To Omar the coincidence did not apparently suggest the remotest suspicion; to us the revelation appears to have been nothing more than a formal adoption of a suggestion of Omar, which the Prophet supposed to represent public opinion. On another occasion, when Omar (or another) bethought him of having the Call to Prayer, so as to avoid imitation of Jews and Christians, when he communicated the suggestion to the Prophet, he found that he had been just anticipated by the Angel Gabriel. On three other occasions he claimed to have coincided with Allah; having made a suggestion to the Prophet, he was presently told that a revelation had come down embodying his idea in his own words.† The occurrence flattered his vanity, but suggested no suspicion of imposture. Other followers were perhaps less simple, but were aware of the danger of ridiculing the Koran. Quarrels occasionally arose between Moslems owing to the fact that the Koran had been repeated to them in different forms, and each naturally claimed that

* *Musnad*, iii., 121.

† *Ibid.*, i., 24.

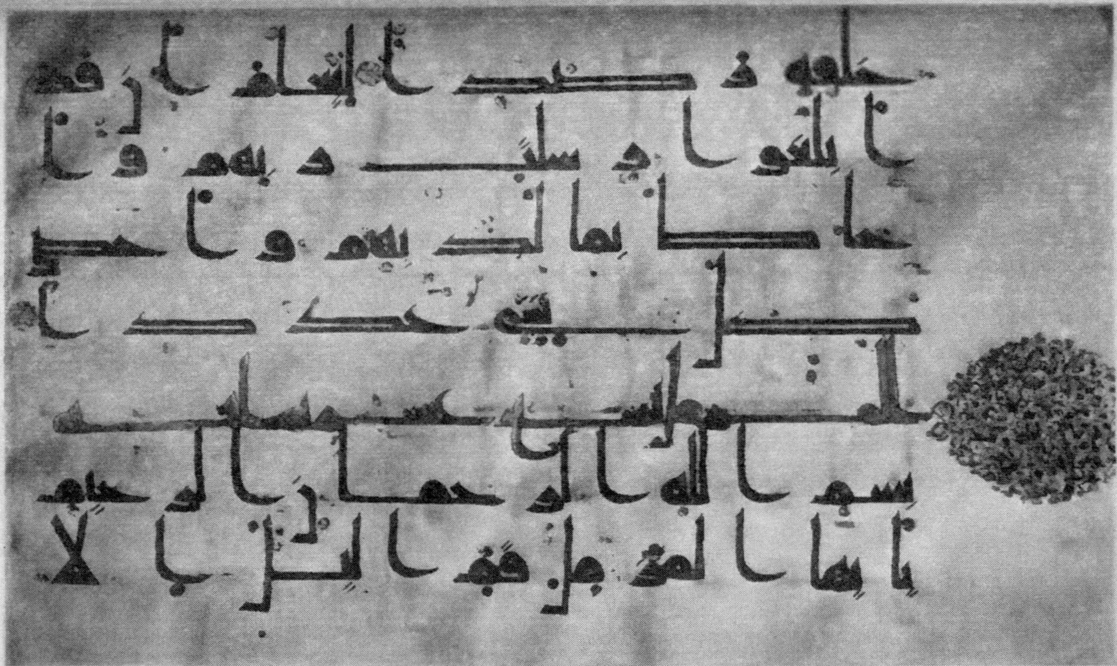

CUFIC KORAN IN THE BODLEIAN LIBRARY, SURAH LXXII., 27, 28, AND LXXIII., 1, 2.

his version only was correct: the Prophet, never at a loss, asserted that the Koran had been revealed in no fewer than seven texts.

Although the notion that the Koran was the word of God in the most literal sense seems to have been present to the mind of both the Prophet and his followers, it is rather surprising that its contents were treated with the sort of carelessness which the above anecdote illustrates, but which also appears in other narratives. According to Ayeshah, a text of enormous importance, that in which stoning was enjoined as the punishment for adultery, was on a slip (of parchment?) deposited under her bed, and afterwards lost. Casual reciters of the Koran reminded the Prophet of texts which he declared that he had himself forgotten. A text of vast importance, recited by Abu Bakr after the Prophet's death, was new to Omar. Persons were ranged at times in order of merit according to the amount of the Koran which they had collected, as though the process resembled that of collecting the Sibyl's leaves; and certain believers in the Prophet's time made it their business to collect it.* When asked by disputants whether a certain Surah contained thirty-five or thirty-six verses, the Prophet only blushed, and gave them to understand that either would do.† The Prophet, who was sometimes taunted with being "all ears," *i. e.*, ready to be guided by any suggestion, could easily be got to produce modifying or abrogating revelations, when convicted of hasty and

* So Kais Ibn Al-Sakan. *Ibn Sa'd II.*, ii., 70.

† *Musnad*, i., 106.

impracticable legislation; but those who pointed out the flaw had to take the greatest care to cast no shadow of doubt on the divine character of the earlier oracles. In consequence of the Prophet and his bodyguard making absolutely no concession on this point, the Prophet was able to the end to maintain his power of producing oracles as a *deus ex machina* to which he could effectively resort whenever a serious emergency occurred; and the dread of being made the subject of a text kept many men from opposing the Prophet in any way whatever.

His first task at Medinah was to build a place of worship, the first church of Islam, unless it be true that the mosque of Kuba was yet earlier. The land selected by his camel is said to have belonged to two orphans, whom the Prophet elected to pay for the site out of Abu Bakr's purse. They were connected in some way with the zealous As'ad, son of Zurarah; yet it would appear that Abdallah Ibn Ubayy had some claim on their land.* Of the erection of the first of the mosques we read various details, some supplied from the imagination. The most probable account seems to be that the Prophet did not go to the trouble of building, but utilised a barn or storehouse which had served for drying dates, and which was to be had for a reasonable sum. Some authorities suggest that this barn had been used as a praying-place before Mohammed came to Medinah, and considering how rarely the Prophet left anything to chance, it is possible that his camel had some reasons

* *Ibn Sa'd II.*, ii., 53.

for kneeling down at this particular spot. The measurements are given variously; perhaps 70 x 60 x 7 cubits is the most probable of those recorded. The barn had a roof of palm branches and clay, not sufficiently solid to keep out rain. In this the Prophet found an analogy to the Tabernacle of Moses, which he appears to have confused with the huts at the Feast of Tabernacles, the roofing of which must not keep out either light or wet. This roof was supported on palm trunks, against one of which the Prophet used to lean when preaching, till the Minbar or pulpit was introduced. The barn faced north, with doors on the south-east and west sides; for the first of these a northerly door was substituted when the direction of prayer was changed. Flooring of pebbles seems to have been gradually introduced by worshippers who were inconvenienced by the puddles which were the consequence of rainy days. An eastern door was a private entrance for the Prophet, who proceeded to provide quarters for himself and his wives on that side of the mosque.

The first of these was for his wife Sauda, and his bride Ayeshah whom Mohammed married shortly after his arrival: ere his death the number had increased to nine. An authority tells us that these too were not new erections, but huts belonging to a certain Harithah, son of Al-Nu'man,* who retired from each as soon as the Prophet required it. Four of them were of mud-bricks, with inner chambers of lath and clay; five were of lath and clay without inner chambers. A curtain of sacking served in

* *Samhudi*, 126 (after *Ibn Sa'd II.*, ii., 52).

most cases for a door. They surrounded the mosque on three sides, only the west being clear of them.

Round this pile of buildings many of the institutions of Islam centre. In the absence of clocks the worshippers assembled for prayer at very different times; and thereby much confusion was occasioned. An early and faithful follower of Mohammed named Bilal had a loud voice; he was employed to summon the worshippers from some eminence, such as the roof of the barn. At some time in the early months of the Prophet's residence at Medinah this practice became regular, and was regarded as an institution of Islam. Those who heard the call were ordered to come to the meeting on pain of having their houses burned down, no excuse being permitted.* Bilal's voice saved his master from the necessity of imitating the Christian hammer and the Jewish trumpet. The former institution he had been near adopting; one Abdallah, son of Zaid, claimed to have had the "Call to Prayer" revealed to him in a dream, which he communicated to the Prophet,† while according to another account the suggestion came from Omar. Minarets, now so familiar a feature of Mohammedan towns, were not added till long after Mohammed's death.‡ With this substitute for a church bell religious worship began to assume a regular and stereotyped form; the details were supposed to have been communicated to Mohammed during his ascent

* *Musnad*, iii., 423.

† *Ibid.*, iv., 43.

‡ *Kamil of Mubarrad*, ii., 66.

into heaven, this being the Moslem analogue of the Jewish phrase "a rule delivered to Moses on Sinai." For clearly the rules of prayer must have been communicated to Mohammed at some time; and when they were not to be found in Koranic revelations, the ascent into heaven was the most likely occasion for their delivery.

The barn had to be enlarged during the Prophet's lifetime and in course of time it was replaced by more magnificent buildings. Other mosques were erected before the Prophet's death, and when a rival faction was started it commenced its short career with the building of a mosque. Till the Prophet's death however the barn served not only as the sanctuary of Islam but also as the town-hall and audience chamber of Medinah. It was here that each fresh revelation was delivered. In the shabby accommodation of the first mosque we may notice a great instance of Mohammed's caution and economy. Any dirhem that was wasted on building would be taken out of the mouths of hungry Refugees: for Mohammed knew men well enough to calculate with precision the time by which the enthusiasm of the Helpers would cool. A story that may be true makes the owner of the barn offer it to Mohammed gratis, and Mohammed insist on paying for it. Whether this be historical or not, he certainly abstained at this time from demanding any needless contributions. If the prayer houses of Jews and Christians were richly decorated, he could urge that Gabriel had forbidden the decoration of that of the Moslems. And indeed he held that the outlay of money in building was the worst that a Moslem could make.

While the mosque was being adapted for worship and the huts being erected for Mohammed's families, he was doubtless being waited on by all the heads of households in Medinah, and exercising his sharp vision upon them. His strong constitution appears to have kept him free from the Medinah fever which for a time struck down some of his most stalwart followers, Abu Bakr, his freedman 'Amir, and Bilal. His mode of dealing with men was ordinarily so fascinating and winning that those visitors who were already converted to Islam were doubtless not disappointed. The Prophet had many ways of making those visits agreeable. He could change the names of visitors who had been called after pagan objects of adoration, or substitute names of good omen for such as were inauspicious.

Among his visitors, or at any rate among those who made his acquaintance were representatives of two parties of whom much will be heard, Jews and Hypocrites. The latter, or disaffected Medinese, are complimented by the Prophet on their fine appearance and melodious voices, but presently he had occasion to compare them to a row of sticks *; men so cowardly and irresolute were by no means to his taste. The Hypocrites on the other hand gave the newcomers the sobriquet, the "Surtouts" † meaning perhaps that Medinah was over full of them. A tradition ‡

* *Surah* lxii., 4.

† *Tabari, Comm.*, xxviii., 68.

‡ *Samhudi*, 8.

makes the Prophet request to be taken in at the house or castle of Abdallah, son of Ubayy, who uncourteously told him to go to the people who had sent for him. Mohammed was not the man to bring such an affront upon himself. A better authenticated tradition * makes the Prophet visit Abdallah, who complained of the odour of the beast which the Prophet was riding; this observation led to an altercation between their respective followers, which the Prophet succeeded in appeasing. These Hypocrites, as they are called by an Abyssinian name in the Koran, otherwise "those in whose hearts is sickness," were destined for long to be a thorn in the Prophet's side. Professedly acknowledging his mission and consequent authority, they were ever thwarting his plans, intriguing with his foes, and calling attention to the inconsistency of his Koran. To Mohammed however the world consisted of only two classes, those who acknowledged his mission and those who rejected it; and though he gave vent to his feelings on the subject of the Hypocrites in the Koran, he was confident that the illogicality of their position must of itself lead them to become either open foes or loyal friends. He therefore put up with many an affront from them, and lived to see their leader left without supporters.

The "Hypocrites" had probably no preconceived notion of what a prophet should be like. But the Jews had, and it is certain that Mohammed wished to conciliate the Jews as far as was possible; one of the problems which he had to face was whether he

* *Bokhari*, ii., 165.

should or should not identify his system with Judaism: and it seems likely that he was inclined to do this. Arriving at Kuba on their Day of Atonement, he adopted it as a fast day, and even sent orders to the tribe Aslam, when it was converted, to keep it * (what the Jews can have thought of this not knowing of the Day of Atonement we can conjecture); and the task of determining the day on which it should be kept was confided to a Jew.† Picking up the piece of information that the Jews expected prophets to come from Syria, he even started on a journey thither, but saw difficulties in the way of executing this, and so desisted.‡ When a Jewish funeral passed, the Prophet and his followers stood up till it was out of sight.§ A Jew, says Anas Ibn Malik (the Prophet's servant), invited him to a meal of barley-bread and rancid fat, and he accepted the offer.‖ Pedantry prevented the Jews from seeing that the sign of a true prophet—or at least the best substitute for one—was the possession of a will and intellect capable of introducing order and tranquillity at Yathrib. Had the Jews been prepared to give him the title Prophet, they might have had him for their disciple. If the Old and New Testaments are trustworthy, even prophets who could produce the most authentic credentials had little chance with the Jews: hence Mohammed, who had none that the Jews would recognise, had

* *Isabah*, iii., 1259.

† *Tabarani ap. Mahmoud Effendi, Le Calendrier Arabe*, p. 25.

‡ *Baidawi* on *Surah* xvii., 76.

§ *Musnad*, iii., 295, etc.

‖ *Ibid.*, 211.

no chance with them. The Rabbis probably expected that a prophet should be able to speak Hebrew, and finding him unable to do that, some vented their opinions of his prophetic claim somewhat freely. Others addressed him questions of no great difficulty (*e. g.*, what were the nine signs given to Moses?), and finding his answers hopelessly wrong, courteously expressed themselves satisfied, but excused themselves from acknowledging him on the ground that their Messiah must be of the seed of David.* In the assemblies at which the Call was discussed he had to put up with serious personal affronts from them, and such meetings were apt to lead to rioting and violence.†

The biographer Ibn Ishak produces a contract, made shortly after his arrival, in which the *modus vivendi* at Medinah is laid down. Wellhausen, who has acutely analysed its contents, throws no doubt on its being the work of the Prophet, but finds some difficulty in its never being cited during the many disputes that arose between Mohammed and the Jews, and also in the fact that there is no record of any formalities attending its introduction such as might have been executed. One placed in Mohammed's position would not, however, have entered into a *treaty;* it is even somewhat surprising that he should have given a rescript, except in the form of a divine revelation. But the Prophet displayed so much caution that he was perhaps unwilling to put into the mouth of God concessions the withdrawal

* *Musnad*, iv., 240.

† *Bokhari*, iv., 4.

of which he may have contemplated from the first. The purpose of the document is to arrange for the relations of the different communities inhabiting Medinah. Blood-money and ransoms were to be incumbent on the respective tribes as before, but Moslems of all tribes are recommended to help in such cases, in order to prevent any of their number being too heavily embarrassed. Protection is promised to the Jews so long as they give no cause for offence. In the case of general warfare each tribe is to pay its own expenses. Only the people of Meccah are excluded from the possibility of friendly relations.

It is not certain whether the contract was made at this time or somewhat later. In any case the position of the Jews was one of some difficulty. It was not forgotten that the sources of information about prophets, revelations, angels, etc., to both Meccans and Medinese were Jews, and that Mohammed had relied on Jewish witnesses. The Jews of Medinah, then, by the mere fact that they were not with Mohammed, were against him. For if they did not welcome the Messiah, either they or the Messiah must deserve reprehension. Moreover, the envy of many of them was doubtless aroused by the reflection that Mohammed's power had been won by his use of their Bible; of which he had not a beginner's knowledge as compared with them. Their efforts lay therefore in the direction of discrediting him before his followers from Meccah and Medinah.

A Jew of the tribe Kuraizah is said to have taken the trouble to translate a portion of the Old

Testament into Arabic, in the hope of ruining the Prophet's reputation. He brought his version to Omar, perhaps expecting that this formidable personage's eyes might be opened thereby. But Omar would not read the book without asking the Prophet's permission, which naturally was not granted.* "If Moses himself were to come to life," he added, "you would have no right to follow him and abandon me."† Others tried the plan of joining the Moslems for a time, and then returning, alleging that they had found some reason for dissatisfaction: hoping thereby to make it easier for others to retire.

A few of the Jews, as might be expected, permanently joined the newcomers. Abdallah, son of Salam, of the tribe Kainuka, was the most celebrated: he is said to have advised Mohammed to ask for his character from his brethren before they knew of his apostacy; and having given him a glowing testimonial, they were greatly embarrassed when they learnt what had happened. Mohammed, enchanted with this accession, told him he was already in Paradise—a compliment which he bestowed on no other person.‡ His two nephews followed his example, and four other Jews, Asad § and Usaid, sons of Ka'b, Tha'labah, son of Kais, and Yasin,‖ son of Yamin, made up the seven converts to Islam from the Jewish community.¶ More than one of these

* *Isabah*, ii., 699; *Musnad*, iii., 387.

† *Musnad*, iv., 266.

‡ *Isabah*, i., 169.

§ The name means *Lion* (Löwe).

‖ Perhaps a Benjamin who took the name Yasin.

¶ *Isabah*, ii., 231.

appropriated to himself the text of the Koran in which the testimony of a member of the Children of Israel is cited.* Probably all did not join at once. The Jews are said to have submitted a case of adultery to him for judgment, and to have expressed extreme dissatisfaction when he ordered the culprits to be stoned. Mohammed declared his ruling to be in accordance with the Law of Moses—as, indeed, it appears to be; but when the Law was produced, the passage could not be found, which Mohammed supposed to be due to fraud. In another† case he ordered a Jew to be stoned for having robbed and murdered a believing slave girl. Nine months‡ after his arrival a serious misfortune befell him in the death of the Jew-hater§ As'ad, son of Zurarah, who had done so much to promote the Flight. The Prophet tried to heal him by cauterisation, but thereby either accelerated or, at least, did not prevent his death. The Jews naturally jeered.‖ Their prophets had tried less painful remedies, and succeeded. A yet worse misfortune befell the Prophet when from ignorance of palmiculture he forbade the fertilisation of the female palms: when a plantation became sterile in consequence he had to confess to having spoken without book.¶

Disputes, leading to violence, broke out between the Jews and Mohammed's fanatical followers.

* *Isabah*, iii., 968.

† *Musnad*, iii., 163.

‡ *Ibn Sa'd II.*, ii. 141.

§ *Wakidi* (*W.*), 414.

‖ *Tabari*, i., 1260.

¶ *Musnad*, iv., 138; *Ibn Sa'd II.*, ii., 140.

Even the traditions show that in these disputes the Jews scored in argument. Abu Bakr came to beg money of them, quoting the words of the Koran: "Who will lend God a good loan?" "If God wants a loan," replied Pinchas, son of Azariah, "He must be in distressed circumstances";—forgetting that in the Old Testament men are advised to "lend unto the Lord." The repartee was answered by a blow; instead of returning it the Jew went to whine before Mohammed and (apparently) denied having said anything. The Angel Gabriel came to Abu Bakr's rescue, * confirming his account of the atrocity—and, indeed, Abu Bakr was not likely to have invented it himself—and raking up the old charge against the Jews of killing the prophets. The same charge served as an answer to those pious Israelites who, looking over their sacred books, discovered how in Elijah's time it had been generally agreed that a prophet could prove himself one by offering a sacrifice, which heavenly fire would devour. "If that be so," Mohammed was divinely authorised to reply, "why did you kill the prophets?"

It is asserted that the Jews attempted to deal with Mohammed by those magic processes in which they were supposed to be adepts. A page-boy had access to the hair on his comb, and the possession of this would give the sorcerer command over the person to whom it belonged. The waxen image, the knots, and the needles were all tried. Labid, son of Al-A'sam is given as the name of the sorcerer who undertook, for a small remuneration, to bewitch the

* *Surah*, iii., 177.

Prophet. It is possible that this expedient was not tried till after the latter had, by his actions, manifested his intention to exterminate the Jewish community; but even shortly after his arrival the Jews boasted that by their magic they had produced barrenness among the Moslem women *; and with plausibility, if it be true that the first child born to the Moslems of Medinah appeared fourteen months after the Prophet's arrival.† A few months were sufficient to produce mutual contempt and dislike. Jewish schoolboys could refute the pretensions of the Koran; Jewish chieftains might with impunity be cuffed by the followers of Mohammed. The Jews, too, professed disgust at a prophet whose chief concern was his harem—though their studies in the Old Testament should have shown them that this was not incongruous. Mohammed got an idea that the Jews were always plotting to murder him, and, in a saying that is probably genuine, declared that whenever a Moslem sat with a Jew, the latter was thinking how he could kill the former ‡; while the Jews, with more obvious justice, asserted the converse.§ In tales that were afterwards invented early harbingers of Islam warn the Prophet's grandfather or the youthful Prophet himself against the hostility of the Jews. There were indeed many causes for collision as we have seen; and want of cleanliness in the Jewish habitations further offended the Pro-

* *Tabari*, i., 1264, 3.

† *Isabah*, iii., 1151.

‡ *Jahiz, Bayan*, i., 165.

§ *Talm. Bab. Erubin*,

phet,* who, in those matters, was somewhat fastidious. Yet, doubtless, the Prophet's ultimate determination to destroy the Jews was due to his secret recognition of their superior knowledge of matters on which he claimed authority. That knowledge was dangerous to him but useless to the Jews. The Jewish learning was sufficient to irritate, but not of a sort which gave its holders any power of self-defence; for to their sorceries it is improbable that the more respectable members of the community attached any importance save under the influence of despair. Failing in courage, they might, by well directed study, have rendered themselves more than a match for a man who did not even know that the year was determined by the relations between the earth and the sun. But the study of their Talmud was valueless for any practical purpose.

One other visitor deserves mention, the "Christian," Abu 'Amir—an influential Medinese chieftain who is said to have discarded paganism before Mohammed's missionaries came. It was not to be expected that Mohammed would find favour with such a man and the interview was stormy. He himself, with his following, left Medinah, and made many an abortive attempt to injure Mohammed. Perhaps it occurred to him that, if what Yathrib wanted was a teacher of monotheism, he could and should have filled the post.

* *Ibn Duraid*, 315.

CHAPTER VII

THE BATTLE OF BADR

A FEW months at Medinah found the Prophet at the end of his resources. Fresh arrivals from Meccah, such as Mikdad, son of 'Amr, who has already been mentioned, found none of the Helpers ready to receive them.* Many of the Refugees had no shelter but the Mosque, had not sufficient clothing for decency, and went almost without food. Mohammed had to teach that what was enough for two was enough for three or even for four.† One date per day, eked out with some of the herbs on which camels browse, counted as a man's rations, ‡ and one garment had to serve for two wearers. How parsimonious the Prophet was compelled to be is shown by the fact that when, seven months after his arrival, he married Ayeshah, there was no wedding feast. Since her father, the faithful Abu Bakr, provided the bridegroom with the indispensable gift to the bride, perhaps this ill-assorted union (for as such we must characterise the marriage of a man of fifty-three to a child of nine, dragged from her swing and her

* *Musnad*, vi., 4.

† *Muslim*, ii., 148.

‡ *Ibid.*, 110.

toys) was accelerated by the desire to obtain some ready money.

It had originally been arranged that the Refugees should assist the Helpers in their field-work *; but knowing nothing of palmiculture, † they could only perform the most menial services; thus some ‡ literally hewed wood and drew water; some § were employed in watering palms, carrying skins on their backs; and Ali at least on one occasion earned sixteen dates by filling buckets with water, and emptying them over mould for brick-making at the rate of a date a bucket; which hardly earned meal he shared with the Prophet. ‖ The Refugees found rather more prospect of earning money by retail trading; thus Abu Bakr sold clothes in the market ¶; Othman, son of 'Affan, ** became a fruiterer, buying dates of the Banu Kainuka, and selling them at a higher price; Abd al-Rahman, son of 'Auf, set up as a milkman ††; Omar too spent much of his time bargaining in the market ‡‡; and others §§ got the name of "the hucksters," altered by Mohammed to "the Merchants." The date-growing industry had however been severely hit by the Prophet's orders forbidding artificial fertilisation, and prohibiting loans

* *Bokhari*, ii., 174.

† *Tabari, Comm.*, xxviii., 27.

‡ *Musnad*, iii., 137.

§ *Ibid*, i., 8.

‖ *Ibid.*, 135; *Tiraz al-Majalis*, 157.

¶ *Ibn Sa'd*, iii., 130.

** *Musnad*, i., 62.

†† *Ibn Sa'd II.*, ii., 77.

‡‡ *Musnad*, iv., 400.

§§ *Ibid.*, 6, 7.

on the security of the prospective produce. The mischief caused by the former of these measures seems sufficient to account for much in the sequel. It produced artificial scarcity at a time when plenty was specially required. One or two of the Refugees appear to have attempted to carry on foreign trade in the style of Meccah, and we shall presently meet Ali starting, though unsuccessfully, in business of this sort. Omar too appears to have had trade connections with Persia.*

It must be admitted that the Prophet shared to the full the misery of his followers: and indeed, as he refused to employ the Alms for his private needs, he had no source of revenue. Like some other great rulers, he connected taxation with unpopularity; and the notion which is familiar from the Gospel, that independent citizens do not pay taxes, was certainly current in Medinah. Hence, when casual and private generosity failed, he was content to starve. Charitable persons used to invite the Prophet, seeing his face pinched with hunger.† Months used to pass, said Ayeshah, without any fire being lighted in their dwelling, their food being dates and water.‡ His daughter Fatimah was stinted, and after her marriage the little recorded of her consists mainly of complaints about the misery of her lot.§ When presents of food were sent to the Prophet, he would share it with the "people of the

* *Musnad*, iii., 347.
† *Tirmidhi*, i., 203.
‡ *Musnad*, vi., 71.
§ E.g., *Musnad*, v., 26.

Shed," the homeless Moslems who were compelled to seek refuge in the Mosque,—where in the course of time a sort of hospital was started by a woman called Ku'aibah, daughter of 'Utbah.* Miracles by which multitudes were fed or a small quantity of provisions was made to last indefinitely were indeed ascribed to him by the fancy of later generations: but it is evident that, welcome as these powers would have been, he neither possessed them nor let it be supposed that he did. Oppressed with this grinding poverty, starved, naked, and frozen, the True Believers naturally felt some resentment against the Jews, from whom nothing was to be had without security, who were merciless about the recovery of debts,† and who were enjoying opulence (as it seemed) as the result of their skill in industries of various sorts, of their thrift and their business capacity. Bitter reproaches on their meanness were consequently heard from the Prophet's mouth and indeed produced in revelations. Nor did a request for a loan of raiment addressed to "Halik, the Christian" meet with a more favourable response.‡ Among the people of Medinah some pious women,§ as might be expected, placed large portions of their possessions at the Prophet's disposal. Some of these undertook to provide for a fixed number of individuals, but it became evident that some new source of revenue must be discovered.

---

* *Wakidi (W.)*, 215.

† Cf. *Musnad*, iii., 423.

‡ *Musnad*, iii., 244.

§ *Muslim*, ii., 379.

One mode of acquiring a living is open to the very poorest, when there is impunity; and that is robbery. We do not know whether the Prophet when he fled to Medinah foresaw that he would assume the character of robber-chief; but his attaching to himself the robbers of the tribe Aslam, and the provision in the contract which has been quoted, excluding the Meccans from all friendly relations, make it likely that even then he expected to have to fall back on plundering their caravans. Having been with these caravans himself so often, he had the most special knowledge of the best mode of attacking them. The idea however of utilising the position of Medinah for attacking the caravans is said to have first occurred to one of the converts of Medinah, who visited the Ka'bah shortly after the Flight.* Mohammed's experience had moreover taught him to regard the fighting powers of the Meccans as of poor quality. The view that the Kuraish were cowards † was held by many in Arabia—not without justice, as the sequel will show,—and the manner in which they had dealt with Mohammed must have enforced this fact on his mind.‡ Their treatment of himself had displayed a degree of cowardice and imbecility which could not fail to be rightly gauged by a man who could estimate his fellows with precision after a single interview. But besides this like many exiles he had a passionate desire to wipe out the

* *Musnad*, i., 400.

† *Jahiz*, *Opuscula*, 61.

‡ He is credited with the assertion, "the strength of a Kurashite is equal to that of two men"; but its import is doubtful. *Musnad*, iv., 83.

insult to which he had been subjected, in being forced to quit his native town. The people who had driven him out were those on whom he wished to force his authority; whom he wished to see repenting in dust and ashes of their insolence. If the Kuraish had been afraid to shed his blood, he was not afraid to shed theirs. A fresh relationship had been substituted for tribal kinship. When he first announced his new policy, some of the more earnest of his followers were shocked at the idea of fighting, remembering how at Meccah they had been told to return good for evil *; but their scruples were silenced by a revelation; and other revelations were required to comfort those Refugees who actually missed the society of their unbelieving friends.†

About the time of Ayeshah's wedding the first of these expeditions took place; and though they were repeated continually, some months passed before they led to any brilliant result. According to the contract only Refugees took part in them: and they did not at first possess the familiar acquaintance with the region which is indispensable to a brigand. Either they arrived on the scene too late, or something occurred to render their efforts unsuccessful. These attempts, however, taught the Prophet something about the capacity of his followers, and brought him into relations with the surrounding tribes. And even the failures impressed on the Refugees the necessity of earning their living by the sword.

* *Wahidi*, 24.

† *Tabari*, *Comm.*, xxvi 48.

The first commanders employed by the Prophet were his uncle Hamzah, and his cousin 'Ubaidah, son of Harith. Hamzah was sent to waylay a caravan returning in the spring from Syria. The spot chosen was in the territory of the tribe Juhainah, where the road into the interior of Arabia passes near the sea, and is crossed by a wady called 'Is. The Meccans, as peaceful merchants, had secured the protection of the tribes through whose lands their caravans passed, and the head of the Juhainah, Majdi, son of 'Amr, discharged his duty manfully in seeing that the caravan was not attacked in his land. On the only other occasion when he figures in history * he is performing a similar duty. Hamzah with his thirty men could not deal with both Kuraish and Juhainah, and went home.

A few weeks later, 'Ubaidah, son of Harith, was sent with a larger party to waylay a caravan at Rabigh, also near the seashore, midway between Medinah and Mecca. Sa'd, son of Abu Wakkas, one of the party, shot an arrow; but the leader appears to have been wanting in courage, and the Meccans were not at present disposed to fight their former brethren, whose attempts they probably ridiculed.

To Sa'd, son of Abu Wakkas, not unnaturally the next expedition was entrusted (May, 623). He was to catch a caravan at a place called Kharrar, near where the pilgrim roads from Syria and Egypt meet, five days from Medinah. He arrived a day too late.

---

* *Agh*, iv., 22.

During the sacred months nothing was attempted; but near the middle of the following August (Safar) Mohammed made another endeavour, heading the expedition himself. This was to a place called Waddan, an emporium in the days of Ezekiel, but at this time of no account. The caravan escaped him, but he made some sort of covenant with the head of the Banu Damrah, in whose territory Waddan then lay.

The notice of this event is so meagre that we have no knowledge of the process by which Mohammed accomplished this small success. It is so worded as to make it appear that the Prophet made a feint of attacking the Banu Damrah themselves, and spared them on condition of their entering an offensive and defensive alliance; while the contract, as it is quoted,* gives the Prophet the extraordinary right of attacking them, if he chose, in order to force them to Islam. This clause must surely be a dogmatic interpolation to mitigate the Prophet's conduct in making an offensive and defensive alliance with idolators; for why (it might be argued) might he make such an alliance with the Banu Damrah, and yet wage implacable war with the Kuraish? But this argument was answered by a special revelation, † excluding the Meccans (as opposed to other idolaters) from friendly relations. The Prophet's course, whether morally defensible or not, was sound politically; experience had shown him that in order to attack the caravans with safety he must secure the co-operation of the tribes in whose territory he proposed

* *Halabi*, ii., 166.

† *Surah* lx., 7, 8.

to waylay them. If it be true that the caravan which had just slipped through his fingers was of twenty-five hundred camels, the arguments by which he won over the Banu Damrah can easily be reproduced in thought.

Fresh attempts were made by him in September and November, both in the direction of Yanbo, and both unsuccessful. In the second he proceeded with his policy of making terms with the neighbouring tribes. The course followed in this expedition (called the "'Ushairah raid") is chronicled with great accuracy, and was long marked by a series of sanctuaries. This was due to the length of the time, nearly a month, which the Prophet waited in the hope that some booty might come in his way. He had returned to Medinah but a short time when the herds of Medinah were raided by a more experienced robber, and an expedition of which the object was to recover the booty ended in another failure.

Mohammed had failed to secure success by methods which were not, in the opinion of the Arabs of his time, inconsistent with the character of a prophet of God. During the raids of the first year of exile he had not disturbed the peace of the sacred months,* and the peace of those sacred months had been one of the institutions which redeemed Arabia from a state of savagery: for some weeks in the year men could go about unarmed and yet secure. But this security offered a chance to any one who was enlightened enough to have no scruples. An armed

* *Wakidi* places one of the raids in Dhu'l-Kadah.

force attacking an unarmed caravan in the sacred months would be certain to bring home some prisoners and booty. Here, then, lay a prospect of obtaining what was becoming more and more necessary, success. The month after the last failure was the sacred month Rejeb,* and in it Mohammed resorted to this expedient.

The historians are not quite agreed about the details, but everything points to this having been Mohammed's reasoning. Let us first hear the account of the matter ascribed to Sa'd, son of Abu Wakkas.†

"When the Apostle of God came to Medinah, the Juhainah came to him and said: Thou hast settled amongst us, so give us a covenant that we may come to thee, and make thee our leader; so he gave them a covenant and they became Moslems. Then the Apostle sent us out in Rejeb, we being less than one hundred, and bade us attack a branch of the Kinanah that dwelt near the Juhainah. So we did so, but they being too many for us, we took refuge with the Juhainah, who protected us. They said to us, Wherefore fight ye in the sacred month? And we said, We only fight in the sacred month against those who drove us out of our country. Then we consulted with one another; some said, Let us go to the Prophet of God and tell him: others said, Let us stay here. I, with some others, said, Rather let us attack the caravan of the Kuraish, and cut it off. So we went against the caravan, and the others went back to the Prophet and told him. And he rose up, his face red with

* Beginning Dec. 29, 623 A.D., in the ordinary tables.

† *Musnad*, i., 178.

anger, and said, What! Did ye go from me in one company and come back divided? Division it is which ruined them which were before you. I shall set over you a man who is not the best of you, yet is the most enduring of hunger and thirst. So he set over us Abdallah, son of Jahsh, who was the first Commander in Islam."

Most of this account cannot be reconciled with the ordinary history, yet clearly Sa'd's memory had been impressed with the fact of their having been sent out in the sacred month. The commander of the force was Mohammed's cousin, Abdallah, son of Jahsh, under whom seven men were placed. The little that is known of this man makes it appear that he was a fanatic; he is supposed to have prayed that he might die in battle and be mutilated. He had shared the double flight to Abyssinia, and was now a poor Refugee at Medinah. Mohammed sent him towards Nakhlah with *sealed orders*, to be opened after two days' march; and when he opened the orders, he was to compel no one to accompany him any farther. These preparations indicate that something discreditable was intended; for service in the sacred months was not dangerous, but, in the opinion of the Arabs, wicked. The text of the orders, as given by the genuine tradition,* contained definite instructions to attack a party who were going without escort under cover of the sacred month. No one of Abdallah's followers took advantage of the permission to retire; but two members of the party, Sa'd, son of Abu Wakkas, and 'Utbah, son of Ghazwan,

---

* *Wakidi* (*W.*), 25; *Wellhausen*, *Ibid.*, 2.

CAMELS OF BURDEN RESTING.
From De Laborde's *Voyage en Syrie.*

contrived presently to lose their camel, and to lose themselves in following it. The remainder came up with a caravan escorted by four persons. Of these one escaped, two were taken prisoners, and one was killed. 'Amr, son of Al-Hadrami (the man of Hadramaut), was the first of the millions to be slaughtered in the name of Allah and his Prophet. Wakid, son of Abdallah of the tribe Tamim, was the slayer. The two prisoners and considerable booty were brought back to Medinah. At last a success had been gained.

This success was in a way the seed of those which followed, and in organising it Mohammed showed his thorough acquaintance with the character of his subjects. Some booty was absolutely necessary, but it was not absolutely necessary that it should be honourably acquired. Claiming to be the Messenger of the Almighty, he had the right to authorise any act; and whether on this or some other occasion, when remonstrated with by his followers for some atrocity, he repudiated their right to criticise his conduct, assuring them that he knew best and was the most God-fearing among them.* The effect of this success was, as he rightly calculated, that the next time he organised a raid, Helpers and Refugees alike pressed to take part in it. Violation by Allah's Prophet of the sacred months which the pagans respected lost Mohammed no vote that was worth retaining. The Jews indeed signalised themselves by offensive sneers and poor epigrams on the names of the persons concerned, Wakid "the Burner," and

* *Muslim*, ii., 220; *Musnad*, i., 45.

Hadramaut, "the presence of death." And so, too, the Kuraish could tell their Moslem fellow-citizens * that Mohammed had now thrown off the mask and revealed the character which had been no secret to them. Mohammed kept his head and satisfied each party that he considered to merit satisfaction, with a statesmanlike disregard for consistency.

To the timid Moslems courage and a clear conscience were restored by the invariable expedient—a revelation. "Fighting in a sacred month is a bad offence: but to turn people out of Meccah a worse one." The Moslems were to infer from this ambiguous sentence either that the atrocity committed by the Kuraish rendered an attack on them in the sacred month permissible, or that, though no such attack had been made, the Meccans might not complain if it had been. The booty was awarded to the brave company who had won it, all but the percentage (one fifth) which the Prophet claimed. The Meccan prisoners he retained as hostages till the two truants had come back; for the prisoners he then accepted a ransom. The death of the Hadramite was of considerable consequence for the sequel. This man and his brother were under the protection of 'Utbah, son of Rabi'ah, a Kurashite of eminence, whom we afterwards meet with playing a heroic part at the battle of Badr; the protector in such a case was bound to avenge the death of his client. At Badr the brother of the dead man, 'Amir, demanded this vengeance of his protector, who offered payment in camels instead, but this 'Amir refused to

* *Ibn Arabi Colloquies*, ii., 157.

take, at the instigation (it is said)* of Mohammed's enemy, Abu Jahl. 'Utbah therefore resolved to fight, with the result which shall be seen. The blood-feud then which finally decided the Meccans to fight the Medinese sprang out of the relation between client and patron which, owing to its uncertain nature, led to many complications, but, like other matters which are left to the conscience, produced a group of rights and duties which the most honourable natures were the most ready to observe.

What Mohammed had to bear from the Jews during this series of reverses, ending with a scandalous success, we do not exactly know; as failure succeeded failure their jeers doubtless became louder and their sarcasms more stinging. We shall find them many times repeating the process of triumphing prematurely, of irritating without hurting. Mohammed lost patience with them after long endurance of their jibes. Their ordinary modes of speech appeared to him to contain some offensive *arrière-pensée*, and Moslems were forbidden to employ the same. Modern ingenuity cannot discern wherein the offensiveness lay. Probably after the affair which we have been describing he decided definitely to break with them. He received a sudden revelation bidding him to turn his back when he prayed to the Jewish *Kiblah* (or prayer-direction), Jerusalem, and his face to the Meccan temple, the Ka'bah. For the Day of Atonement he substituted a new fast, the month Ramadan, to be kept in the style familiar to visitors of Eastern

---

* *Wellhausen* (*Wakidi*, p. 14) regards the introduction of Abu Jahl in these cases as due to the development of a myth.

states; no food (liquid or solid) may be consumed from sunrise to sunset, but even revelry is permitted at night. Some have connected this institution with one of the Sabians of Harran; this sect are said to have fasted a whole month, and Mohammed, where compelled to differ from both Jews and Christians, may have gone to them.* Others† suppose the fasting month to have been an institution of the old Arabic religion to which Mohammed went back; and this, considering the nature of the change in the prayer-direction, is not impossible. Besides wounding the Jews, it would serve to keep his followers in training for the pursuit which they had been practising for many months, for bandits kept concealed in the day and only moved at night. The feast which follows the fasting month was to serve as a substitute for one of the two public holidays which the Medinese had celebrated in their pagan days,‡ and on it the Prophet ordered drums to be beaten.§ With it some of the ceremonies of the old worship of the dead got united.‖ With these institutions we may further connect the adoption of the Friday as a day for public worship. This was not indeed to be a Sabbath; for that institution he had no desire to imitate, but it was to correspond with the sacred week-day of the other communities, and since the Christians had seized the day after the Saturday, he had no choice but to take the day before it. The

* *Winckler*, *Altorientalische Forschungen*, ii., 348.

† *Nielsen*, *Altarabische Mondreligion*, 168.

‡ *Musnad*, iii., 105.

§ *Ibid.*, 422.

‖ *Goldziher*, *M. S.*, i., 240.

suggestion that such a day was desirable is said to have been made by a Medinese named Rabah or Riyah, son of Rabi'.* The change of the prayer-direction was also not merely anti-Judaic; he had no sooner spilt Meccan blood than he resolved to open the road to an agreement with the Meccans. Their temple then was to be retained in its proud position of central sanctuary of Arabia. Mohammed's religion would not affect the solemnities which had made Meccah wealthy and famous. We fancy, too, that he had learned by some accident that the Temple at Jerusalem was no longer standing, and he got an idea that the rebuilding of it would mean the ruin of Medinah.†

The Jews, it appears, were thoroughly alarmed at this new move of Mohammed, and, it is asserted, offered to acknowledge his mission, if he would go back to his former praying direction. But Mohammed had by this time resolved on their destruction, and even if the offer had been meant earnestly, would have done unwisely to accept it. Had the Jews not been afraid of him, they would never have made it; had they any plan, any resolution, any courage, they would have utilised this period of failure and ignominy to crush him. How cordial co-operation on the part of the Jews would have affected Mohammed at Medinah we do not know; resolute and courageous opposition might for some time yet have effected a good deal.

---

* *Usd al-ghabah. Ibn Sa'd*, iii., 83, states that it was instituted in the correspondence between Mohammed and Mus'ab, son of 'Umair.

† *Jahiz, Bayan*, i., 165.

From this time the breach widened: and whereas Mohammed had a few months before carefully imitated Jewish practices, he now forbade his followers to do anything like the Jews.* If they fasted for the Day of Atonement, they were to keep the fast one day before or after the Jewish day.† Having altered his mode of doing his hair from the pagan style, in which it was parted, to that of the Jews, who let it hang loose, he now reverted to the pagan fashion,‡ and in his ordinances about dyeing the hair forbade imitating the Jews. § He ruled that the pagan as opposed to the Jewish mode of burial should be employed by his followers,‖ and that they should stand at funerals instead of sitting, which was the Jewish practice.¶ The rules concerning menstruating women were altered in a manner which implied opposition to the Jewish code.** Consultation of the Jews on doubtful points was forbidden.†† A long revelation, somewhat in the style of Stephen's Apology,‡‡ was fulminated against them. This tirade, which constitutes most of the second Surah, is regarded by Moslems as a marvel of eloquence, and appears to have produced a profound impression—not on the Jews themselves, but

* *Musnad*, i., 165.

† *Ibid.*, 242.

‡ *Ibid.*, 246.

§ *Ibn Sa'd*, iii., 157, 27.

‖ *Musnad*, iv., 363.

¶ *Ibid.*, 85.

** *Ibid.*, 132.

†† *Ibid.*, 338.

‡‡ *Preserved Smith*, p. 84, makes this comparison.

in stirring up the feelings of the people of Medinah against them. It was followed by others. To these repeated philippics we may, in part, ascribe the circumstance that in the severe measures which he proceeded to take against the Jews he met with little or no opposition on the part of their former allies.

Meanwhile the luck had turned. The violation of the sacred month had shocked some followers, but it had caused no apostasies: the net was still further spread over the consciences of those who by assenting had compromised themselves therein. To the revelations which now served so many purposes the old argument of Abu Bakr was applied by an ever-increasing circle. Having believed so much, why should they not believe more? Having overridden so many scruples, why be delayed by any from following the Prophet's career?

Between the people of Meccah and the Prophet there was now a blood-feud. 'Amr, son of the Hadramite, had been killed, and under specially disgraceful circumstances. Vengeance was due for him, which might be exacted not only from Mohammed and his co-Refugees, but also from the Helpers who had undertaken their protection. The next scene, therefore, represents a very considerable advance. The Meccans are not all bent on avoiding a conflict with their robber-kinsman; some of them are no less anxious for it than he. And the natives of Medinah follow the Prophet to the battle-field as well as the Refugees.

The caravan which had escaped Mohammed the

previous November was on its way home in March. It was under the command of Abu Sufyan, whose descendants afterwards reigned over Islam, forming what is known as the Umayyad dynasty. They had done good business in Syria and were bringing home goods of the value (it is said) of five hundred thousand francs. The prize was worthy of an effort and Mohammed resolved to make it.

How news travels in the East is to this day a wonder. Probably the carrier-pigeon does more work than is ordinarily credited to it; speculators of different kinds have agents who thus keep them informed of various events, primarily for commercial purposes; but the information can also be used for other objects. There are other organised modes of signalling of which the secret is rarely revealed. Moreover, members of the Khuza'ah (in Meccah) were already in league with Mohammed, assisting him against the Kuraish.* Mohammed on this occasion sent spies to a point in the road some time before the caravan actually passed: but these were outwitted by the chieftain in whose territory they waited; yet the news reached Mohammed none the less, according to one account, through one Busaisah.† On receiving the information he called to arms; and the memory of the spoils which had at last reached Medinah acted like the display of nuggets brought as specimens from a gold-mine: every one wished to share in the plunder. Of the multitude who answered the appeal some 60 Helpers and 240

* *Musnad*, iv., 325.

† *Ibid.*, iii., 136.

A CARAVAN HALTED.
From a photograph.

Refugees were selected * (perhaps with the view of reproducing the numbers employed by "Talut," *i. e.*, Gideon-Saul in the battle recorded in the Koran †). Two horses and 70 camels were all the beasts that could be got together, many of the latter being taken from agricultural operations. The owners of the camels were requested by the Prophet each of them to permit two or three of their unmounted comrades to ride by turns with themselves; which they did. ‡ Probably the men took with them small stores of dates § by way of commissariat. On some expeditions the soldiers trusted to locusts ‖; whereas the dried strips of cooked meat used by the pilgrims at other times furnished them with food.¶ When the Moslems had become richer, camels were sent by wealthy members of the community to be slaughtered at the rate of one camel for a hundred soldiers**: the Meccan commissariat was similar, the soldiers also carrying with them supplies of meat. One Abu Lubabah was sent to govern Medinah during the absence of the army; and a governor was also sent to keep Kuba quiet, where there seemed danger of disturbance.†† Abu Sufyan, however, got

* Different estimates of the Moslems who fought at Badr: Ishak, 314 (83 Refugees, 61 Aus, 170 Khazraj); Abu Ma'shar, 313; Ibn 'Ukbah, 316. *Ibn Sa'd, II.*, ii., 134.

† *Musnad*, iv., 291.

‡ *Ibid.*, iii., 358.

§ Cf. *Musnad*, iii., 446.

‖ *Musnad*, iv., 353.

¶ *Ibid.*, iii., 85.

** *Wakidi* (*W.*), 231.

†† *Ibn Sa'd, II.*, ii., 36.

early information—at Zarka*—of the fact that Mohammed planned an attack in great force, and while hurrying to Meccah by routes known to few besides himself, and by forced marches, he also sent a scout to call the Meccans to help. The scout, according to custom, disfigured his camel and rode it backwards. Hearing his message, the Meccans resolved on a general rally in which all men either joined or sent substitutes. It had been Mohammed's plan to infest the route where it passed near Medinah. Thither the Meccans' army, some thousand strong,† after three days' preparation, hastened.

Owing to the importance of the battle of Badr such a number of conflicting legends grew round it that each statement about it must be received with some distrust, there being so many grounds for falsification.

It is stated that when the Meccan force, having started, learnt by messenger of the safety of the caravan, several persons were of opinion that the wisest course would be to return to Meccah without fighting, and one or two tribes actually did so (notably the Zuhrites, to whom Mohammed's mother belonged, and the Banu 'Adi). This counsel is assigned by the tradition to 'Utbah, son of Rabi'ah, whereas the determination to proceed is ascribed to Abu Jahl, the old opponent of Mohammed. One ground for the proposed retirement was the fact that the Meccans were at feud with another tribe, the Bakr Ibn Kinanah, who might be expected to attack the city when its

---

* *Wakidi*, 21.

† Nine hundred and fifty men, seven hundred camels, one hundred horses.—*Wakidi* (*W.*), 44.

defenders were away. It was also remembered that the Refugees, though enemies, were their own kin; albeit, on the other hand, the blood which Mohammed had spilled cried for vengeance. To us, endeavouring to recall the situation, with, it is true, imperfect knowledge of the facts, it is difficult to say which course would have savoured most of true wisdom. If the caravan had been in danger, there would have been no question: but it had reached safety well before the battle, and if Mohammed had been suffered to return to Medinah having gained nothing, bankruptcy and failure combined might have injured him as much as a lost battle. On the other hand, an important factor in the situation, Mohammed's military ability, was unknown to them, as indeed it was to his friends: they were enormously superior in numbers, and, in some respects, in equipment. Retreat might bring them into contempt, when there was blood to be avenged. Mohammed's raids occasioned some inconvenience, though till then no serious damage; and a chance of getting rid of him should not be neglected. It is probable that to most of those who had a voice in the matter the arguments in favour of advancing seemed weightier than those on the other side. Their resolution turned out to be disastrous: we do not know whether the opposite course would have proved more beneficial.

The scene of the famous battle, Badr, lies at the end of a westerly ramification of the great chain of mountains which follows the Arabian coast-line. It is said to have been the locality of an annual fair, held on the first eight days of the month preceding the pilgrim month. It lay near the point at which the Syrian road to Meccah leaves the coast to wind through difficult passes. From the number which Mohammed took with him it would seem that he hoped to overwhelm opposition.

The route followed by Mohammed is recorded in detail*; of the names which meet us in it the most familiar is Safra, a village about a day's journey from Badr, visited by Burckhardt. The ordinary route from Safra to Badr passes through a very narrow and difficult valley: Mohammed is said to have avoided it, because some of the names wounded his sense of delicacy: and to have chosen a pass through a valley called "Sweet-smelling" instead. The motives by which this remarkable man was swayed were so numerous that this story need not be rejected. It is not probable that this fancy lost the precious time in which the caravan could have been caught; but doubtless it lost some.

The day before the battle (Ram. 18)† the parties were separated by one sand hill. A couple of men from the Meccan army, trying to find water, found their way to the Prophet's camp, and one of them‡ being captured brought the news that the caravan had escaped, but that the Meccan army was at hand. This statement occasioned the bitterest disappointment; the Moslems tried hard to discredit it by torturing the messenger till he retracted: but Mohammed

* *Ishak*, 433.

† March 16, 624 A.D., according to the ordinary Tables.

‡ *Memoirs of Ali.*

appears to have satisfied himself that the statement was true. He had, therefore, the same problem before him as the Meccans had faced when the news of the safety of the caravan reached them; and he (it is said) left it to the Helpers to decide; justly acknowledging that the contract which they had made by no means bound the Helpers to aid him in aggressive warfare. The Helpers were, however, eager for battle—perhaps doubting whether the caravan had got into safety after all. There is, however, a story that Mohammed sent Omar to offer the blood-money for 'Amr the Hadramite: which his brother 'Amir, at Abu Jahl's instigation, refused. The story is told with details which give it some plausibility: 'Amir is said to have practised the peculiar rites by which the demand for blood was enforced. Such an act may perhaps be alluded to in the pride and ostentation with which Mohammed in his comments on the battle charges the Meccans, while he rather implies that the Moslems were not anxious for battle. After the victory it was natural that the latter should represent themselves to have been eager to fight from the commencement.

Experience has shown that the military career can, more than any other, be started successfully late in life; but if Mohammed, entering his first battle as commander at the age of fifty three, succeeded beyond all hope, the result must be attributed to his readiness to receive suggestions. The help of the angels or other supernatural agencies was gratefully acknowledged *ex post facto*, but for the attainment of the end much more commonplace expedients were adopted. Hubab,* son of Al-Mundhir, the Prophet's junior by twenty years, having ascertained that they were engaged in ordinary warfare, and possessing a special knowledge of the wells in the neighbourhood, advised the Prophet to get in front of all, except one, round which they should make a reservoir, so as to have a constant supply of water for the troops: the possession of this valuable element would then save the day. The Prophet welcomed the suggestion and placed his force under Hubab's guidance. One Meccan is said to have rushed at the reservoir, and to have paid for a drink with his life; but when a number of the enemy approached they were allowed to drink unmolested—in accordance with a principle laid down in Persian treatises on tactics.†

Of the battle that followed we have no clear or detailed account: but we know at least some of the factors which brought about the result. The discipline of the *salat* or "prayer," in which the Moslems were arranged in rows, and had to perform after a leader certain bodily exercises,‡ and falling out of line was threatened with divine punishment,§ had served as a rough sort of drill, and Mohammed before the battle discharged the duty of making the troops fall into line. The Meccan general, 'Utbah, son of Rabiah, was struck with their appearance: they were kneeling on their knees, silent as though they were dumb, and stretching out their tongues

*Since Hubab was the name of a demon, it is strange that it was not altered.

† *'Uyun al-Akhbar*, 140, 12.

‡ *Musnad*, iv., 228.

§ *Ibid.*, iv., 27[illegible]

like snakes.* They were all subject to the single will of their Prophet, who was aware that the general should not risk his life; for him therefore in the rear of the army a hut was built, where, attended by his most trusted counsellors, he could issue orders; and to which camels were tied ready to be used by the leaders for flight in case of disaster. When the first blood was shed the Prophet retired into his hut and fainted; when he had come to himself he devoted the time to impassioned prayer, showing that he was thoroughly alarmed.† The members of the cabinet, who regarded these prayers as unseemly, remained by their master in his hut, issuing orders when necessary. The soldiers had probably been supplied with armour by the Jews of Medinah, who could judge well of such goods, though unskilful in using them. The armour, when complete, covered the whole person except the legs‡; the helmet was provided with a continuation for the throat§; thus the holes for the eyes and the legs offered the most promising places for blows.

Opposed to them was a horde of Arabs, far superior in numbers (six hundred to three hundred), and well provided with cavalry and camels; but justifying otherwise the reproaches levelled against the Arabs in later days when foreign Moslems maintained that the Arabs were inferior to other races. The Arabs,‖ they urged, were unacquainted with

* *'Uyun al-Akhbar*, 135.

† *Muslim*, ii., 55.

‡ *Wellhausen* (*W.*), 153.

§ *Wakidi* (*W.*), 110.

‖ *Jahiz*, *Bayan*, ii., 50.

the rudiments of military science. They fought in no order, with no leadership, with no suitable weapons or attire, with no scouting, no artillery, and no camp defence. Of the hundred or more technical terms which the warfare of Islam evolved, the Arabs of the Ignorance had no knowledge. And indeed the Meccan leaders fell out before the battle; 'Utbah, son of Rabi'ah, killing his colleague Abu Jahl's horse. He then, in order to show his courage before his rival, abandoned the duty of director of operations, and demanded that a champion of the enemy should meet him in single combat; and in the miniature combat between 'Utbah with two other Meccans, and Ali with Hamzah and another, all three Meccans were killed. One tradition speaks of a Meccan leader having deserted in the middle of the combat, and so having broken the line of fighting men; but the source of this statement appears to be a rather too literal interpretation of the realistic language of the Koran about Iblis or the devil. The other general, Abu Jahl, being on foot, was forced to fight and was killed. There being no recognised leader left, the Meccans were seized with panic and turned their backs, losing seventy slain and seventy captives; the Moslem loss was fourteen.

It certainly appears that the winning of this most important fight was in the main due to the prowess of Ali (who fought without armour to his back)* and Hamzah. The Prophet is said to have bestowed especial praise on the valour of Simak, son of Kharashah, Sahl, son of Hunaif, al-Harith, son of al-Simmah,

* '*Uyun al-Akhbar*, 162, 18.

and Kais, son of al-Rabi—all of them Medinese.* The armour of Abu Jahl is said to have been worn by three men in succession, each of whom perished in single combat; after the death of the third no one was found willing to don it. For the greater part of the day the Moslems remained in serried formations, "fighting (or rather defending themselves) like a wall," except when a champion went forward to answer a challenge: of any sort of order or discipline on the Meccan side we do not hear. The greater number of deaths and captures seem to have taken place late in the day, when the Meccans turned their backs. What we cannot understand is how, if any sort of purpose was to be found in the Meccan tactics, their cavalry failed to trample down the enemy. Sprenger supposes that the cavalry was deterred by fear of the Moslem archery; and their attack on the square appears to have been resisted. But with their superiority in numbers there should have been no difficulty in outflanking, for the accounts of the battle do not suggest that the Mohammedan position was particularly strong. Mohammed himself seems to have been puzzled by the result, and to have on the whole regarded it as due to an erroneous estimate of the forces on both sides. The Meccans thought the Moslems twice as many as they actually were, whereas the Moslems similarly underestimated the Meccan force.† Mohammed's statements on this matter are likely to be based on accurate knowledge. At the next meeting the

* *Isabah*, iii., 491.
† *Surah* iii., 11, viii., 46.

victory of Uhud was rendered fruitless to the Meccans by their erroneous supposition that Mohammed had still an enormous force at his command. In the Boer war grossly mistaken estimates of the forces in action seem many times to have been made, and to have been of influence on the course of the campaign. The statement of the Koran forces us to reject, as biographical fiction, the story that Mohammed made before the battle an exact computation of the force arrayed against him based on their daily consumption of camels; and that a Meccan scout by inspection of the Moslem force was able to estimate it exactly, and also to tell that it had no reinforcements and no men in ambush. It is more likely that the Meccans were firmly convinced that Mohammed had an enormous reserve.

Mohammedan writers, arguing from a hint in the Koran, further imagine that the heavy rain which fell the night before the battle was of advantage to the Moslems, but the opposite to the Meccans. They suppose that the rain by moistening the sand rendered it firmer and better suited to infantry—perhaps taking the words of the Koran too literally. And indeed the very recent writer who "went on the track of the masked Tawariks" declares that the feet of *camels* are useless when the ground is wet. Further, they interpret the passage as meaning that the Moslem forces actually slept the night before the battle, and so came to the fight fresher than the Meccans, who had kept awake, fearing a surprise, and perhaps also doubting the fidelity of different detachments after the loss of two by desertion. If the night was spent in this way by the armies, there can be no doubt that Mohammed was correct when he declared that each was quite mistaken in its estimate of the numbers of the other.

Too much confidence must not, however, be placed in the Prophet's statements. Thus he declared that God had promised them (before the battle) one of the two—either the caravan or the Meccan host; yet it appears that of the arrival of the latter Mohammed had no knowledge till the day before the battle, and the same messenger who brought news of the arrival of the Meccan force, must also have brought intelligence of the safety of the caravan. Then to the Moslem prayer for help, he says, there came an answer that a reinforcement of one thousand angels, each with a back rider, would be sent. Finally even these angels had to be encouraged by a special promise of the divine assistance. We cannot very well believe that the promise of the angels' help was made till after the victory was won. Had Mohammed known the size of the force opposed to him, it is not probable that he would have fought; and he was too cautious to promise angelic assistance when there was no chance of its arriving. Once, however, the angels had been called in, it cost nothing to multiply them; and the next year the angels who fought at Badr had grown to three thousand.* But in the popular tradition the credit of the battle was ascribed not to the angels, but the prowess of the family of Abd al-Muttalib,† who years after

* *Surah* iii., 120.

† *Jahiz*, *Mahasin*, 140.

continued to fling it in the face of Abu Sufyan's descendants.

Discipline and steadfastness of purpose are said to win battles, and it is clear that these qualities were to be found on the Moslem side, not on the Meccan. Mohammed, in getting his troops into line, is said to have hurt one of his followers with his staff; the injured man, by way of obtaining amends, kissed his leader's stomach. We have but to contrast this scene with the unseemly brawls between the Meccan leaders to understand one reason why the Meccans failed. And further, there is evidence that the motive which worked wonders in so many Moslem battle-fields helped largely too in this. Death in the path of God was regarded by not a few of the fighters as a better thing than victory. Overwrought with desire for their gaudily painted paradise they chafed at the chains which bound them to this world: they flung themselves with rapture on the enemy, whose swords formed so many keys to the gates of the eternal kingdom. Well able to assist by their counsels, and to impart strength and endurance, Al-Lāt and Al-'Uzza had in store no Garden of Delight, to be entered by the grave and gate of death. Those who died in their service, if they did not, as Mohammed declared, enter the Fire, yet at best, according to their account, had a continuation of their personality similar to that enjoyed by Mr. Myers's discarnate spirits: the sovereign among whom might be thought worse off than a poor slave up above.

And finally early satirists of the Kuraish accuse

them without hesitation of cowardice. As merchants they had obtained some immunity from fighting, and by putting some bark or other sign on themselves when they left their houses, they could pass safely where others would be challenged. The poet who refers to this practice taunts the Kuraish with their abandonment of the Ka'bah at the time of the invasion; and the unwillingness to shed blood and readiness to leave the field which characterise their actions till the taking of Meccah seem to show that the poet was right in his estimate.*

But it is likely that the point on which Sir William Muir insists, the horror of shedding kindred blood on the one side, with the desire to shed it which prevailed on the other side, was after all the leading factor in deciding the battle in favour of the Moslems. The cases in which members of the same family were ranged on opposite sides were numerous; and Islam, as appears from the most authorised traditions, had the effect of making men anxious rather than otherwise to signalise their faith by parricide or fratricide. The Tradition records a case, presumably later than this time, when a man told Mohammed he had killed his father for speaking slightingly of the Prophet; who received the intelligence calmly.† And lest any filial affection should remain, he expressly forbade men to pray for the souls of their unbelieving fathers. When it was pointed out that according to the Koran Abraham had done this for his father, a special revelation came down, explaining

* *Jahiz*, *Opuscula*, 61.

† *Isabah*, iii., 708.

that Abraham had specially promised "Azar" that he would do this—one wonders how or when; and in quite late revelations this act of Abraham is noticed as a slur on his character.* Abu Bakr's son (it is said), who was converted long after, told his father that he had intentionally spared him on the day of Badr. Abu Bakr answered that had he had the chance he would have slain his son. Abu 'Ubaidah, son of Al-Jarrah, actually killed his father, who was fighting on the Meccan side; he is credited indeed with having endeavoured to avoid the necessity. Abu Hudhaifah, not being permitted to fight with his father, 'Utbah, son of Rabi'ah, in single combat, still assisted in dispatching him.† Mus'ab, son of 'Umair, urged the captor of his brother to demand a heavy ransom, because their mother could well pay it, declaring the captor to be of nearer kin to himself, being a Moslem.‡ Probably Moslem earnestness was a case of that principle of human nature by which "what before was too much feared is all the more eagerly trampled under foot." Mohammed indeed appears to have endeavoured to obtain immunity for his own relatives and former benefactors, and thereby to have incurred the reproach of one of his followers, who thought the Prophet should have set a better example—the Prophet who for years had owed the continuance of his existence to the respect felt for kindred blood! But the Prophet was him-

---

* *Surah* lx., 4.

† *Wakidi* (*W.*), 54.

‡ *Ibid.*, 79.

self at no time a gloomy fanatic: unlike some of his followers; for it may be a true anecdote which makes one of the Meccans before the fight compare the healthy faces of the idolators with the woebegone, melancholy looks of the monotheists, and warn the Meccan leaders against a course which might reduce the Meccans to the same miserable condition. The French revolution exhibits well-known cases of men in whom principle took the form of a thirst for blood. This passion indeed seized possession of the victorious ranks at Badr. Some men who had yielded themselves prisoners could not be rescued by their captors from the fanatics, who preferred blood to ransoms. Those who had endured torture at Meccah seized the opportunity to exact vengeance from their persecutors.* Omar (always ready to be executioner) was for slaughtering all the prisoners; one fanatic, the poet Abdallah, son of Rawahah, suggested that they should be burned,† and Mohammed in his revelation declared that a massacre would have been more pleasing to God: bloodshed on a great scale being calculated to impress the imagination. Economical considerations probably decided him against carrying this out. For though the spoil amounted to one hundred and fifty camels and ten horses, besides some goods which Meccan speculators had taken with them in the hope of finding a market, and the clothes and armour of the slain, seventy prisoners formed an asset which the condition of his followers did not allow him to squander.

* So Bilal and 'Ammar.

† *Musnad*, i., 383.

The Prophet spent three days at Badr before he commenced the triumphal journey home. Some, it is said, urged him to make a rush on Meccah, but for that enterprise he was probably not prepared.* Before they left Badr a pit was dug or cleared into which the corpses of the unbelievers were thrown; and the exultant conqueror, though ordinarily reverent to the dead,† could not refrain from asking them whether they were now convinced, telling his astonished followers that the corpses could hear, though unable to answer. Truly he might exult over his deliverance from Abu Jahl, thanking Allah who had helped his servant and strengthened his religion‡; and a few days more were to deliver him from Abu Lahab. Two of the prisoners were slaughtered on the way, Al-Nadir, son of Al-Harith, and 'Ukbah, son of Abu Mu'ait. The latter is said to have treated the Prophet with roughness; he had also had early connection with the Jews, and may have at some time helped the Prophet with information; he had even at one time formally espoused Islam, but had afterwards withdrawn. The dirge§ uttered over the former by his daughter (or sister) is one of the most affecting in the pathetic dirge literature of the Arabs, and is said to have moved Mohammed himself to tears and regrets. The man's offence is said to have been that he bought the books of the Greeks, Persians, and Arabs of Hirah,

* *Musnad*, i., 229.

† *Ibid.*, iv., 252.

‡ *Ibid.*, i., 442.

§ *Zahr al-adab*, i., 28.

and recited their contents; and argued that if story-telling was the criterion of a prophet he had as good a right to the title as Mohammed. His daughter thought a brave man might have pardoned even such an affront, but she was in error.

No event in the history of Islam was of more importance than this battle: the Koran rightly calls it the Day of Deliverance, the day before which the Moslems were weak, after which they were strong. Its value to Mohammed himself it is difficult to overrate; he possibly regarded it himself as a miracle, and when he declared it one, most of his neighbours accepted the statement without hesitation. His own share in the fighting appears to have been small—was indeed confined to flinging a handful of pebbles in the enemies' faces*; but he wisely claimed the whole not as his own work, but as that of God. The fate that had befallen the enemy was a just retribution to those who had presumed to resist God and His Prophet. As we have seen, the want of the power to perform a miracle was a thing that embittered his life. Now at last the trial had been removed.

Wealth, fame, honour, power, all of them were secured or at any rate brought within reach by the Day of Deliverance. At a later time to have taken part in the battle of Badr was a letter of nobility, and when the proceeds of the treasury were divided among the Moslems, in Omar's time, the Badris received five thousand dirhems apiece.† Mohammed

* Ali however asserted that he had fought bravely.

† The Badri who survived longest was Sa'd, son of Abu Wakkas. *Bokhari* (*Kast.*) vi., 274.

was ready to the end of his life to forgive any offence committed by one who had taken part in the fight; God, he declared, might for all he knew have given them a license to do what they pleased.*

Almost immediately after the battle gifts were offered Mohammed by neighbouring chiefs, anxious to win his favour; but he would only accept them on condition of the givers embracing Islam. Some who refused had afterwards occasion to regret that they had not at this time taken shares in the new venture.†

The time was approaching when the Refugees would depend no longer on the charity of the Helpers: the latter were beginning to enjoy the profits of their speculation in joining Islam, and those who had stayed at home wished they had joined the expedition. The share which accrued to each soldier was to starvelings comparative wealth. Ali's was a couple of camels. Mohammed's slave Salih, who was given charge of the prisoners, got gratuities from them which amounted to more than a share in the spoil.‡ The Meccan prisoners were not made of the stern stuff which Horace has taught us to admire in Regulus. Little difficulty was made about offering ransoms. The highest sum so given was four thousand dirhems; for others, who were poorer, a smaller sum was taken. In the case of quite poor men (it is said) the sum was paid in writing-lessons given to Medinese

---

* *Musnad*, iii., 350.

† *Ibid.*, iv., 68.

‡ *Ibn Sa'd*, iii., 34.

lads; the teachers at times recouping themselves with blows.* The importance of this art was now fully recognised by Mohammed, who† urges the utility of drawing up deeds connected with property and loans, and having them attested. The mode in use was clumsy, and ere long a new fashion was brought to Medinah, which Abu Sufyan took the trouble to learn.‡ Among the prisoners were Mohammed's uncle Abbas, and the sons of his uncle al-Harith: from one of them, Naufal, Mohammed demanded as ransom a thousand spears which he kept at Jeddah; Naufal is said to have turned Moslem at once, supposing the Prophet to have learned of this store by supernatural means.§ To Abbas himself the Prophet is said to have displayed some similar knowledge. "Redeem yourself, your nephews, and your confederates," he said to Abbas, who declined, declaring that he was a Moslem at heart, and had served against his will. "God knows best about that," was the reply; "externally you were against us, so ransom yourself."—"You have twenty ounces of silver that I lent you, take them as my ransom."—"They are a present to me from God."—"But I have no other money."—"Then where is the money which, when you left Meccah, you secretly deposited with your wife Umm Fadl, with instructions how it should be shared between your sons, in case of your death?" Abbas

* *Musnad*, i., 247.

† *Surah* ii., 282, 283.

‡ *Ibn Duraid*, 223.

§ *Isabah*, iii., 1090.

(according to his imaginative son) testified that Mohammed was the Prophet of God, when he heard this secret revealed: yet he appears to have paid his ransom none the less, in order to go back to Meccah.* More credit attaches to the tradition which makes Mohammed endeavour by impressive religious rites to make proselytes among the visitors who came to redeem their friends‡; and that attempts were made by kindly treatment of prisoners to win them over to Islam.

One man only is said to have determined not to swell Mohammed's treasury. Abu Sufyan, now the recognised leader at Meccah, instead of sending a ransom for his brother whom Ali had captured, waited till a man from Medinah came to Meccah on pilgrimage; this man he seized and exchanged for his brother. The whole sum which Mohammed thus acquired was probably not less than one hundred thousand dirhems. His first idea was to claim the whole on behalf of God and His Prophet. But he was induced to modify this claim. Of the whole sum taken, God and His Prophet were to have a fifth. Each captor was otherwise to have the ransom of his prisoner. It is stated that the claim to the fifth was a reduction on the leader's perquisite enjoyed by the pre-Mohammedan sovereigns. They not only had a fourth of the plunder, but also certain other privileges which Mohammed abandoned.

The news of the defeat was brought to Meccah by one Haisuman; the scene which followed on the

* *Musnad*, i., 553.

† *Ibid.*, iv., 83.

arrival of the defeated army is recorded in fragments only. Some perhaps excused their flight on the ground that they had been confronted by supernatural antagonists; but the excuse was received with derision and indignation. Hind, daughter of 'Utbah, demanded of the Hashimites her father, brother, and uncles, whose faces were wont to shine like beacons to the travellers in the dark night.* An attempt was made to sequestrate the goods belonging to the Banu Zuhrah in the caravan which Abu Sufyan had saved: but their leader pointed out that Abu Sufyan himself had commanded the Meccans to desist from the expedition against Mohammed, and they had in returning obeyed his orders. On this act of justice therefore he did not insist, but the profit made by the expedition and saved from the enemy was devoted to the equipment of a force to be sent against Medinah.† All eyes apparently now looked to Abu Sufyan: the battle had taken off the stage all possible rivals to his influence, while inflicting on him losses which he was bound as a man of honour to avenge. And indeed it was evident that on the ability of the community to avenge their losses depended not only their honour but their very existence. The ransom money would not last for ever; when it was near exhaustion Mohammed would be ready for an attack on the caravans, and find no difficulty in obtaining helpers for so profitable a speculation.

Numerous verses on the battle of Badr are given

* *Ghurar al-Khasa'is*, 200.

† *Wakidi*, 199.

by Ibn Ishak in his biography: to leave the fallen at Badr unmourned would have doubtless been disrespectful*; yet the genuineness of most of the dirges produced is disputed; some may have really been sung on the occasion. The note of all is the same,—vengeance cannot be delayed. Another time the Meccans will show to greater advantage. It will be seen whether they did so. Meanwhile some poetic talent was rising in Medinah also, since a war of force in Arabia would have been incomplete without a war of rhymes†; and Abu Bakr's genealogical knowledge was once again found useful in the Prophet's cause.‡ For the satirist, though not scrupulous in his statements, still had to be supplied with material which he could adorn or expand. Just as the Refugees were suffering from Meccan satire, so versified retorts could now be taught the slave-girls of Medinah. §

---

* *Goldziher*, *W. Z. K. M.*, xvi., 307.

† *Id.*, *M. S.*, i., 44.

‡ *Zahr al-adab*, i., 26.

§ *Musnad*, iv., 263.

CHAPTER VIII

PROGRESS AND A SETBACK

THE herald sent on by Mohammed to announce his victory at Medinah, Abdallah, son of Rawahah,* was at first treated as a liar—the sole survivor of a routed host. The Jews, whose ill-luck rarely failed them on such occasions, appear especially to have enjoyed a short-lived triumph. Many, many a man at Medinah utilised the day that passed between the arrival of the herald and the triumphal entry of Mohammed to curse the new ruler; for after a few hours it would be unsafe. Near the end of Ramadan he entered the city, preceded by the prisoners. The triumphant rhapsody which forms the 8th Surah was doubtless delivered at a thanksgiving service. With the enthusiasm of one who has performed a successful coup in a new career, he dilated on the glories of fighting; and arguing from the losses on either side declared that for purposes of war, one Moslem was equal to ten unbelievers.

The institution, which the Greeks called tyranny,

* According to *Ibn Sa'd*, iii., 38, Zaid Ibn Harithah.

seems everywhere to produce similar effects. Let one man be given absolute and uncontrolled authority in a community, a number of parasites are sure to arise, ready to plunge into any sort of mire in the hope of gaining a smile from their master. Ramadan was not over before this breed began to show itself. If any one had incurred the Prophet's displeasure, the Prophet could be served by that person's assassination. There were people at Medinah who gave trouble to the Prophet; the sort whose misfortune it is that they are unable to share the aspirations of their neighbours. To these persons the victory of Badr was not so much a triumph as an outrage. The slain whom the conquerors had left on the field were their fathers and brothers; those whom they were bringing back with their hands bound and tied to their camels were their nearest kin. This sort of triumph shocked those in whom the old humanity had not been killed by the new religion. Even the Prophet's wife, Saudah, asked the Kurashite Sulaim, when he was brought in, tied and bound, why he could not have died like a man? The wives and children of the victors are likely to have re-echoed these sentiments, and a warning was revealed against them, with a request, however, not to punish them too severely.* In the tribes resident at Medinah there were satirists who expressed their opinions freely on public affairs. The race did not die out even late in the Caliphate; but in the great cities of later times they were not detected quite so easily and their satires circulated in writing.

* *Surah* lxiv., 14.

At Medinah satires may indeed have been written,* but are more likely to have been declaimed with the normal formalities; the satirist anointed one side of his hair, let his mantle droop, and wore only one shoe.† 'Asma, daughter of Marwan, the wife of a member of the tribe Khatmah, mother of five sons, had the poetical gift; she taunted the people of Medinah with obeying a stranger, who was waiting for the city "to be done brown," when he might enjoy the gravy; and invited some one to nip these hopes in the bud. Abu 'Afak, a member of the tribe 'Amr Ibn 'Auf, failed to see that the Prophet's arrival had united the people of Medinah, and taunted them with being divided by this stranger whose notions of right and wrong were quite different from theirs. He thought that if they believed in force and tyranny, they had better have obeyed the old Kings of Yemen. Mohammed expressed a wish to be delivered from these satirists, and a couple of assassins readily offered their services. Both were run through at dead of night, when sleeping peacefully in their homes, and the assassins publicly applauded and held up as patterns of conduct.‡ These executions were perpetrated in the week immediately following Badr.§ And perhaps about the same time 'Umair, son of Umayyah, finding his sister by the seashore, killed her for a similar offence.‖

Before the arrival of the Prophet there would have

* *Goldziher*, *Z. D. M. G.*, xlvi., 18.

† *Ibid.*, 5; *Abhandlungen*, i.

‡ *Ibn Ishak* (pp. 995, 996) puts these events after Uhud. *Ibn Duraid* gives the name of 'Asma's murderer as Ghishmir, son of Kharshah (p. 265). § *Wakidi.* ‖ *Isabah*, iii., 56.

been no doubt about the effect of these acts. The murderer's life would have been forfeit without question. The son of the murdered mother would have been as much in duty bound to avenge her death as ever was Orestes to avenge his father. The tribesmen of the old poet would have fallen on the first member of the murderer's tribe who came in their way. It appears that in ordinary cases, even apart from the superstitions connected with blood, the filial feeling was not less keen among the Arabs than among other races. But the result of these executions shows how well Mohammed understood the people among whom he sojourned. When the slayer of the woman 'Asma asked whether he need fear the consequences of what he had done, the Prophet, coining a new proverb, told him that there would not be as much disturbance about it as two goats can make. The historians tell us that the tribes of the murdered persons adopted Islam in consequence. Translating the scene into modern language, we might say that they treated the acts as legitimate executions ordered by the sovereign power; which they found it beyond their power to resist, and whose protection they thought it expedient to enjoy. Since, if the verses ascribed to 'Asma be genuine, she had deliberately incited the people of Medinah to a murderous attack on the Prophet, her execution would not have been an inexcusably ruthless measure, judged by any standard; and it must not be forgotten that satire was a far more effective weapon in Arabia than elsewhere *; and

* *Goldziher*, *Abhandlungen*, i.

that during the Caliphate it was at times penalised.* The employment of the assassin where the executioner might reasonably have been employed is what excites horror.† Mohammed could urge that in dealing with tribes which had not adopted Islam he had no executioners at his disposal; that discipline is to be maintained by the exhibition of power rather than of authority. Hence the dexterity manifested in the selection of the right time and the right agent for effecting a result was, in a partly organised state, the only possible substitute for the legal and judicial procedure which would suit a completely organised state; and from the fact that only the culprit suffered, it was a decided improvement on the existing system, by which satire on an individual meant war between whole tribes. The principle that each person shall suffer for his own fault was introduced instead. If any people felt horrified by these assassinations, they either left Medinah, or kept their horror for private conversations; but presently criticism of the Prophet in private was condemned in a revelation,‡ and True Believers who heard such communications felt it their duty to inform their master.

A more serious step had to be taken against the Jews (Banu Kainuka) who inhabited the chief market of Medinah; said to be three hundred men capable of bearing arms, and four hundred unarmed. They

* *Goldziher*, *Z. D. M. G.*, xlvi., 19.

† Both Muir and Sprenger treat these acts as cold-blooded and treacherous murders.

‡ *Surah* lviii., 9.

were goldsmiths, and doubtless the wealthiest of the inhabitants of Medinah. They had pursued the policy of aimless irritation which has already been noticed. Before acknowledging Mohammed as a prophet, they had desired a miracle in the style of Elijah on Carmel. The Prophet, in the pride of the victory at Badr, had stalked into their market, asking if they were satisfied; whether the miraculous multiplication of their numbers on that battle-field was not as good in its way as a sacrifice devoured by heavenly fire? The reply is stated to have been a good-humoured sneer at the cowardice of Mohammed's countrymen, and a boast of what they themselves would do should Mohammed ever fight with *them.* What they actually did was to shut their doors for a fortnight and then surrender at discretion. Mohammed, however, probably about this time began to challenge the Jews to be eager for death if they believed themselves to be the chosen of God, and to guarantee that they would show no such eagerness.*

About a month after the Prophet's return from Badr,† a dispute broke out between him and the Banu Kainuka. It appears to have commenced thus. Ali's share of the booty at Badr had been two camels. Since he was anxious to make money in order to marry his master's daughter, Fatimah, he bethought him of employing his camels in the export trade, and some of the Kainuka Jews agreed to start him. They were to supply the goods which

* *Surah* lxii., 6.

† *Halabi*, ii., 274.

Ali was to sell abroad, bringing back others. The camels were left in the street awaiting their load; when the other hero of Badr, Hamzah, passing by, like an old Arab chieftain, slaughtered the beasts, and proceeded to give a banquet off them to his friends. When Ali, arriving on the scene, perceived that his prospects of merchandise and marriage were ruined, he went to Mohammed to complain. The Prophet came to the carousers, intending to remonstrate with his uncle, who by this time was so drunk that he even forgot the reverence due to God's Messenger. Surveying the Prophet from foot to head and head to foot, he asked him, "Are you not my father's slave?" To this point the anecdote rests on unimpeachable authority.* A few more steps we must ourselves supply. When the Jews who had promised to furnish Ali with goods for exportation arrived, they found the beasts that should have been laden, killed and eaten, the Lion of God dangerously intoxicated, Ali whining, and the Prophet himself seriously ruffled. Being flesh and blood, they expressed, or at any rate looked, contempt and abhorrence at the Holy Family.

The complication was one of those which at the time are exceedingly serious, though afterwards they appear trifling. Ali and Hamzah were both heroes of the late triumph of Badr; it was impossible to recoup Ali for the loss of his booty at Hamzah's expense, and yet most undesirable that Ali should lose his capital; it was also undesirable that Ali should go on commercial travels when his strong

* *Bokhari* (*K.*), ii., 270; *Muslim*, ii., 123.

arm might soon be again needed. The marriage of Ali and Fatimah was also desired by the Prophet both for domestic and economic reasons; probably, too, desired by Fatimah herself, whom the additions to her father's harem vexed. The revelations denouncing the Jews had by this time prepared the Moslems for an attack on the former; and, therefore, the plunder of their shops would furnish an easy and satisfactory way out of the inconvenience occasioned by Hamzah's excesses. There was no difficulty in finding in their conduct on the occasion that has been described something that would form a plausible pretext for an attack. Nor need we doubt that the Jews had been excommunicating those of their number who had embraced Mohammed's creed, and passing ridicule on the religious performances of the Moslems.*

The disgraceful conduct of Hamzah suggested one important innovation to the Prophet—the abolition of the use of wine and other intoxicating liquors. Questions on this subject had apparently been addressed him by persons who were aware that the practice of some ascetics forbade their use, and his first answer was a compromise, in which he declared that the uses of wine (which he couples with the arrow-game) were considerable, though the injury produced thereby was great, and indeed greater than the profit. Apparently the disorderly scene in which Hamzah and Ali figured, and in which it is likely that the arrow-game was not wanting, led him

* *Wahidi*, 148, 149.

presently * to forbid both without exception; and Ayeshah remembered how, when the revelation which dealt with them was delivered, the Prophet went to the Mosque, and forbade the sale of liquor. According to one account † due notice had been given to the owners of liquor that such a text would be revealed and they were advised to sell it while they could; but when the revelation came, zealous followers went the round of the houses of the Moslems and emptied their vessels of all liquor which was supposed to be intoxicating, in many cases breaking the vessels themselves; and trading Moslems who brought wine home from Syria after this event were compelled to pour their earnings away ‡; nor was milder treatment meted out to those orphans whose property had been invested by their guardians in wine. The prohibition was extended to vinegar made of wine, and a categorical denial was given to the suggestion that wine had medicinal value; there was (he was by this time convinced) no good in it at all. "All possible mischief is gathered into one chamber and locked there; the key of that chamber is drunkenness." § This prohibition probably did the Jewish trade some harm, since the making of wine (ordinarily got from dates) is likely to have been largely in their hands. It was also a trial to the faith of the Moslems, under which many of them

* The date is uncertain. An account represents the Prophet drinking wine just before the battle of Uhud—*Ibn Sa'd*, iii., 63. So too four months before Uhud—*Wakidi* (*W.*), 101.

† *Jauzi, Adhkiya*, 14.

‡ *Musnad*, iv., 336.

§ *Jahiz Misers*, 39.

sooner or later broke down. But the Prophet appears at no other time to have been the victim of drunken insolence.

The altercation with the Kainuka probably led directly to the denunciation of the treaty and an attack on the dwellings of the goldsmiths. They appear to have had no lands or fields; but their houses, like the rest of those in Medinah, were so built as to be able to stand a siege. The Mohammedans declare that they had the reputation of being the most courageous of the Jews, and their shops were filled with excellent armour.

At the blindness of the other Jewish tribes, who failed to help their brethren at this crisis, we should marvel, did not the rest of the history of those tribes make us marvel more. The chronicles tell us that about this very time members of the Banu Nadir bethought themselves of scheming with the Meccans, but of any attempt at aiding the Kainuka on the part of the Jewish tribes there is no suggestion, nor does any appear to have been made. Certainly the Kainuka ought by themselves to have been sufficient in numbers to deal with Mohammed and his three hundred followers, but their brethren could without difficulty have brought into the field a force four times in number that with which he was attacking. The Prophet came to the conclusion that the fear of death was with these people an overpowering motive; not, it would seem, more overpowering than the attachment to that religion which has brought them so much suffering; but one which made them seek peace at any price, except that of acknowledging the Prophet. This explanation of the conduct of the Jews is probably correct; yet, as the Israelites of Medinah left no Josephus, posterity knows very little of the causes which determined their fate. The Koran suggests* in one place that there were serious internal dissensions in the Jewish colonies; and this is highly probable. Against each other they were courageous enough, but they could form no united front.

Of their two allies, 'Ubadah Ibn Al-Samit, the Ausite, washed his hands of them so soon as the dispute commenced. The other, Abdallah, son of Ubayy, leader of the "Hypocrites," was more loyal. He remembered (according to the chroniclers) that at the battles which preceded the coming of the Prophet these Jews had caused his life to be spared. Had he had any policy, this was certainly the time to come forward with it. His strong objection to bloodshed prevented him from attempting a diversion, but when the Jews, being starved out, were in danger of being massacred by the Prophet's order, he is said to have seized the Prophet bodily and refused to leave hold till their lives had been guaranteed. They marched off, leaving all their possessions, except, it would appear, their mounts, in the direction of Syria, being kindly treated by their kinsmen in Wadi Al-Kura. They do not appear to have found permanent work at Adhri'at, and dispersed or perished.† Their goods were treated by

* *Surah* lix., 14.

† One or two seem to have contrived to stay in Medinah, since we hear of Rafa'ah, son of Zaid, a member of this tribe, being the

the Prophet as the spoils of war. He took his fifth, and divided the rest among his followers. The houses and property of seven hundred of the wealthiest of the community doubtless made the Moslems comparatively opulent. Ali could now provide the necessary wedding-gift for his bride Fatimah, and the auspicious ceremony was performed.

There is no moral to be drawn from the fate of the Kainuka except the uselessness of superior knowledge unless it produce the means of self-defence, and be combined with courage. At a later period of Islam the banishment and plunder of an industrious section of the community would have been highly impolitic besides being criminal. At this period it is not clear that it was impolitic. Many towns and countries remained to be plundered before the Moslems could be compelled to work.

The banishment of the Banu Kainuka apparently led the other Jewish tribes to reflect on the fate that was in store for them. It did not move them to any act of courage, but one of their number, Ka'b, son of Al-Ashraf, a Nadirite, went to Meccah to urge on the Meccans to come quickly. This man had a high reputation as a poet. The critic Kudamah* quotes some of his verses as models of style. What passed between Ka'b and the Meccans is not known; we can only imagine that his purpose was to arrange for some united action between the dis-

rallying-point of the disaffected party as late as the year 5, and of another, Zaid Ibn Al-Lukaib, taking part in an expedition in the year 9. *Wakidi* (*W.*), 398.

* *Nakd al-Shi'r*, 11.

affected in Medinah and the Meccans when the invasion should take place. But Mohammed, as we have seen, had ways of learning what took place in Meccah; by employing his court poet Hassan, son of Thabit, to satirise Ka'b's hosts at Meccah, he rendered the place too hot to hold him*; and when the man returned, Mohammed determined that he should be slain.

If there be any truth in the story of his assassination, it must have happened somewhat differently from the mode described. The biographers make Mohammed publicly demand to be relieved of Ka'b, son of Al-Ashraf; whereat Mohammed, son of Maslamah, otherwise known as a libertine, † having ascertained that the Prophet desired his assassination, undertakes to do the deed; four other Medinese join him, and obtain permission from the Prophet to lie to the victim. The five Medinese come and complain to Ka'b of the poverty in which Mohammed's enterprise had landed them, and request from him a loan of food for which they offer to pledge their arms. They return at night, at an appointed time, which however Ka'b has so far forgotten as to be asleep with his bride. Instead of depositing their arms and taking the food, they take him out with them on the pretext of wishing to hold a nightly conversation: and when they have got some distance fall upon him and murder him. One account increases the horror by making two of the assassins Ka'b's foster-brothers, which occasions the question to be asked, How came

* *Wakidi* (*W.*), 96.

† *Musnad*, iv., 225.

a Jew to be foster-brother of two of the Medinese? But we cannot believe that the purchasing of food against a deposit would be an act requiring any secrecy, and unless the story of the night attack be an invention, must suppose that Ka'b had been summoned out with the ostensible view of making a night attack on Mohammed: an enterprise to which the perfidy of his companions gave an unexpected direction.

Our authors proceed to make the Prophet declare the Jews outlawed, giving any Moslem who found one the right to kill him. Of this right a certain Khazrajite, Mahisah, is supposed to have availed himself, to kill a Jew named Ibn Subainah, from whom he had experienced much kindness; an act which so impressed his brother with the sublimity of Islam that he immediately became a Moslem:—we might rather see in this conversion the feeling of the futility of resistance to a system which recognised no moral obligations when they opposed its progress. But if the Jews were really declared outlawed, some ostensible reason must have been given for such an order: and the conspiracy of Ka'b would furnish an adequate ground for it. Without fresh orders from the Prophet the Jews could not have continued to remain in Medinah.*

For a whole year after the battle of Badr the Prophet's power kept on increasing and fortune continued favourable. Partly by conquest and partly

---

* The "Sawik expedition" which is put here is omitted, because the name is given to another expedition, and there are other improbabilities connected with the story.

by treaty the country which lay between Medinah and Meccah towards the coast had been won to the Prophet's side: and a Prophet who went in for cattle-stealing probably seemed to most of the tribesmen a very worthy character. The growing wealth of Medinah also attracted marauders, but these had no chance against the Prophet's disciplined forces.

The Meccans had therefore to bethink them of a new road for their caravans, unless they were to be starved out; and it was discovered that it was possible in winter to work eastwards to the Euphrates Valley, the want of water which renders the Nefud impassable in summer being at that season less of an obstacle. A guide was engaged and a heavily laden caravan despatched in December. News of it was brought to Medinah by a Meccan who went to a feast given by one of the Nadirites, and who became communicative in his cups. A follower of the Prophet who was present immediately told his master, who sent an expedition to catch the convoy: the Prophet's adopted son, Zaid Ibn Harithah, was made captain. He was completely successful, and came near capturing Abu Sufyan himself. The property seized is said to have been of the value of 100,000 dirhems.

This accession of wealth enabled the Prophet to add to his harem, which now began to assume princely dimensions. He further gave Othman his daughter Umm Kulthum, as a substitute for Rukayyah, who died during the battle of Badr. About the same time occurred another domestic event, which culminated the Prophet's joy—the birth of his grandson Hasan, son of Ali and Fatimah. On the seventh day he was named and circumcised, his head shorn, and a ram sacrificed for him. Al-Hasan, "the beautiful," is said to have been then first used as a proper name: in giving it his grandson the Prophet fancied he was translating the name of a son of Aaron.*

Thus after little more than two years at Medinah, Mohammed and his followers found themselves in possession of wealth, power, and domestic happiness. The Prophet could begin to entertain projects of conquest on a great scale: the horizon began definitely to expand. There were, however, to be still some setbacks.

Rather more than a year after the victory of Badr, while Mohammed and his family were in the midst of their domestic joys, the news arrived at Medinah that a well-equipped force, thrice the size of that which had been defeated at Badr, was on its way to retrieve that misfortune. Abu Sufyan had, it would appear, risen to the occasion; he had persuaded his fellow-townsmen to devote to preparation the whole of the profit which he had brought safely home at the time of Badr; he had some allies in the coast-tribes and the Kinanah; and he had pressed into the service such poetical talent as was at Meccah. He had been joined by an influential man from Medinah, Abu 'Amir, "the monk," the Ausite who before Mohammed's arrival had manifested a disposition

* He is sometimes called by his Syriac name—*Mez, Baghdader Sittenbild*, 5. Mez regards the connection with Aaron as Shi'ite invention.

ARAB WOMAN ATTENDING WOUNDED MAN.
From Mayeux's *Bédouins*.

towards reformed religion, but whom a little of Mohammed had convinced of the superiority of paganism; he is said to have brought fifty followers with him.* Abu Sufyan appears to have done his best; and, as a substitute for military music, caused or permitted the army to be followed by a company of ladies, who, by threatening and promising, reciting verses, and beating drums, were to keep the courage of the troops to its proper level; for nothing did the refugee from the battle-field dread more than the reproaches of his women-folk.† Besides, they could tend the wounded, and stitch the water-skins.‡ In Beckwourth's wars the women were in charge of the horses that were not being ridden, and brought fresh ones to the warriors when requested.§ The Kurashite ladies may have had some similar duty, and some certainly did curious service. The wife of Abu Sufyan made the suggestion that the body of Mohammed's mother should be exhumed and kept as a hostage; but the Kuraish rejected this suggestion (of which the practicability was surely doubtful) for fear of reprisals. One of them, 'Amrah, wife of Ghurab, raised up the Kurashite standard when it had fallen, and enabled the Kuraish to rally to it. Others, it is said, helped the actual carnage, and were spared by chivalrous Moslems, who would not dishonour their swords by striking women. Before the rout, stationed behind the

---

* *Wakidi*, 205.

† *Wellhausen*, *Ehe*, 451.

‡ *Ibid.*, *Wakidi*, 283.

§ *Autobiography*, 158, etc.

troops, they encouraged acts of valour, and launched reproaches against those who showed any disposition to flee.

Where the history of a defeat is told by the defeated, so many are interested in misrepresenting what occurred that it is difficult to disentangle the truth. Mohammed was defeated at Uhud—of that there is no question. Since a Prophet could do no wrong, the blame for that defeat could not be his; hence at two stages of the story the Prophet's followers are said to have disobeyed him, and so brought on the disaster.

It is said that the Kurashite army appeared on the west of Medinah, on a mountain called 'Ainain, "the two wells," and proceeded to send their cattle to feed in the fields of some Medinese, at a place called 'Uraid. Mohammed summoned his followers to attack, promising them the aid of five thousand angels, a promise, he had afterwards to explain, intended as an encouragement, not to be literally fulfilled. Abdallah Ibn Ubayy, always cautious, advised the Medinese to stay in the city, and wait till the Meccans thought fit to go away; believing that an assault on Medinah would either not be attempted, or, if attempted, could easily be repelled. Mohammed had not yet the experience which would have shown him the wisdom of this counsel; he doubtless expected a second Badr, and determined to save the crops. He called to arms, and of those who assembled about one thousand were passed.

At a later time Mohammed was represented as advising the Moslems to stay in Medinah, but afterward suffering his hands to be forced by the more eager and ardent of his followers. He also had revealed to him in a dream exactly what was about to occur—even to such details as the death of his uncle. The leading article on the battle of Uhud—Surah iii. —proves this statement to be unhistorical; and in the description of the fight which is professedly by the court poet, Ka'b Ibn Malik,* the Prophet is represented as from the first urging his followers to fight. From the same authentic source we are able to modify the account of another incident which was supposed to alleviate the shame of defeat—the supposed desertion of Abdallah Ibn Ubayy. When the Moslem army got half-way between Medinah and Uhud, the biographers tells us, Abdallah Ibn Ubayy deserted with three hundred followers, thus reducing the force by a third. But the Koran says two parties (supposed to be the tribes Banu Salamah † and Banu Harithah), whose fields had been wasted by the invaders, ‡ *meditated* cowardice; implying that the courageous language of the Prophet braced them up; and, indeed, many members of those tribes were known to have fought at Uhud; and from the text § we may justly infer that Abdallah, son of Ubayy, simply stayed at home—did not desert after the expedition had started. Hence the incident of Abdallah's desertion was magnified at a later time; nor,

* *Ishak*, 614.

† *Wakidi*, 207.

‡ They had at one time begged leave to change their residence and come near the Mosque. *Musnad*, iii., 371.

§ Verses 162-167.

from what we read, does he appear to have enjoyed sufficient influence to have effected such a desertion.

Uhud, the mountain which gives its name to the battle, lies to the north-west of Medinah, "forming part of the great chain, whence it breaks off into the plain in such a way that it is almost isolated"*; its whole length from west to east is about four miles.† Its distance from Medinah is variously given as two thirds or three quarters of an hour; but this refers to a time when a broad road led from Medinah to Uhud, which is visited by every pilgrim, and by pious Medinese on Thursdays. In Mohammed's time there was no such road, and even for that short distance a guide was required; the Prophet's purpose being to secure the shelter of Mount Uhud for his rear, and to reach this position without being seen and surrounded by the Kuraish. He took great pains to make the troops fall into line, remembering how effective this precaution had been at Badr.‡

He wound up the courage of his followers by an oration, recorded or imagined by Wakidi, in which he utilised the ordinary topics which provide material for harangues on such occasions, adding a little more than a commonplace general can urge, of his consciousness of being the channel through which God's commands and prohibitions were conveyed to mankind, and of having explained to them ex-

---

* *Burckhardt*, ii., 104.

† *Ibid.*, ii., 107.

‡ The date of the battle of Uhud is given as Saturday, 7 Shawwal, A.H. 3 = March 24, A.D. 625.

haustively everything that God either required or disapproved.

A way was found through the "Harrah of the Banu Harithah," amid date plantations, the blind owner of which is said to have played the part of Shimei, and pelted the Moslems with mud. The Prophet's force, however, succeeded in reaching Uhud before the Kurashites had perceived their tactics. To the east the mountain 'Ainain overlooks the path by which the Moslem position could be turned; there Mohammed placed a detachment of fifty archers, it was said (perhaps after the event), under strict orders to remain there till they were told to come down. The Kurashites were stationed in the low ground of the Wadi called Kanāt (or the channel), which separates Medinah from Uhud. The ground has been greatly altered since the Prophet's time by flood and earthquake,* whence the descriptions of modern visitors are of only partial help for understanding the situation. What is clear is that the Prophet secured a strong position, but in doing so had placed the Kurashites between his army and Medinah. He assumed that the enemy would not attack the city, and the event showed that he had calculated rightly. He assumed that the disaster of Badr would have taught the Kuraish nothing; and that the valour of Hamzah, Ali, and a few others would produce a panic as before. On the other hand he was not aware that the ground had, at the instance of Abu 'Amir, "the monk," been dug so as to injure the Moslems.

* *Samhudi*, 20.

The fight began, it is said, by this Medinese exile, Abu 'Amir, presenting himself to his relatives the Aus, with the expectation that they would troop over to him at once. How many an exile has similarly mistaken his value! His brethren answered his advances with reproaches and contempt.

It appears, too, that at the commencement events were going as the Prophet had imagined. The champions of Badr, Ali and Hamzah, dealt out death as unsparingly as before; the heroism of the Kuraish compelled them to meet these champions in a series of single combats, in which their own champions were killed, and their overthrow spread discomfiture and panic. Wakidi gives a list of the persons who successively took the Kurashite standard: it passed through the hands of seven men of the family Abd al-dar, each of whom was in turn slain by a Moslem: no one attempted to co-operate with the standard-bearer, who was simply left to his fate; in one case the brave comrades, who had done nothing to protect his life, succeeded in saving the spoils. As we picture the scene, the standard-bearer probably was in advance of the line, and, his hands being incommoded by the standard, furnished an easy victim to any champion who chose to rush on him from the enemy's side. The Moslem standard was not allowed to court destruction in the same way. Hamzah, however, was killed by an Abyssinian slave, who had practised throwing the lance; and who, having done his side this very considerable service, resolved to take no further part in the fray, lest he should never enjoy the liberty which had been promised him as the reward of success. After the death of a few standard-bearers and champions the Meccan army turned to fly, leaving their camp to the enemy, who proceeded to pillage it in disorder. The women dropped their drums and rushed towards the hill: many who were less agile yielded themselves captive to the Moslems.* Abu Sufyan himself narrowly escaped death. The archers who had been posted to protect the Moslem rear came down to join in the plunder; and this gave Khalid, son of Al-Walid, afterwards a doughty captain of Islam, the chance of a descent with his cavalry on Mohammed's rear; this diversion checked the rout, and the Moslems found themselves caught between two fires. Discipline could not be restored, nor was it easy to distinguish friend from foe. Some of the riders saw that the important matter was to kill Mohammed, and a whole series of martyrs threw themselves in front of him till a rescue party came; though even so they could not prevent his suffering some slight wounds about the face and head: treatment which naturally seemed shocking in the last degree to the man who had already shed no little blood for his ideal. The Prophet also appears to have done what he did on no other occasion—take to weapons and fight for himself (even to the extent of killing a man), besides letting men and women fight for him, and, indeed, offering a place beside himself in Paradise to any one who kept the enemy off his person.† The

* *Halabi.*

† *Musnad*, iii., 286.

Prophet is said to have owed his life to his resemblance to Mus'ab, son of 'Umair, whom Ibn 'Kami'ah mistook for him *; Ibn Kami'ah, having slain Mus'ab, fancied that he had achieved a stroke which would have ended the war. The cry that the Prophet had been killed was soon heard, and if, as was said, Satan uttered it, his object must have been to save Islam rather than ruin it; for while it discouraged many of Mohammed's followers, it roused to desperate valour many others who were too deeply committed to Islam to care for life after a crushing defeat; while the conquerors, who bore no sort of ill-will to Mohammed's followers, supposing their chief business had been accomplished, cared less to proceed. Hence it is probable that the cry, "Mohammed is slain," saved Mohammed and his cause; and indeed the Prophet, who asserts that he tried to stop the flight, was shrewd enough, amid his wounds, to perceive the advantage of the false rumour being circulated. The doughty Ali with other brave men finding him, huddled him into a ravine, where he could be tended while the supposition that he was killed might be left to do its work. He even changed armour with one of his followers that he might escape recognition if found in his hiding-place.† Ibn Kami'ah assured Abu Sufyan that Mohammed had fallen by his hand, and this assertion was accepted by the commander, till having time to search the battlefield with Abu 'Amir he found the story unconfirmed.

Had the Kurashite army preserved their original

* *Diyarbekri*, i., 483.

† *Wakidi*, 233.

position between Medinah and the Moslems, the latter must have been destroyed to a man, when the rout began; but the first part of the battle had cleared away those who had their backs to Medinah, and thither, as well as in other directions, therefore the defeated Moslems could escape. The names of the fugitives are not all preserved: among them, however, figures Sa'd, son of Mu'adh,* destined erelong to wash out this stain with Jewish blood; Anas, son of Nadir, tried to make him return to the field, but vainly. Another against whom the charge of flight from the battle-field was afterwards brought was the Prophet's son-in-law Othman, son of 'Affan, who had also the year before found in his wife's illness an excuse for absenting himself from Badr. The first of the runaways brought to Medinah the news of the Prophet's death, which, however, seems to have gained little credence; and fresh arrivals from the battle-field soon contradicted it.

Flight was doubtless facilitated by nightfall, when pursuit on the part of the enemy would have been dangerous. But while the Prophet was in hiding considerable carnage continued, and though fine tales were afterwards invented of the courage displayed on this occasion by faithful followers of the Prophet, others describe them as having become wholly disorganised. Of all the plunder secured in the assault on the Kurashite camp only two men retained any; two purses of gold secreted by two men of Medinah were the sole relic of this initial victory. Of the persons who fell in the slaughter, some plainly

* *Musnad*, iii., 253.

declared that they were not fighting for Islam, but for Medinah; while others, it is said, had come out to battle in the hope that they might win martyrdom, and had received the Prophet's blessing on their purpose. One Moslem at least seems to have made use of the confusion to wreak on a fellow-Moslem vengeance dating from a pre-Islamic blood-feud; for which he was afterwards executed by Mohammed.*

The deaths on the side of the Kurashites amounted to twenty-two; those of the Moslems to seventy—exactly the number of the victims of Badr; to these one account, which is likely to be correct, adds seventy wounded,† among whom Abu Bakr, Omar, and Ali figured; and indeed we cannot suppose that these champions escaped scot free, or that the number of wounded was not proportioned to that of slain. Detailed accounts, true or imaginary, are preserved of most of the contests in which the Kurashites perished; the slaughter of a Moslem came presently to be an inglorious souvenir, and the acts of prowess which ended thus were allowed to fall into obscurity. The Kuraish appear to have made no prisoners. We need scarcely doubt that the discovery of seventy corpses on the field was what moved the Kurashite general to mistake his victory for a conquest, and depart without delay.‡ For each victim at Badr the equivalent life had been paid; the people of Meccah and Medinah were now quits; and presently one (ordinarily ener-

* *Wakidi* (*W.*), 140.

† *Diyarbekri*, i., 482.

‡ So in *Ibn Sa'd II.*, ii., 78, a Kurashite declares himself satisfied, having killed an equal number of the foe.

getic) Meccan discouraged following up the victory on the ground that last year the Moslems had not followed up theirs.* So little did these Meccans understand what warfare meant. Savage cruelty was wreaked on some of the corpses by the women, whose desire for vengeance was a deep-seated passion rather than respect for tribal usage; but it seems clear that the Meccans were absolutely innocent of what is now called imperialism, and, having satisfied the demands of honour, were anxious to resume the occupations of peace. The Medinese, when their retreat had been effected, fully expected an attack on their city, and steps were taken to guard the house whither the wounded Prophet had been carried; but Abu Sufyan contemplated no such measure, and his forces, mounting their camels and leading their horses, were shortly seen to be departing. Omar is said, at the Prophet's request, to have answered the Kurashite thanksgiving to Hobal with an ascription of praise to Allah; and having assured Abu Sufyan of the survival and safety of Mohammed, to have made an appointment (in the style of the Fijar wars) for a renewal of hostilities the following year at Badr.

At nightfall then, it would appear, the army of Abu Sufyan commenced its departure from the battle-field; and by the next morning news reached the Prophet that there was no prospect of Medinah being attacked. Notwithstanding his wounds the Prophet succeeded in mounting his horse, and even persuaded his followers, in spite of the effects of the

* *Wakidi* (*W.*), 138

previous day's disaster, to accompany him in a demonstration as far as Hamra al-Usd, about twelve miles from Medinah, in the direction which the Meccans had taken. Meanwhile the Meccans had reached Rauha and are there said to have become awake to the folly of leaving their work unfinished, and to have begun to consider the advisability of returning to attack Medinah. They were deterred from this by the counsel of Safwan, son of Umayyah, whose father had perished at Badr, who warned them of the danger of bringing the heroes of that fight to bay. And the chief of one of the local tribes is said to have done Mohammed the service of conveying to the Kuraish an exaggerated account of the army of reserves still at Mohammed's disposal, which Mohammed artificially confirmed by causing camp-fires to be lit at night over an immense area. The operations of this day resulted in the capture of two men on either side. Mohammed remained in the field five days, on the chance of the Meccans changing their plans, and returned to Medinah on the Friday. To the courage of the soldiers, who, in spite of wounds and defeat on the Saturday, were ready to take the field on the Sunday, a just compliment was paid when the Prophet delivered the revelation which dealt with these events.

In dealing with an ordinary enemy, probably Abu Sufyan's procedure would have been justified: he had severely punished the attack on his own people, and could have counted on this punishment intimidating the enemy, and preventing a renewal of such attacks. But with such an enemy as Mohammed he should have known that a defeat could have no such effect: his energy would not be quieted this side of the grave. The Allies however who sent Napoleon to Elba appear to have understood human nature no better: and perhaps Abu Sufyan indulged in the hope that so decisive a victory over Mohammed would break the spell which enchanted the Moslems, who now had ocular demonstration that Mohammed had no allies of a supernatural order, and that even his sacred person was not proof against material weapons. The experience of a later invasion of Medinah also shows that Abu Sufyan had not the least notion of the way in which a city could be stormed or even attacked: and having narrowly escaped death in the battle on the Saturday he may have been unwilling to risk his life again on the Sunday. What views on the subject were held by the able lieutenants who had secured the victory, we know not: but after a little more of Abu Sufyan's leadership we find them desert his cause for that of the energetic and daring commander over whom they had scored a victory.

It was however, after the conversion of Meccah, difficult for the victors of Uhud to explain the motives by which their conduct was guided on that day: and inquisitive archæologists were put off with ambiguous answers.

Like every other event which had happened since Mohammed's arrival at Medinah the battle of Uhud tended to accentuate the hostility between Moslems and Jews. In spite of its being fought on a Sabbath some Jewish troops were prepared, it is said, to follow

Abdallah, son of Ubayy: but Mohammed refused their assistance, though one individual named Muchairik late in the day joined in the fray, and, dying a hero's death, won from the Prophet the title Best of the Jews. As on other occasions individuals appear to have taken the opportunity of taunting the non-fighting Moslems with the Prophet's difficulties: we hear of no effort on the part of the enemies inside Medinah to take serious advantage of the humiliating return of the Prophet: the numbedness and stupidity with which he taunts the unbelievers seem indeed to have beset them so often as they had a chance of doing their own side any service.

The "leading article" on the battle of Uhud is one of the longest continuous passages in the Koran, and was doubtless composed and delivered after the first unfavourable impression caused by the defeat had begun to fade away. Its purpose is in part to convey an answer and a menace to those persons who had found fault with the Prophet's strategy, and who, pointing to the disaster, were trying to dissuade the people of Medinah from further expeditions. As might be expected, the Prophet throws the blame for the defeat on every one but himself: he calls attention to his own mild and lenient character, to the blessing which his presence was to his followers: he finds the reason for the defeat now in the disobedience to his commands, now in the eagerness of the Moslems for plunder, and now in the purpose of God, who would "know" which were believers and which hypocrites: an explanation which has given the theologians much trouble. Nevertheless the divine advice to the Prophet "to take counsel of them in future" implies that he had committed an error in failing to take it on this occasion. The rest of the matter is commonplace consolation, such as might well be employed by a brave man after a defeat; recognition of the vicissitudes and uncertainty of war, of that fate which cannot be avoided, so that no man by staying at home can outwit death, which will come at its time no matter where its victim be found; repetition of some of the commonplaces of religion, which tries to assure the believers that death is better than life, that the martyrs of the holy war are not dead, but alive, enjoying happiness rendered incomplete only by the absence of the brethren who have not yet joined them; eloquent praise of those whom no danger deterred, and whose ardour no discouragement cooled when told to renew the fight the day after defeat.

Besides this harangue many poems are produced by the biographer, of which the battle of Uhud is supposed to have been the occasion, and of which the authors were either the court poets of Medinah, or persons who had taken part in the fray. The genuineness of most of those verses is questionable: but if they give us any correct account of the impression which the battle left on the minds of contemporaries, it would appear that the death of Hamzah was the calamity therein which overshadowed everything else. The poems ascribed to the Medinese are little more than dirges on Hamzah: and even the Meccans boast of this more than of any other event in the battle. According to the tradition the Prophet took some pains to conceal this disaster from Hamzah's sister, Safiyyah, but found, when he communicated it to her, that she bore it bravely. Sa'd, son of Mu'adh, compelled the Medinese women to forego weeping over their own dead in order to weep for Hamzah; and the custom remained among them when any death occurred in a family, of weeping for Hamzah before they mourned their own dead.* The Koran makes no allusion to it, and though Mohammed is supposed to have felt it deeply, his power had now reached a point when the loss of one strong arm mattered little: his newly learned tactics were also destined to render individual prowess of less consequence than it had been to the handfuls who fought his first battles. The mutilation of Hamzah's corpse † at first caused him to indulge in passionate threats of reprisals when he got the chance: but he presently saw the impropriety of imitating the barbarity, and is said to have urged his followers in repeated discourses to abstain from the mutilation of the dead: and we are told that these acts had not had the authorisation of the Meccan generals but were due to the fury of the women. Hamzah, valuable as was his arm in battle, is scarcely one of the prominent figures on the earlier stage of Islam: reliance could be placed on his strength and courage when a hard blow was to be

* *Ibn Sa'd*, iii., 4.

† Hind, daughter of 'Utbah, bit his liver. According to Sir S. Baker, *Isma'ilia*, ii., 354, this practice is maintained by some tribes in the belief that the liver acts as a charm.

TOMB OF THE MARTYRS NEAR MEDINAH.

struck, but the Prophet seems to have placed no confidence in his brains: and his abuse of Ali, and even Mohammed, when in his cups, was probably not forgotten. The death of the husband of Omar's daughter Hafsah gave the Prophet the chance of allying himself with this faithful follower; Omar offered his daughter to Abu Bakr and Othman, but these persons preferred leaving her to the Prophet. She was a woman of violent temper who had often to be put down.

The great bulk of the losses fell, however, not on the Refugees but on the people of Medinah: if the lists given be accurate, only four of the former perished, but over sixty of the latter. At the commencement of the conflict, Abu Sufyan is said (perhaps through Abu 'Amir) to have requested the Helpers to stand aside, and leave the Kuraish to fight out their dispute between themselves: but this proposition was indignantly repudiated. Probably the heavy loss undergone by the people of Medinah only consolidated their attachment and loyalty to the Prophet: the grumbling of a few malcontents was scarcely heard amid the acclamation of those who declared that so long as the Prophet was safe the death of all their nearest and dearest was of no consequence. Had the Prophet himself lost heart, the effect would have been different: but he had the strength of mind and of will to throw the blame of the defeat entirely on the action of his subordinates, and also to take advantage of the retirement of the enemy to claim a moral victory. The wounds which he had sustained did not trouble him for more than a month: and his appearance in the Mosque, leaning on the arms of his comrades, and, with the wounds still showing, delivering messages so warlike and so encouraging as the third Surah, was not without theatrical effect. The persons who at such times see the real situation are at a disadvantage. Men were not impressed but shocked, when told that the promise of Paradise was illusory, and that under the Prophet's rule blood was shed in rivers where previously it had been shed in rills. The defeat of Uhud did not shake the faith of a single proselyte: and even from the first it was probably penal to speak of it as anything but a victory.

CHAPTER IX

THE DESTRUCTION OF THE JEWS

WHAT feelings were excited in Arabia by the news of the Kurashite success we are not told directly: but the next event recorded * is the treacherous capture of some of Mohammed's followers by two tribes (called 'Adal and Kārah) who sent to the Prophet for missionaries to come and explain to them the principles of Islam. Their purpose was to get possession of the person of 'Asim, son of Thabit, for whose head a reward of a hundred camels had been offered by the mother of men slain by him at Uhud. Mohammed, not often caught napping, sent a party of six, of whom 'Asim was one, who were betrayed into the hands of the tribe Hudhail, famous for their lays. The Hudhail meant to sell them to the Meccans, whether in exchange for prisoners of their own tribe or for gold: but three of them died fighting, and one died attempting to escape. Two (Khubaib and Zaid, son of al-Dathinnah) were taken to Meccah and there sold, and given to the families of men who had fallen at Uhud, to be slain.

---

* *Safar* A.H. 4; identified with July–August, A.D. 625.

They were crucified, cursing their captors: and the Caliph Mu'awiyah,* first of the Umayyads, afterwards recorded how his father had made him lie on his side at the execution, that the curses might *slip off him:* so hard was it for them to distinguish word from weapon.

With the followers of a sect who, as has been seen, practised treachery whenever it was deemed advisable, we cannot sympathise when they suffer from a similar crime: but the event is of interest as showing how deep an impression Uhud left on the mind of the neighbours; and we can reproduce in thought the gibes with which Mohammed's former boasts of heavenly aid were now recollected. Mohammed had recourse to the expedient which had already been so useful in dealing with refractory Jews. He sent an assassin to murder the Hudhalite chief, Sufyan, son of Khalid: the chief was with the women of his family, mounted on camels, seeking a summer residence for them. The assassin came on him unawares and left the women weeping.†

Another assassin, 'Amr, son of Umayyah, was sent on a more promising project—to murder Abu Sufyan at Meccah. 'Amr was a Meccan, thoroughly familiar with Meccan ways, and he was given as a companion a native of Medinah. The story of his exploit is preserved by Tabari, and vividly depicts the character of the desperadoes whom Mohammed had in his service. His pious companion wished before attacking Abu Sufyan to perform his devo-

---

* *Aghani*, iv., 40. *Ibn Duraid*, 262, with some errors.

† *Diyarbekri*, i., 507.

CARAVAN FACING JEBEL NUR.

tions at the Ka'bah, and by the time this ceremony was over the Meccans were seated in groups outside their houses. 'Amr, son of Umayyah, was recognised and pursued: but he was familiar with modes of escaping justice, and found his way to a cave outside Meccah,—not, we suppose, the same in which his master had hidden: a Meccan pursuer discovered the cave and was transfixed by 'Amr before he could indicate the assassin's whereabouts to his fellows. When, after a day or two, pursuit had slackened, he made an attempt to carry off the cross on which Khubaib had been impaled. Disturbed in this bold attempt he found the road to Medinah, and skulked for a time in another cave, where he succeeded in murdering another man of Meccah; and meeting two more emissaries from Meccah he killed one and forced the other to render himself prisoner. Meanwhile he had provided for the safety of his companion, who reached Medinah before him: whither he presently arrived himself, bringing his prisoner, to earn the warm praise of the Prophet.* Besides despatching assassins, Mohammed thought it desirable to make a display of force, hearing news that other tribes were emboldened by the Kurashite success to try a fall with him. Against the Banu Asad, who were thought to be doing this, a troop of 150 was sent, which, however, encountered no resistance, and had to be satisfied with raiding camels on a moderate scale.

The success of the Hudhail in entrapping Moslems encouraged another chief to try the same plan. A demand for missionaries to Nejd was made by Abu

* *Tabari*, i., 1441.

Barā 'Amir, son of Malik, chief of the Banu 'Amir. The Prophet after some hesitation sent a company of seventy, consisting of devotees, whose studies in the Koran had earned for them the name of the Readers. "They used, at nightfall, to go to a teacher in Medinah, and spend the night in study: when morning broke, the strong ones would gather wood and draw water, while those who were better off would buy a sheep, dress it, and leave it hanging in the Prophet's Precincts." * Seventy—if the number be correctly given—was a large force, if intended for preaching: but not too large if fighting also was intended. At the well of Ma'unah, not far from Medinah, they were attacked by 'Amir, son of Tufail, chief of the great tribe Sulaim: Abu Barā's promise of protection could not be carried out, though he and his tribe took no part in the assault. The seventy theologians were slaughtered all but to a man: only one escaped, having been left for dead. 'Amr, son of Umayyah, figures on this occasion also: he was with the baggage of the expedition, and was also taken by the enemy, but let go because of some plausible pretext that he had alleged, though with his forelock shorn. On his way homewards he found two of the Banu 'Amir, whom he waylaid and slew. But this act turned out to have been an unnecessary display of zeal since the Banu 'Amir had ostensibly broken no contract: and Mohammed had to pay blood-money for them.

The death of the seventy emissaries is said to have shocked Mohammed more than the disaster of

* *Musnad*, iii., 137.

Uhud; for thirty, or, according to others, forty mornings he cursed its authors, and he even published a divine message dealing with the affair which, for some reason, was not afterwards incorporated in the Koran.* With a cause like his, discredit such as results from a series of failures was likely to have serious consequences; and the cross of martyrdom, so eagerly desired by some, was by no means coveted by others. Hence the pathetic message which came from the murdered men in Paradise, stating that they had met their God, and been satisfied with each other, may have been found unwelcome after this second disaster.

It is a sign of the Prophet's being alarmed that he undertook to pay the blood-money and return the plunder taken from the two 'Amirites whom the desperado 'Amr had slain. And for this he went to demand assistance from the Jewish tribe Nadir—to the end of his life he would always apply to the Jews when he wanted money. That the Jews were more and more elated by each disaster that he underwent is attested and is easily credible; we shall never know whether Mohammed's visit to them on this occasion was the first step in a preconceived plot or turned to account by an after-thought. Moreover, the death of the Nadirite Ka'b, son of Al-Ashraf, if indeed it did not take place about this time (which there is some ground for thinking), is not likely to have been forgotten by either party; the request, therefore, from Mohammed for help in paying blood-money might well have seemed impudent

* *Diyarbekri*, i., 510.

to a tribe who had a right to demand it of him. Still the reception given him was favourable; but a voice from heaven informed him that his hosts had bethought them of taking advantage of his weakness, and that one of them, 'Amr, son of Jihash, was mounting the roof, with the view of throwing a stone on the Prophet's head. We know not, having no Jewish account of the matter, whether this bold design was really contemplated; but since the Prophet had a fixed idea that the Jews always wanted to murder him—an idea which owed its origin to the accusation of "killing the Prophets" launched against them by the Founder of Christianity—he may have sincerely believed such an attempt was meditated. He therefore rushed back to Medinah, asserting that he was escaping from a treacherous assault, and summoned his followers to besiege the Banu Nadir. The followers were quite ready. Of the fighting ability of the Jews, and of the energy of their partisans in Medinah, they had ample experience; there was not the least chance of any resistance to an energetic attack. One account indeed informs us that Mohammed sent a messenger offering them eight days in which to remove their possessions, and that this proposal would have been accepted immediately had not the unfortunate Abdallah Ibn Ubayy urgently advised them to resist, and promised them assistance in the event of their doing so. The Banu Kuraizah, to whom an appeal was made on behalf of their brethren, flatly refused to break with Mohammed. This act of cowardice prepares us to feel less sympathy with them for the fate that afterwards befell them. The fortresses occupied by the Nadir were probably no worse than the others at Medinah; and legend, if not history, recorded how the fortresses of Yathrib had held out against the great Yemenite King Tubba' and forced him to raise a siege.*

Experience shows that the most inexpugnable and best provisioned fortresses are useless unless there are men inside them. Abdallah Ibn Ubayy had good grounds for believing that the Jewish forts were easily able to resist an attack, and that the defenders were well supplied. Let the Jews (he reasoned) weary Mohammed by successful defence for some months at least, and meanwhile he could marshal his concealed forces, and attack Mohammed from the rear or flank. With Abdallah the tradition mentions certain other Hypocrites, who, however, are to us merely names. Apparently they all shared the peculiarity of the Jews—readiness to do anything rather than fight. From Meccah, too, an expedition might erelong be expected. Huyayy, the chief of the Banu Nadir, was persuaded by those fair promises, and prepared to defend his lands. But the forts, defended by cowards (who, moreover, were divided amongst themselves) † and attacked by disciplined soldiers, proved themselves untenable. The pride of the Nadirites was a sort of date so clear that the stone could be seen through the pulp. Mohammed cut or burnt those date trees, and the heart of the Nadirites melted. In vain did they

---

* *Aghani*, xiii., 120.

† *Surah* lix., 14.

remonstrate that such wanton destruction of property was in contradiction to the precepts of the Koran and of the law which the Koran professed to confirm; the Prophet's notions on these matters were elastic. After three weeks' resistance the Nadirites offered to capitulate, on condition of being allowed to go away unmolested, taking with them such property (except armour) as their camels could carry. Some of the Moslems assisted them in dismantling their houses. There were only two renegades who retained their lands. The rest marched away with all the honours of war. The Prophet's victory was bloodless, giving him the right to dispose of the whole of the plunder.*

The "leader" inserted in the Koran † on the subject of the expedition charges the Nadirites only with resistance to the Prophet; possibly by the time it was "revealed" he had discovered that his former suspicion was groundless. The purpose of the revelation apparently is to justify the proceeding whereby the land of the Nadirites was exclusively assigned to the Refugees. But the author cannot refrain from sarcasms on both the Jews and the Hypocrites. He compares the latter to the Tempter, who urged man to rebel against God, and when he rebelled, washed his hands of him. They might promise to share any danger or disaster which befell the Jews, but they would never fulfil their promise. Their fear of the Moslems was greater than their fear of God. There was no unity among them, each person having a design or object of his own. In fact, he sums up, they

---

* *Rabi' I*, H.S. 4; identified with August–September, A.D. 625.

† *Surah* lix.

have no understanding. This revelation also contained an *ex post facto* justification of the destruction of the palm-trees. It had all been done in accordance with the command of God.

The poets whose commemorative verses are cited by the biographers connect the banishment of the Nadirites with the murder of Ka'b, son of Al-Ashraf, which indeed can scarcely have failed to elicit some remonstrance, and even threats of vengeance. The Prophet seems to suggest that the fortresses of the Nadirites were rendered indefensible by some sort of surprise—God came upon them whence they expected not. Whatever was the exact series of events, Mohammed had proved himself equal to dealing with internal adversaries, notwithstanding his failure in external warfare.

The banishment of the Banu Nadir put some valuable cards into the Prophet's hand. In the first place permanent provision was made for the Refugees, who had no longer any occasion for dependence on the Helpers' charity, which is likely to have become less enthusiastic as the years passed. Indeed this accession of property seems to have enabled the tide of charity to turn, and a few of the needy but faithful Medinese got some of the plunder. On the other hand the feebleness, irresolution, and incompetence of the hostile party had once more been demonstrated. They heartily wished for Mohammed's destruction: but this motive was as nothing compared with their anxiety for their own skins. To break openly with the Prophet undoubtedly meant danger, for Ali, Omar, and the others would die hard, and at the price of many lives. But the Prophet taunted them with folly in not perceiving that by allowing him to cut off his enemies, party by party, they were making certain a doom which union and energy might still avert. Abdallah, son of Ubayy, has left no memoirs in vindication of his conduct, but his energetic action on behalf of the Banu Kainuka makes it possible that he played the part of a Demosthenes, or of Cicero after Cæsar's death: of the man who vainly endeavours to inspire courage and confidence into the half-hearted.

The banishment of the Banu Nadir was followed by a futile attempt to finish the battle of Uhud. We are told that, on parting from Mohammed, Abu Sufyan there made an appointment to renew hostilities the next year at Badr, but that for some reason or another the appointment was not kept. It is most likely that Abu Sufyan found that he had sadly overestimated the blow which he had dealt the Prophet's power at Uhud; that he committed the mistake, so often made, of confusing victory with conquest. When therefore he found that he had in no way weakened the Prophet's hold on his followers, and that by plunder and expatriation of internal enemies the Prophet had in the interval considerably strengthened his position, he was not anxious for the return match. One account tells us that he endeavoured to make the Prophet break the engagement by sending to Medinah a spy, hired to circulate false rumours of the strength of the Meccans, which Mohammed, having himself practised the same stratagem successfully the previous year, correctly interpreted as a sign of weakness. When this failed Abu Sufyan appears to have made an abortive expedition to Badr, whence he almost immediately returned, on the ground that the season was unsuitable. The army that he brought was sarcastically termed by the Moslems the "water-gruel army," it is said, because Abu Sufyan withdrew it owing to the scarcity of the materials requisite for that dish. This explanation of the gibe seems far-fetched, and its real origin was probably forgotten. Mohammed brought an army of fifteen hundred men (with ten horses) to the rendezvous, and the size and equipment of this force proving to the Meccans that the Moslem cause had scarcely been injured by the affair of Uhud, spread something like consternation in Meccah.* We are surprised to learn that the annual fair took place at the intended battle-field, and that the Moslems, though unable on this occasion to carry on the commerce of war, carried on with profit that of peace.†

The successes which we have just recorded seem to have given the Prophet leisure to attend to his domestic affairs, and at the same time to test the endurance of his followers. One of the abuses which Mohammed had abolished was marriage with a father's wife—a usage which seems to have prevailed before his mission, when the father's wives were inherited by the son with his other possessions. Now, as we have seen, Mohammed had many years before adopted Zaid, son of Harithah, and the old system

---

* *Wakidi*, (*W.*), 168.

† *Dhu'l-Ka'dah*, A.H. 4; identified with April–May, A.D. 626.

knew of no difference between an adopted son and a real son.* Zaid had been married first to a freedwoman, and afterwards to a cousin of the Prophet's own, named Zainab, daughter of Jahsh. For some reason or other the Prophet desired to add this lady to his own harem, or at any rate to bring her under his influence; his motive is not known, but it may have been admiration for her piety, which was celebrated. She at one time went to the length of hanging cords between the pillars of the Mosque to support herself on during prayer,† an act which, if prior to her marriage with the Prophet, rather implies that she wished to attract his attention. From the account of the matter in the Koran it appears that Zaid became aware that the Prophet wanted his wife, and thought it wisest to yield his rights without further delay. It also appears that the Prophet was unwilling to take advantage of Zaid's complaisance, but found it to be the best course; and, indeed, Zainab refused to assent to this step without a special revelation,‡ which speedily was produced. Zaid, therefore, divorced Zainab, who was married by the Prophet, who foresaw that this act would give rise to grave scandal, but gave the usual marriage feast, and, indeed, with special luxury, his followers being entertained with bread and mutton,§ whereas on other similar occasions they had to be

* *W. R. Smith, Kinship and Marriage*, 2d ed., 53. *Wellhausen* (*Ehe*, 141) says the scandal was caused by Mohammed's breach of his own law.

† *Musnad*, iii., 101, etc.

‡ *Ibid.*, iii., 195.

§ *Ibid.*, iii., 98, 242.

content with dates and whey.* This liberality did not prevent severe comments from those who regarded adopted sonship as real sonship—for which view Mohammed's institution of brotherhoods gave some support—and who, therefore, regarded this union as incestuous. How deeply the scandal agitated the Prophet is evinced by the fact that Zaid's name is mentioned in the revelation in which this delicate business was afterwards handled. The whole responsibility for the event is thrown on God; the Prophet's hesitation to marry Zainab was due to his fear of men, whereas God only ought to have been feared. Zaid is described as a person whom both God and the Prophet had favoured, and the Moslems are assured that there was no occasion for the Prophet to *gêner* himself (the French word renders the Arabic exactly) in privileges which belonged to the Prophetic office. An adopted son was not the same as a son, and was not to count as such. The jealous Ayeshah at a later period, sarcastically proved from this verse how faithfully the Prophet delivered the messages which were entrusted to him to deliver; for if any verse of the Koran might have been concealed with advantage, this one might.† It seems as if the Prophet did not venture to communicate this revelation till another victory had secured his position. And Ayeshah had little reason to find fault with it, since she herself presently profited by the divine interest in the Prophet's domestic irregularities. The figure

* *Musnad*, iii., 99, 172.

† *Muslim*, i., 63.

of Zaid himself in the story is mute. We should gather that he was not a man of strong domestic attachments, since he repeatedly went through the form of marriage and divorce. He is credited (we know not with what truth) with having at the outset of his career preferred Mohammed to his parents, who having lost him by captivity, wished to reclaim him, and Mohammed to the end placed in his powers an unlimited confidence which the Moslems did not share, and was so little convinced by the revelation in which adoption was declared to have no legal value that, if Ayeshah may be believed, he intended to make Zaid his successor.* The revelation, however, was regarded as law, and adopted sons were handed up to their parents or former owners.† Even a man who had been adopted by a Meccan in pre-Islamic times, Mikdad, son of Al-Aswad, resumed his original filiation as Mikdad, son of 'Amr.‡

The Jews, who had so easily abandoned their strongholds, were now trying hard to get others to fight; to one centre and another they sent deputations, denouncing the impostor who wished to subjugate all Arabia. As in old times their ancestors had denounced Christianity before pagans, so now they told the Meccans that their religion was better than Mohammed's. Possibly the Meccans remembered how a few years before the Jews were the witnesses whom Mohammed cited to attest his statements, and to whom he appealed when in doubt

* *Isabah.*

† *Ibid.*, ii., 109.

‡ *Ibid.*, iii., 932.

about himself. The indignation displayed b hammed when he heard of the Jewish patronage idolatry appears to have been unfeigned. However, their emissaries had succeeded in making a treaty with the Meccans within the curtains of the Ka'bah, by the terms of which the parties were bound to oppose Mohammed so long as any of them were alive.*

Besides the Meccans the Jewish emissaries had succeeded in stirring up the tribes called Ghatafan, of which three, the Banu Fazarah, the Banu Murrah, and the Banu Ashja', made their way to Medinah under their leaders 'Uyainah, son of Hisn, Al-Harith, son of 'Auf, and Mis'ar, son of Rukhailah. The tribes Asad and Sulaim also joined.† These tribes had, it was said, been stirred up by Jews from Khaibar, who had promised them a year's date harvest for their trouble: and the Prophet, to warn the Jews of Khaibar, sent Abdallah, son of Rawahah, to lure some of them away from the city, on the pretence of an honourable visit to the Prophet, and murder them on the way: a mission which was successfully executed, the Arabian Jews being as incautious as they were cowardly.‡ The purpose of the great expedition was to take Medinah and thus stop the mischief at its source. Two years before Medinah had been supposed by its inhabitants to be inexpugnable. Perhaps the feeble resistance made in the Jewish quarter to an attacking party had

---

* *Wakidi* (*W.*), 190.

† *Ibid.*,

‡ *Ishak*, 980.

convinced both Mohammed and his enemies that this was an error. Pickaxes, shovels, and baskets were lent by the Banu Kuraizah.

To a certain Salman the Persian is attributed the idea of defending Medinah by a trench. This person appears to have been a slave at Medinah when the Prophet arrived there, and to have adopted Islam, perhaps thereby gaining his liberty, since the freeing of slaves was one of the earliest acts of charity imposed on the Moslems who could afford it. The accounts given of his antecedents are so evidently fabulous that we cannot quote them here: we should be inclined to guess from his name that he was a Nabatæan, who had, perhaps, been born, or lived, in Persia: certainly the name which he gave to his "trench" (Khandak) is pure Persian. It would also appear that the plan of defending one's possessions by this simple expedient was displeasing to the Arabs, whose notions of war were, as we have seen, rather chivalrous than practical. But in any case there was one side where the buildings of Medinah were not sufficiently close together to constitute a defence. The Prophet, with the good sense which he so often displayed when occasion required it, took a pickaxe himself, marked out the line of entrenchment, and divided the work of digging between his three thousand followers, who worked continuously in relays. The tradition records how the Prophet, as he worked, sang:

> "There is no life save that of Paradise.
> Pardon the Helpers, Lord, and Refugees";

and how his followers answered :

> " Unto Mohammed we have pledged our faith,
> To fight his foes and flee not until death." *

The line went " from the 'fort of the two old men' to Al-Madhad, then over Dhubab and Husaikah towards Ratij—including the mountain of the Banu 'Ubaid in Khusbah " † — all these names became obsolete shortly after: the places appear to have lain to the north-east of Medinah, beyond the elevation called Sal', where the Moslem army was stationed. The women and children were meanwhile placed for security in the towers.

The digging of the trench is one of the episodes in the history of Islam that gave most occasion for mythical embellishment.

The numbers of the invaders are put by the biographers at ten thousand ‡; whether this be an exaggeration or not, apparently what was wanting was not force, but strategy. The trench planned by Salman the Persian proved an insurmountable hindrance to their advance. The Prophet and his

---

* *Musnad*, iii., 205, etc.

† *Wakidi* (*W.*), 192. *Tabari*, i., 1407.

‡ Kuraish with their allies........................ 4000
Sulaim.. 700 §
Fazarah....................................... 1000
Ashja'.. 400
Murrah.. 400

The numbers of the Asad and probably some other tribes are not given.

---

§ *Wakidi* (*W.*), 191.

followers had, indeed, to endure considerable hardships, in guarding it during the cold winter nights; but only a few of the latter lost courage. The campaign, which lasted close upon a month, may be summed up as follows: the invaders waited outside the trench in the hope that the Moslems would come out and fight. When they discovered that the latter had no intention of doing so, the invaders went away again. A crossing, indeed, at one point * was effected by a venturous party, but it never even occurred to the general to see that they were supported, and the result was a duel, in which a Kurashite champion, 'Amr, son of Abd Wudd, was slain by the redoubtable Ali. A few casualties also were due to the archery practice, among which a wound inflicted on the chief of the Aus, Sa'd, son of Mu'adh, was destined to have serious consequences. Khalid, son of Al-Walid, commander of the Kurashite cavalry, had some opportunities of furbishing his Uhud laurels, but failed to use them; and a number of futile attacks were made by the other Meccan leaders which were frustrated by the vigilance of the Moslems, and their own inability to co-operate. This was the best and also the last chance given to the Meccans and Jews of breaking Mohammed's power. And it was utterly wasted, partly for want of physical courage, but chiefly because there was no man with brains in command. The unforeseen stratagem of the trench seems to have paralysed them as completely as the machine gun might paralyse an enemy who had never heard of gunpowder.

* *Ishak*, 678.

An army must be well organised and well disciplined to stand delay. These hordes were neither: and even if the commander of the Kuraish had some notion of what his purpose was, the auxiliary tribes were very much in the dark about it. It is said that Mohammed started negotiations for buying their retirement, and that these were abortive, not for any loyalty on the part of the tribes to their allies, but because of the fanaticism of Mohammed's followers, who then, as often, took a more exalted view of the honour of Islam than its founder took. The chief sufferers were destined to be the Jews, those Banu Kuraizah whose tender sense of their obligations to Mohammed had kept them from making common cause with the Banu Nadir the year before. The Nadirite agitator, Huyayy, son of Akhtab, who had failed to obtain their help at that time, found a readier hearing now that he appeared in company with ten thousand troops of Arabs. The Jewish tribe was not very numerous, but such an internal enemy could have done serious work, when the whole force which Mohammed could muster was occupied with an external foe three times its number. Without authorisation Huyayy appears to have offered them hostages from the Meccans as a pledge that the latter would not leave them in the lurch *; and by this promise the head of the tribe, Ka'b, son of Asad, was induced to tear up their contract with Mohammed: Zubair, son of 'Awwam, sent by the latter to watch their proceedings, reported that they were highly suspicious. A

* *Wakidi* (*W.*), 206.

deputation of eminent Medinese was then sent by the Prophet to urge the Kuraizah to remain quiet: they failed to produce any effect, but did not inform the Moslems of their failure, which they reserved for Mohammed's private ear *; according to a custom of which Palgrave's history of the Wahhabis gives illustrations. The Kuraish were not destined, however, to profit by their alliance with the Jews, though the latter seem to have shot an occasional arrow. When the Kurashite chief sent to demand a vigorous demonstration inside the city, once again the Jewish tenderness of conscience stood in the way: it was the Sabbath, and they could not fight on that day. It is also asserted that a man of the tribe Ashja', of Ghatafan, named Nu'aim, son of Mas'ud, a deserter and convert, undertook to sow discord between the Kuraizah and the Kuraish, and persuaded the Kuraizah to refuse to move unless the Kuraish gave them the promised hostages, while on the other hand he assured the Kuraish that the purpose of these hostages was to enable the Kuraizah to make their peace with Mohammed. In another form of the story † the treachery on the part of the intermediary is made out to be unintentional and due to a lie told by Mohammed; and this is more likely to be true since Nu'aim was unable to keep a secret, ‡ and the Prophet is unlikely in such an emergency to have trusted to his discretion. Whichever story be true, it is evident that the Kuraizah were desirous

* *Wakidi* (*W.*), 197.
† *Isabah*, iii., 844.
‡ *Ibn Duraid*, 168.

that other people should fight their enemies for them, and unwilling to risk their own necks. We may easily believe that during this hour of stress members of the clan went about the streets in which the women were entrenched, exulting over the disaster which was overtaking the Prophet: nor is there any improbability in the story that one of those men was killed by Safiyyah, the Prophet's aunt. Had they been faithful to either the Prophet or the Kuraish, they would probably have been saved, and saved others. The course they took was that middle road which inevitably leads to destruction.

It does not appear that Abu Sufyan and his friends had any idea of starving out the people of Medinah, and indeed within their entrenchment the latter appear to have been able to carry on some of their normal industries. What finally drove the Meccans away was bad weather. The cold nights were too much for them. The faint-heartedness of the Kuraizah had communicated itself to their allies. The trench had done its work. The plan of taking Medinah was abandoned and Abu Sufyan with his allies returned to their homes. The Moslems lost only six martyrs.*

Mohammed, it is said, had spent most of the time of the siege praying, though any advisers who had a feasible plan to suggest, or who offered to execute any useful project, always found a ready hearing. And when he learned that his prayers had been

* *Ishak*, 699. *Dhu'l-Ka'dah*, A.H. 5; identified with March-April, A.D. 627.

answered, and the great gathering of the Gentiles had dispersed, he would not put off his armour before he commenced the work of vengeance on the Kuraizah, and that this vengeance was to be summary was indicated by the delivery of the standard to the notorious Ali. Huyayy, son of Akhtab, who had organised the original campaign, loyally remained with the Kuraizah in their extremity. The Moslem forces invested the dwellings of the Kuraizah, and apparently offered no terms of any sort. By the advice of Hubab Ibn al-Mundhir, communication between the different forts was cut off, the Moslems stationing themselves between them.* Little fighting seems to have been attempted; yet one Moslem, Khallad, son of Suwaid, is said to have been killed by a millstone hurled by one of the Jewish women; for which inglorious death he was promised a double share of martyr's earnings. The story told of the council that was held among the besieged may be an invention of the fancy, but it probably gives a faithful picture of what did take place where one or two men were trying to inspire a herd of nerveless followers with something like resolution. Should they abandon Judaism and become Moslems? No, their consciences would not permit them to do that. Should they make a holocaust of their families and possessions and, having thus saved their honour, risk their lives in a final encounter? Should they then be successful, wives and children would easily be replaced. No, they could not be so cruel. Then should they try a sortie on the

* *Ibn Sa'd II.*, ii., 109.

Sabbath, when the Moslem vigilance would probably be relaxed? Oh, no, to violate the Sabbath would be too shocking! There remained the plan of falling at the feet of the conqueror and supplicating mercy. But what mercy could they expect who a few days before had been in jubilation over his distress, and who still refused the only homage for which he cared?

At their request a member of their former allies, the Aus, named Abu Lubabah,* at times employed by Mohammed as lieutenant-governor of Medinah, was permitted to visit them, in order to advise, and he seems to have told them to hold out like men, as the Prophet would show no mercy—sound advice for which he afterwards atoned by tying himself to a pillar of the Mosque, only to be released by Mohammed after six days or a fortnight, when Allah had revealed his pardon. After some four weeks' siege they apparently capitulated on condition that their fate should be decided by a member of the Aus — hoping doubtless that as favourable terms would be procured for them as the chief of the Khazraj had three years before procured for the Banu Kainuka. The man to whom their fate was committed was however no half-hearted partisan like Abdallah Ibn Ubayy. Sa'd Ibn Mu'adh, formerly a friend of the Jewish tribe, had but a few days before been wounded during the skirmishes about the trench, and was in no merciful mood. Three times had his median vein been cut and cauterised by Mohammed, the hand swelling more and more in consequence.

* *Wakidi*, 373, conceals his name.

By an act of will he is said to have kept himself from bleeding to death till he was avenged on the Banu Kuraizah.* His award was a foregone conclusion. The men were to be killed, their goods to be seized, and the women and children to be enslaved; which of the lads were to count as men and which as children was determined by medical examination.† A great trench was dug, into which the Jews after decapitation were cast. Such a trench, into which the Martyrs of Najran had been cast, not many years before, had roused the horror and indignation of the Prophet, to which he gave expression in a revelation; so true it is that the acts which men most abhor are those which they themselves commit. Care was taken to make some of their former allies assist in the execution. The lives of a very few were begged of the Prophet by their friends, who found little difficulty in obtaining their request. Some of the captives were exported to Nejd by Sa'd, son of Zaid, of the Banu Abd al-Ashhal, and arms and palm-trees obtained in exchange.‡ In order to encourage mobility, the few horsemen among the Moslems were rewarded with threefold shares of the rich booty—two for the horse and one for the man. In one case at least the gift of life was not accepted by the man for whom it had been granted: Al-Zabir, son of Bata, preferred to die with the great men of his tribe, though his family seem to have survived.

---

* *Musnad*, iii., 350, 363. *Wakidi* (*W.*), 222, puts the operations *after* the massacre.

† *Isabah*, iii., 873.

‡ *Ibid.*, ii., 152.

On Sa'd son of Mu'adh, who had pronounced the doom of the Israelites, Mohammed bestowed the highest compliments to which his fancy could rise. He declared that Sa'd's death, which followed shortly after, shook the Throne of God; that the room where his body lay was so crowded with angels that a seat could scarcely be found; and that if any Moslem corpse might escape the pressure of the grave, it would be Sa'd's.* Years after when a rich robe was presented him he declared that one of the kerchiefs of Sa'd in Paradise was superior to it.†

The facts as recorded by the historians elicit little sympathy and little admiration for any of the parties. The great invasion, which Mohammed declared to have been miraculously frustrated, was due or believed to be due, to the propaganda of members of the Banu Nadir, whom the Prophet had been satisfied with banishing. Should he banish the Kuraizah, he would thereby be setting free a fresh set of propagandists. On the other hand, those who had taken part openly with the invaders of Medinah could not very well be permitted to remain there. To banish them was unsafe; to permit them to remain was yet more dangerous. Hence they must die. Only a few of the disaffected Medinese were shocked by the execution. And since it would appear that the Kuraizah had turned against the Prophet merely because he was in extreme danger, having received no fresh provocation from the time when they had lent him tools to dig his trench, their fate, horrible as it was, does not

* *Musnad*, vi., 55 (Ayeshah).

† *Ibid.*, iii., 207.

surprise us. If they had not succeeded in harming him, they had manifested the will to do so. We must also try, in estimating this matter, to think of bloodshed as the Arabs thought of it: as an act which involved no stigma on the shedder. The Prophet indeed offered them one more alternative—to accept Islam, and not only preserve their lives and possessions, but become one with the conquerors. Most stormers of cities have not been willing to sacrifice to an idea the whole fruits of victory.

It seems surprising that so very few of the conquered availed themselves of this escape. The poet Jabal, son of Juwal, is mentioned as one such convert.* Even a woman, Raihanah, whom Mohammed made his slave-concubine, long preferred concubinage as a Jewess to wifedom as a Moslem.

The theoretical love and practical hate of Mohammed for the Jewish race is a phenomenon so easy to illustrate that it scarcely calls for attention. That the Israelites were "chosen out of the world" is a theme which the Koran never tires of repeating. He used to spend whole nights in telling stories about the Children of Israel,† and Sprenger is probably right in thinking that for a long time the dearest wish of Mohammed's heart was to be recognised by them. Their failure to do so at Medinah cut away the ground on which he had built at Meccah; but it was like the temporary wooden bridge which is removed when the stone fabric, erected with its aid, is complete. Each victory of the Prophet, and especially

* *Isabah*, i., 453.

† *Musnad*, iv., 437.

each accession of plunder, rendered the arguments of the expert Jews less and less weighty; and after the destruction of the Kuraizah it became a matter of indifference to him whether the Jews followed him or not. The change from a basis of reason to a basis of force had taken place gradually, but now was finally achieved.

One other party was also given its *coup de grace* by the campaign of the trench. The disaffected Medinese, called in the Koran the Hypocrites or the Faint-hearted, had given encouragement and futile promises to the Banu Nadir; but they are not mentioned by trustworthy authorities in connection with the attack on the Banu Kuraizah. They endeavoured to shirk the task of digging, and, on the ground that their houses were exposed, endeavoured to leave the defenders of the trench and return to their homes. The unexpected termination of the campaign extinguished their hopes. If Mohammed asserted that the forces of nature had taken his part, and that the Kurashites had been driven off by hosts of angels, the event was on his side. We can but admire his wisdom and forbearance in contenting himself with sarcasms on their behaviour, delivered in the Koran, and avenging himself in no more practical way. To the principle, however, of accepting as final a man's utterance about Islam, and declining to enquire into the sincerity of such profession, he finally adhered. Victories and success were environing Islam with fame and glory; and whereas the profession of it was at first a matter of shame, it was becoming a subject of pride.

The triumph over the Kuraizah was completed by the assassination of Sallam, son of Abu Hukaik, one of the organisers of the late attack. He had taken refuge at Khaibar, and five cut-throats went with the Prophet's blessing to murder him in his bed. They were members of the Khazraj and their purpose, we are told, was to emulate the glory of the murderers of Ka'b, son of Al-Ashraf, who were members of the rival tribe. The Jews of Khaibar, when they heard of the fate of the Kuraizah, had bethought them for a moment of uniting the whole Jewish population of Arabia in an attack on Medinah; but their courage evaporated very quickly.*

Of the effect on public opinion of the result of the whole campaign we have no record, but it is likely to have been very great. A victory won by the help of angels and spirits was far more valuable than a triumph secured by physical force. Those who would not rest quiet when defeated by mortal champions, feel no shame in acknowledging themselves incompetent to deal with angels. Whether Mohammed, who resorted so readily to the aid of the assassin's dagger, believed in these supernatural allies we know not. Of the Arabs who were disinterested spectators, some were sufficiently thrilled by the Prophet's success to join him unsolicited. Such an accession was Abbas, son of Mirdas, son of the poetess Al-Khansa, and of great renown in the tribe Sulaim, which extended over a large portion of the Hijaz. This man, according to one account, was, after the retirement of the Kuraish, led by a series of portents

* *Wakidi* (*W.*), 224.

to burn the family idol and visit Mohammed in Medinah; he at first incurred the reproaches of his tribe, but presently succeeded in converting them; and at the battle of Hunain, after the taking of Meccah, a troop of a thousand men led by Abbas's father-in-law, Dahhak, succeeded in regaining the field.

CHAPTER X

STEPS TOWARDS THE TAKING OF MECCAH

FREED from the controversy with the Jews and the fear of invasion from his older enemies, the Prophet could now turn to schemes of vengeance and conquest. Vengeance was necessary for the treacherous murder of Khubaib and his followers by the Banu Lihyan—an act precisely analogous to the assassinations authorised by the Prophet; but whereas the Jews were incapable of retaliation, the Prophet was not. His strategy was similar to that which has proved successful in many campaigns: since the Lihyan dwelt to the south of Medinah the Prophet's expedition commenced by a march northward, on the Damascus road. At a point called al-Batra he turned to the left, and came gradually back to the Meccan highroad, whence he made a dash on the dwellings of the Lihyan, in a valley called Ghuran, going westward from one of the Harrahs to the sea. But the Lihyan had received timely warning of his approach and betaken themselves to inaccessible heights; and there would be nothing in their dwellings worth plundering. The property of tribes in this condition consists entirely in live-stock, which they take with them when either war or stress of weather compels them to leave their houses. They possess no furniture that cannot easily be loaded on their persons or on their mounts. The expedition was therefore a failure.

Still they were near Meccah and the Prophet thought a demonstration of force in the neighbourhood of that city might enhance his prestige. He accordingly advanced with two hundred followers sufficiently near Meccah for the fame of his expedition to reach the ears of the Kuraish.

The whole of the sixth year was occupied with expeditions in which sometimes Mohammed himself, but more often Abu Ubaidah, Ali, and Zaid took the command. They were ordinarily though not invariably successful; and the restless energy of the Prophet spread the fame of Islam over a constantly widening area, and won for it the respect which success inspires.

The campaign against the Banu Mustalik in the same year (6)* was remarkable for two events. This tribe, a branch of the Khuza'ah, led by Al-Harith, son of Abu Dirar, appears to have meditated a raid on Medinah. Mohammed, by the aid of a spy, learned of their movements and attacked them by Muraisi', a spring near the coast between Medinah and Kudaid, "capturing two thousand camels, five thousand sheep, and two hundred women" †; among the last Barrah, a daughter of the chieftain, whom the

---

* *Ishak* says Sha'ban, A.H. 6, identified with Dec. 627–Jan. 628. *Wakidi* puts it a year earlier.

† *Wakidi* (*W.*), 178.

Prophet made his wife, in order to consummate his victory. The division of the booty—or some other incident—nearly led to a battle between the Helpers and Refugees, and the party of Abdallah Ibn Ubayy showed some signs of recrudescing. It is asserted that on this occasion the dangerous words, "if we return to Medinah, the stronger of us shall turn out the weaker," were used. The old story of the dog which, when pampered, bites, seems to have naturally suggested itself to Abdallah as an illustration of the conduct of the Refugees towards the Helpers. Omar would on this occasion have settled the difficulty of Abdallah Ibn Ubayy with his sword, but the Prophet would not give permission, and broke up his camp in the midday heat, in order that the soldiers in their fatigue might forget this unpleasantness.* Presently Mohammed received a request from the son of the Arch-hypocrite to be allowed to kill his father, should the act be necessary. Omar was forced to agree that the Prophet's method was superior to his, and, though the crime of parricide was not permitted, Abdallah's son is said to have treated his father with a dose of water in which the Prophet had washed, in the hope that it might soften his heart.†

A yet more serious event which marked the raid on the Banu Mustalik was the disgrace of Ayeshah. The last time we met her she was torn from her playthings to marry the Prophet, for whom she had shown a childish and natural aversion ; having now reached her fifteenth year, she had learned to ap-

* *Wakidi* (*W.*), 182.

† *Tab.*, *Comm.*, xxviii., 69.

THE DROMEDARY OF THE DESERT.

Etching by R. Swain Gifford.

preciate the advantages of the post of royal favourite, and had developed a haughty ill-nature which had made her many enemies. The Prophet, who found it difficult to keep the peace in his harem, had adopted the plan of letting them draw lots for the honour of accompanying him on his expeditions, and to Ayeshah the lot had fallen on this occasion. She had stopped behind (she said) when the army was starting homeward to pick up a necklace, which she had dropped in the sand, had been found by a youth named Safwan, son of Al-Mu'attal, who had also loitered, and by him been escorted to the camp. Why evil should have been thought of what seems to us a perfectly natural occurrence we know not, but we must remember that the Moslem mind had by this time been somewhat tainted by licentiousness, whence any meeting between persons of different sex gave rise to sinister rumours. The supposed delinquency of Ayeshah was greedily seized by a variety of persons; some were scandal-mongers, like the cowardly poet Hassan Ibn Thabit, who had probably suffered from Ayeshah's tongue; whereas others were moved by interest in Ayeshah's rivals in the harem, or wished to use the matter as political capital for the purpose of occasioning the Prophet trouble, and in this context the notorious Abdallah Ibn Ubayy is mentioned. For indeed they argued that by punishing Ayeshah he would necessarily offend his most faithful ally, her father, whereas by condoning her offence he would make himself contemptible, and give the poets employed by his enemies a handle. To hush up the matter was impossible, and the violent discussions which it produced threatened to lead to civil war. Meanwhile the Prophet had treated Ayeshah with marked disfavour, and permitted her to return to her parents —possibly for good. This last (divorce) was the course recommended by Ali, who also endeavoured to get some witness against her. Those, however, were not wise who matched themselves in intrigue, either against Mohammed or against Ayeshah. The latter, being openly questioned by the Prophet in her parents' presence, indignantly refused to answer; she would follow the example of Joseph's father (she confessed that she had forgotten Jacob's name), who under trying circumstances, took refuge in "becoming patience." Happily for her the Prophet was no Othello, but a man whose judgment was not often put out of balance. Even if he believed Ayeshah guilty, it was not desirable to acknowledge such suspicion, since discredit falling on Abu Bakr would affect his own cause, even if that faithful ally were not alienated. He had recourse to a revelation, covered himself up, and presently exhibited himself in a violent state of perspiration. While this operation lasted the audience were probably in a fever of anxiety as to the result. Some there doubtless remembered how when a case of adultery among the Jews had been referred to him, he had deliberately rejected the more merciful alternative, and condemned the parties to be stoned; and even in the case of the wife of one of his followers he is said to have adhered to the rule.* Would this horrible fate

* *Bokhari* (*C.*), ii., 69.

really befall the blooming girl who claimed the premiership in the harem, the pert minx, as others called her, who made so many victims of her laziness and her caprices, who even made the Prophet feel that he was her father's debtor? And had Islam extinguished the natural instincts sufficiently to allow her father to remain at the Prophet's right hand, should such a disaster happen? It was a very dark cloud, but the Prophet's revelation caused it to clear away —to break on the heads of the persons who had had the hardihood to meddle in the Prophet's domestic affairs. God Almighty declared Ayeshah innocent, and protested against the conduct of those who had entertained the suspicion for a moment. The queenly Ayeshah told her husband that she thanked God, but owed him no thanks.* Violent personal chastisement was admistered to the gossips, including, according to one account, the court-poet, Hassan, son of Thabit; according to another,† he was wounded by the co-respondent Safwan, son of Mu'attal; the evidence of adultery to be demanded in future was of such a sort as was practically impossible to procure. The Prophet's privacy was in future to be undisturbed by gossiping tongues. Ayeshah's temporary depression was amply expiated by the honour and glory of a communication from Almighty God of which the direct intention was to clear her character. And Ali, doughty warrior as he was, had won for himself in this girl an enemy whose vengeance

* *Musnad*, vi., 30.

† *Wakidi* (*W.*), 189.

followed him relentlessly for thirty-five years.* In order to disseminate no ill-feeling among his followers the Prophet presently compensated Hassan for his wound or his beating by a present of an estate and a concubine.

The fact that Medinah was not safe from internal foes suggested to the Prophet to take some steps in the direction of regaining Meccah. In the month before the pilgrimage month (March, 628) he determined to make an attempt to keep the festival and announced that God had promised him in a dream that he should enter the sacred Mosque.† According to custom it should have been quite safe for Mohammed like any other Arab or foreigner to make the pilgrimage during the sacred month, but having violated the sacred month himself before the battle of Badr, he had forfeited the right which every one else enjoyed. It is stated that he issued a proclamation to the Arab tribes round Medinah, inviting them to accompany him on this sacred expedition: hoping thereby to impress them with the fact that he was bent on maintaining the national religion. This appeal met with a cold response; but of his followers in Medinah seven hundred or fourteen hundred were ready to go with him, and they started accordingly, taking a number of camels for sacrifice. These beasts were decorated for the purpose at Dhu'l-Hulaifah, said to be six miles from

* Abu Bakr one day was shocked at hearing Ayeshah addressing her illustrious husband in a loud and shrewish voice; she was taunting him with preferring Ali to her father. *Musnad*, iv., 275.

† *Surah* xlviii., 17.

PANORAMA OF MECCAH.

Medinah; he then sent one of his Khuza'ite spies to find out what the Meccans were doing; the spy rejoined him at the pond of Ashtat near 'Usfan, with news that the Meccans had assembled a great force, had posted a series of scouts between the Sarawi and Baldah, had encamped in force at the latter place, and sent Khalid with two hundred horsemen to Kura' al-'Amim.* On hearing of the Meccan preparation he whined his regrets that the Meccans did not leave him to be dealt with by the Arabs, in which case they might either be rid of him without trouble to themselves, or, without loss, join him if he proved successful. The possibility however occurred to him of taking Meccah by surprise, if he approached it by a circuitous route, known to few, through the pass of Dhat al-Hanzal, which with some difficulty his guides managed to find; thence they emerged at Hudaibiyah, some eight miles from Meccah, to find that the Meccan force, having obtained knowledge of his plans, was prepared to meet him. The reason however which he afterwards alleged for declining to proceed against Meccah was either fear for the fate of the Moslems who were living (in retirement) in that city, or that his camel had been divinely stopped on the road by the same power that had restrained the Ethiopian's elephant.

If however the idea of storming Meccah had to be given up, the pretence of the pilgrimage still remained; and also he was not unwilling to impress the Meccans with a sense of his might, wealth, and the reverence and awe which he inspired. It is not

* *Wakidi* (*W.*), 244.

probable that any actual engagements took place between the believing and unbelieving parties, but the Kuraish sent repeatedly to know what Mohammed wanted, and expressed themselves determined not to let him inside their city whether he came as a friend or as an enemy: while the assurances brought them of the Prophet's pacific intentions were received with extreme scepticism by Budail, son of Warka, the Khuza'ite, and 'Urwah, son of Mas'ud, the Thakafite (both of them figures who will meet us in the sequel).

Finally the Meccans sent the leader of their allies, Hulais, son of 'Alkamah, whom Mohammed knew to be subject to religious scruples. He took care that this man should see the sacrificial camels and the uncombed pilgrims; affected by the sight, Hulais urged the Meccans to compromise with their unwelcome visitors.*

Presently it was determined to send a representative to Meccah, but the consciousness that most of the Moslems were stained with Meccan blood rendered the heroes of Islam unwilling to risk their lives on such an errand; even Omar, ordinarily so ready with his sword, hung back. At last the Prophet's son-in-law, Othman, son of 'Affan, who had preferred nursing his wife to fighting at Badr, was sent as a *grata persona:* he stayed away some three days, taking the opportunity to visit those Moslem families that remained at Meccah; and on a rumour that he had been killed, a solemn league and covenant was made by the Prophet's followers, in which they shook the

* *Wakidi* (*W*.), 252; *Musnad*, iv., 323.

Prophet's hand under a tree, vowing not to turn their backs should they have to fight.* Ma'kil, son of Yasar, held a branch over the Prophet's head. The rumour turned out to be false. Othman had succeeded in persuading his former townsmen that the Prophet really meant no harm, and that there was now an opportunity for the communities to make a treaty for some years, since both had suffered so much from this continued warfare. Probably the Meccans were all the more ready to listen, because some of their weak-minded allies felt shocked at worshippers being debarred from doing honour to God's holy house, and threatened to rebel if the Kuraish persisted in their impiety. They sent, as plenipotentiary to Mohammed, Suhail, son of 'Amr, a man of fame as an orator, who had been captured at Badr and ransomed. He appears to have regarded as so much "bluff" the display with which Mohammed had endeavoured to impress his enemies, and obtained terms from the Prophet which made the Moslems blush—indeed would have made Omar turn renegade, could he have found a following.† The Prophet was not allowed to call himself God's messenger in the document which they drew up, and Allah was not suffered to be identified with the Prophet's Rahman. There was to be peace between the Kuraish and the Moslems for ten years, and tribes who chose to enter the confederation of either the Prophet or the Kuraish were to be free to do so.‡

* *Musnad*, v., 25; *cf.* iii., 292.

† *Wakidi* (*W.*), 255.

‡ *Ishak*, 803.

Runaways from Meccah to Medinah were to be reclaimed, but renegades who escaped to Meccah were not to be delivered up. The Mohammedan force was to return to Medinah, but in the following year an unarmed party of Moslems was to be suffered to perform the pilgrimage, for which purpose Meccah was to be evacuated for three days. And to show that Mohammed meant to be loyal to this treaty, no attempt was made to rescue Suhail's son, who, having turned Moslem, was in chains at Meccah. On the night which followed the signing of the treaty, hostilities nearly broke out, owing to the reported murder by the Meccans of a Moslem named Zanim or Ibn Zanim, but the Prophet succeeded in allaying the disturbances.* The Moslems, however, were sulkily silent when told by him to shave their heads and offer their sacrifices. At last (by the advice of his wife Umm Salamah) he performed the operations himself, and his followers did the same.†

The motives which guided the Prophet throughout this scene (which is described with unusual vividness by the biographers) can be divined. He certainly submitted to humiliation, since though his followers slaughtered their camels, and shaved their heads, they could only by straining words be said to have entered the sacred precinct safely. Moreover, the terms on which the right to pilgrimage had been conceded by the Kuraish involved one condition which favoured them above the Moslems—the clause about the extradition of deserters, but then Moham-

* *Musnad*, iv., 49.

† *Ibid.*, iv., 325.

med thought any who abandoned him were as well away.* Medinah, he remarked in reference to a Bedouin who, after experiencing the fever, wished to be relieved of his oath of allegiance, was like a furnace which discharges the dross, while it brings out the purity of the gold.† He also was aware that treaties are of little avail when they can be safely broken by either party, and at no time was stingy of verbal concessions. If Omar had fallen away, as he threatened to do several times during those scenes, the Prophet could have endured the loss. But the Prophet knew both Omar and his other followers too well to fear such a catastrophe; and he had in his hand the card of Khaibar.

The chapter of the Koran which the tradition connects with this episode adopts a triumphant tone which the circumstances would not appear to justify. It is, however, addressed to the Arabs who refused to follow the expedition, whom it charges with expecting that the Prophet would never return. It asserts that the Moslems gained a victory over the Kuraish in the Vale of Meccah, and that further bloodshed was then prevented by divine interposition. This statement must have been intended for "those who were left behind." They are, however, promised the chance of a call to arms against a mighty power, and threatened with "terrible punishment" if they refuse to obey it. Apparently, then, the tribes to whom he refers had been experiencing the same change in their circumstances as had fallen

* *Musnad*, iii., 268.

† *Ibid.*, iii., 365.

to the lot of the people of Medinah. Originally entangled in a defensive alliance, they were compelled by force of events to offer themselves for foreign service.

The clause in the treaty whereby proselyte Kurashites were to be returned to Meccah without corresponding extradition, was shortly found to be as unworkable as the Prophet had probably foreseen when he accepted it. The pomp and parade of the expedition to Hudaibiyah had been effective; still more the magnificence of the offerings to the House of God. When the new religion led to increasing reverence for the Meccan sanctuary, the question of the dogma interested few. The Kuraish were growing proud of their kinsman, and beginning to pay him in his own country the honour which was lavished on him elsewhere. When this son of Meccah was treated by strangers with adoration such as no earthly monarch enjoyed, were they wise in continuing to repudiate this honourable connexion? 'Utbah, son of Usaid, escaped from Meccah to Medinah and was claimed back by the Meccans, who sent two men to fetch him. Mohammed was true to his word and let them take the proselyte back; but the example of 'Amr, son of Umayyah, was not lost on the neophyte; under the pretence of examining the sword of one of his guards, he got hold of the weapon and proceeded to attack his captor, upon which the captor and assistant fled. Returning to Medinah, he received from the Prophet a hint that if he could raise a gang of proselytes the treaty with Meccah might be broken; and this enterprising Moslem found little difficulty in raising one, which for a time waylaid and robbed the Meccan caravans. At last, in despair, the Meccans implored the Prophet to break the treaty and give these zealots a refuge in Medinah.

A certain number of Meccan ladies were, as might be expected, moved by the fame which the Prophet had now acquired, to desire to join him in his place of refuge, sometimes, perhaps, in a fit of vexation after a conjugal dispute,* and for these a simple arrangement was made. To a woman the wedding-gift, a substitute for the older purchase-money, constituted the most important part of her identity. If, therefore, the women remained, but the wedding-gifts which had been brought them by their unbelieving husbands were returned, no substantial injustice had been committed. These welcome visitors easily found new ties at Medinah, though some sort of examination † had to be undergone by them, to test the genuineness of their faith; perhaps to see that they were not decoys, whose flight was with the purpose of turning True Believers away from their faith. At a later time, when the Prophet's weakness was generally known, fair women either presented themselves or were sent to him from various parts of Arabia, or the husbands of fair and fruitful women offered to hand them over to the Prophet ‡; and indeed at Medinah, whenever a woman became a widow, her relations would not

* *Tabari, Comm.*, xxviii., 42.

† *Surah* lx., 10.

‡ So 'Uyainah, son of Hisn. *Isabah*, iii., 108.

find her a husband before asking whether the Prophet wanted her.* An anecdote in which the Prophet rejects a girl on the ground that "she never cried nor complained"† shows the sort of qualifications which he required in a wife.

One other recruit who came to Meccah at this time, and at first occupied a humble place among the homeless in the Mosque of Medinah, was destined to occupy a remarkable position in the evolution of Islam. This was Abu Hurairah, a man about whose origin and original name there were many various opinions—amounting in number to from thirty to forty. When the Prophet was no more, and his sayings became precious, Abu Hurairah won himself fame and importance by being ready with an inexhaustible stock of them. His place in Islam might be compared with that which (according to some theories) the author of the Fourth Gospel occupies in the evolution of Christianity. Wherever a saying ascribed to Mohammed is mystical or sublime, wherever it is worthy of a mediæval saint or ascetic, Abu Hurairah is most likely to be the authority for it. His wonderful acquaintance with what the Prophet had said excited some scepticism about its genuineness even in his own time: but he could account for his knowledge partly by a miracle wrought by the Prophet, and partly by the assertion that when the Helpers were occupied with their palms, and the Refugees with their retail trade,‡ he made it his business to hear and recollect

* *Musnad*, iv., 422.

† *Ibid.*, iii., 155.

‡ *Muslim*, ii., 261.

what the Prophet said. The transformation of Mohammed in men's minds from the character of statesman and warrior to that of saint and philanthropist is due in the main to the inventions of Abu Hurairah, the first Traditionalist. His method was adopted by many Moslems in later ages, and has probably done far more good than evil: but the honour of inventing it appears to belong to this ingenious convert.

The return of the Prophet from Hudaibiyah was marked by a slight success, illustrating the degree of courage and competence which might now be expected from a Moslem fighter. The story may be told in the words of the chief actor, who is likely indeed to have exaggerated his achievement, but perhaps has not seriously misrepresented the facts.*

"We reached Medinah," said Salamah, son of Al-Akwa', "after Hudaibiyah with the Prophet. Rubah, the Prophet's slave, and I took the Prophet's camels out to pasture, and I also led the horse of Talhah, son of Ubaidallah. At dead of night a raid was made on the camels by Abd al-Rahman,† son of 'Uyainah, who killed the herdsman, and proceeded to lift the camels with the aid of some men mounted on horses. I bade Rubah mount the horse, ride it to its owner Talhah, and inform the Prophet of the raid on his camels. Mounting a hill, and turning my face towards Medinah, I proceeded to shout 'Raid!' three times; I then went after the raiders with my sword and my

---

* *Musnad*, iv., 52, 53. Others give the event a different date.

† This name, which could only have belonged to a Moslem, is incorrect.

arrows, and proceeded to shoot them down and wound their horses. The ground was here covered with trees, and whenever a horseman turned upon me, I sat down at the foot of a tree, and shot at the horse under him, crying out my name. When the ravine became narrow, I got on the top of the hill, and hurled stones down on them. This went on till I had got every camel that belonged to the Prophet behind my back, in safety. This continued till they had aimed thirty lances at me, and thrown down thirty cloaks, to lighten the burden on their horses. On each one of these I threw a stone. Near midday reinforcements were brought them by 'Uyainah, son of Badr, of the tribe Fazarah; the enemy were in a narrow ravine, and I on the mountain above. 'Uyainah asked them who I was, and they replied that I had been giving them great trouble and had rescued from them all their plunder. 'Uyainah said that I must certainly have some reinforcements behind me, or else I should have let them alone. Four men then at his command climbed the mountain to attack me. When I had told them who I was, I also assured them that not one of them could come up with me or outrun me if I followed him. One of them replied, 'I think otherwise,' but at that moment I saw some of the Prophet's horsemen entering the wood. The first were Al-Akhram of the tribe Asad, followed by Abu-Katadah, the Prophet's best horseman, followed by Al-Mikdad. The enemy immediately turned their backs and fled. I ran down the hill, and seizing Al-Akhram's rein, bade him be careful, as the enemy might cut him off. He had better wait, I said, till the Prophet and the rest of his followers had come up. 'Salamah,' he replied, 'if you believe in God and the last day, and know that the Garden is real and the Fire real, then do not stand between me and martyrdom.' So I let go his rein, and he galloped up to Abd al-Rahman, son of 'Uyainah, who turned upon him, and the two exchanged sword-thrusts, in which Al-Akhram was killed, and Abd al-Rahman's horse disabled. Abd al-Rahman leapt on Al-Akhram's horse, but was immediately attacked by Abu Katadah, and this time Abd al-Rahman was killed, and Abu Katadah's horse disabled. Abu Katadah leapt on Al-Akhram's horse, but meanwhile I ran on far in front of my friends, and drove the enemy by my arrows from a well at which they had intended watering, called Dhu Karad, and seized two of their horses which I brought to the Prophet, who had now come up with five hundred men. I then begged the Prophet for a hundred men, promising to overtake and annihilate the whole of the enemy with them. But before I could start, news reached the Prophet that they had rested in the Ghatafan country, where a chief had slaughtered a camel to entertain them ; but finding the flesh of the camel, when flayed, to be ashy in colour, they had been alarmed by the omen, and fled hurriedly to their homes. The Prophet thereupon assigned me a foot-soldier's as well as a horseman's share of the spoil, and set me on his camel behind him, as we returned to Medinah."

Each time the Prophet had failed, or scored an incomplete success, he compensated for it by an attack on the Jews; the policy had served too well to be abandoned after the unsatisfactory affair of Hudaibiyah, and therefore a raid on the Jews of Khaibar was speedily planned.* Khaibar was famous as the richest village in the Hijaz ; it would appear from its

* Muharram, A.H. 7, identified with June, A.D. 628.

name (Hebrew, "community") to have been originally a Jewish settlement; it is divided from Medinah by about a hundred miles chiefly of *harrah*, or lava-formation.* Rarely visited by Europeans, it was the residence of the great explorer Doughty for some months in the year 1877. The oasis at the edge of which it is situated is luxuriantly fertile, and was skilfully cultivated by the Jews. But the place was also well fortified; many names of fortresses are mentioned by Ibn Ishak; some parts of the old fortifications remaining to this day. The Hisn, or citadel rock of basalt, stands solitary in the Wadi Zeydieh; and upon its southern skirt is built the clay village. The length of the walled platform is two hundred paces, and the breadth ninety. Mohammed by this time knew the Jews too well to fear that there would be any difficulty in storming their fortifications, however strong. Following the principle of his raid after Uhud, he only permitted those to accompany him who had shared the expedition to Hudaibiyah. The route which he followed required three days; the names of the places at which he rested are preserved by the biographers but seem otherwise to be unknown.

Abdallah Ibn Ubayy (whose name the Jews must by this time have heard with curses) is said to have sent word to the inhabitants of Khaibar of the coming storm; and the Jews, from whom this could scarcely have been concealed in any case, sent to the Ghatafan tribes, whose home was in their neighbourhood, requesting their aid. Mohammed, whose guides were

* *Doughty*, i., 73.

skilful men of the tribe Ashja', succeeded in finding his way between the Ghatafan and Khaibar, and, by a feigned attack on the possessions of the former, averting the danger of a confederation. It would seem that cordial assistance was rarely extended to the Israelites, who, as has been seen, regularly abandoned each other to destruction.

The Prophet's prayer on the occasion of this raid is faithfully recorded. His God had by this time acquired the chief attributes of the Roman Laverna or goddess of gain; and he prayed that rich booty might be accorded them. Indeed it is probable that he had already pledged God's word for the success of the expedition; when he published his revelation about Hudaibiyah, God had promised them much plunder, and was giving *this* (*i. e.*, Khaibar) at once. This raid on a town so distant as one hundred miles from Medinah, in the opposite direction to that which his previous raids had taken, shows that he already contemplated the conquest of Arabia, if not of the world.

Wakidi has given a long account of the siege, and the Jews appear to have defended themselves better than might have been expected. Some accounts protract it for a couple of months, during the first of which the Jews are supposed to have been aided by their Arab allies; who, however, took the opportunity of quitting on a rumour reaching them that their homes were attacked. The Jewish forts held out well—over one called Sa'b many lives were lost. Some of the Khaibar Jews even won respect for their fighting powers; one Marhab, before he died, killed the brother of the assassin Mohammed, son of Maslamah, to perish afterwards by that assassin's hand; not, it would seem, in fair fight, but when Khaibar had surrendered, the prisoner was handed over to Mohammed Ibn Maslamah, and slain by him.*

As time went on, the Moslem army was near having to retire for want of food. However, there were traitors among the Jews of Khaibar, and with their assistance some forts were stormed; and other traitors even revealed to the Moslems the place where siege machinery was hidden and instructed the enemy in its use.† Presently Mohammed bethought him of the plan which presently became a prominent institution of Islam. To kill or banish the industrious inhabitants of Khaibar would not be good policy, since it was not desirable that the Moslems, who would constantly be wanted for active service, should be settled so far from Medinah. Moreover their skill as cultivators would not equal that of the former owners of the soil. So he decided to leave the Jews in occupation, on payment of half their produce, estimated by Abdallah, son of Rawahah,‡ at two hundred thousand *wasks* of dates. These Jews of Khaibar were then to be the first *dhimmis*, or members of a subject caste, whose lives were to be guaranteed, but whose earnings were to go to support the True Believers. Later on the fanatic Omar drove out the poor cultivators whom the Pro-

* *Isabah*, iii., 788.

† *Wakidi* (*W.*), 269.

‡ *Musnad*, iii., 367.

phet had spared. Meanwhile the Jews, though they retained their lives and lands, forfeited their goods —all save their Rolls of the Law. How else could Allah's pledge be redeemed? The *dhimmis* or subject races derived their name from the relation of client to patron, which, as we have seen, was of great consequence in Arabia; the client being ordinarily a man who, for some reason or other, put himself under the protection of a tribe not his own, which, doubtless for some consideration, defended him from his enemies. Thus the Moslems undertook to protect and fight for the non-Moslem races who acknowledged their supremacy, though they rejected their Prophet. Severe penalties were threatened against Moslems who killed members of those protected communities.* His recognition of the principle that a money payment would serve instead of a religious test shows us how little of a fanatic the Prophet was at heart.

The taking of Khaibar was marked by two events which, though of no permanent importance, make the scene vivid. Huyayy, son of Akhtab, had been the Prophet's most earnest adversary among the Jews, and had been assassinated, as has been seen, by Mohammed's order. His daughter "Safiyyah,"† was married to Kinanah, grandson of one Abu'l-Hukaik, like her father one of the Nadirites who had taken refuge at Khaibar. The Prophet's greed

* *Musnad*, iv., 237, etc.

† This word means "titbit," *i.e.*, an article specially selected by the conqueror out of the booty. It is unlikely to have been the woman's real name.

was excited by the thought of some rich silver vessels which Safiyyah's father had owned, and which had been the glory of his house. The family were told to bring out all their possessions and conceal nothing, under pain of execution. Those vessels they were as anxious to save as was the Prophet to rob them: they concealed them, and vowed that they had been sold or melted down long before. The angel Gabriel revealed to the Prophet where they were—not a difficult thing to reveal, as we know from *I Promessi Sposi*: the practised pillager knows what are the possibilities of concealment in the case of a besieged house; he knows the secrets which are revealed by the newly upturned soil, the disordered brickwork, the cobwebs or dust that have been cleared away. Some precious things had been concealed perhaps when Medinah was besieged; and men act in these matters instinctively or uniformly, like ants. But the production of the cups meant death to the men, and captivity to the women.* Safiyyah was invited to accept Islam and become the bride of the murderer of her father, her husband, and her brothers, of the treacherous enemy who had all but exterminated her race, and she accepted the offer. Some Moslems paid her the compliment of thinking she meant to play a Judith's part, but they did her more than justice. Just as the Jewish tribes had

* So *Wakidi*; but *Wakidi* (*W.*) and *Ibn Ishak* make another Jew betray the hiding-place; after which Kinanah is tortured by Al-Zubair, and killed by Mohammed, son of Maslamah. The Kurds still endeavour to wrench treasure out of their captives by similar means. In *Musnad*, iii., 123, the story of Safiyyah is told in a manner that is inconsistent with the above.

each played for its own hand, careless of the fate of the others, so to this woman a share in the harem of the conqueror made up for the loss of father, husband, brethren, and religion. So Beckwourth found that a few hours were sufficient to reconcile the American squaws to captivity. Dragged from the blood-baths in which their husbands, fathers, and brothers perished, they in a little time became cheerful and even merry.*

Another Jewess, Zainab, the wife of Sallam, son of Mishkam, who figures as a partisan of Mohammed, tried with partial success a plan which others had attempted—to fail entirely. She found out what joint was the Prophet's favourite food, and cooked it for him, richly seasoned with poison. The Prophet's guest, Bishr, son of Al-Bara, took some and swallowed it; and presently died in convulsions. The Prophet bethought him in time of the enemies who bring gifts; and spued the morsel before it passed down his throat, and had his shoulder bled at once, as a means of excreting the poison.† But when three years after he died of fever, he thought it was Zainab's poison still working within him, and among his other honours could claim that of martyrdom.

When the Moslems came to apportion their spoils they found that the conquest of Khaibar surpassed every other benefit that God had conferred on their Prophet. The leader's one fifth enabled him to enrich his wives and his concubines, his daughters and their

* *Autobiography*, pp., 147, 180, 296, 297.

† *Isabah*, iv., 400.

offspring, his friends and acquaintance, down to the servants. Eighteen hundred lots were portioned out for the fourteen hundred fighters; the two hundred horsemen got, according to custom, treble lots. To one flatterer, Lukaim the 'Absite, as a reward for some felicitous verses, all the sheep of Khaibar were assigned. Moreover there was no fear of this wealth melting away as the former booty had melted; for the Jews remained to till the land which became the property of the robbers. The news of the victory alarmed the neighbouring settlement of Fadak: its people sent to the Prophet half their produce, ere he came and took away their all: and he accepted it, for thus the whole profit fell to him, since it had been won without sword or lance. The rich Wadi al-Kura, the chief oasis of the Hijaz, also after a brief struggle fell into his hands; and the Jews of Taima accepted the same conditions as the others.*

The taking of Khaibar marks the stage at which Islam became a menace to the whole world. True, Mohammed had now for six years lived by robbery and brigandage: but in plundering the Meccans he could plead that he had been driven from his home and possessions: and with the Jewish tribes of Medinah he had in each case some outrage, real or pretended, to avenge. But the people of Khaibar, all that distance from Medinah, had certainly done him and his followers no wrong: for their leaving unavenged the murder of one of their number by his emissary was no act of aggression. Ali, when told

* *Wakidi* (*W.*), 292.

to lead the forces against them, had to enquire for what he was fighting: and was told that he must compel them to adopt the formulæ of Islam.* Khaibar was attacked because there was booty to be acquired there, and the plea for attacking it was that its inhabitants were *not Moslems.* That plea would cover attacks on the whole world outside Medinah and its neighbourhood: and on leaving Khaibar the Prophet seemed to see the world already in his grasp. This was a great advance from the early days of Medinah, when the Jews were to be tolerated as equals, and even idolators to be left unmolested, so long as they manifested no open hostility. *Now* the fact that a community was idolatrous, or Jewish, or anything but Mohammedan, warranted a murderous attack upon it: the passion for fresh conquests dominated the Prophet as it dominated an Alexander before him or a Napoleon after him.

He was joined at Khaibar by the Abyssinian refugees, and declared the arrival of some of them to be more welcome to him than even the taking of Khaibar. There were sixteen men and about the same number of women, for whom the Abyssinian monarch had provided two vessels: we suppose that after the massacre of the Kuraizah the Prophet had sent for them, having no lack of land to offer them; forwarding as a present to the Abyssinian King a silken *jubbah*—a robe which had been presented him by a monk †—perhaps out of respect for the

* *Muslim*, ii., 237. On the other hand in *Wakidi's* narrative the people of Khaibar are made out to have been planning attacks on Medinah.

† *Musnad*, iii. 3.37.

man who had massacred so many Jews. Of the Abyssinian refugees not a few had ended their lives in exile: one had turned Christian, telling his fellows that *his* eyes were fully opened, while theirs were still half closed. Until his death the Abyssinian King maintained friendly relations with Mohammed: but the well-meant hospitality of the Christian won no favour for his co-religionists when the process of rapine had reached Christian frontiers. Perhaps a man would never rise high unless he turned away each ladder whereby he had ascended: others coming after might overtake him. When the homily which had originally won the Christian's favour was incorporated in the Koran, fresh texts were inserted, condemning the Christian theory of their Master's nature in no ambiguous terms. The doctrine of the Son of God was branded as a blasphemy sufficient to cause an earthquake or general convulsion of the universe. Hence Christians might with impunity be plundered. And indeed a Christian living at Medinah was summoned to adopt Islam on pain of forfeiting half his goods.*

About the time of the campaign of Khaibar he published his programme of world-conquest by sending letters to the rulers of whose fame he had heard. Being told that such letters must be sealed, he had a seal of silver made, with the words "Mohammed the Prophet of God" inscribed thereon on an Abyssinian stone.† This seal is said to have adorned the finger of his three successors, till the last of them let

* *Isabah*, i., 482.

† *Muslim*, ii., 158.

LETTER OF THE PROPHET TO THE "MUKAUKIS," DISCOVERED BY M. ÉTIENNE BARTHÉLÉMY; BELIEVED BY SEVERAL SCHOLARS TO BE THE ACTUAL DOCUMENT REFERRED TO IN THE TEXT.
From the "Hilal," Nov., 1904.

it drop into a well. Learning further that douceurs should be given to foreign ambassadors, he started a state chest, reserving part of the tribute from Khaibar for this and other extraordinary expenditure.* The following is a specimen of those letters—according to the tradition †:

> In the name of Allah the Rahman, the Merciful. From the Apostle of Allah to the Mukaukis, chief of the Copts. Peace be upon him who follows the guidance. Next, I summon thee with the appeal of Islam: become a Moslem and thou shalt be safe. God shall give thee thy reward twofold. But if thou decline then on thee is the guilt of the Copts. O ye people of the Book, come unto an equal arrangement between us and you, that we should serve none save God, associating nothing with Him, and not taking one another for Lords besides God. And if ye decline, then bear witness that we are Moslems.

How many of his letters ever reached their destination we know not. Arabic and Greek ‡ writers agree in making 628 the year in which Mohammed's letter reached Heraclius, though the following year would agree better with the tradition that he received it in Emesa, or at Jerusalem, whither he had gone on pilgrimage to give thanks for his great victories; and both give fabulous accounts of the result. Yet the story told by the Arabs, if it be false, contains no

* *Musnad*, iv., 37.

† *Husn al-Muhadarah*, i., 47 (new ed.). The document of which a facsimile is given contains this text. If Dr. Butler's theory be correct (see below) it must certainly be spurious.

‡ *Muralt, Essai de Chronologie Byzantine*, gives the date as April, 628. Cp. also *Drapeyron, L'Empéreur Heraclius*, Paris, 1869.

chronological errors. Heraclius, according to this account, receiving the letter of Mohammed at the hands of the handsome Dihyah, in whose form the angel Gabriel was accustomed to appear,* asked whether any of the Prophet's countrymen could be found in Syria. It was the time of truce between Meccans and Moslems: hence Abu Sufyan, son of Al-Harith, † was quite near at Gaza. He was summoned to the presence of the Emperor to explain the conduct of his kinsman: and gave answers which, without any intention on Abu Sufyan's part, effected the Emperor's conversion, which only fear of his subjects forced him to conceal. This story, variously embellished, is supposed to go back to Abu Sufyan himself, who was deeply impressed by the terror which Mohammed's name inspired in the Emperor of the Greeks: of the ultimate success of Islam he now became convinced. What elements of truth lie hid in this anecdote it is hard to discover. The coincidence of Abu Sufyan being in Syria, which is likely to be historical, was sufficient to produce the fabrication of his being summoned to give an account of his famous countryman. Had he really been summoned, he could scarcely have lost the opportunity of endeavouring to obtain help for Meccah against the dangerous exile; of pointing out the menace to the neighbouring provinces which was contained in the rise of the Moslem power. And in-

* *Isabah*, i., 973.

† So *Wakidi* (*W.*), 329, n. In the story Abu Sufyan is represented as a near relation of Mohammed, which does not suit the more famous Abu Sufyan so well.

deed according to one story* Abu Sufyan accused the Prophet before Heraclius, but his charge was answered by a poet named A'sha of Kais. Probably the missive in an unknown tongue was thought unworthy of the monarch's notice. How many lunatics in our time worry royal personages with their inspirations! Or, if its reception was really favourable, we know of one tie between Mohammed and the Emperor which may have secured it. To Heraclius, fresh from a massacre of Jews, came the news of a Prophet in Arabia who had slaughtered six hundred Jews in one day; who, having ruined their settlements at Medinah, had just brought desolation on their greatest and most flourishing colony, killing the men and making the women concubines. His claims to a divine mission might seem plausible, till for Jews Christians came to be substituted.

Another letter was sent to the Persian King,—according to the tradition,—whom Heraclius had defeated, and who was presently to be slain by his own son. The date of this King's death is given with great appearance of precision †—Tuesday, the tenth of Jumada I of the year 7 ‡: some three months after Khaibar had been taken. The Persian King is represented as treating the Prophet's message far otherwise than Heraclius: he tore it in pieces, and sent to the governor of Yemen to bring him the slave who dared to send such a letter to his suzerain.

* *Aghani*, xv., 58.

† *Diyarbekri*, ii., 39.

‡ The true date was Feb. 29, A.D. 628 (*Nöldeke*, *Sas.*, 432; *Gerland*, *Persische Feldzüge des Kaiser's Herakleios*). The above is identified with Sep. 15, A.D. 628.

That official's messengers went first to Ta'if, whence the inhabitants, overjoyed at the thought that Mohammed had incurred the displeasure of the Great King, sent them on to Medinah. There the Prophet received them not without reluctance, owing to their having after their national style shaved their beards and let their moustaches grow*; whereas his own practice was the converse. While they were parleying with the Prophet the news reached them of their master's death; and they had to wait for further orders. These were that they should leave the Prophet unmolested.

The environment of this story is even more mysterious than that of the other: in each form of it the Prophet announces the death of the Persian King at the time when it actually took place, and thereby makes the emissaries hesitate to arrest him till they had verified his statement: so poor was the discipline maintained among the Persian King's retainers. Now, that Mohammed had many secret agencies for obtaining intelligence speedily cannot be doubted: but that the messengers would have refrained from doing their duty in consequence of such an assertion we do not believe. If, however, the date of the Persian King's death be correct, the story will hang together best if we suppose that amid the confusion arising from the assassination of the King, this seemingly unimportant matter was overlooked. The message was either never delivered, or never answered.

---

* *Ibn Arabi*, *Musamarat*, ii., 73. According to him the families of the messengers were extant in Yemen in his time (7th century A.H.)

Another letter was to the "Mukaukis" of Egypt, or to the governor of Alexandria, wrongly identified by the Arab chroniclers with Cyrus, viceroy and archbishop at the time of the Arab invasion, called by the Copts Pkauchios.* What is certain is that the letter, to whomsoever addressed, had a favourable reception: for the Mukaukis sent handsome presents when he received it, with Jabr, son of Abdallah †—a horse, a mule, an ass, and a present that went near perpetuating the Prophet's dynasty: for the concubine Mary, a Copt, sent by this governor, erelong brought forth a son of whom Mohammed claimed to be the father, his fatherhood being attested by the infant's features—though the rival wife, the childless Ayeshah, would not see the resemblance. This governor could not from Mohammed's letter only have divined so well its author's tastes: a couple of concubines would have been a suitable present for Achilles, but how came the Alexandrian to know that they were equally suitable to the founder of a new religion? He must have learned of this from the messenger—Hatib, son of Balta'ah, whose description of the massacres of Israelites may have secured this man's partial acceptance of Mohammed's claim. Of his conversation with the Mukaukis a specimen is preserved. ‡ "If Mohammed is a Prophet," he asked, "why did he not curse the people of Meccah when they drove him out?"—a proceeding for which authority could be found in

---

* See *Butler, Arab Conquest of Egypt*, Appendix C.

† *Isabah*, i., 480.

‡ *Usd al-ghabah*, i., 362, etc.

both Testaments. Hatib was equal to the occasion: "If Jesus be a Prophet," he replied, "why did not *he* curse the people who wanted to crucify him?"

Other messengers went to the heads of small states in Arabia, to whom the claim to hegemony on the part of one of their number perhaps came as less of a surprise; for the history of Arabia apparently had been one of ups and downs: when a competent ruler had shown himself in a province he aspired to the homage of the others. These princes seem to have temporised, waiting to see whether the new power would crush the resistance of its neighbours, or itself succumb. It is not claimed that the effect on these persons was as remarkable as that which had been produced on the three Christian potentates: and perhaps the series of battles which bards had celebrated in copious verse had by this time brought them news of Mohammed and his claims. And since the Meccan party were as boastful as those of Medinah, they would have learned that if one day had been for him, another had been against him. With the southern Arabians also Mohammed's massacres of Jews may have rendered him popular: since the recollection of the Israelitish hegemony was not sweet. Haudhah, the Christian ruler of the Banu Hanifah in Yemamah, must have sent a courteous reply: since at the Khaibar campaign Mohammed's beast was held by a Nubian slave whom that monarch had sent him as a present.* Presently Haudhah offered to accept Islam on condition of being

* *Isabah*, iii., 588.

appointed the Prophet's successor; a condition which was, of course, declined.*

As the end of the year 7 approached the time came for the execution of the Prophet's project of a pilgrimage, leave for which had been extorted from the Meccans the year before. The Prophet's cause had materially advanced since his visit to Hudaibiyah. and he had all the interest of a royal personage attaching to him. He had, moreover, taken into his harem the daughter of his resolute opponent Abu Sufyan: for at his request Umm Habibah, widow of one of his followers, had been sent to him by the Abyssinian King, with a handsome dowry provided by the monarch himself. Meccah, according to the terms agreed on the previous year, was to be vacated by the Kuraish for three days, during which Mohammed might have the Ka'bah to himself: after that he was to quit. Probably neither party was sure of the good faith of the other: Mohammed brought with him two hundred horsemen, in case of emergencies: and so little were the Kuraish disposed to prolong the visit of their guest, that they refused him permission to give at Meccah the entertainment which should have followed one of his numerous weddings, which he prepared to solemnise in his native town.

An accurate record is preserved of the Prophet's road and of the direction from which he approached Meccah. His escort of two hundred riders was left behind at Yajuj, an elevation whence the images at this time surrounding the Ka'bah could be seen.

---

* *Khafaji*, *Comm. on Durrah*, 46.

The procession of sixty camels for sacrifice, followed by the twelve hundred Moslems, proceeded from Kada past the graveyard on the road to Abtah and Mina.* Lest the Meccans should think the Moslems still worn and jaded, as they had seemed at Badr, they were ordered to do part of their procession racing, and this custom remained till after times. They had requested a meal of camel's flesh to make their countenances cheerful; but the Prophet, regarding this as too costly, had given them a feast of dates instead.†

This pilgrimage,‡ then, like the last, was to impress the Meccans with a show of power and wealth, and doubtless materially assisted the capture of Meccah, which was now within easy distance. Much vexation must have been occasioned to the steady, though not always judicious, opponents of Mohammed, like Abu Sufyan, by the Ciceros of the time—the faint-hearted partisans, whose fears regularly foreboded ill to their own cause, and who now could point to the fulfilment of their forebodings. If there were any there who had urged vigorous measures the day they let Mohammed escape from their daggers, any who had advised that the victory of Uhud be not left unfinished, and whose calculations had not been put out by the stratagem of the Ditch—such persons could look back with justifiable pride on valuable counsel given and neglected.

In the marriage with Maimunah, a beautiful widow

* *Diyarbekri*, i., 690.

† *Musnad*, i., 221, 306.

‡ Dhu'l-Ka'dah, A.H. 7, identified with March, A.D. 629.

VIEW OF MINA.
From *Ali Bey's Travels.*

whom the Prophet now added to his harem, his uncle Abbas is said to have acted as the bride's guardian. The marriage took place at Sarif, some eight miles from Meccah, and the question whether the Prophet was in a sacred or profane condition at the time interests Moslems, though it has no interest for us, who know the elasticity of the prophetic conscience. Owing to the fact that the empire founded by Mohammed had fallen to the descendants of Abbas at the time whence our chief documents emanate, determined attempts were made at representing him on all occasions as Mohammed's close ally. The lady herself is supposed to be referred to in the Koran as a believing woman who offers herself to the Prophet. According to some she was the last wife.

Mohammed's fame began to attract to Medinah the bards who went from court to court to sell their compliments. The poet of Yemamah, A'sha, of Kais, who enjoyed an exaggerated reputation, bethought him of earning something in this way, and there attached to his verses a superstition similar to that which in old times belonged to the words of Balaam: those whom he praised became great, those whom he ridiculed sank low. On the way to Medinah he came to Meccah, probably not knowing the relation between the two cities, and he showed his verses to Abu Sufyan. The latter offered him a hundred camels if he would go far away and watch the turn of events before he published his praise of Mohammed. The poet was sufficient of a business man to close with this offer, but one of his newly acquired camels killed him.

The spectacle of the pilgrimage produced one important convert, Khalid, son of Al-Walid, presently destined to earn the name of the Sword of Allah. He and the other great Moslem general, 'Amr, son of Al-'Asi, were converted about this time, and are even said to have met each other on their way to Medinah. Khalid had gone away from Meccah in order not to have the humiliation of seeing the Moslems enter it; and a letter from his brother, Al-Walid, who had been converted shortly after Badr, written at the Prophet's instance, was decisive in causing him to join the conquering side.* The conversion of 'Amr is sometimes assigned to that Abyssinian potentate at whose palace his was a not unfamiliar figure. Thither, according to his own account,† he had retreated after the affair of the Ditch, thinking that Mohammed's success in his war with the Kuraish was now assured, and that the court of his Abyssinian friend would be a safe harbour for him, whence, even if Mohammed failed, he could easily return to Meccah. It is worth noticing that his return from Abyssinia must have followed on that of the Moslem exiles. The defection of these two deprived Meccah of the only strategic skill which it possessed, and it is an unsolved puzzle why that skill, which proved so valuable to Mohammed and his followers, had been useless to the Meccans. From the paralysis which held the Meccans in their undertakings these men of war were not free till they had put themselves under the reso-

* *Isabah*, iii., 1318.

† *Musnad*, iv., 199.

lute and resourceful founder of Islam; under him they were to win no fruitless victories as before. Khalid, the greater captain of the two, proved himself under the Caliphs better able to command than to obey; unwilling to be bound by rules, or to be checked in his movements by the central authority. But he fell behind none in blind reverence for Mohammed, who had occasion to rebuke him for excesses as well as to praise him for saving many a day; a word from the Prophet could cool this hero in his most savage moods,* and he wore some of the Prophet's hair as an amulet in his soldier's cap.† 'Amr counted as one of the Arab diplomats, on whose sagacity reliance could be placed, though under the Meccan régime it does not appear to have been successful. These persons' conversion is rightly regarded by Sprenger‡ as an acknowledgment on the part of far-seeing men that the progress of Islam could no longer be resisted; they were not so much betraying their fellow-citizens as setting them an example, which indeed the faint-heartedness of Meccan policy rendered easy of imitation. The great accession of wealth and strength which the last years had brought the Prophet made his countrymen anxious to obtain some of the glory which he was reflecting on all connected with him. Abu Sufyan § had hard work to persuade many of his countrymen to adhere to the religion of their fathers. Hakim, son of

---

* *Musnad*, iv., 89.

† *Wellhausen*, *Reste*, 166.

‡ Cf. *Wakidi* (*W.*), 304.

§ *Jauzi*, *Adhkiya*, 95.

Hizam, Khadijah's nephew, went to the expense and trouble of buying a robe that was said to have belonged to the hero Dhu Yazan, for fifty dinars, and bringing it to Medinah * as a present to his distinguished relative, who, however, refused to take a present from an unbeliever. Our wonder is not that Mohammed so easily took Meccah the next year, but that he had then to conciliate so many of his old opponents with bribes.

* *Musnad*, iii., 403.

CHAPTER XI

THE TAKING OF MECCAH

THIS year (8) was marked by the first collision between the forces of Islam and of Byzantium. It does not appear to have been deliberately planned by the Prophet, but was rather the result of his ignorance of Byzantine politics, and of the general want of communication between one part of the Byzantine Empire and another. Among the letters sent out by Mohammed at the time when he felt it his duty to summon all mankind to follow his doctrine, was one addressed to the governor of Bostra and conveyed by Al-Harith, son of 'Umair.* The messenger had been attacked and slain by the Ghassanide Shurahbil, son of 'Amr, also said to be an official in Cæsar's pay; and, as has been seen, Mohammed never allowed such an outrage to remain unavenged. He immediately † collected a force which was to go and avenge the murder, but we can scarcely believe that he was aware that an attack on Shurahbil meant an attack on the great Roman

* *Wakidi* (*W.*), 309.

† Jumada I, A.D. 8; identified with September, A.H. 629.

Empire. He would not have sent a force of three thousand to cope with the unlimited armies of the great Emperor: nor could he be expected to know that persons with such truly Arabic names as the Ghassanides were politically Roman rather than Arabs. He regarded this as one of the many raids on Arabic tribes which kept his treasury full, and sent a force strong indeed for him, but wholly unequal to that which the Byzantine Empire could bring against him. The horses are described by the poet Abdallah, son of Rawahah, as brought from Aja and Far' —mountains in the Shamr country. Zaid, son of Harithah, a not unsuccessful leader of raids, was chosen to command, and told to conclude treaties, if necessary, in his own name, instead of the Prophet's, so as to make them easier to break.* Among the rank and file was Khalid, son of Al-Walid, fighting now for the first time under his new allegiance. A few orders were given for the succession to the command in case of disaster: but of a hierarchy of officers the Mohammedan warfare at present knew nothing; indeed such a system would probably have seemed to violate the equality of all Moslems.

The authorities have not taken the trouble to chronicle the route taken by Zaid on this the most distant of the Moslem raids. Probably they followed the road which is now the pilgrim route from Damascus to Meccah, and which was the old caravan route. Their first destination was Mu'an or Ma'an, on the verge of the desert: it is a point at which the road to Meccah converges with another from Akabah.

* *Wakidi* (*W.*), 309.

It was at this time an important fortress, with an Arab governor, subject to the Byzantines. There they heard that the Greeks were in great force at Maāb (near the Dead Sea) with the fighting men of numerous Arab tribes: Heraclius himself, having recently recovered Palestine from the Persians, was said to be among them: but we need not repeat the fabulous numbers which the Moslems assign to the Byzantine army in order to excuse the sequel. A council of war was held, some suggesting that information should be sent to the Prophet, who clearly had nothing so serious in view: but Abdallah, son of Rawahah, a poet and enthusiast, who had been the first to advance and the last to retreat from every other fight, pointed out the inconsistency of losing a chance of martyrdom, which the Moslem should welcome even more than victory. After two days' deliberation they advanced. The spot at which they came in sight of the enemy was a plain called Masharif, not, it would seem, identified in modern times, but connected by the Arabs with Bostra, or Bosra, which has repeatedly been visited, in the region known as the Hauran. At the sight of the Byzantine force the Moslem army fell back on a village called Mutah, which has given its name to the campaign. There battle was given. Some of the Moslem leaders descended from their horses and deliberately lamed the beasts in order that they might not be tempted to flee.

Of the order of events in the battle we learn very little. Three standard-bearers (Zaid, Ja'far, the Prophet's cousin, and Abdallah, son of Rawāhah) being killed in succession, some difficulty was found in getting any one to take this dangerous charge: and, to judge by what happened at Uhud, it would appear that the Moslems were on the verge of a rout. Khalid, whose ability at Uhud had been displayed when his party had begun to fly, was again ready for the emergency: he stepped into the position of leader, at the instance, it is said, of Khalid, son of Arkam. By means not recorded, he succeeded in rallying the broken forces of the Moslems, and getting them safely away from the field. Even so, the Moslem losses were doubtless considerable; but on these their historians are unwilling to dwell. Probably the work of the victorious army was chiefly done by the tribes Lakhm, Judham, Kain, Bahra, and Bali, who spoke the same language and used the same weapons as their Moslem antagonists.

In Mohammedan history Ja'far, son of Abu Talib, is as much the hero of Mutah as is Hamzah the hero of Uhud. Ja'far had only returned from Abyssinia in the preceding year, so that his enjoyment of his cousin's regal position was of short duration. The general, Zaid, son of Harithah, had been connected with one of the worst scandals of the Prophet's domestic life, whence his not returning was perhaps not without its consolation. Abdallah, son of Rawahah, who is made responsible for the forward march from Ma'an, is represented as having shown some tendency to flinch: probably cooler men had more real nerve. He was one of Mohammed's court poets, but his satire fell flat on the Kuraish, because he taunted them with that unbelief of which they boasted.* High honours in Paradise were awarded to all by the grateful Prophet: but for Ja'far he found wings, to carry him to God's throne. With tears in his eyes he harangued the Moslems, narrating the order of the deaths, and saying he could not wish them back.† The survivors of this disastrous fight were greeted by the Moslems as deserters, and some were even afraid to appear in public for some time: such Spartans had the people of Medinah become in their eight years of warfare. The Prophet, whose mind was always clearest in times of stress, by no means echoed this taunt: if the numbers of the enemy had been one tenth of the figures given by the historians, no single Moslem should have escaped. To have come in collision with the great world-power and not have been exterminated, if not a victory, was very near one. Moreover, the Arab tribes who were now serving under Byzantine commanders were to the Mohammedans as wheat ready for the harvest.

It was the Prophet's custom, as we have often seen, to redeem a disaster as quickly as possible by some striking success. So long as there were Jews left, he was always sure of an easy victory; they were by this time exhausted; but Meccah remained, and his experiences of the last years showed him that it was ripe to fall. All then that was required was a decent pretext for attacking it, and this was provided by the treaty which he made with the Meccans at the time of his abortive pilgrimage.

---

* *Aghani*, xv., 29.

† *Musnad*, iii., 118.

We have repeatedly seen that blood once shed was never forgotten, unless there were formal atonements. Of the clause in the treaty of Hudaibiyah which permitted different tribes to enter the rival confederacies of Meccah and Medinah advantage had been taken by the Khuza'ah, who entered that of Medinah, and the Banu Bakr, a section of the Kinanah, who entered that of Meccah. Between these two tribes there was a blood-feud, dating from the time before the commencement of Islam; it had begun, as so often had been the case at Medinah, by the murder of a foreign trader, whom the Banu Bakr had undertaken to protect. A member of the Khuza'ah had been murdered in return, and in return for this three noble Bakrites had been murdered at Arafat. At the time of Badr, it will be remembered, an attack on Meccah by the Kinanah was feared, but did not take place: and for reasons not known to us, during the years in which the Meccan caravans were raided by Mohammed the feud seems to have slumbered. But the cessation of the danger from Medinah gave the Kuraish courage to assist their allies, the Kinanah, and in a nightly raid they killed one of the Khuza'ah within the sanctuary. The relations between the two confederacies were severed by this bloodshed; and a gap had been made through which the Prophet could enter. Indeed, so obvious was the occasion for the intervention of Mohammed that a variety of busybodies among the Khuza'ah hastened to be the first to solicit the Prophet's aid. The historians record the names of 'Amr, son of Salim, and Budail, son of Warka, in this contest.

PILGRIMS LEAVING ARAFAT.

The former is supposed to have presented himself in the Mosque at Medinah, and recited some flaming verses. The Prophet pointed to a cloud in the direction of Meccah, and declared that it contained help for the oppressed Khuza'ah. The other man had probably been in the Prophet's confidence long before. His family long preserved a letter from the Prophet, in which he is invited to come to Medinah, or to "migrate" without leaving his country: it would seem, by abstaining from communication with the people of Meccah, except at times of pilgrimage, lesser or greater. The letter ran as follows *:

"In the name of Allah, the merciful, the clement. From Mohammed, the Apostle of God, unto Budail, son of Warka, and the chieftains of the Banu 'Amr. I praise unto you Allah, than whom there is no other God. To proceed: I have not vexed your heart, nor set a burden on your back (?). Ye are the most precious of the people of Tihamah in my eyes, and the nearest akin unto me, with those among you that do well. Now I have taken for him of you that shall migrate the like of what I have taken for myself: even if he migrate in his own land, not dwelling in Meccah save for the lesser or greater pilgrimage. And I have laid no burden upon you in that I have made peace, and ye need not fear nor be alarmed by me."

This curious letter bears the marks of genuineness, and contains phrases on which some comment would be desired. As Wellhausen explains it, it refers to the time after the Hudaibiyah treaty, when Mohammed, having less need of the services of the Khuza'ah,

* Text in *Isabah*, s. v. Budail; a translation in *Wakidi* (*W.*), 306.

might seem to think less of them. The man to whom it was written now seized the opportunity for a visit to Medinah, in order to give the Prophet the good news that the time to invade Meccah had come. Little credibility attaches to the legend that the Prophet, distrusting Budail, sent spies to Meccah to find out the truth or to demand the extradition of the actual criminals before resolving on an advance to that city.

Neither party is likely to have deceived itself as to the issue of such an invasion. The biographers make Abu Sufyan himself head a deputation to Medinah with the view of securing the renewal of the terms which the Meccans found so beneficial to their commerce: the men, women, and children whose intercession with the Prophet he besought, all refused it; so mighty a matter of state could be settled by the chief alone: the Prophet himself received his distinguished suppliant with sardonic smiles. It was true that the Kurashites who had fought with the Khuza'ah had been disguised and unauthorised: but of their complicity there was apparently no question. The Prophet was not the man to throw away such a card, now it had come into his possession at a time when it was welcome. Abu Sufyan returned to Meccah with the knowledge that his long rivalry with Mohammed was nearing its termination.

Then came the expedition to Meccah, which started on the 10th of Ramadan,* and for which no fewer than 10,000 troops had mustered: it was the

* Identified with Jan. 1, A.D. 630.

Prophet's wish to conceal his purpose from the Meccans, and indeed he was near Meccah before he made it clear whether the Kuraish or the Hawazin were his object, and indeed whether he meant war at all.* The Meccans, however, fostered no delusions on the subject, and each step from Medinah made the Kurashite resistance melt faster away. Early in the journey Mohammed was joined by his uncle Abbas, whom Mohammedan authorities suppose to have for years been a secret aider and abettor of the Prophet: we know not whether this was so, or whether when the Caliphate came into Abbaside hands, the founder of the line had to be whitewashed. Nearing Meccah, at Marr Zahran they fell in with a scouting party, containing Abu Sufyan himself, Khadijah's nephew, and Budail, of whom we have just heard. Abu Sufyan was told by Abbas that it was not too late for him to save his head by a profession of faith in the mission of the man whom it had been the object of his life to prove an impostor: and that such an example might save many lives, seeing that Meccah must in any case fall. To this humiliation Abu Sufyan not without reluctance resigned himself: obtaining thereby not only his own safety, but the right to offer the same to all Meccans who took refuge in his house, who locked their own doors, or who went into the Meccan sanctuary. He had to listen to some hard words from the women folk when he got back to Meccah with his coat (metaphorically) turned inside out. They would have preferred one who, if he could not live for a cause, would dare to

* *Wakidi*, 329.

die for it. Still he had brought back good terms, and the Meccans gladly availed themselves thereof.

The course adopted by Abu Sufyan was similar to that adopted by wise and patriotic leaders when the alternatives of submission and annihilation have been before them. That his poor generalship was to blame for the state to which Meccah was now reduced must be conceded; but having at the last realised how affairs lay, he acted with prudence in saving life and property to the utmost of his power. He acknowledged that his gods had been defeated by Mohammed's God, and therefore that he owed the former no further allegiance.

Not quite all the Meccans were of the same mind as their chief. Some few knew that they had offended Mohammed too much to be forgiven—such were persons who had once believed in him, but afterwards abandoned him. A few others had personal wrongs which still cried for vengeance. They included Safwan, son of Umayyah, by whose counsel the battle of Uhud had not been followed up; Suhail, son of 'Amr, who had arranged the compact of Hudaibiyah; 'Ikrimah, son of Abu Jahl, who since his father's death had been a prominent opponent of Islam. They had some arms and ammunition, and formed a troop which stationed itself at Khandamah, a mountain which is close to Abu Kubais*—according to Burckhardt the culminating point of the Meccan mountains. Since Mohammed was bent on entering Meccah from the top (*i. e.*, from the north-east), his force would necessarily be men-

* *Azraki*, 155.

THE KA'BAH WITH THE STATION OF ABRAHAM.

aced by a body of men who occupied this position. There was a skirmish between them and the cavalry commanded by Khalid, with slight losses on both sides; and then the heroes abandoned their position and fled. Meccah was now the Prophet's. The idols which so many years before had roused the Prophet's scorn, and to which he owed his banishment, could now be utterly abolished. The pictures (probably rude artistic efforts) within the Ka'bah were effaced by Omar with a cloth * wetted in Zemzem water: whom or what they represented we know only on Mohammed's authority, which we are not inclined to trust; a curious tradition says that Mohammed put his hands over a picture of the Madonna and so saved it from destruction. † The images which surrounded the Ka'bah, and were fixed to their supports with lead, were overthrown and removed. The call to prayer resounded from the top of the Ka'bah, chanted by Bilal the Abyssinian slave—not without evoking expressions of horror and disgust from some who were not yet accustomed to the new régime. ‡ Yet the sanctity of the Ka'bah was to suffer no diminution by the religious innovations: whatever treasure its store contained—said to be seventy thousand ounces of gold!—the Prophet refused to touch §: a new mythology was substituted for the old: but the ceremonies, more important to the majority, were to remain. All Meccah was now

---

* *Musnad*, iii., 396.

† *Azraki*, 111.

‡ *Id.*, 192, quotes what they said.

§ *Ibid.*, 172.

to be an inviolable sanctuary: no blood was to be shed within its precincts, of which the landmarks, partly effaced, were now (with the angels' help) renewed.* If the Prophet had himself shed some, the privilege of God's favourites was not to be claimed by those of lower rank. Like Motley's cardinal preaching religious toleration, Mohammed took the earliest opportunity of impressing on his townsmen the abhorrence with which bloodshed should be regarded. And indeed though at the first he had drawn up a short proscription list, for one reason or another he reduced it to the modest number of two. Therein we can see not only an example of the Prophet's clemency, but also evidence of the excessive gratification which the taking of Meccah caused him. All old injuries were forgotten on that day of final triumph. The Refugees were not even allowed to reclaim their houses which had been seized or sold by the Meccans: they had to be satisfied with the promise of houses in Paradise instead †—Mohammed setting the example with Khadijah's former dwelling. Even the keys of the Ka'bah were not taken away from their hereditary holders, but returned to them, though the meritorious Ali put in a claim.

The taking of Meccah was the outcome of the series of events which began on the day when Mohammed was allowed to become the master of a community that lay between the Kuraish and their markets. An interest similar to that which attends the efforts of a tight-rope walker attaches to his

* *Azraki*, 360.

† *Chronicles of Meccah*, iv., 67.

career in the meanwhile. Destruction menaces him on all sides: but he surmounts the dangers, because he has a will, and his enemies have none. The historians tell us little of the internal history of Meccah during the past eight years, whence the gradual shifting of opinion in Mohammed's favour can only be guessed, and knowledge of the details fails us. We are justified in supposing that much was effected by Mohammed's campaign against the Byzantines, which, though not for the moment successful, made him the champion of a national idea, which the Arabs till then had scarcely been able to realise: even the enterprise of Saif, son of Dhu Yazan, had been only to substitute Persian for Abyssinian sovereignty. With this attitude agreed his ordinary tenderness for the lives of Arabs, when he massacred Jews without mercy. Moreover, experience seems to show that a man who can for a number of years force attention to be concentrated on himself acquires popularity even among his enemies.

Levées (if that be the right term) were held for the admission of the new converts—first for men and then for women; the latter not being permitted to shake the Prophet's hand.* A reasonable time was indeed granted for studying the evidences of the new religion in the case of those who were not prepared to accede to it at once: but of his resolve ultimately to tolerate no other the Prophet made no secret. The appearance of the neophytes at these levées revealed many traits of character: poets who had employed their facility of versification in lampooning the

* *Tabari*, *Comm.*, xxviii., 49.

Prophet now showed that it could be turned to his glorification; adulation and sycophancy were rife. On the other hand, among the women who had to swear allegiance some even at the risk of offending the conqueror could not restrain a sarcasm at the character of the code for which they had been compelled to suffer and to do so much. "All this I have kept from my youth up" was the comment of Hind, Abu Sufyan's wife, in response to some of the regulations: to the command "not to slay your children" she replied that the women at Meccah had reared their children to be slain by Mohammed's partisans at Badr. Still, when she returned from the levée, she took an axe and hewed her domestic idol into bits, taunting it with having deceived her all that time.* And similar iconoclasm now became rampant at Meccah.

The Prophet's stay at Meccah did not exceed a fortnight, as he was anxious to assure his friends of Medinah that he had no intention of leaving them for his former home: of which indeed there was some danger, since he did not conceal his opinion that Meccah was the best spot on earth and the dearest of all places to God.†

The day after his entry into Meccah, and proclamation of the sacrosanct area, one of his followers, a Khuza'ite, had exercised the blood-right by assassinating in Meccah a Hudhalite who had murdered one of his tribe; Mohammed repeated his oration, and paid blood-money for the victim‡ to the, as yet,

Azraki, 78.

† *Musnad*, iv., 305.

‡ *Azraki*, 353.

unconverted Hudhalites: he was only deterred from handing the assassin over to their vengeance by the doctrine that a Moslem must not be killed for an Unbeliever. Missionaries—which name occurs for the first time in Islam in this context—were sent to the neighbouring tribes, summoning them to put away their idols and submit to the new religion. Khalid, son of Al-Walid, being sent on a mission of this sort to the Jadhimah, took the opportunity of avenging an old wrong—the murder of his uncle which had happened years before: he attacked the tribe at Ghumaisa and dealt considerable slaughter. The Prophet, who now regarded all Arabs as his natural subjects, readily paid blood-money for all the slain, and gave the tribe a bonus as well. It was not his custom, however, to find fault with his subordinates for excessive zeal, and Khalid was employed to destroy other idols and sacred houses in the neighbourhood. The priests appear to have left the idols to see after their own defence—on Jerubbaal's principle, and with the like result. The House of Allah was therefore relieved of some rather dangerous rivals: for, as has already been seen, we have little or no reason for supposing that the House at Meccah stood alone as a centre of pilgrimage. The theory was now started that the House at Meccah was the first ever built: an assertion which gave rise to much speculation, and thence to many myths. Of it (the Ka'bah) these other houses would be bad imitations, not deserving to be maintained as Houses of Allah, for whose worship they had not been intended. How, we are inclined to wonder, would

Mohammed have treated "the furthest Mosque," the Temple wall at Jerusalem, had he lived to conquer that sacred city? He would have learned (what he perhaps did not know) that the Temple no longer existed: and since he forbade pilgrimage to Jerusalem, he would probably have secured in some way that special sanctity should no more attach to Zion. The political value of centralised worship was not learned by him from the example of the Jewish kings; but he was alive to it none the less. Not without deliberation did he decide what ritual he should retain, till he finally drew up a scheme whereby a number of rites belonging originally to different sanctuaries were grouped into a lengthy performance: the inequalities which in the older system had distinguished different clans were all abolished; all Moslems being equal. Into those ceremonies there was little difficulty in working the Abraham myth in place of the tales which former cicerones had told. If stones were in one place thrown to keep down the body of some fallen enemy, or to secure that certain land should not be appropriated for a year,* it could now be said that they were thrown at Satan. Was not Satan called "the stoned" in the Koran?

One serious alteration was presently to follow when the Prophet conceived the unhappy idea of altering the Calendar without knowledge of the elements of astronomy or even of the purpose of the year. Previously, by unscientific intercala-

* *Chauvin. Le Jet des Pierres au Pélérinage de la Mecque*, Anvers, 1902.

tion, the months had been made to correspond roughly to the seasons: Mohammed, by making it twelve lunar months, destroyed all relation between them. Of any accommodation of the pilgrimage months to the needs of commerce there could no longer be any question. Mohammed had not intended this result, of whose certainty he was ignorant: but it came, and the markets of the "Days of Ignorance" quickly fell into oblivion. The commerce of Meccah was ruined, but the city was the gainer—at first by a fair share in the plunder of the world, presently by a concourse of visitors unprecedented in number at the sacred seasons: a stream at rare times diverted by sedition and fanaticism, increasing in peaceful times since Meccah was taken, until now, when railroad and steamer help to swell it. If Mohammed took anything from Meccah, he gave it more.

Of cities that existed in the seventh century of our era probably few have carried on an existence so continuous, ruffled only by superficial troubles. Its population, after it had been made the great sanctuary of the world, quickly forgot politics and commerce: they turned into show-managers, the keepers of an exhibition which it was the duty of all the world to visit. To the faithful whose lives had been spent in dreams of Meccah before the chance of pilgrimage arrived, the heavenly city became clothed with a fantastic glamour, and was with difficulty dissociated from that Paradise for which a visit to it was the preparation and of which it was the symbol. "Blessed be they that dwell in Thy House, they shall be always praising Thee." It does not appear that the population of Meccah spend all their time in this edifying manner: but they have the great advantage of knowing that their business will come to them without their having to go to seek it.

By giving the empire of Islam a religious capital, at no time utilised as a political capital, the founder got for it a mainstay which has secured the continuity of the system amid the most violent convulsions. A political capital once sacked is often abandoned by the victorious dynasty for another: and various commercial and military considerations render the substitution of one for another desirable or even imperative. Hence the political centre of Islam was shifted as the dynasties succeeded each other, and was at each time where the most powerful Mohammedan sovereign chose to hold his court. But with each of these sovereigns Meccah was equally honoured: each took pride in conferring lavish gifts on the city of God: each regarded its protection and adornment as duties specially incumbent upon him. Identified thus with Islam as a religion, the city which had offered the most stubborn resistance to its rise speedily became its most fanatical adherent. Elsewhere in Islamic countries one who is not a Moslem may live and even thrive. At Meccah he must conceal his unbelief, being sure, if detected, of death.

The capture of Meccah was followed almost immediately by a dangerous struggle with a host of nomad Arabs, led by some of those pagan heroes with whom the old poetry and the works of the

THE HOLY CARPET.

archæologists are constantly occupied, but who have not hitherto figured much in the life of the Prophet, which had been mainly spent in debate with the civilised Jews or the partly civilised denizens of the towns. The growth and consolidation of the Moslem state had thoroughly alarmed these Bedouins, to whom the liberty of the desert was dear: and the expedition against Meccah, of which the purpose was at the first concealed, was thought to be directed against them. But even when it was known that it had been aimed at Meccah, and had terminated successfully, the leaders of the assembled forces determined to make a stand for the liberty of Arabia.

The tribes who had assembled bore the names Hawazin and Thakif; their pastures were in the neighbourhood of Meccah. Like many races in a primitive condition they made one man chief when they went to war: and their head at this time was Malik, son of 'Auf, of the clan Nasr, a branch of the Hawazin. But they also took with them to the battle-field on a litter the aged hero of a hundred fights, Duraid, son of Simmah, of the clan Jusham.* He was brought to the battle somewhat as the bones of dead heroes were sometimes taken to it—owing to a belief in what the Maoris would call his *mana*, and the Arabs his *nakibah*, a combination of fortune, skill, and efficiency, which would make his presence desirable in any enterprise. Not a few anecdotes are told of the life of this hero, who, like many of

* Jusham is called by *Al-Akhtal* (*Kamil*, ii., 60) the worst of the tribes; like *Katas*, neither black nor red. A war between Thakif and Nasr is mentioned, *Bayan*, i., 55.

his clan, had some reputation as a poet, and especially as an encomiast * of fortitude, though we cannot say whether any of the verses attributed to him are genuine. His prime was spent in the usual pursuit of camel-stealing—where possible, from hostile tribes, when otherwise, from friendly clans. Reprisals led to bloodshed: all Duraid's brothers died in camel-raids: for each it was Duraid's duty to demand many lives in return, as well as to record their praises in verse. His exploits as a lover were naturally no less considerable than his achievements as a warrior: in both fields he met with occasional rebuffs, but more often with success. At one time he escaped from slaughter by feigning to be dead—a ruse practised also by the American Indians. The camel-stealer's wealth endures not: if secured, it is speedily lavished on wives new and old, and clansmen and guests: "Rascaldom" of this sort, too, "has no strong box." Old age finds him poor, unfit for war or love: but not yet stripped of his *mana*, and perhaps anxious to die in a battle-field: ready even to give his bungling slaughterer some useful hints of the way in which he should proceed. This sort of man has an instinctive horror of order and discipline and organisation. Where blood may not be shed freely, he cannot find his true level.

The coalition of Hawazin and Thakif took up a station in a wadi called Autas, not many miles, it would seem, from Meccah, though the place seems not to have been visited in recent times. It would appear to be somewhat to the south-east of Meccah,

* *Goldziher*, *M.S.*, i., 252.

close by a place called Dhu'l-Majaz or "the Pass," one of the market-places of old times. Thither came the tribes, accompanied (in true savage style) by their wives and children, and their flocks and herds, a proceeding said to be disapproved by the aged Duraid, but probably sanctioned by constant usage: we have seen that at Uhud the women played a not unimportant part. He also is said to have advised retreat, partly owing to the absence of some of the best of the Hawazin tribes: but, seeing that every day added to Mohammed's power, the leader was right in resolving to try his fortune at once. Men were placed under cover on both sides of the valley of Hunain, whither the Moslems were descending; the number of Mohammed's * forces is given as 12,000—the 10,000 with which he had invaded Meccah, reinforced by 2000 of the new converts or allies. The united forces of Hawazin and Thakif are put at 4100. Probably the latter estimate is an exceedingly rough one. But the Moslem chroniclers deserve credit for making their own force on this occasion greatly superior to its antagonist. At early morning † the Moslem forces entered the valley of Hunain, and were speedily attacked on all sides by the enemy, who had been ordered to break their scabbards when the engagement commenced, as a sign that they were to be whole-hearted in their enterprise. The plan of

* For this campaign Mohammed borrowed 30,000 or 60,000 dirhems from Abdallah Ibn Abi Rabi'ah, which were honestly repaid. —*Musnad*, iv., 36.

† Shawwal, A.H. 8; identified with Jan.-Feb., A.D. 630.

Malik, son of 'Auf, was, for the moment, completely successful. The Moslems turned and fled in headlong confusion: not, according to some, without the set purpose of some of the new converts, who thought the occasion a good one for dealing the conqueror a blow. Indeed, one of these unwilling followers is even said to have nerved himself to attack the Prophet, only to find his nerve fail him. One Moslem woman, who had armed herself with a scimitar to be used in emergencies, afterwards advised that these traitors should be killed.* Some of the fugitives are said † to have carried the tidings to Meccah, where they were received with acclamation. One of the Meccans declared (somewhat prematurely) that that day had seen the last of the witchcraft.

The Moslems had been discomfited by a shower of arrows, with which the Hawazin were skilled marksmen. The Prophet was clad in such complete armour that he had no occasion to fear this weapon: but besides, as at Uhud, he exhibited presence of mind, and consciousness of the fact that a defeat in the neighbourhood of Meccah, so long obstinate and so recently overcome, was a disaster of very different magnitude from one near his devoted Medinah. If the biographers can be believed, he stood still, surrounded by a few of the innermost circle, while the others were flying past: and he utilised the stentorian lungs of his uncle Abbas to remind the fugitives of their oaths, their duty, and their glorious victories. The heroes of Badr gathered round the

* *Musnad*, iii., 286.

† *Halabi*, 157.

Prophet, and stemmed the rout. Men who found their mounts uncontrollable descended from them and put on the armour of infantry. Ali aimed a blow at the camel on which one of the Hawazin leaders was riding, and with the aid of a man from Medinah dispatched the rider. What happened then is not known exactly: it appears however that the Hawazin general had not the ability to make use of his initial advantage, and that the fierce resistance of a company of a hundred men who gathered round the Prophet was sufficient to turn the tide. The gigantic Abu Talhah is said to have alone killed twenty men.* The poet of the Banu Sulaim however claimed that the merit of the victory lay with his own tribe, led by Dahhak, regarded as the equal in prowess of a hundred men: "when the Prophet cried to the Banu Sulaim, 'rise up,' they rose: else had the enemy swept away the Believers, and seized their possessions." And indeed it appears that the chief achievements in the slaughter of the foe belonged to the Banu Sulaim, who pursued the enemy as far as "Buss and Aural," places in the Jushamite territory. Of the Thakafites the clan called Banu Malik fought like heroes, and lost seventy men: others fled and saved their skins—including a leader called Karib who got safely to Ta'if, the headquarters of the Thakif tribe: for this act of discretion he receives the warm praise of a poet, to whom we are indebted for a vivid account of the battle. The general, Malik, son of 'Auf, is said to have rallied his horsemen sufficiently to make them hold their

* *Musnad*, iii. 279, etc.

ground till the weaker members of the party were covered, and then to have brought them safely to an eminence whence they could make their way to Ta'if. There apparently some of the women were saved, though others fell into the hands of the Moslems. Khalid, son of Al-Walid, whose savagery had already won a rebuke from the Prophet, earned a fresh one by thinking it his duty to kill these amazons: an act which was totally against the Prophet's ideas of gallantry; just as he found it necessary to rebuke others who had thought it their duty to slaughter the children of the unbelievers. "What are the best of you," he asked, "but children of unbelievers?" * Among the captive women was one who claimed to be the Prophet's foster-sister—known only as Al-Shaima, "the woman with a mark," which she declared was due to the Prophet's having bitten her when a child: the relationship was recognised, and the woman sent with presents to her kindred. So too Beckwourth found among the Crow tribe a woman who recognised him by a wart as her son, and it suited his purpose to acknowledge the evidence. Duraid, son of Al-Simmah, found (in his litter) a soldier's death; he was slain by a Sulamite, member of a tribe which Duraid's prowess had saved, but "Islam had cancelled all that was before it." His son Salamah contrived both to escape and to save his wife.

The whole number of Moslems killed on this occasion is given as *four*—surprisingly small, if true: yet when the Moslem force numbered twelve thousand

* *Musnad*, iii., 435.

it is not probable that deaths were noted as carefully as when the troops only amounted to hundreds. In this battle, as in that of Badr, supernatural combatants were supposed to have taken part: and indeed in some verses attributed to the general, Malik, son of 'Auf, and which may conceivably be his, he ascribes the ultimate defeat of the Hawazin entirely to the intervention of Gabriel: which, since in any case the Moslem force was treble that of the Hawazin, was scarcely to be expected. Though it is probable that Mohammed gladly encouraged the belief in supernatural aid, the poets of his side do not resort to this explanation of their success: except indeed that they admit that Allah, in whose cause they had violated all ties of friendship, was on their side. The chief of the poets on this occasion is Abbas, son of Mirdas, of whom we have heard before; like many of those champions he had a grudge of old standing against some of the Hawazin, which he was glad to have the opportunity of avenging. The piety of his verses renders them unusually edifying, though an accident unfortunately revealed to him the curious fact that his Prophet could not possibly distinguish verse from prose.

Whether however the angels had a hand in the matter or not, a highly important success was gained, and the Prophet's fortune proved constant at a time when a reverse would have had serious consequences: for Abu Sufyan might have been equal to taking advantage of a disaster, though not sufficiently energetic to help to bring one about. A sarcastic comment of his is reported to the effect that the headlong flight of the Moslems would have to be stopped by the sea: an observation which provoked no assent from the unbelievers to whom it was made, who regarded submission to a Kurashite as less humiliating than submission to the Hawazin. The name of Hunain was, like that of Badr, thought worthy of mention in the Koran: a sign that the Prophet attached great importance to the victory. Just as the defeat of the Kuraish was commenced at Badr, so it was consummated at Hunain.

After the victory of Hunain it was naturally the Prophet's desire to take Ta'if, the headquarters of the Thakif tribe. Of that tribe some members had already visited the Prophet at Medinah, where he had a tent (*Kubbah*) erected for them, and after evening prayer discoursed with them for hours; complaining of the Meccans, and showing how the condition of his followers had bettered since the Flight.* Ta'if was a walled town, as perhaps its name signifies; situated in an oasis of sweet water and fertile soil; not more than thirty-six hours' journey from Meccah.† It lies in a plain surrounded by mountains in horseshoe form, with the opening facing the east. These mountains are diversified by little valleys descending to the plain, which all round the city is divided into gardens. Fruit trees of fourteen kinds are enumerated by Tamisier as cultivated in the orchards: but the cultivation of the vine gave Ta'if the greatest celebrity in ancient times; the raisins made from them looked like flasks

* *Musnad*, iv., 343.

† Visited by J. Hamilton, Tamisier, and Doughty.

of purified honey*: and even now great quantities of grapes are grown there for the Meccan market. Various kinds of grain are cultivated besides: and of some there are several crops. In the neighbourhood there is abundance of clay suitable for brickmaking. Here then was plunder even more desirable than that of Khaibar. Of the fabulous history of Ta'if we need repeat nothing here: its inhabitants, owing to the accumulation of wealth and the cultivation of peaceful industry, had acquired some knowledge of the arts of building and of war: the biographers declare that at the time when Hunain was being fought two of their chiefs, 'Urwah, son of Mas'ud, and Ghailan, son of Salamah, were away at Jurash in Yemen, to learn the making of engines of artillery. 'Urwah was the man "honoured in both towns," to whom, according to the Meccans of old time, God should have sent a revelation if He sent one at all. Ghailan was one of the sages of his time, whose adages had so pleased a Persian king that a royal architect had been sent to build a fort for him at Ta'if.† Before the siege was over they were back, with some knowledge that proved of service: though we know not why Jurash should have been the school for this sort of learning. Against Malik, son of 'Auf, the unsuccessful leader at Hunain, they closed the gates.‡ His castle, which lay not far off, was destroyed by the Prophet, and he was presently forced to become a Moslem.

* *Mez, ein Baghdader Sittenbild*, 48.

† *Isabah*, iii., 377.

‡ So *Wakidi*. But *Ishak*, 879, puts him at Ta'if.

The Prophet's course to Ta'if is thus given: Nakhlah Yamaniyyeh, Karn, Mulaih, Buhrat al-Rugha, then a road called the Narrow which the Prophet after his fashion renamed the Easy; then Nakhb. Of these places Karn (or Karn al-Manazil) is marked on Doughty's map: it is there at the head of the curve which the road, directed by the wadis, follows, going first directly to the north, and at this point turning round to the south, towards Ta'if, which lies to the east of Meccah. Mosques were founded by him or by his followers at the places at which he alighted during his route. He entered the horseshoe plain wherein Ta'if lies, and destroyed some of the plantations. When he found the gates closed and a determined resistance offered he endeavoured to frighten the Thakafites into submission by wholesale destruction of their property. This was how he had dealt with the Banu Nadir. But the Thakafites were not Jews.

The siege of Ta'if marks a great stage in the progress of Islam, in that the Prophet resorted to the employment of engines of war, the sort of siege artillery which was in use before the invention of gunpowder. We are not told on this occasion (as at the Battle of the Ditch) who his engineer was, but by this time he had been joined by Arabs who were acquainted with Byzantine modes of warfare, and perhaps were equal to the not very advanced mechanical knowledge requisite for a first attempt. According to the plans of these persons a wooden shed was built, similar to those under which the Romans had been accustomed to advance in order to effect a breach in the enemies' walls: but the Thakafites burnt it over the soldiers' heads by a shower of red-hot iron bars: and then took aim with their arrows at the Moslems as they fled out of their untenable cover. That day was called the "day of the sword," and was indeed notable: hitherto the Prophet's forces had met with no power of self-defence; the Thakif showed that prosperity and wealth might be accompanied by some knowledge of war.

How long the Prophet persisted in the siege is not known: the accounts vary between twenty and forty days. The classical expedient of promising liberty to slaves who joined him brought him a score of deserters who let themselves down from the wall.* The Thakafites declared that they were provisioned for two years: which was certainly a longer period than the Moslems could afford to wait. The Prophet presently had a dream which suggested that he was not to succeed this time: this gloomy prognostication is said to have leaked out through a woman who wished to secure for herself the jewels of some wealthy lady of Ta'if, and was told by the Prophet that there was no chance of her getting them: and the news that the siege was to be abandoned causing serious disappointment, the Moslems were exhorted to make a final attempt at carrying the place by storm: in which they were again repulsed, and Abu Sufyan's conversion was confirmed by the loss of one of his eyes. The Moslems no longer objected to the order for retreat: and the brave resistance of Ta'if even extorted some compliments from

* On these slaves see *Isabah*, ii., 717.

Moslems whose nature had not been changed entirely by the new religion.

The resistance of Ta'if, coming at this period of Islam, was of no permanent importance. But it showed that if other fortresses had yielded with scarcely a blow when the Moslem members were still few, it was because there were no men behind them. Meccah had had plenty of time to prepare for a siege, and might have made common cause with Ta'if, if Abu Sufyan's party had been in earnest.

The Prophet with excellent forethought had kept the spoils of Hunain undivided: they were stored at Ji'irranah, some dozen miles from Meccah, doubtless under good custody. The folly of the Hawazin in bringing their families and possessions to the battle-field caused the plunder of Hunain to be peculiarly rich: therefore although the Prophet would have gladly seen it merged in the spoil of Ta'if, there was enough to allay discontent, and cause the failure of the siege to be forgotten. Yet the whole of this was not to go to the conquerors. The defeated Hawazin had meanwhile decided to be converted, and sent to Ji'irranah to announce their reformation to the Prophet: with the request that, as they were now Moslems, they might receive back their families and their goods. Obviously they could not have both: and being given their choice they preferred their women and children; there being some question whether the Moslems would consent to part with this valuable half of the plunder: the more so, as in order to quiet the consciences of those who hesitated to violate the married women (whose husbands had not been killed), the Prophet had, on divine authority, declared that *marriage is annulled by captivity.* The older followers of the Prophet readily consented to sacrifice their slaves and concubines: the newer converts, anxious to taste the blessings of the religion they had adopted, kept a tighter hold on their prizes: which however they were induced to give up on the promise of a large share in the next booty which the Prophet could secure.

With regard to the property of the Hawazin, about the division of which there was to be no question, the Prophet took a hint from the willingness of the Medinese to sacrifice their worldly advantages. To them he gave nothing: instead he bestowed enormous gratuities on his former enemies, the chieftains of the Kuraish, such as Abu Sufyan and his sons, and the Banu Sulaim who had won the battle for him. While persons who had no faith were given one hundred camels apiece, others who were acknowledged to be the salt of the earth were told to find in faith its own reward.* Nay, even the leader of the Hawazin, Malik, son of 'Auf, was offered one hundred camels if he would turn Moslem: and the brave warrior was persuaded and joined the fold. The Prophet confessed with naïve frankness that these presents were meant to confirm the new converts in their faith; as we have often seen, he never troubled himself about the motives which produced conviction. The motives which dictated this strange policy are hard to fathom: ill-gotten gains are consumed too quickly for us to suppose that he hoped

* *Isabah*, i., 688.

to win the permanent gratitude of his former enemies by such bribes: perhaps the sour faces with which the Kurashites met the members of the Prophet's family made him devise a plan for saving his relatives from annoyance *; perhaps he thought it all-important to impress the Meccans with the magnificence of his gifts, as he had impressed them before with his regal state: and this, he knew, could safely be done at the expense of the Medinese—as indeed some professed to be convinced of his divine mission by his lavish munificence, which exceeded all human performance †; and casual visitors to Medinah were treated so handsomely that they could promise their tribesmen independence for life if they became Moslems. ‡ The Medinese indeed felt they were not fairly treated, and their indignation found voice: which led to a scene of the sort beloved by the theatrical, in which the quarrels of lovers lead to the renewal of love. The Prophet summons his faithful "Helpers" and laments that they are dissatisfied with his conduct. The thought that any words of theirs have given the Prophet pain banishes from their hearts the memory of their wrong: the Helpers declare that they owe everything to the Prophet, and the Prophet gladly acknowledges that he owes everything to them. Tears flow copiously on both sides: and the deputation leaves the sacred presence with the proud thought that they are coming off with a greater prize than their new allies. If the others take home with them sheep and camels,

* *Musnad*, i., 207.

† *Jahiz, Misers*, 170. ‡ *Musnad*, iii., 108.

they will go home with the Prophet of God. So the Prophet, not for the first time, paid words instead of gold and silver, and had no difficulty in passing this coin. Omar indeed was near, ready to behead any one, friend or foe, who charged God's messenger with injustice: but God's messenger had no real occasion for his services. Malik, son of 'Auf, turned out to be well worth the buying: for he harassed his former allies the Thakif as unremittingly as Mohammed himself had raided the Kuraish.

The visit to Meccah which had been accompanied with so many vicissitudes was terminated by the Prophet going through the ceremonies of the lesser pilgrimage. Afterwards, 'Akib, son of Usaid, was appointed governor of Meccah at a salary of a dirhem a day: this was the first permanent civil appointment made in Islam; at Khaibar, the only other city of importance which the Moslems had captured, the local government had been left. Besides the governor a spiritual officer was left, Mu'adh, son of Jabal, a native of Medinah, in whose competence to teach the new religion the Prophet had confidence. He is said to have been a man of attractive appearance, and free-handed: the latter virtue had at one time brought him into the bankruptcy court.* Both these men were under thirty years of age. After thus settling the affairs of Meccah, the Prophet went home, followed by the portion of the booty of Hunain which he had reserved.

* This expression is not inaccurate. Mohammed, to whom the creditors applied, was requested to hand Mu'adh's person over to them; instead of this he collected enough to pay them a dividend of $\frac{5}{7}$.—*Ibn Sa'd*, *II.*, ii., 123.

CHAPTER XII

THE SETTLEMENT OF ARABIA

THE return to Medinah * was probably somewhat in the nature of a triumphal entry, and, as has been seen, Mohammed had reserved some of the plunder of Hunain for display on this occasion, lest the victory should appear barren or ambiguous. Medinah was now in the position of the capital of an empire — sending out rulers to subject tribes, and tax-gatherers to collect tribute. Moreover the prospect of the subjection of the heroic Thakafites had brightened, as before the Prophet had reached his home he received the submission of 'Urwah, son of Mas'ud, one of the pair whose ability had saved Ta'if from storm. What can have occurred to make this man change his mind so quickly we know not: his townsmen were for the moment less fickle, for when he returned to Ta'if expecting his example to be followed without hesitation, he was undeceived: a shower of missiles ended the turncoat's life.

Another visitor to Medinah about this time was the poet Ka'b, son of Zuhair. His father was a

* Dhu'l-Ka'dah 24, A.H. 8; identified with March 16, A.D. 630.

Bedouin poet of great and deserved celebrity: of the verses ascribed to these early bards those which bear his name are of the highest quality: for they embody many a wise and noble sentiment. The son, like other rhymesters of the time, had employed some of his energy in lampooning Mohammed, and taunted his Moslem brother with following a system of which their parents had known nothing. Arabia was quickly becoming too hot to hold an idolator, and the poetic gift might be turned to profitable account in the services of the new monarch. At Medinah he was directed to where the Prophet sat (or squatted) in the centre of a throng: round him were a series of ever-expanding circles; listening with bated breath to his wise utterances. To the very centre of this audience the poet found his way and recited his apologetic ode—containing some loud praise of the Prophet and the Refugees, some hidden sneers at the Helpers.* The Prophet bade the audience listen, and when the poem was concluded accorded the poet forgiveness, with a request (easily granted) that he would compose some verses in praise of his Medinese friends.

Although this poem counts as one of the classical compositions of Arabia, its beauties were very likely lost on the Prophet, who, however, was not unwilling to be shown how the land lay. The poets had before this given him considerable trouble. In nomad Arabia they were part of the war equipment of the tribe: they defended their own, and damaged hostile

* This suggests that the dispute recorded above had attracted attention.

tribes, by the employment of a force which was supposed indeed to work mysteriously, but which in fact consisted in composing dexterous phrases of a sort that would attract notice, and would consequently be diffused and remembered widely. The attraction to Medinah of poets who had no connection with the tribes who had given the Prophet shelter showed that it was coming to be recognised as the residence of a sovereign who had it in his power to reward dexterous encomiums of himself. Ka'b, the son of Zuhair, was the first of the legion of poets who haunted the courts of the Moslem monarchs, and by whose efforts the Arabic encomium became a rather remarkable work of art: and the example which he set of veering with every wind was also not neglected by his followers.

When the Arabs hastened to accept Islam they were apt to overlook one portion of its requirements, viz.: the regular payment of a tax, called by a euphemism Alms. The stages by which the Alms had reached the character of a tax cannot now be traced: it began without doubt in voluntary contributions which the wealthier members of the community were desired to provide for the support of the poorer members: and indeed the names for the institution seem quite certainly Jewish terms, of which one signifies "righteousness" and the other "merit," but of which the former even in biblical times had a tendency to signify "alms-giving." In the Koran, however, as in the Bible, alms-giving is rather recommended as a virtuous act than definitely assessed as an amount which each believer must contribute: nor do the Jewish codes appear to assess it,* though the modes in which it can be given and the purposes to which it can be applied are clearly defined: and it is assumed that officials will be appointed whose business is to collect the Alms. The Jewish Alms resembled therefore the Christian informal collections, and while the Moslem community embraced a modest number of persons it was recommended rather than enforced: and when the Prophet declared that "true charity would not be attained till men spent of their favourite possessions," the valuable gifts which that aphorism called forth all came under the head of "Alms." Abu Bakr is said to have "given in Alms" all that he possessed: Othman, son of 'Affan, redeemed some serious shortcomings by his liberality in alms-giving. But the idea of enforcing Alms as a yearly tribute appears to belong to the period when the necessity for organisation of the state on some sort of financial basis had arisen; when money was wanted, and the expedient which had till now been employed, robbery of Jews, was no longer available, owing to the Jews having all been either massacred or despoiled. Experience had shown the Prophet that the new converts were much more anxious to receive than to give: lavish presents had been deemed advisable in the case of the Meccans to induce them to remain faithful to Islam. There was, therefore, no prospect of the new accessions offering to contribute of their own account: the idea of imposing a contribution upon them in the form of a tax appears to have

* Cp. *Saalschütz*, *Mosaisches Recht*, 284.

originated with Abu Bakr, who at the commencement of his Caliphate made the refusal to pay it a ground for war; it is said, against the opinion of Omar, who however eventually accepted this doctrine. Abu Bakr was quoted in after times * as the possessor of a code drawn up by the Prophet, which went into the details concerning contributions in kind and afterwards became the law of Islam. The assessment which eventually prevailed makes the contribution on each sort of produce amount to about one fortieth (two and a half per cent.), although in the case of contributions in kind many special regulations enter: a camel is in general made the equivalent of ten sheep, and one sheep of twenty dirhems. It is not probable that this tariff was settled till a variety of experiments had been tried.

Early in the ninth year Bishr, son of Sufyan, went to the tribes Khuza'ah and Tamim to collect the Alms. The Banu Ka'b, a clan of the former, allowed their contribution to be collected: but the Tamim dissuaded them from letting the collector take it, and both denied that the religion which they had joined involved any such sacrifice. The Prophet, on hearing the news of this insubordination, took rapid measures to quell it. 'Uyainah, son of Hisn, was sent with a force of fifty Arabs, who practised the manœuvre regularly employed on these raiding expeditions—journeying at night, and hiding during the day. They succeeded in effecting a considerable capture of men, women, and children, whom they brought to Medinah. The Banu Tamim there-

* *Nasa'i.*

upon sent a deputation to the Prophet, containing their chief orator, 'Ut arid son of Hajib, and their chief poet, Al-Akra', son of Habis. They probably despaired of gaining any advantage over the Moslems in the field: but the difference between the shafts of the quiver and those of the mouth was ill understood by the Arabs, and they hoped to compensate for their inadequate equipment for actual warfare by outboasting the Prophet; and indeed they are said to have summoned the Prophet with a certain amount of brusqueness to a boasting-match. The Apostle of God naturally declined to enter the lists himself: if nothing else had prevented him, his reminiscences of similar matches at Meccah were not altogether encouraging: but he had his champions ready: the poet Hassan, son of Thabit, whom Mohammed had taken pains to conciliate after he had been justly punished, and the orator Thabit, son of Kais. With these allies he had no hesitation in letting the old-fashioned debate commence. The rival poets and orators boasted of the achievements of their respective tribes in fluent phrase and rolling verse. The conclusion however was a foregone one: the Tamim would not have resorted to a verbal contest had they had any intention of fighting; nor would the Prophet have permitted it, except as an act of courtesy. When the prize compositions had been delivered, the Tamim delegates naturally declared themselves satisfied with the superiority of the poetry and rhetoric which had been enlisted on the side of Islam. The prisoners were restored to the Tamimites and their delegates given the douceur ordinarily granted to ambassadors; but they were doubtless also given to understand that the tribute must be paid. For Hassan Ibn Thabit, owing to his successful defence of the Prophet, a pulpit was erected in the Mosque.*

Another incident also illustrated the unwillingness with which the Alms were contributed. To the Banu Mustalik, whose name has already met us, a tax-gatherer was sent who was involved in a blood-feud with this tribe dating from the time before Islam. The mode in which the tribe came to meet him suggested to him that they meant mischief: and he accordingly hurried back to Medinah. The Mustalik, now that their prize had escaped them, were unwilling to bring on themselves a raid from Medinah, and sent the most solemn assurances that their intentions had been most honourable. The Prophet sent Khalid with a force to find out: and, if there were any signs of falling away from Islam, to raid them. Finding the tribes were punctiliously performing their devotions, he was compelled to bring home a favourable report, and there was no further difficulty about the Alms.

Some part of this year (9) was also taken up with domestic troubles, of which a variety of accounts are given, but none quite edifying: nor would allusion to them have been desirable had not a place in the Koran been assigned to them. Hafsah, the daughter of Omar, who, after the death of her husband at Badr, had some difficulty in getting another, and was taken by the Prophet for political reasons, was a woman of violent temper: and, finding her rights

* *Musnad*, vi., 72.

infringed in favour of the concubine Mariah, made a disturbance in which the other members of the now numerous harem took her part. The Prophet would appear to have given his word to Hafsah that he would for the future avoid the society of Mariah: and having given it, obtained divine permission not to keep it; his breach of faith with Hafsah being excused by her having revealed a secret which she had promised to keep. Owing to the violent reproaches bestowed on him by the members of the harem, he resolved to quit their society for a whole month, and even threatened to divorce the whole set. The harem probably knew him too well to fear this threat: and the month had not expired before he made his peace with them; to account for which he produced a half-serious, half-comic revelation,* in which they are assured that the Prophet would have no difficulty in getting another set of wives, their equal in every respect, should extreme measures be necessary. Some of the biographers reproduce for our benefit the curious scene—the Prophet lying in an upper chamber, accessible by a ladder: nothing but a reed mat separates him from the floor. Close on a month of domestic broils has rendered the Prophet haggard and woebegone in the extreme. Omar mounts the ladder in extreme distress of mind and asks the Prophet whether it is true that he has divorced his wives. The Prophet, who has now made up his mind, replies in the negative, at which Omar shouts "Hurrah!" ("God is mighty") in a voice that can be

* *Surah* lxvi.

heard over a large part of Medinah. The painful incident is at an end. Another of those domestic scenes is somewhat different in character. Abu Bakr and Omar knock at the Prophet's door and at first cannot obtain admission. When they are admitted they find the Prophet seated gloomily silent with his wives around him. They have been asking for household supplies which the Prophet cannot provide. Omar, hoping to cheer the Prophet, narrates how *his* wife had been demanding money, and he had replied by a sound blow on her neck. The Prophet, exploding with laughter, explains that his wives were equally importunate. The two friends wish to try Omar's expedient with their respective daughters. This the Prophet does not permit: but he gives his wives the choice of quitting him if they prefer the present world. Ayeshah declines the offer, and the others follow suit.*

After the conclusion of this trial of forces, in Rejeb of the year 9,† the Prophet summoned his followers to arms to attack the Byzantines at Tabuk. Tabuk is a station on the Pilgrim road, visited in recent times by Doughty and Huber: it is half-way between Damascus and Medinah. Information had been brought the Prophet by some Nabatæan merchants that a great Byzantine force was assembled there, with Arabian allies of the tribes Lakhm, Judham, Ghassan, and 'Amilah. The report was probably a false one‡ and indeed ac-

* *Musnad*, iii., 328.

† Identified with Oct.–Nov., A.D. 630.

‡ *Diyarbekri*, ii., 136.

cording to one account the Christian Arabs had prematurely announced to Heraclius the Prophet's death; whence there would have been no occasion for such a levy. Nevertheless the Prophet believed it, and was probably anxious by a brilliant victory to bring into oblivion a variety of troubles that had accumulated: the defeat of Mutah, the domestic disputes, and the unfair division of the booty of Hunain.

The effects of this last scandal now began to appear. The people of Medinah showed themselves unready to join in an expedition of which the profits would probably fall to others. Complaints were made of the season of the year, of distress, and sickness: the party of the "Hypocrites," began to raise its head, and even a Jew named Suwailim had the folly to allow his house to be made a rendezvous of malcontents: with the very natural and indeed inevitable result that the Prophet sent an emissary to burn the Jew's house over his head; the malcontents escaped from the flames not without personal injury. We are asked to believe that Abdallah Ibn Ubayy got a fresh opportunity of acting as he had acted at Uhud before: he is said to have equipped a force, no smaller than Mohammed's, to have encamped outside Medinah when the Prophet encamped, then to have refused to come farther, on the ground that the Moslem force was quite unequal to a contest with the Byzantines. Unless the discontent at Medinah went far beyond all that has been recorded or even hinted at, we cannot well believe that the arch-Hypocrite can after all that had passed have been still in a position to adopt his old tactics.

Whether Abdallah, son of Ubayy, came to the front again or not, it is stated that the Prophet used his utmost efforts to collect a force sufficient for any emergency, to which end he demanded help from all the new accessories to Islam: and in equipping the force (said to have reached 30,000) he exhausted the money at his own and his friends' disposal. He resolved to lead the army himself, and some criticism was occasioned by his sending Ali home to take care of the royal household.

The expedition was of interest to the Prophet as leading them past those ruined cities of whose history the Koran was so full; the rock-dwellings, as he supposed them to be, of the Thamud, who, having refused to hear the voice of their prophet, had been destroyed, their rock-mansions remaining as a monument and a warning. Recent explorers have proved that what the Prophet supposed to be mansions were tombs: but Mohammed, passing by this notorious country, could not fail to take some notice of the fact that they were in presence of the great theatre of the divine vengeance. The Moslems were to pass by those deserted habitations with veiled faces, spurring their steeds: they were to eat and drink nothing that was to be found there, and after nightfall when they encamped they were to keep together. Fables were afterwards invented showing the need for these orders by the fate that befell those who violated them. Many years had elapsed since Mohammed had first heard the thrilling story of the fate of the Thamud from some story-tellers attached to a caravan: and truly the seed had been sown on wondrous soil.

The record of the expedition to Tabuk is characterised by a number of narratives illustrating "Hypocrisy," faint-heartedness, and even desertion on the part of the troops. Of the expressions of disbelief to which some were hardy enough to give vent the Prophet soon heard, whether miraculously, or in virtue of the system of espionage which had worked so well at Medinah: and according to the biographers these were in no case punished, but confuted by a series of exhibitions of prophetic power.

It is further interesting to notice that the Moslems were deeply impressed with a sense of the greatness of the Byzantine power, and the idea that to fight them would be wholly different from fighting the Arabs.

Any fears which they might have entertained were not realised. The rumour which had caused the Prophet to start on his expedition was a false one: there was no Byzantine army to be met. The Prophet, however, was determined that his march should not be fruitless, and the plan of imposing tribute on Christians as well as Jews was now matured in his mind. The governor of Ailah, at the head of the Gulf of Akabah, whose name, Johanna, son of Rubah, shows him to have been a Christian, was induced to undertake to pay a tribute to the Moslem leader: good authorities tell us * that the amount came to three hundred dinars—being one dinar or ten

* *Baladhuri*, 59.

francs per head. The way was thereby prepared for the invasion of Egypt. A couple of Syrian communities, those of Jarba and Adhruh, also sent in their allegiance and undertook to pay at the same rate: the money was to be paid every Rejeb. From the people of Makna, being Jews, harder terms were demanded: they were to pay one quarter of their produce. A document was in the hands of the Jews of this place, ensuring their full protection on condition of their paying this proportion of the product of their palms, their fisheries, and their looms, and admitting the right of the Prophet to their slaves, horses and mules, and arms. It further informs us that the inhabitants were called Banu Habibah. Twenty-five per cent. of the produce meant ten times the amount imposed on the Moslems as alms. These terms are so hard that the document might be thought to be genuine: yet the signature shows it to be spurious—unless, indeed, the agreement was not made on this occasion.

To a Christian prince, Ukaydir of Dumat al-Jandal, the biblical Duma, a force was sent under Khalid, who is said to have met the King out hunting, and taken him captive, having killed his brother. The prince appears to have readily accepted Islam, but the terms made with him and his people were somewhat harsh, as they appear in a document the genuineness of which is attested by its archaic language.* All their arms and horses were to be put in the possession of the Prophet, who also claimed their fortresses and their unoccupied or uncultivated

* *Baladhuri*, 61.

lands. The rest of their property was left them, but they were to adhere to the ordinances of Islam, which are here specified as Prayer and Alms; for the collection of the latter certain regulations were made, securing that it should not be unnecessarily onerous. Probably the distance of this community from Medinah rendered it impossible for the Prophet to impose on its members the necessity of military service, and the overpopulated condition of Medinah rendered it undesirable to encourage further emigration thither. His policy with this outlying acquisition was tentative, and not imitated by the Caliphs.

The time spent over these negotiations is variously given at a fortnight or two months. At their conclusion he started homeward, with only a moderate amount of gain: the coat, embroidered with gold, of the brother of the prince of Duma, whom Khalid had slain, was the most important trophy that he took home. Omar is made responsible by some authorities for the retreat. The Byzantines, he supposed, had heard of the Prophet's expedition and would be prepared for it.

The homeward journey showed that the Prophet, like other founders of tyrannies, was becoming unpopular. A fresh attempt at assassinating him is supposed to have been made on the way: frustrated, as others had been, by want of determination on the part of the conspirators, and by the Prophet's constant vigilance. More serious still was the fact that Islam had begun to develop dissent: a mosque, he was told, had been built near Kuba, "with the view of spreading dissent among the Moslems, and helping the Prophet's enemy" : and this enemy is further defined as "Abu 'Amir the Monk," the citizen of Medinah who had embraced monotheism before the Prophet's arrival, who had been frightened away by the Prophet's religion, who had vainly endeavored to cause desertion on the part of the Helpers at Uhud, and who after Hunain had fled to the Byzantine monarch to obtain help against the successful founder of Islam. The new mosque had not been founded with any secrecy and the Prophet had been requested to inaugurate it. The leader of prayer there was one Mujammi', who had won fame (and perhaps his name) from his zeal in collecting the Koran. But the secret which eked out, or the account which the Prophet saw grounds for accepting, was that this mosque was meant to serve as a centre for the followers of Abu 'Amir, when he should arrive with his Byzantine allies: and meanwhile be the headquarters of a secret society whose purpose was to oust the Prophet. Mohammed's method with such designs was short and effective. Invited for the second time to inaugurate the mosque, he sent a party of men to burn it to the ground, and turn it into a dunghill for the future.

Of the rights and wrongs of this affair nothing decided will ever be known : the revelation in which it is mentioned, and which contains a variety of oracles delivered in connection with the expedition to Tabuk, is in a tone of bitterness and vexation such as disappointment and opposition are likely to engender in a man of the Prophet's temperament. The people of Medinah and their new Bedouin allies are charged with harbouring Hypocrites: and it also appears that the Koran was beginning to give rise to criticisms of the sort from which the Prophet had suffered at Meccah. When a new revelation comes down, the people at Medinah ask each other sarcastically whether their faith had been increased. Knots of people are found talking and laughing: and in spite of the most earnest denials, the Prophet is of opinion that the Koran has provided the materials for their amusement. This recrudescence of unbelief was probably due to the Prophet's policy of "reconciling hearts," *i. e.*, persuading men by bribes to become Moslems. Persons converted in this style are likely to have retained some of their choice sarcasms to communicate when occasion required. There is also one verse in the tirade suggesting that some of the malcontents disliked the plan of living on plunder which was now characteristic of Islam, and wished a more honest system to be inaugurated. Of the builders of the Mosque of Dissent not sufficient is known to enable us to estimate their purpose correctly. If it was rightly interpreted by Mohammed, it would follow that his example had already deeply impressed the Arabs with the notion that a political movement must be preceded by a religious movement: that the preliminary operation necessary for one who would start a revolution is to build a church. The programme of these unsuccessful conspirators is likely to have been a form of Abrahamism—such as Abu

'Amir is said to have practised: which he charged Mohammed with having corrupted. Mohammed retorted that the mosque built for him was on a quicksand, ready to collapse into Hell-Fire.

Both at the time when the expedition to Tabuk started and during the course of it there had been many desertions. The return of the Prophet filled the guilty with alarm, and we learn from the Koran that the Prophet reserved some of the cases for very special deliberation. One of these persons has left us an account of his sufferings, illustrative of the Prophet's ways.* Ka'b, son of Malik, was a Khazrajite who had received eleven wounds at Uhud, and who had earned an estate at Khaibar. He was besides a poet whose muse served the Prophet, and is even said to have intimidated the tribe Daus into adopting Islam. But he was comfortable at Medinah during the hot weather, and through indolence failed to be ready in time for the expedition, and also to join it afterwards. He made a clean breast to the Prophet, who reserved his case with that of two others for future revelation: meanwhile neither the Prophet nor any Moslem would speak to him. During the time of his excommunication a message (he stated) came to him from the Ghassanide prince in Syria, offering him patronage and protection, if he chose to leave Medinah: but this temptation of the Devil he rejected. Presently a message came from the Prophet enjoining on the three delinquents a penance which the Prophet undoubtedly regarded as a severe one: for a time they were to be parted

* *Muslim*, ii., 330.

from their wives. Meanwhile all three continued practising their devotions with punctilious regularity in the hope that the Prophet's wrath might pass over. And after fifty days it did pass over. A revelation came assuring them of forgiveness. Warm congratulations poured in from all sides. In the enthusiasm of the blessed moment Ka'b was ready to give away everything he possessed, as a thank-offering for his readmission to the society of the faithful. When the people of Medinah were children of this type, what wonder that a grown man could mould them to his will! Similarly we read of others who were kept faithful in moments of extreme temptation by the fear of being made the subject of a text in the Koran.

Fortune was too true a friend to the Prophet to permit of his success suffering more than a temporary eclipse. Shortly after his return envoys came from Ta'if, announcing the submission of the brave and stubborn Thakif. The last that has been heard of the Thakif was that they had killed their chieftain 'Urwah, son of Mas'ud, for embracing Islam, and that Malik, son of 'Auf, their former ally, was proving his sincerity as a Moslem by making it unsafe for them to go outside Ta'if. Their submission was hastened on by the belief that Mohammed was irresistible; that protracted resistance would only ensure their suffering loss, and would in the end be ineffectual. There would also appear to have been a want of any cause for which many of them consciously cared, and for which they were prepared to suffer or die. Their procedure appears to have been rather more methodical and dignified than that of their predecessors in submission. A party of six persons were sent as a deputation to Medinah, drawn from different strata of the population: a smaller number might, they feared, on their return fall victims to another wave of popular feeling. These envoys also when they reached Medinah acted with caution, and endeavoured to make terms with the Prophet: they would fain have retained the right to worship their idols for a period of time, and been excused the five daily prayers, which many of the converts found exceedingly irksome; and the washings, which were disagreeable in their cold country*; and have been permitted to take interest, drink wine, and commit certain sexual irregularities.† Abu Bakr and Omar took care that the Prophet did not concede too much: experience had shown them that Mohammed, when the main concern had been settled, was over-facile about details. Instructions however were given to Othman, son of Abu 'l-'Asi, a young man who was appointed governor as a reward for the desire which he evinced to master the Koran, not to be too exigent in the matter of the ceremonies of Islam. The terms granted to Ta'if were far less onerous than those to which the people of Allah had had to submit. The old sanctuary of the goddess Al-Lāt was to be respected under its new owner.‡ The *idah* (an herb on which camels browse) and the game of Bajj

* *Musnad*, iii., 347.

† *Wakidi* (*W.*), 384.

‡ *Wellhausen*, *Reste*, 30.

(the old name for Ta' if) were to be left alone under severe penalties. However the Thakafites were to be relieved of the Alms and the obligation to fight: Mohammed observing that when once they had accepted Islam they would wish both to pay Alms and to take part in the sacred war. *

The Thakafites had further stipulated that they should not be compelled to break their own idols. So many Moslems were willing to undertake this pious task that the stipulation might have seemed unnecessary: the two who were finally entrusted with it were a former priest of the goddess,† Mughirah, son of Shu'bah, a Thakafite who had come to Medinah as a convert some years before, and Abu Sufyan, in whose ability and loyalty Mohammed was now placing extreme confidence. The goddess of the place—a white stone—was possessed of some wealth, as might be expected from the prosperous condition of Ta'if: it was lodged in a hole half a fathom deep, under the stone. ‡ Precautions were taken to prevent the destroyers from becoming the victims of popular fury, but they turned out to be unnecessary. The women indeed bared themselves and wept, and even taunted the men with the betrayal of their goddess: but the Arabs had a doctrine that a god should be able to defend himself, and they did not interfere with the execution of the Prophet's orders. The money and jewels of the goddess were taken by Abu Sufyan, who, we

* *Musnad*, iii., 341.

† *Wellhausen*, *Reste*, 31.

‡ *Ibid*, 31.

suppose, was accountable for them to the Prophet. We are not told in these cases what became of the idolatrous priests who hoped against hope that their gods would show some signs of resentment: however new converts could easily be put in the way of acquiring plunder, whence we suppose that they earned their living as most of the Moslems at this time earned theirs.

This year was marked by an important event in the history of Islam: the first Pilgrimage over which a Moslem official presided. Abu Bakr was sent to perform this honourable task: shortly after he had started the Prophet remembered that further instructions were desirable. A revelation was therefore produced, being indeed a manifesto to the Arabs who might gather for the Pilgrimage: and Ali was sent post haste to communicate it to Abu Bakr while there was still time.* This sanguinary document† showed that affairs had now advanced very far: the Arabs were given four months' grace, after which the Prophet would raid them if they did not accept Islam: and it was announced that after this year no unbelievers might take part in the Pilgrimage. The crime of keeping people from God's house, which had been so serious when the Kuraish were guilty of it, assumed a different aspect when the Apostle had the power to perform it. The unhappy notion of the Prophet with regard to the

* In *Musnad*, i., 3, Abu Bakr is said to have been recalled in order that one of the Prophet's house might deliver it: but this looks like a Shi'ite invention.

† *Wellhausen*, *Sturz*, 14, accepts the ordinary date for this document; *Grimme* would place it after the taking of Meccah.

Calendar was enforced, thereby causing the ruin of Meccan commerce, so far as it depended on the Pilgrimage and the sacred months: but for the loss they were to be indemnified by the plunder of Jews and Christians, whose place as a tributary caste had now been definitely settled. The Prophet was not unaware of the character of these expedients: he defended them by a series of charges levelled at the persons whom he was now bent on oppressing or exterminating. The effects of the recent discontent at Medinah are not unapparent.

The delivery of the manifesto at Meccah now led to a series of embassies to the Prophet, on the part of persons anxious to make friends with the new ruler of Arabia, or to learn about his system. Petty princes and governors of tribes or provinces were eager to obtain confirmation of their rights, and secure possession of the domain * which they had appropriated, or possession of domain which had belonged to some god: and since war had been proclaimed against all who did not accept the new system, men were left no choice but either to come into it, or prepare to fight against it. The iconoclasm which had raged in Medinah at the time of the Prophet's arrival spread far and wide, now it had been clearly proved that the old gods were incapable of defending themselves or even of taking vengeance on those who broke them. Facts which had remained unheeded for generations suddenly began to suggest important inferences: one man observed that his god suffered himself to be

* *Wellhausen*, *Reste*, 107.

desecrated by beasts, and declined henceforward to worship a deity on whom the foxes staled.* The persons who hurry to place their incense on the altar of success are familiar figures in all ages: and many a comedy was enacted at those visits. Some of the visitors † professed to examine the prophetic claims of Mohammed with the utmost care: they had made out a whole series of questions which the Prophet must answer satisfactorily or else they would have none of him: they required the most positive assurances on one subject and another, that the needs of tender consciences and sceptical intellects might be satisfied. The Prophet succeeded in satisfying even these stern examiners, who were then confirmed in their privileges, or accorded fresh ones; some trying to rob their neighbours by trading on the Prophet's ignorance of local conditions. ‡ Doughty warriors, who had won fame in many a fight, came to express their conviction in the truth of Islam: a poor part for them to play perhaps, which they endeavoured to lay aside so soon as the Prophet was gone; but their prowess and command of the camel served them in this sort of scramble as it had served them in the field. A couple of chieftains bethought them of visiting the Prophet, and had arranged that while one occupied the Prophet with his questions the other should plunge his dagger into God's messenger. Easier

---

* *Isabah*, i., 1012.

† *Musnad*, i., 264.

‡ *Ikd Farid*, i., 104. Not all the envoys were converted—*Ibn Duraid*, 236, mentions Wazar Ibn Jabir in this context.

said than done! 'Amir Ibn Tufail talked glibly enough with the Prophet and arrested his attention: but his colleague, Abrad, considered the fate which Mohammed's murderer would undergo at Medinah, and the native hue of resolution was sicklied o'er with a pale cast of thought. Abrad accounted for his cowardice by a miracle: during the interview the Prophet had become invisible, so that Abrad knew not where to strike. To us Charlotte Corday's conduct seems the more miraculous of the two.

Unlike most of the embassies was that from the Christian state of Najran: the one community of Arabian Christians of whom traces are left in the martyrology, and whose sufferings under the temporary rule of Jews suggested one of the earliest inspirations of the Koran. A great deputation of those persons came to Medinah: they expected, it would appear, that the Prophet would welcome them as co-religionists, and indeed declared that they were "Moslems": a pretension which Mohammed refused to recognise on the ground of certain doctrines and practices of which he disapproved. It is stated that their spokesman was anxious to argue with him about the nature of Christ: supposing doubtless that, since Mohammed accepted the doctrine of the Virgin Birth, his view of this difficult subject would not differ very seriously from theirs; or, if it differed, he might be open to argument. Mohammed knew enough about Christianity to be aware that much blood had been shed on this controversy: but instead of arguing, which would have exposed him to very serious disadvantage, he had recourse to revelation. Some years before, when endeavouring to obtain a refuge for his followers in Abyssinia, he had composed a Gospel: with success, if viewed from the result. All he had now to do was to reproduce this Gospel, insisting on the points which he was aware that the Christians of Najran would resent. Finally, if this direct communication from God was not found convincing, he was commissioned to offer what seemed reasonable terms. Each party was to invoke God's curse on himself and all his nearest and dearest if his account of the matter was not correct. After the receipt of this message the delegates desired a little time for consideration. They resolved that the risk of invoking the curse was too great, and that it was best to submit to the tribute. They undertook to supply each year thirty cuirasses and two thousand of the garments which were manufactured in their country: an undertaking which would have been made with grim satisfaction had they known that within two years some of their garments would constitute the Prophet's winding sheet.* Omar desired to be sent to administrate, but the Prophet preferred the less fanatical Abu Ubaidah.

This is the story told to illustrate the passage in Surah iii. in which the Christians are invited to this simple ordeal. Of its truth we cannot be quite sure: but some features in the accounts seem veracious. If the Christian leaders refused to settle the matter by the process recommended from Heaven, it was probably because they regarded it as a trap:

* *Musnad*, i., 222.

the Prophet would merely have to send some legions to Najran, with orders to destroy the persons on whom destruction had been invoked, and the truth of his doctrine would be demonstrated. There were persons at Medinah ready to tell them some of the disasters that had befallen the Jews, who had presumed to maintain for their religion a position of independence, and assure them that their submission was necessary, if physical resistance were impossible. The Prophet was secure of a triumph whether they accepted the challenge or refused it: by refusing it they were spared some bloody scenes. Yet the refusal of the Christians to acknowledge him left in his mind no less bitterness against them than he had harboured against the Jews. He declared the Najranites and the Christian Taghlibites to be the two worst tribes in Arabia.* He forbade fasting on Friday,† doubtless with the view of avoiding Christian practice. Ali declared that the Prophet had left him private instructions to turn the Christians out of Najran.‡ Christians and Jews were, the Prophet declared, to serve as substitutes for Moslems in Hell-Fire.§ Isolated converts from Christianity to Islam, such as Tamim al-Dari, who came to Medinah about this time, received a warm welcome, and their confirmation of the Prophet's statements was loudly advertised.‖

---

* *Musnad*, iv., 387.

† *Ibid.*, iii., 296.

‡ *Ibid*, i., 87

§ *Muslim*, ii., 329.

‖ *Ibid*, ii., 380.

Of other visitors there are stories that are interesting, and even touching. Tufail, son of 'Amr, who had offered the Prophet a refuge in his castle, came to Medinah bringing with him a friend, who caught the Medinah fever, and in his pain cut off his fingers till he bled to death.* Zaid of the Horses, a chevalier known all over Arabia, came with a number of the Tay'ites, heard the Prophet preach, and declared himself a believer. Others of whose fame Mohammed had heard disappointed him when he saw them: Zaid, whose feet touched the ground when he rode his horse, came up to his reputation. Wonderful tales are told of this hero, called Zaid of the Horses because he possessed many, whose names he immortalised in verse. He played in earnest a part like that which Beckwourth played for sport: always ready for a fight, helping now one tribe, now another; for the pleasure of war rushing to the rescue of the vanquished; enriching the poor with spoil when they begged of him. Like Odysseus he could send arrows from his bow through the loops of a strap as unfailingly as if he had inserted them with his fingers. When vengeance for blood was his quest, he knew no mercy. At times he took feigned names, but Zaid of the Horses could not be disguised. His life was the aimless career of a Knight-errant, interesting as a romance, useless and dangerous to any state that hoped for quiet development. Mohammed welcomed the famous warrior, gave him of the gold which Ali had sent from Yemen, to the envy of

* *Musnad*, iii., 370.

A BEDOUIN ON A CAMEL.

both Refugees and Helpers,* assigned him lands and honours, and hoped to direct in serious warfare his wasted energies: but saw in him ere he left Medinah the taint of fever, contracted by a short stay in its pestilential air: whénce he died before he reached his home. And his wife, unconverted, burned the rescript of the Prophet who, claiming to be sent from Heaven, was less resourceful against sickness than the humbler medicine man. And other deputations of persons, who had intended to embrace Islam, were frightened off by the death of some of their numbers.†

The son of another of the Arabic Knights, 'Adi Ibn Hatim, also of the tribe of Tay, was brought into the fold. His father had been a famous hero, and so great was the reflected glory that once when taken prisoner by a raiding tribe he had been released without ransom.‡ As the Moslems were gradually forcing Islam on the whole of Arabia, this man, who was professedly a Christian, fled towards Syria, having prepared for the contingency, but waited till the last moment to carry out his project. A sister of his was taken captive, brought to Medinah and released by Mohammed, to be sent as a decoy to her brother, who, not to be outdone in generosity, could do no less than come to Medinah with an open mind about Mohammed's prophetic mission, of which a very little experience was sufficient to convince him. And indeed the

* *Musnad*, iii., 68.

† *Isabah*, i., 655.

‡ *Ibn Duraid*, 224.

reasoning of the Prophet seems to have been powerful enough. He pointed out (in some form or other) his intention of spreading a *pax Islamica* over Arabia: a bond of religion uniting the whole, firmer even than had been the bond of blood uniting the clans: and what then would become of the trade of such men as 'Adi and Hatim his father, who had lived and thrived by raiding? The advantage that the Christians had enjoyed, by being free from the institution of the sacred months, had now become common to the greater part of Arabia: if therefore marauding was to be done at all, it could be best practised by joining the new power to prey upon the Christians. The son of Hatim may have seen the force of this argument, perhaps faintly, yet effectively: for when, after Mohammed's death, the Arabs rose, hoping to shake off the yoke, he remained steadfast, and sent the Alms. Exile and helplessness had taught him his lesson. For the rest this Christian's converse with Mohammed seems to have been less on points of doctrine than on subjects connected with the chase.* With his name the tradition connects the curious rule that dogs employed in coursing must have the name of God pronounced over them; game killed by an unconsecrated dog is unfit for food.

And so one by one the Arabs who had been nominally Christians became nominally or actually Moslems. The change in most cases brought no sacrifice: the Byzantine power was not ordinarily in a position to persecute. The governor of Ma'an

* *Muslim*, ii., 107, 108.

whom they imprisoned first and then crucified was a solitary example.

On the return from Tabuk the Prophet was met by messengers from the historic state of Himyar, bringing a letter in the names of Al-Harith, son of Abd Kulal (in a poet's opinion the second best man in the world*), and his brothers Nu'aim and Nu'man, *Kail,* or chieftains, of Dhu Ru'ain, Ma'afir, and Hamdan. These persons had been invited to the faith two years before: the wary chieftains waited for fortune to declare herself more decidedly; and when they were satisfied about it, they made haste to show their earnestness by killing and plundering. Their letter was conveyed by a man of the clan Ruha, of the Yemenite tribe Madhhij, who appears to have been noted for his beauty. Besides the letter he conveyed some private intelligence, which Mohammed thanked him for concealing with diligence. The reply was on parchment, and was entrusted to the messenger with four of the Prophet's followers. It is said to have run as follows:

"From Mohammed, God's messenger, the Prophet, to Al-Harith, son of Abd Kulal, and Nu'aim, son of Abd Kulal, and Al-Nu'man, chieftains of Dhu Ru'ain, Ma'afir, and Hamdan: for the rest I praise unto you God than whom there is no other God: next, we were met by your messengers on our return from the land of Rum, who met us at Medinah, and conveyed to us your message, and instructed us concerning your state, and showed us how you had become Moslems and had slain the

---

* *Ibn Duraid*, 308.

Idolators. And know that God has led you aright if ye shall do well, and obey God and His apostle, and be steadfast in prayer, and give Alms, and bestow out of your booty God's fifth, and the Apostle's share and perquisite. And the Alms or land produce which is enjoined on the Believers is a tenth of what is watered by springs or by rain, and half a tenth of what is watered by irrigation, and of camels one female two years old out of forty, and one male two years old out of thirty, and one ewe for five camels, or two ewes for ten. And for every forty head of oxen one cow, and for thirty a calf of one year, a she-calf or he-calf, and for every forty sheep a ewe that can feed by itself: for this is the prescribed alms which God prescribed for the Believers: but whoso adds thereunto it is well for him. And whoso pays it, and testifies that he is a Moslem, and helps the Believers against the Idolators, he is one of the Believers, having the same rights and the same duties as they, and enjoys the protection of God and of His Apostle. And if any Jew or Christian become a Moslem, he is one of the Believers, with the same rights and duties as they. But if a man persist in his Judaism or Christianity, he shall not be made to leave it, but shall pay the Tribute, a dinar of full weight for every male or female of mature age, free or slave, out of the price of the garments which they weave, or the equivalent thereof in garments. And whoso pays this unto the Apostle of God, he shall enjoy the protection of God and His Apostle. But he that withholds it shall be an enemy to God and His Apostle. And know that God's Apostle Mohammed the Prophet has sent to Zur'ah Dhu Yazan saying: When my messengers come unto you, I commend them unto you, Mu'adh, son of Jabal, Abdallah, son of Zaid, Malik, son of 'Uba-

SABÆAN INSCRIPTION.
In the British Museum.

dah, 'Ukbah, son of Namir, Malik, son of Murrah, and their fellows. Collect ye the Alms and the Tribute from your districts and bring it to my messengers, so that their chief Mu'adh, son of Jabal, shall not return discontented. And next, Mohammed testifies that there is no God save Allah, and that he is His servant and Apostle. And know that Malik, son of Murrah, of Edessa has shown me how thou didst become a Moslem among the first of Himyar, and didst slay the Idolators, and know that it is well unto thee, and I bid thee do good unto Himyar: deceive not neither betray each other: for God's Apostle is the patron of rich and poor among you. And know that the Alms is not lawful for Mohammed nor his family: it is a charity to be bestowed on the poor of the Moslems and on the beggar. And know that Malik has delivered his message, and kept his secret, and I bid you to treat him well. And know that I have sent unto you of the best of my company and of the pious and learned amongst them, and I bid you treat them well, for our eyes are turned unto them. And upon you be peace and God's mercy and His blessings."

The genuineness of this letter is probably beyond suspicion, and it shows that the Prophet and his new subjects understood each other very well. The guidance of God, Paradise, and all other religious topics are now relegated to a very modest place: the main thing is the payment of taxes by Believers and the tolerated sects. Of the pious and learned official who is sent the main business is tax-collecting. Other business between the princes and the Prophet was of too private a nature to be committed to parchment: the messenger had his instructions, but the allusion made to the matter is faint. The Prophet carefully clears himself of the charge of having a personal interest in the collection of taxes: but yet also provides against his privy purse being quite neglected.

The public declaration of war delivered by Ali at the Pilgrimage of the year 9 was thus having its effect. It might, had there been any man of consummate ability in Arabia, have led to a union of forces in defence of religious liberty: for what happened at the Prophet's death showed how much the Arabs appreciated the Prayers and Alms. If however any persons cared to fight, it was not for liberty, but for their gods; and Mohammed had certainly exposed the Arabian deities effectively: their houses and images had been destroyed, scarcely any of them having made even a display of resistance.

In general it was Mohammed's policy not to disturb the existing order of affairs. The chieftains and princes who gave in their submission to Islam were confirmed in their rights, and even retained their old titles: the Prophet merely sent back with them an official whose business was to collect the Alms, and tribute where there were any Jews or Christians, and another who was to instruct the new converts in the principles of Islam, and especially to conduct the religious services, and recite the Koran. These two officials formed the prototypes of the governors still sent out from Islamic capitals to the provinces. Neither of them at first was meant to reside permanently in the new province. The former paid annual visits, returning to headquarters

THE REMAINS OF A PALACE AT AXUM.

From an engraving.

when he had goods or money for the capital. Thither the tribute certainly went, and also the fifth of the spoil which Mohammed claimed for himself. The conditions made by the Prophet rather imply that the Alms were retained in the province to be distributed there among the poorer Believers. We have however no authentic record of the mode in which the distribution was organised.

Some deaths marked this year: that of the Prophet's daughter, Umm Kulthum, who had after her sister's death been married to Othman; and Abdallah, son of Ubayy, who is said to have sickened and died shortly after the retreat from Tabuk. He had however long been harmless, and his death now made little difference. A scene which romancers have tried to reproduce is Abdallah sending for the Prophet on his death-bed, and even then maintaining a sort of proud independence in the presence of the man who had so often outwitted and humilated him. At the request of his son,* the Prophet performed his obsequies, not without expostulation from Omar. Another death which could not fail to move the Prophet was that of his Abyssinian friend at Axum, the Negus who had nursed Islam when it was likely to have been extinguished.

* *Musnad*, iii., 371.

CHAPTER XIII

THE LAST YEAR

AS the tenth year came to a close the Prophet determined to lead the Pilgrimage in solemn state, and on this occasion was accompanied by his numerous harem. "People flocked to Medinah, anxious to imitate the Prophet and do as he did: he started on the 20th of Dhu'l-Ka'dah [Feb. 17, 632], and we went with him,—and I looked and as far as my eye could reach there were crowds of riders and pedestrians in front of the Prophet and behind him, and on his right and on his left." * He took this opportunity of fixing for ever the ceremonies which, together, bear that name: rites connected with different places, and commemorating very different events, were all grouped together, and transferred from whatever may have been their original purpose to the cult of Abraham and Ishmael. Mohammed took care that the neighbouring sanctuaries should as far as possible lose their independent local significance, be brought into close and necessary connection with the Ka'bah, and be-

* Jabir, son of Abdallah, in *Musnad*, iii., 320. Others date the expedition some days later.

THE HOLY MOSQUE AT MECCAH.

From the "Hilal.'

come, so to speak, dependencies thereof; he succeeded so well that there is no longer a feast of Arafat, but only of Meccah.* A solemn address was delivered by him to the assembly, all of them Moslems, who were gathered to worship and to be exhorted. The reproduction of it which his talented biographer offers can scarcely be regarded as authentic †; yet the Prophet's sermon may have dealt with the same subjects. These are (among others) the doctrine of brotherhood of Islam: that there was an end to the pride in ancestry which marked the Days of Ignorance, all Arabs who adopted Islam being equal, or only differentiated by their piety, and that a wholly new epoch was started by its introduction. The planets had, he declared, come back to the places in which they were situated when the world began: the world was to begin afresh, and no pre-Islamic feud was to be permitted to survive. On the other hand he had no intention of founding a communistic state, and urged that property should be respected no less than life. Something was said of the rights of women, and, on the whole, humane treatment of them was prescribed. That day ‡ God had completed their religion; and it must be admitted that for a great length of time the Mohammedans had no need of legislators, but only of commentators on the law which their founder had given them. Those who wrote the history of that day make the Prophet

---

* *Wellhausen*, *Reste*, 70.

† It is discussed by *Goldziher*, *M. S.*, i., 70–99.

‡ *Musnad*, i., 28.

prophesy that it might be his last visit to Meccah, and it is known as the "Farewell Pilgrimage."

While the despatch delivered by Ali in the previous year represented the offensive side of Islam, the sermon at the Farewell Pilgrimage insisted on the aspects in which it constituted a reformation of previous conditions. The sacrosanct area of previous times was greatly extended, and an earnest attempt made by the Prophet to abolish the blood-feud. The only cases in which we find him act with severity towards his followers is when they carry into Islam the memory of the feuds of former days; and, as has been seen, the lessons of the Fijar war never faded from his mind. But, indeed, the cross-division occasioned by the brotherhood of Islam left little room for the tribal feud. Murder within the religious community became a crime which the ruling authority was bound to punish; whereas outside the community it became a mild offence with which the Moslem rules had little concern; it being the business of Islam to attain to a degree of strength which would render retaliation on the part of the outsiders impossible.

Hence it may be said that the invention of an Islamic brotherhood secured a certain degree of peace among the Arab tribes. On the sanctity of that brotherhood the Prophet never ceased to insist, whether in his revelations, or in his ordinary sermons.* Divine punishment was threatened for any act whereby one Moslem injured another.†

* *Musnad*, iv., 66.

† *Ibid.*, 229.

Like members of the same body, when one felt pain all others must necessarily share it.* With the same idea he recommended fathers to divide their estates equally among their sons, and give no preference to one.† Raiding (such as is now carried on in Arabia, as the journal of the murdered Huber attests) was forbidden; a man who asked whether he might go raiding with his tribe was told that the pride of Ignorance was over.‡ For a time, at any rate, the tribe showed a tendency to sink to the level of those provincial and municipal divisions which, though useful for the purpose of organisation, arouse no sentiments comparable in force with those of nationality and religion. That society is an institution for securing life and property was naturally a notion which neither Mohammed nor his followers ever harboured; but the abolition of the tribal unity certainly rendered better government possible, since an offender could no longer count on being backed by his natural allies. Moreover, that without justice the state could not exist was not unknown to Mohammed; and he therefore made it characteristic of the Moslems that they should prescribe right and forbid wrong.

The notion that a profound difference existed between intentional and unintentional manslaughter appears to have made little way before Islam, obvious though it would seem to be.

Although in cases of the latter sort the Prophet

* *Musnad*, iv., 268.

† *Ibid.*

‡ *Isabah*, ii., 6.

ruled that the slayer be handed over to the avenger of the slain, he informed the latter that he would incur Hell-Fire if he exacted the penalty.* But for other offences it was the merit of Islam that it provided both a system by which they could be checked, and also a code by which they could be judged.

Ever since the taking of Meccah the Prophet had worked as hard as the most industrious of sovereigns, organising expeditions, giving audiences, despatching ambassadors, dictating letters; besides hearing plaints, administering justice, and interpreting the law. He worked continuously, allowing himself no day of rest.† Always ready to hear and take advice, whatever the subject, he kept all the reins in his own hand; and till his death managed both the external and internal affairs of the vast and ever-growing community which he had founded, and of which he was both the spiritual and the temporal head. In later times a whole hierarchy of deputies was established for the purpose of discharging those duties; and in the Prophet's time, though no definite officer as yet existed, the duties attaching to such had to be performed. "Kais, son of Sa'd, son of 'Ubadah," says a trustworthy authority, "was to the Prophet what a chief of the guard is to a Caliph." As political secretary, Abdallah, son of Abu'l-Arkam, served after the taking of Meccah; though converted so late, this man enjoyed the Prophet's complete confidence, and was even allowed to answer foreign correspondence without showing his replies to his

* *Isabah*, i., 1000.

† *Musnad*, vi., 55 (Ayeshah).

master. For the no less important business of taking down "revelations," Zaid, son of Thabit, acted as secretary; on him afterwards fell the duty of publishing the Koran. When these persons were not at hand, other educated Moslems took their place.*

His last years were brightened for a time by the birth of a son to his Coptic concubine Mary whom he acknowledged as his own, and whom he called after the mythical founder of his religion, *Ibrahim*. This concubine having been the object of the extreme envy of his many childless wives, the auspicious event occasioned them the most painful heartburnings; which indeed were speedily allayed by the death of the child (who lived only eleven months)—it is unknown whether any of them assisted nature. The survival of this child would have enormously complicated the beginnings of the Islamic realm, since its stability was certainly due to the fact that the Prophet's immediate successors were the most earnest believers and the most competent rulers in the community, and the men who had the firmest grasp of the principles by which the Prophet had won his successes.

Besides this event of passing importance the Prophet's matrimonial affairs went on as they had done since the battle of Badr had first given him the means of establishing a princely harem. His taste being generally known, and doubtless the subject of much concealed amusement, tribes that were anxious to gain his favour presented him with the

* *Isabah.*

fairest of their women, some of whom indeed took the initiative themselves; though one or two cases are recorded in which the Prophet's suit was rejected.* The history of these persons is given at length in one of the biographies, but there is little in it that repays excerpting. The residence of some of them in the Prophet's harem was short, owing to unsuitability of temper; in one or more cases the newcomers were taught by the jealous wives of the Prophet formularies which, uttered by them in ignorance of the meaning, made the Prophet discharge them on the spot. One was discharged for declaring on the death of the infant Ibrahim that had his father been a prophet, he would not have died—a remarkable exercise of the "reasoning power."† Of the whole number of inmates Ayeshah alone by force of character and keenness of wit won for herself a place in the political and religious history of Islam. By the Prophet's death she had scarcely reached womanhood according to European ideas. But from the time of her emergence from childhood till her death at the age of sixty-six, she exhibited a degree of ability and unscrupulousness which should earn her a place beside the Agrippinas and Elizabeths of history. Fatimah and Zainab, the heroine of the Zaid scandal, in vain endeavoured to obtain from the Prophet some reduction of her privileges in favour of the rest of the harem; Fatimah was told that she should love the beloved of her father, and Zainab, after an encounter with the shrewish favourite,

* *Ibn Duraid*, 176. The lady became leprous in consequence.

† *Al-Kanz al-Madfun*, 5.

retired hopelessly vanquished.* Just as when a child she had, by manifesting abhorrence of the Prophet, riveted his fancy on her, so to the end she possessed the art of making herself valued. When her husband displeased her, she refused him the title Prophet of Allah; and regularly submitted his revelations to a searching criticism which would have cost an ordinary Moslem his head.

A more healthy and respectable form of domestic felicity was provided by the Prophet's grandchildren, the family of Ali and Fatimah. Like Jacob of old Mohammed thought of his grandsons Hasan and Husain as his own sons, and many stories exist to illustrate the Prophet's affection for them. Al-Hasan was said to resemble his grandfather in face more closely than any member of the family; when the former prostrated himself in prayer, his grandchild would mount upon his back; or when the Prophet was standing Al-Hasan would plant his feet upon his grandfather's and climb on to his breast.† At times the Prophet would appear in public with one of the grandsons on each shoulder; and legend, unaided by art, made the holy family consist of Mohammed, Fatimah, and the two boys; in time, when a figure corresponding to the Christian Virgin was required, Fatimah could take the place. The relations between her and her husband do not seem to have been of the most peaceful description, and indeed Ali wished to espouse in addition Abu Jahl's daughter, much to Fatimah's indignation‡; but

* *Muslim*, ii., 245.

† Cf. *Musnad*, iv., 172.

‡ *Muslim*, ii., 248.

these disputes did not often embitter Mohammed's relations with either, though his wives were naturally jealous of her influence and of her offspring. Born at a time when fortune had declared herself in Mohammed's favour, these pampered princes received a training which would have fitted them to mount a secure throne, but by no means prepared them for the rôle of an Augustus or Third Napoleon. The sons of the bravest of champions, the grandsons of the astutest of statesmen, the one proved himself a coward, and the other an incompetent leader; and they transmitted to their descendants their ill-fortune, but none of the gifts which adorned the founders of their line. The Prophet's affection and his blessings were of no efficacy in their case.

Besides these lineal descendants there were many nephews, grand-nephews, and cousins often seen about the Prophet's house; and pleasing stories were told of the games which the Prophet played with them.* But even with his grown-up followers Mohammed appears at times to have thrown aside the gravity which belonged to his office. A story which appears to be authentic is told of his throwing his arms suddenly from behind round the head of a dwarfish convert named Zahir, who was selling goods in the market, and offering him for sale.† One of his followers declared that the Prophet was almost always smiling.‡ The nephews and cousins who had arrived at manhood were naturally anxious to

* *Musnad*, i., 216.

† *Ibn Duraid*, 168.

‡ *Musnad*, iv., 191.

profit by their relationship to the great man, and applied for posts in the new administration; collectorship of the Alms was the easiest of their offices, and the one that offered the best opportunities for peculation. The Prophet, while acknowledging the claims of his kin to support, did not readily grant such requests,* and appears in no case to have injured his administration by nepotism; nor did he allow his relatives to interfere with the course of justice.†

The *deputations* form a more important chapter in the Prophet's biography, and though fact and fiction are greatly mixed in the accounts of them which have reached us, there is no question of their historical character. The defeat of the Hawazin had decided the fate of Arabia. After that event unimportant raids were not indeed unfrequent; but the greater number of the Arabian dynasties or communities, in all parts of the peninsula, from Yemen to Bahrain, from Hadramaut to Yemamah, hastened to throw themselves into the arms of the new power. It would seem that the boastful chieftains had deeply ingrained in them the notion that they must be under some one's suzerainty; for centuries their suzerains had been Byzantines or Persians; by a change of yoke something was probably to be gained, and perhaps the waking consciousness of nationality made them incline to a suzerain whose language was Arabic. Moreover the achievements of Mohammed, and the exaggerated reports of his miraculous powers, probably determined many to seek his favour at the earliest opportunity.

---

* *Musnad*, iv., 166. † *Ibid.*, iii., 395.

Throughout the correspondence, of which fragments are preserved, the Prophet claims the right to dispose of the whole of Arabia, of Syria,* and even of Egypt. The man whose example Mohammed is thought to have followed when he first began to prophesy, the forgotten Maslamah of Yemamah, hoped that his disciple would be satisfied with half the world, and asked, perhaps on the ground of his seniority, for the right to dispose of the other half; but in vain. Two prophets cannot exist in the world at once. "The earth is the Lord's and He bestows it on whom He will." Squatting in his poor apartment, with a veil over his face and a palm-branch in his hand, the outcast of Meccah gave and took away crowns, granted amnesties, and guaranteed rights, bestowed mines,† forced enemies to remain at peace, or compelled sluggards to go to war. Each day's couriers would seem to have brought messages from places whose names till then no one at Medinah had heard. What surprises us as much as anything is that the same language, and indeed the same script (with the slightest of provincial variations), would appear to have been current over the whole peninsula. We nowhere hear of interpreters being required for either the messengers or messages from the distant communities who were now brought into touch with the Sanctuaries.

Many of the visitors' names which were redolent of paganism, or were otherwise displeasing to the Prophet's delicate ear, were altered by him to some-

---

* *Isabah*, iv., 401; *Ibn Duraid*, 226.

† *Musnad*, i., 306.

thing better. So "Zaid of the Stud," whose fate has been described already, found himself renamed "Zaid of the Good"; "the Wolf, son of the Cub" (Dhuaib Ibn Kulaib) was turned into "Allah's Servant"; an "Oppressor" (Zalim) was altered into a "Well-doer" (Rashid); and many a servant of an idol was compelled to call himself servant of Allah or of the Rahman. At times this delicacy extended itself to the names of places: "Wanderer" from "Straying" was altered into "Directed" from "Direction" (Rashdan) and the place retained its new name unto all time. Sometimes these alterations were not to the taste of their objects: a clan named "Sons of Bastardy" whom he wished to rename "Sons of Chastity" preferred the title by which their fathers had been known.* Ordinarily the visitors were too anxious to secure some immediate benefit from their visit to be particular about such points. Men who had been partners in estates hurried to Medinah to embrace Islam, in order to obtain sole possession.† Recognising that the Prophet's assignation had become the only title to property, men hastened to get him to assign them wells.‡ Some, distrusting the honesty of the collectors of Alms, got letters from the Prophet, securing them against injustice.§

The Prophet's letters were now known to be documents of terrible seriousness. If any disrespect

* *Isabah*, i., 701.

† *Ibid.*, i., 994.

‡ *Ibid.*, i., 1054; *Ibn Duraid*, 113.

§ *Musnad*, i., 164.

were shown them, it was speedily avenged. To Ru'ayyah, of Suhaim, the Prophet wrote a letter, with which Ru'ayyah patched his water-skin. The Prophet sent a force which captured his children and all his possessions. He came to Medinah, accepted Islam, and begged that his children and his goods might be restored. The latter had already been divided, but he was allowed to rescue the former. Whether this particular story be true or not, it is a type of many actual events. From the time when the Prophet first governed a state, he never let an insult remain unavenged.

The last of the deputations was that of the Banu Nakha', received in the first month of the eleventh year, and said to consist of two hundred men: their home was in Yemen.

If the Prophet's extraordinary success had cast something like a spell over the whole of Arabia, and subdued the pride of champions who had never recognised authority before, we may be sure that to the persons in his immediate neighbourhood, who had been able to watch his progress, the superstitious reverence which attached to his person knew no bounds. The occasions, therefore, on which he had to punish any one who had adopted Islam were exceedingly rare: and except in the case of Moslems who had avenged on other Moslems injuries which dated from the Days of Ignorance his punishments were extraordinarily mild. Recognition of his prophetic claim was to the end a sort of incense whose perfume never staled. In one case, that of Al-Hakam, the ancestor of the future dynasty of Marwan, he punished an offence with banishment to the charming city of Ta'if; the nature of the offence is not certainly known; but if it really consisted, as is asserted, in intrusion on the privacy of the Prophet, the penalty was not severe. When a man was caught in open treachery, holding private communication with the Prophet's enemies, the latter refused to do any serious mischief to one who had shared the perils and the glories of Badr. On the other hand, his ruling in the case of the Jews that adultery must be punished by stoning led him to cause this barbarous penalty to be inflicted on occasions when he would probably have desired to be less severe, and even suggested to the culprit to perjure himself.* He is said to have crucified one offender,† it is uncertain for what. The penalty of death was also exacted by him in the case of a man who, after pagan usage, married his father's widow.‡ In two cases of theft on the part of Moslems he carried out the horrible penalty of hand-cutting,§ which his code retained probably rather than introduced,‖ and which was clearly not to his liking¶; and one of the heroes of Badr ** even was repeatedly beaten for drunkenness, against the wishes of Omar, who would have exacted a severer penalty. A man found drunk †† on the day of Hunain was by the

---

* *'Uyun al-akhbar*, 95.
† *Ibid.*, 94.
‡ *Musnad*, iv., 292.
§ *Isabah*, iii., 792; *Musnad*, iii., 395.
‖ *Baihaki*, *Mahasin*, 395.
¶ *Musnad*, iv., 181.
** *Isabah*, ii., 823. †† *Musnad*, iv., 88.

Prophet's orders beaten with all available instruments, while the Prophet himself pelted the offender with clods. In dealing with enemies he often showed what may be called a good heart: violent orders given in the heat of passion were retracted after a little reflection; the tradition records how he ordered some enemies if caught to be burned, but remembered in time that it was the privilege of God to punish with fire. The Christian Arabic kings had been less scrupulous,* and the nineteenth century had begun before all Christian nations had attained to this degree of humanity. The one case on record in which Mohammed exercised ingenious cruelty was where a tribe had sent for missionaries, on the pretence that they were adopting Islam, and had murdered these missionaries on their arrival. The culprits, when caught, were indeed barbarously tortured. It cannot be denied that there had been provocation. His principle was however averse to such practices; and many a horror was afterwards prevented by the knowledge that mutilation and torture were forbidden by the Prophet.†

His humanity even extended itself to the lower creation. He forbade the employment of living birds as targets for marksmen ‡; and remonstrated with those who ill-treated their camels. When some of his followers had set fire to an anthill he compelled them to extinguish it. § Foolish acts of cruelty

* *Ibn Duraid*, 230.

† *Musnad*, iv., 292.

‡ *Ibid.*, i., 273.

§ *Ibid.*, 396.

which were connected with old superstitions were swept away by him with other institutions of paganism. No more was a dead man's camel to be tied to his tomb to perish of thirst and hunger.* No more was the evil eye to be propitiated by the blinding of a certain proportion of the herd. No more was the rain to be conjured by tying burning torches to the tails of oxen and letting them loose among the cattle.† Horses were not to be hit on the cheek‡; and their manes and tails were not to be cut, the former being meant by nature for their warmth, and the latter as a protection against flies.§ Asses were not to be branded or hit on the face.‖ Even the cursing of cocks¶ and camels** was discouraged. When a woman vowed to sacrifice her camel if it brought her safely to her destination, the Prophet ridiculed this mode of rewarding the beast's services, and released her from her vow.††

To the same genuine humanity we may ascribe the one innovation of Islam which ordinarily receives praise even from its enemies: the abolition of the practice of burying girls alive. The tradition records the thrill of horror with which the Prophet heard the recital of a man who had covered with earth a girl whom her mother, owing to the father's

* *Hariri*, *Mak.*, xxxiii.
† *Baihaki*, *Mahas.*, 441.
‡ *Musnad*, iv., 131.
§ *Ibid.*, 183.
‖ *Musnad*, iii., 323.
¶ *Ibid.*, 115.
** *Ibid.*, 420.
†† *Ishak*, 722. *Preserved Smith* adds some more examples.

absence, had ventured to save and bring up. Our sources do not tell us within what limits this practice prevailed: some of the archæologists confined it to particular tribes, whereas from the Koran we should imagine that the fate of each daughter born hung in the balance. On the other hand one of the women who adopted Islam at the taking of Meccah indignantly repudiated the charge of infanticide. Though modern political philosophy would view the practice with less severity than Mohammed, regarding it as not the most cruel solution of an apparently hopeless problem, recognition is due to the humanity which prompted the prohibition, both in raising the estimation of the weaker sex, and in hedging human life round with additional sanctity.

For the latter Mohammed's system otherwise accomplished little: but for the female sex it certainly achieved much, and there too it is best to hush the voice of sentiment and treat his rules and innovations as an attempt to grapple with a hopeless problem: hopeless in the sense that no community of any magnitude has ever found a blanket (to use Isaiah's image) that will cover the whole frame. The seclusion and veiling of women were, as Muir has well observed, a direct consequence of polygamy and facility of divorce. Polygamy is itself an attempt at solving a problem which Indo-Germanic nations solve by harbouring prostitution. In the latter system a portion of the female population is wholly degraded, in the former the whole female population is partially degraded. If by the introduction of the veil Mohammed curtailed

THE KA'BAH WITH PILGRIMS PRAYING.

women's liberty, he undoubtedly secured for them by laws the rights of inheriting and holding property, which under the older system were precarious. And though wife-beating is recommended in the Koran, the Prophet himself quite certainly never practised it *; and is said to have forbidden their being beaten on the face, or reproached except indoors. † On the other hand he deprived them of the power to repudiate their partners at pleasure (by altering the direction of the tent), while retaining this right for the men. ‡ The abolition of slavery was not a notion that ever entered the Prophet's mind, and we are too near the date of its abolition in Christian countries to be able to make this a reproach. Some of his regulations in the matter were humane: the parting of a captive mother from her child was forbidden, and threatened with an appropriate punishment in the next world: those who committed the crime would there be parted from their friends. § The parting of brothers when sold was similarly forbidden. ‖ On the other hand the parting of husband and wife was permitted: captivity *ipso facto* dissolved marriage; and the captive wife might at once become the concubine of the conqueror. On the whole however the Prophet did something to alleviate the existence of captives. At the Farewell Pilgrimage he is said to

* *Musnad*, vi., 32.

† *Ibid.*, iv., 447.

‡ *Perron*, *Femmes Arabes*, 127.

§ *Isabah*, ii., 252.

‖ *Musnad*, i., 98.

have ordered his followers to feed and clothe their slaves as they fed and clothed themselves, and if the slaves offended, to sell them rather than punish them.* The scourging of slaves was made by him characteristic of the worst of men†; manumission was also declared by him to be an act of piety, and many an offence might be expiated by the setting free of a neck. A Himyari chief is said to have freed four thousand slaves at the Prophet's request.‡ A system was further encouraged by which slaves might contract for their own manumission, and assistance of such persons with presents was regarded by the code with favour. When a man died without heirs, but leaving a slave, the slave was manumitted by the Prophet, § and received the inheritance. His last words according to one account were an injunction to treat concubines with mercy. ‖ A man who shared one slave with seven brothers, and had cuffed the slave, was made to manumit him ¶; and murder or maiming of slaves was to be punished by retaliation. **

Some of the legislation which was rendered necessary by the occurrence of difficult or doubtful cases was embodied in the Koran: even at an early period, as we have seen, the revelations were the result of protracted deliberation, and when the community

* *Musnad*, iv., 37.
† *Jahiz, Misers*, 182.
‡ *Ibn Duraid*, 308.
§ *Musnad*, i., 221.
‖ *Ibid.*, 78.
¶ *Ibid.*, iii., 447.
** *Ibid.*, v., 18.

had come to be numbered by myriads, the oracles by which it was to be guided were framed with great care. To his elaborate regulations on inheritance some tribute is still paid by those who in India administer the law according to them: he has left out no member of the family who can have any equitable claims, and, so far as his arithmetical knowledge went, endeavoured to settle those claims fairly. But it was rarely that the machinery of revelation was employed. More ordinarily the question which had to be settled admitted of an answer which the Prophet's common-sense could improvise: there were persons who eagerly noted his ruling, which became a precedent for the guidance of magistrates. If the traditionalists are to be believed—and their theory is in the main likely to be correct—there was no detail of conduct too trivial to be made the subject of an appeal to the Prophet, much of whose time, when he was not organising or executing campaigns, or receiving embassies, must have been occupied with the functions of judge. Where his own kin were concerned, he did not escape the charge of favouritism, often brought against him by followers who thereby incurred serious rebuke: but where they were not concerned, such judgments as appear to be faithfully recorded exhibit the shrewdness and fairness which might be expected. Though he declared his system to be brand new, he was doubtless under the influence of custom in his decisions.

But amid all the duties of general, legislator, judge, and diplomatist, the Prophet did not neglect those of preacher and teacher: his advice was demanded on all possible questions, and the occasions were few on which he failed to give it. Certain subjects were indeed forbidden: questions that savoured of metaphysics or rationalism were excluded; the Prophet holding (perhaps rightly) that such had been the occasion of infinite mischief to the religious systems that had preceded his. A rather fantastic eschatology is indeed ascribed to him in the tradition, but Parsee influence is very conspicuous in this, and the bulk, if not the whole, may safely be ascribed to some professional inventor of tradition. Although his early threats of the approaching end of the world must have been partly forgotten during these eventful years, he appears to have maintained the belief in a modified form: asked at Medinah when the end of the world was coming, he said that a boy named Mohammed might, if he lived, witness it before he was an old man.* Among the numerous sayings ascribed to the Prophet we should probably regard those as most likely to be genuine which are characterised by shrewd common-sense. A man intending to marry requested the prayers of the Prophet that he might find a good wife. The Prophet told him that marriages were made in heaven, and that his prayers, even though backed by Michael and Gabriel, could make no difference.† Men, he said, are like camels; out of a hundred you will scarcely find one fit to ride.‡ A woman is like

* *Musnad*, iii., 270.

† *Jahiz*, *Mahasin*, 218.

‡ *Musnad*, ii., 7.

a rib; if you try to straighten her, she breaks.* However old a man be, two things about him retain their youth: desire for money and desire for life.† Asked what God likes best, he used to reply, that in which a man persists though it be slight. Being told that a woman had vowed to make the pilgrimage on foot, he declared that God could do well without His creatures undergoing voluntary torment.‡ "When you boil your meat use plenty of water, so as to get broth in quantity even if you do not get meat."§ Being asked at a time of scarcity in Medinah to regulate the price of provisions, he replied that God only could fix the prices.‖

A whole series of aphorisms is probably with justice ascribed to him, in which he recommended economy, and warned against lavish generosity.¶ The upper hand is better than the lower (*i. e.*, to be creditor is better than to be debtor). Waste of money is to be avoided no less than idle loquacity. Charity begins at home. The best alms are such as leave wealth behind. These aphorisms are the more remarkable, because he himself was never able to hoard money, and died in debt.

The journey from Medinah to Meccah which has been previously described appears this time to have been more than the Prophet's strength could support; and he is said to have felt signs of ill-health

* *Musnad*, vi., 278.

† *Ibid.*, iii., 256.

‡ *Ibid.*, iv., 143.

§ *Jahiz, Misers*, 12.

‖ *Musnad*, iii., 85.

¶ *Jahiz, Misers*, 201.

immediately after his return. News also reached him of risings in South Arabia, which however did not come to a head till after his death; and he determined to organise an expedition against the Byzantines in Syria in order that the defeat of Mutah might be wiped out. As leader of this expedition he chose the son of Zaid, Usamah, a proper person to avenge his father's death, yet in the opinion of the Moslems unsuited from his age, which was twenty, to command an army destined to fight the greatest known power. Some criticism of this appointment reached Mohammed's ears, to which he replied with bitterness. It would appear that his mind became somewhat unhinged because of his illness; at dead of night, it is said, a fit took him to go out to the cemetery called Al-Baki', and ask forgiveness for the dead who were buried there. This indeed he had done before; Ayeshah once followed him like a detective when he started out at night, supposing him to be bent on some amour: but his destination she found was the graveyard.* This time he roused his slave or freedman, Abu Muwaihibah, of whom little is otherwise known, whom he bade accompany him to the cemetery; there he raised his hand to heaven and interceded for the dead in a lengthy prayer, after which he congratulated them on being better off than those who remained behind. He then returned to Ayeshah who complained of a headache; he also complained of one in answer, and asked Ayeshah whether it would not be better for her if she died first, since she would

* *Musnad*, vi., 221.

have the advantage of having her obsequies performed by the Prophet of God; to which she retorted that he would also be able on returning to install a fresh bride in her place. He then spent the night restlessly wandering over his harem till he collapsed in the chamber of Maimunah; whence he begged to be transferred to the chamber of the favourite Ayeshah. Thither he was carried, in a high fever, by some of his relations or followers. Though women are ordinarily doctors among the Bedouins,* and indeed a woman named Rufaidah † ordinarily treated the wounded at Medinah, male physicians were not wholly unknown in Arabia at this time, and one Harith, son of Kaldah, a man of Ta'if, enjoyed a great reputation, and is said to have been called in by the Prophet when his followers were ill ‡; nor is the tradition wholly silent about male physicians resident at Medinah; a Taimite or Tamimite physician, Abu Ramthah,§ had offered to remove the excrescence on the Prophet's back which was supposed to be the "Stamp of Prophecy." Ayeshah further declared that the Prophet's health had long been precarious, and that his numerous visitors from all parts of Arabia used to favour him with a variety of prescriptions which she used to make up.‖ But of course the Prophet like other prophets was himself a medicine man, and was accustomed to heal by incantations,¶ cauterization,

* *Wellhausen*, *Reste*, 161; *Ehe*, 448.

† *Ibn Sa'd II.*, ii., 7.

‡ *Muslim*, ii., 184.

§ *Musnad*, iv., 163; *cf.*, iii., 315.

‖ *Ibid.*, vi., 67. ¶ *Ibid.*, iv., 259.

and other approved methods. He had therefore in the first instance to prescribe for himself in virtue of his office, and demanded a cold-water douche, which was carried out with the aid of a bath belonging to one of his wives. The ground for this treatment was that fever came from sparks of Hell-Fire, which might be extinguished with water*; just as a cold bath was a remedy for anger, which had a similar source.† The douche would have probably been recommended by other doctors of the time, and even now is sometimes prescribed for the reduction of temperature. The exact consequences of this treatment in the Prophet's case are not recorded; it seems however to have ended in convulsions and loss of consciousness, from which he was aroused after a time by the forcing of some Abyssinian drug into his mouth.

The accounts of what happened after the Prophet had been flung on the bed of sickness are for the most part untrustworthy, evidently fictions intended to support the political interests of rival claimants to the succession, or to glorify the Prophet, and make his death, if not the result of choice, at least foreknown—on the principle which has already been seen at work in the accounts of his defeat at Uhud. And indeed the same man whose advice had been followed on the memorable day of Badr, Hubab, son of Al-Mundhir, claimed that on his deathbed too the Prophet followed *his* counsel: asked whether their Prophet should go or stay, the other Moslems desired him to remain with them, but Hubab coun-

* *Musnad*, vi., 91. † *Ibid.*, iv., 226.

selled him to go whither his Maker summoned him, and to this counsel the Prophet consented. It appears to be certain that he fell ill on a Thursday and died on a Monday; and that during these last days Abu Bakr, probably according to his wont, performed public worship in his stead. Between the stroke and his death there may or may not have been a lucid interval; Ayeshah seems to have declared that there was none, and thereby to have refuted the pretensions of Ali to have been nominated successor*: but her interest in this question deprives her evidence of some of its value. Thus she refused to allow that Ali was one of those who carried the Prophet to her chamber.† Moreover her statements appear to have been quite inconsistent. In one account she makes the Prophet lie peacefully with a cup of water by his side, with which he occasionally moistened his brow—suffering indeed terribly, but not unconscious.‡ At one period he is said to have asked for parchment or for "a blade bone" and ink, that he might write a body of rules for the guidance of Moslems; a request which was attributed to delirium, and therefore refused. This anecdote appears to be genuine, because it is difficult to conceive any motive which can have led to its invention: but we know not why the request should have been refused. Another specimen of his dying words is a treble injunction, of which however the third member was forgotten: the two that were remembered were a desire that all non-Moslems

* *Bokhari*, ii., 185.

† *Musnad*, vi., 32. ‡ *Ibid.*, vi., 34.

might be banished from the Arabian peninsula, and a request that deputations might be paid according to the rate which he had instituted. This, if really said, was probably said in delirium: for the second precept was too trivial for so solemn an occasion; and the first (in the spirit of the sanguinary Omar) was directly opposed to the policy which he had urged in his most recent dealings, according to which Christians and Jews were to be left undisturbed provided they paid a poll-tax. Another utterance which he is supposed to have made was a prayer for assistance in bearing the pangs of death. More credence attaches to the stories that the pain which he endured was extremely severe and that owing to the fierceness of the fever he could not endure the hand of any one on his person. Nor is it necessary to reject a story that he told his daughter Fatimah that she would follow him speedily: for predictions of this sort from dying mouths seem to be attested even in these days—whatever may be their psychological explanation.

So the strong man was stricken down, and the business of Islam was for the time at a standstill. Usamah waited with his army outside Medinah, not knowing whether he should start, since perhaps the need for fighting was over. The Moslems assembled in groups, discussing eventualities. Abbas, the uncle, who could tell from the look of a Hashimite when he was going to die, would have asked the Prophet to leave the throne to his family; but Ali dissuaded him, urging that if the Prophet refused, the Moslems would never give it them;

whereas, if he named no successor, his kin would be likely to succeed.*

The treatment which the women followed is not recorded, and is not likely to have been wise or scientific. The length of time occupied by the fever is also uncertain; but probably it was not more than five days. There is nothing surprising in a man of over sixty succumbing to a fever. But his collapse may have been helped by his excesses, or (as many thought) by the poison of the Jewess of Khaybar; or by his belief that water could not be contaminated, whence he drank unhesitatingly from a well that served as a sink; or finally by the anxieties of royalty. Presently,† when Ayeshah was nursing him, his head sank, and a drop of cold moisture fell from his mouth on the hollow of her chest. The inexperienced nurse took fright, and fancying that he had fainted, called for help; her father coming in found the Prophet dead. On Monday, June 7, 632, the curtains were drawn and the Moslems with Abu Bakr in front of them took a last gaze at the face of their Prophet, which looked like a parchment leaf of the Koran.‡

His political work was not left half finished at his death: he had founded an empire with a religious and a political capital; he had made a nation of a loose agglomeration of tribes. He had given them a rallying-point in their common religion, and therein discovered a bond more permanent than a dynasty. The old faiths which had survived so

---

* *Musnad*, i., 263.

† *Ibid.*, vi., 220. ‡ *Ibid.*, iii., 110.

long in secluded Arabia had been given their deathblow: some of their practice was indeed taken over unaltered, but the old names were utterly destroyed. "Though Mohammed is dead, yet is Mohammed's God not dead."

Twenty-three years had transferred him from his shop in Meccah to the throne of an empire which threatened to engulf the world. Had he lived he could scarcely have increased it faster than his successors, though the brief setback in the period of the rebellion might have been avoided. Broader-minded than Omar he might have made Islam weigh less heavily on the subject populations: though, having no notion of a constitution, he could not have inaugurated any permanent or self-righting political system.

In the course whereby he reached his eminence we have had constantly to admire a genius equal to the emergencies, but, if the phrase be intelligible, not too great for them. Security for his person he wisely regarded as the first condition of success: a crown would be useless if he had no head to wear it. He also held that chances must not be thrown away, and while regularly profiting by other men's scruples, allowed no scruples to stand between him and success. He estimated accurately what the emergencies required, and did not waste his energies in giving them more.

INDEX* AND GLOSSARY†

* (M. = Mohammed.) † Arabic words in italics, and translation in inverted commas.

B